THE AMERICAN CLOCK

1 (above). Statue shelf clock. Metal case with painted decoration. Porcelain dial. Brass 8-day, spring-driven movement with strike. Made by Seth Thomas Sons and Company, Thomaston, Conn., c.1870. H. 17¼". (William J. Haggerty Collection)

2 (left). Tall case clock. Painted and decorated case.
Pennsylvania German. Maker unknown. c.1790. H. 91″.
Photograph: Alfred J. Wyatt. (Philadelphia Museum of Art:
The Titus C. Geesey Collection)

3 (above). Lighthouse clock. Wood case painted white. Brass
8-day, weight-driven movement with strike (once on the hour).
A most unusual form of "Bride's" clock that is probably
unique. Made by Simon Willard, Roxbury, Mass., c.1822.
H. 27″. Photograph courtesy Israel Sack, Inc. (Private collection)

4 (opposite). Clock dial. Painted wood. Signed by Abraham
Edwards, Ashby, Mass., c.1810. H. 17″; W. 12″.
(Private collection)

THE AMERICAN CLOCK

A Comprehensive Pictorial Survey 1723-1900
With a Listing of 6153 Clockmakers

WILLIAM H. DISTIN
and
ROBERT BISHOP

E. P. DUTTON & COMPANY, INC.

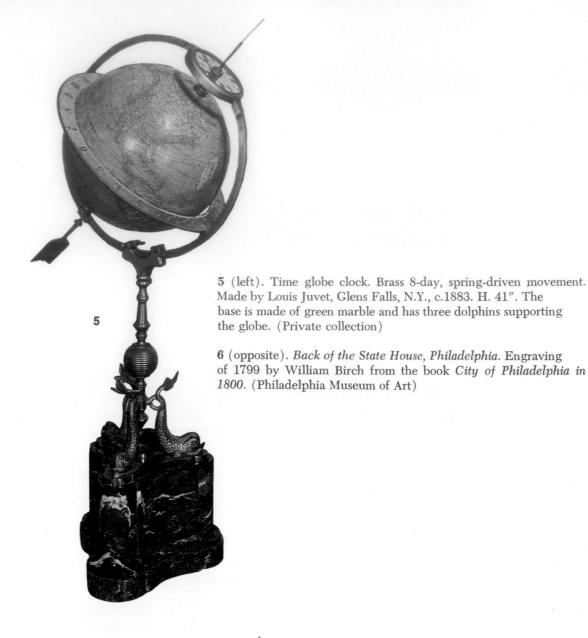

5

5 (left). Time globe clock. Brass 8-day, spring-driven movement. Made by Louis Juvet, Glens Falls, N.Y., c.1883. H. 41″. The base is made of green marble and has three dolphins supporting the globe. (Private collection)

6 (opposite). *Back of the State House, Philadelphia.* Engraving of 1799 by William Birch from the book *City of Philadelphia in 1800.* (Philadelphia Museum of Art)

Designed by Robert Bishop.

First published, 1976, in the United States by E.P. Dutton & Co., Inc., New York. / All rights reserved under International and Pan-American Copyright Conventions. / No part of this book may be reproduced or transmitted in any form or by any means, electronic or mechanical, including photocopy, recording, or any storage and retrieval system now known or to be invented, without permission in writing from the publishers, except by a reviewer who wishes to quote brief passages in connection with a review written for inclusion in a magazine, newspaper, or broadcast. / Published simultaneously in Canada by Clarke, Irwin & Company Limited, Toronto and Vancouver. / Printed and bound by Dai Nippon Printing Co., Ltd., Tokyo, Japan. / Library of Congress Catalog Card Number: 76-20201. / ISBN 0-525-05310-7.
First Edition

CONTENTS

COLOR ILLUSTRATIONS

Drawn Engraved & Published by W. Birch & Son   Sold by R. Campbell & Cº. Nº 50 Chesnut Street Philadª 1799.

BACK of the STATE HOUSE, PHILADELPHIA.

7

7 (above). Bracket clock. Mahogany case. Brass 8-day, spring-driven movement with strike and calendar aperture. Strike-silent dial in the lunette. Silvered dial. Made by Pearsall & Embree, New York, N.Y., 1785–1795. H. 21″. (The White House Collection)

8 (opposite, above). Shelf clock. Painted and gold-leaf case with mother-of-pearl inlay. Brass 8-day, spring-driven movement with strike. Made by The American Clock Company, New York, N.Y., c.1880. H. 21¾″. (J. Alford Jones)

ACKNOWLEDGMENTS

This book clearly would not have been possible without the kind and always gracious assistance of a great many museums, historical societies, libraries, the White House and Department of State, and antiques dealers, who were most generous in providing us with photographs and data on clocks in their collections. Very special thanks must also be given to the many wonderful private collectors who opened their homes to us so that we could photograph clocks that have never before been illustrated.

William M. Distin II of Dearborn, Michigan, was most cooperative in taking photographs of clocks not supplied by the various museums and individuals. It also gives us

great pleasure to give special acknowledgment to Arline M. Ehrle for doing all the typing of the manuscript, sometimes over and over again, to Helen M. Distin for arranging the files containing hundreds of photographs and for proofreading, and to William J. Haggerty for his valuable critique of material contained in this book. The help of our editor at E. P. Dutton, Cyril I. Nelson, and his assistant, Julie McGown, is also deeply appreciated. We are most grateful to them all.

WILLIAM H. DISTIN
ROBERT BISHOP

INSTITUTIONS AND DEALERS

Abby Aldrich Rockefeller Folk Art Collection, Williamsburg, Va.

Albany Institute of History, Albany, N.Y.

American Clock and Watch Museum, Bristol, Conn.

Architect of the Capitol, Washington, D.C.

The Art Institute of Chicago, Chicago, Ill.

Association for the Preservation of Virginia Antiquities, Richmond, Va.

Athenaeum of Philadelphia, Philadelphia, Pa.

Atlanta Historical Society, Atlanta, Ga.

The Baltimore Museum of Art, Baltimore, Md.

The Bayou Bend Collection, Museum of Fine Arts, Houston, Tex.

The Brooklyn Museum, Brooklyn, N.Y.

Museum of Art, Carnegie Institute, Pittsburgh, Pa.

Chicago Historical Society, Chicago, Ill.

Childs Gallery, Boston, Mass.

Gary C. Cole, New York, N.Y.

Colonial Williamsburg Foundation, Williamsburg, Va.

The Currier Gallery of Art, Manchester, N.H.

DAR Museum, Washington, D.C.

Dedham Historical Society, Dedham, Mass.

Department of State, Washington, D.C.

The Detroit Institute of Arts, Detroit, Mich.

Drexel Museum Collection, Philadelphia, Pa.

Eastern National Park & Monument Association, Philadelphia, Pa.

Fond du Lac County Historical Society, Fond du Lac, Wis.

Greenfield Village and Henry Ford Museum, Dearborn, Mich.

Hammond-Harwood House, Annapolis, Md.

Hirschl & Adler Galleries, Inc., New York, N.Y.

Historic Deerfield, Inc., Deerfield, Mass.

The Historical Society of York County, York, Pa.

Huntington Galleries, Huntington, W.Va.

8

9

9 (right). Shelf clock. Mahogany veneer case with carved
half columns and splat, paw feet. Wood 30-hour, weight-
driven movement with strike. Made by Mark Leavenworth
and Company, Waterbury, Conn., c.1830. H. 28¾".
(Private collection)

10

United States Department of the Interior,
  Arlington House, McLean, Va.

Valentine Museum, Richmond, Va.

The Western Reserve Historical Society, Cleveland, O.

Westmoreland County Museum of Art, Greensburg, Pa.

The White House, Washington, D.C.

Henry Whitfield State Historical Museum, Guilford, Conn.

The Henry Francis du Pont Winterthur Museum,
  Winterthur, Del.

Yale University Art Gallery, The Mabel Brady Garvan
  Collection, New Haven, Conn.

INDIVIDUALS

Amos G. Avery

Chris H. Bailey

Gene L. Bagwell

Ivan F. Belknap

Joe J. Brincat

M. S. Burroughs

Herschel B. Burt

O. Harry Burt

Irving Cooperman

Theodore R. Crom

Gary R. Davenport

John H. Distin

William M. Distin II

Paul H. Ernest

Thomas E. Eurich

Burton and Helaine
  Fendelman

Alfonso J. Finamore

David C. Foust

Robert Guthrie

William J. Haggerty

J. Alford Jones

Frank L. Kemp

Harold Klock

Bernard Levy

S. Dean Levy

Bertram K. and Nina
  Fletcher Little

Robert G. Matthews

Robert G. Mindrup

Charles S. Parsons

Jennifer Parsons

Rocco A. Romeo

Lawrence I. Ruby

Robin K. Ryan

Stan P. Sax

Samuel and Esther Schwartz

Mark E. Shanaberger

Anthony J. Sposato

David Stockwell

Edward Thomas

Eric M. Wunsch

11

10 (opposite). Massachusetts shelf clock. Mahogany veneer case. Original
tablets in excellent condition. Brass 8-day, weight-driven movement.
Made by Daniel Hubbard, Medfield, Mass., c.1820. H. 35¾".
(Private collection)

11 (right). Presentation banjo clock. Mahogany and gold-leaf case and
bracket. Brass 8-day, weight-driven movement. The tablet painting shows
"The Constitution escape from the British Squadron." Made by Aaron
Willard, Jr., Boston, Mass., c.1820. H. 39¾". (Dr. Paul H. Ernest Collection)

INTRODUCTION

Collectors need and welcome reference books in their field, for such books can become good friends by providing the help collectors need to acquire more knowledge about their subject of specialization. For this reason we have set out to put together as comprehensive a volume as possible on the subject of American clocks, hoping that it will serve as a basic reference work for clock collectors at all levels for many years to come.

We must make it clear from the beginning that it has not been our intent to produce a history of clockmaking in America; such books are already available and will be found listed in the selected bibliography included at the end of this volume. Instead, we have consciously brought together a very large number of photographs of significant clocks of all types so that collectors will have in this volume a substantial pictorial reference with which to compare the clocks already in their collections or to check the points of a clock to be acquired. Each clock illustrated is identified by its general type, the kind of movement, the maker (where known), his location, and the approximate date when the clock was made. The height of each clock is also given as an additional factor for proper identification.

Thus the reader will find in *The American Clock* almost 700 black-and-white illustrations, which, generally speaking, are chronologically arranged within the nine major sections of the book: Tower Clocks, Tall Case Clocks, Dwarf Tall Case Clocks, Bracket Clocks, Massachusetts Shelf Clocks, Lighthouse Clocks, Shelf Clocks, Novelty Clocks, and Wall Clocks. For advanced collectors we have also included a section showing many types of tools used in making clocks.

12

12 (above). Massachusetts shelf clock. Mahogany case. Brass 8-day, weight-driven movement. Brass dial. No. 14 above the center post. Inscribed on the painted iron plate beneath the dial is: "For/Samuel Fisk/Roxbury." Made by Simon Willard, Grafton, Mass., c.1785. H. 34½".
Photograph courtesy Israel Sack, Inc. (Stan P. Sax Collection)

12a (opposite). Close-up of the dial and iron plate of the Massachusetts shelf clock made by Simon Willard.

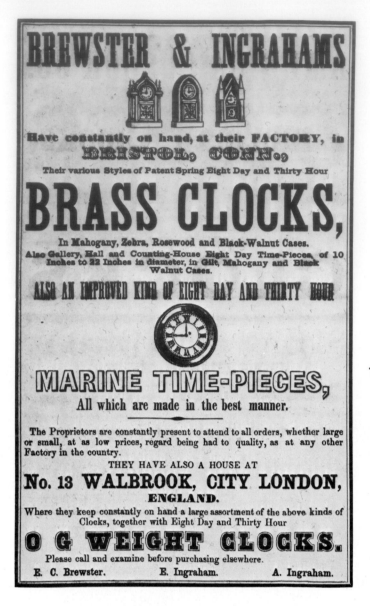

13

13 (left). Clock advertisement of Brewster & Ingrahams, Bristol, Conn. (The New York Public Library)

14 (below). Tall case clock. Cherry case. Brass 8-day, weight-driven movement with strike. Brass dial. Made by Benjamin Willard, East Hartford, Conn., c.1765. H. 94". Case made by Vine Welch. Originally, this clock had one of the finest wood movements made by Welch; it has been replaced with the present one. (Julie and Van Belknap)

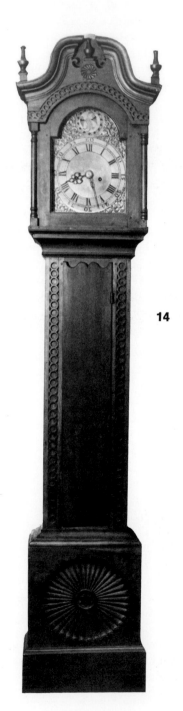

14

One of the major reasons for collecting American clocks is, quite naturally, their beauty. While black-and-white illustrations convey a good deal about the lines, proportions, and details of clock cases, color does much more. For this reason we felt it would prove a valuable addition to this survey to include as many color plates as possible. The 84 color illustrations are grouped together in sections, and the reader will find the color sections listed following the table of contents on page 5.

Believing as we do that clock collectors are chiefly interested in having a reference work that is heavily pictorial, we felt it could be made even more valuable by our selecting examples from private or little-known public collections throughout the country. For this reason, the majority of the clocks shown in *The American Clock* are published here for the first time. They are fine examples that most collectors would normally never have a chance to see.

Many of us, of course, have a special interest in the dials and movements of clocks. Thanks to the generosity of the collectors and institutions who provided material for this project, we are able to include over 100 close-up photographs of dials and movements, and in several instances these elements are shown full page so that they can be even more closely examined.

15a

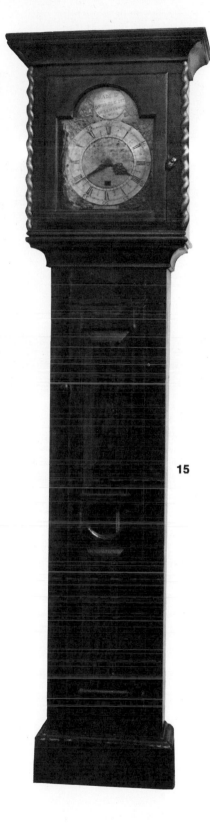

15

15 (right). Tall case clock. Walnut case. Probably a 30-hour, pull-up brass movement. Brass dial with calendar aperture. Made by David Blaisdell, Amesbury, Mass., 1750. H. 93". (Private collection)

15a (above). Dial of the David Blaisdell clock. Inscribed "David Blasdel" on dial.

A useful reference work should include material that up to now has been available only through several different sources. Vital to any study of the American clock is the basic information about the clockmakers—their names, locations, and dates. As mentioned above, this information has been provided in the captions for each of the illustrations, but, obviously, we could show examples by only a very small portion of the total number of American makers. The list of American clockmakers, which occupies 65 pages at the end of this book, has been made as complete as possible up to this point. Actually, of course, such a list is an endless project, for thanks to the diligent research efforts of dedicated collectors, new makers are discovered almost daily. The 6153 makers are given in alphabetical order with the individual makers listed first, and they are then followed by companies and partnerships under the same letter.

Each of the main sections of the book contains some comments about the type of clock illustrated in that section; we hope that the introductory words combined with the clocks themselves will prove an inspiration to the reader to go more deeply into this subject, which has proved endlessly fascinating to so many of us in the clock-collecting field. The index at the close of the book provides an alphabetical listing of the makers whose clocks are represented in the illustrations, and the clocks shown are arranged under the name of each maker.

In essence, this book is a tribute to all those who learned to love clocks and wanted to own and learn more about them. It is they who have cared enough to acquire and care for great examples of American clockmaking; it is they to whom we dedicate this book, for it is only through their efforts that this book was at all possible.

16 (above). Tower clock. Made by Ebenezer Parmalee in 1726 and placed in the steeple of the First Congregational Society's second church building located on the Guilford, Conn., Green. In 1830 it was transferred to the steeple of a new church, where it remained until replaced by a modern one in 1893. Diam. of face: 70″, Hand: 52″. **16a** (opposite). Wood dial of the tower clock made by Ebenezer Parmalee. Photograph: James M. Pennock, Jr., Creative Camera. (The Henry Whitfield State Historical Museum)

TOWER CLOCKS

16a

16

Probably the first clocks known in the Colonies were tower clocks or clocks that were brought here from England or Europe by the colonists. Many of the churches or public buildings in New England had clocks installed in their towers for use by all of the townspeople, since the ownership of clocks by individuals was scarcely a necessity in those early years of colonizing.

Possibly the first tower clock that is definitely known to have been constructed in the Colonies was made by Benjamin Bagnall of Boston, Massachusetts, about 1717. Bagnall was born in England and served his apprenticeship there, migrating to Boston about 1712 or 1713. Although town records indicate that tower clocks were installed as early as 1650, when various townspeople were employed "to keep them in good running order and repair," it is most likely that they were brought here from abroad.

The Diary, or Evening Register of January 8, 1794, printed the following: "Robert Joyce.—Watch & Clock-Maker, No. 4, Beaver Street, Takes the liberty of informing his friends and the public, that he has commenced business in this city. Having served his apprenticeship in London, and afterwards wrought with the most eminent in his line there, and in Dublin; and in the latter place for seven years carried on

17

18

business on his own account, in the course of which he has been employed in making time pieces for astronomical observations, Airometers for shewing the point of the wind, and the Clocks for the principal part of all the public buildings; so that his experience gives him confidence to assert, that with his strict attention, he will execute every command in his line of business in the best and most satisfactory manner."

Before 1850 most of the tower clocks were made on special order by the various clockmakers for churches and public buildings. After that date they were produced in quantity until about 1925, when their popularity ceased. Movements of the clocks were either of iron, brass, or wood, with metal being the most predominant. The Terrys of Connecticut were known for their wood movements, one of which is preserved in the American Clock and Watch Museum at Bristol, Connecticut. In addition, movements could be obtained that were constructed for time only, for strike and/or chime, and with anywhere from one to four dials, depending, of course, on the amount of money available for construction.

Due to fires, replacements, and other causes, comparatively few tower clocks have survived. Most of the earliest ones are either in their original locations or have been removed to be preserved in museums.

Some of the better-known makers of tower or public clocks were the Willards, Eli Terry and Samuel Terry, Thomas Harland, Enos Doolittle, Daniel Burnap, Seth Thomas, and Edward Howard.

17 (above, left). Wood 8-day, weight-driven tower movement with strike. Made for the Congregational Church of South Glastonbury, Conn., and apparently installed when the church was built in 1836. Maker unknown. c.1836. H. 36″. Photograph: Edward H. Goodrich. (American Clock and Watch Museum)

18 (below, left). Cherry wood, 8-day, weight-driven tower movement with strike. Made by Samuel Terry, Bristol, Conn., for the Bristol Congregational Church and presented to them in 1832. H. 38″. It was replaced in 1923 by a Seth Thomas movement. Photograph: Edward H. Goodrich. (American Clock and Watch Museum)

19 (above). The Great Clock in Machinery Hall, Centennial Exposition, Philadelphia, Pa., 1876. Strikes the quarter hour on two bells. The main frame is 10′ long by 3½′ wide and 7′ high, weighs 7,000 lbs. Pendulum is 14½′ long; the bob weighs 500 lbs. Made by the Seth Thomas Clock Co., Thomaston, Conn., c. 1875. Illustration reproduced from *Masterpieces of the Centennial Exhibition*, Vol. 3 (Pub. Gebbie & Barrie, 1875).

20 (right). Michigan Central Railroad Station in Detroit, Michigan, showing a tower clock, before 1900. (Ford Archives, Greenfield Village and Henry Ford Museum)

22

21 (left). Hanging wall clock. One-hand brass dial. 30-hour brass movement with forged iron frame. Made by Isaac Blaisdell, Newburyport, Mass., c.1760. H. of dial: 14″. Photograph: Donald F. Eaton. (Old Sturbridge Village)

22 (above). Wag-on-wall clock. Brass 30-hour movement, made by David Blaisdell, Amesbury, Mass., c.1752. H. of dial: 14″. (Private collection)

21

23 (below). *The Ohio Land Speculator* by James Henry Beard, c.1840. Oil on canvas. Note the hang-up clock at upper left. (Hirschl & Adler Galleries, Inc.)

23

TALL CASE CLOCKS

Originally, tall case clocks were nothing more than wall or hang-up clocks (see fig. 21). Generally speaking, the transition to a tall case clock came about in England during the years 1670 to 1700. At first probably only a hood was added to keep dust and dirt from the movement, and later a case was added to hide the exposed pendulum and weights.

The craft of making tall case clocks in America was first developed in Massachusetts and Pennsylvania and later in Connecticut, which, incidently, became the birthplace of mass-produced clocks about 1840. It is quite possible that the earliest American tall case clock was made by Abel Cottey, who had his shop in Philadelphia. As far as we know this clock still exists in the Philadelphia area.

The clockmaker did not make the cases for his clocks except in rare instances. Usually the cases were made by a cabinetmaker on order from the clockmaker or from the purchaser of the movement. If the case was sold to the maker of the movement, the cabinetmaker was paid either in cash or in trade: so many movements for one case. An example of this arrangement is the Bachmans of Pennsylvania, who made clock cases as well as other types of furniture.

Generally speaking, case styles reflect the furniture styles of the period, although the cases often tend to date somewhat later than the period styles generally known as William and Mary, Queen Anne, Chippendale, etc. Each area developed its own regional style. With practice, one can learn to distinguish whether a clock was made in Philadelphia, New York, Boston, and so forth. Thus, cases with flat tops, no feet, and square brass dials are of the William and Mary style. "Bell tops" appeared on cases and bun feet were sometimes added, and this is a continuation of the William and Mary style. Between 1715 and 1725 arches appeared on the dial, and the hoods were arched to conform. Bun feet were continued, and at the same time the ogee foot gradually appeared, and the style slowly developed into that known as Queen Anne. The true Queen Anne style in clocks developed around 1725 and was popular to about 1750 or 1760.

As the Chippendale style developed about 1760, broken arches became popular on the hoods and some fretwork was used, brass or wood finials made their appearance, and ogee feet became standard. The Hepplewhite style, of which many Willard clocks are excellent examples, appeared around 1780. The cases of this period often feature inlay work and are more delicate in design compared to the Chippendale style, which can be rather heavy in appearance.

24

24 (above). Wood dial with brass spandrels. Made by Vine Welch, Norwich, Conn., c.1750. H. 13½". (Amos G. Avery Collection)

24a (below). Side view of the wood dial and movement made by Vine Welch.

24a

20

25a

Although clock hands can be useful in dating clocks, they will not be discussed here in detail. It is enough to say that early hands, at least up to about 1825, were rather heavy and were often cut and filed into intricate designs. The hands of later periods, especially those on shelf clocks, were much thinner and usually stamped from sheets of metal.

Dials of tall case clocks are another means of dating clocks. The earliest ones were about ten inches square and made of brass with spandrels of pierced brass, and usually had a silvered chapter ring that contains the numbers. They were in use from about 1600 to around 1740. With the advent of the arched dial, a moon phase frequently appeared in the lunette, which before had carried the maker's name on a boss. Numerals were usually Roman with IIII being used instead of the more familiar IV. The painted dial appeared around 1780 along with Arabic numerals.

Movements of the tall case clocks were most often made of brass and ran for eight days. However, some brass movements were of the pull-up variety and ran for thirty hours. Wood movements were also used to a lesser extent, both in the eight-day and the thirty-hour type. The Willards of Ashbury, Massachusetts, used wood movements, as did the Terrys and others. Depending upon the whim of the clockmaker, additions could be made, such as a date dial or slot, seconds hands, musical bells, different types of moon phases, and in the case of scientists like David Rittenhouse, astronomical sightings and orrerys, which showed the movements of the planets around the sun. A notable example of such a complex mechanism is the Rittenhouse astronomical clock (fig. 55) owned by the Drexel Museum of Philadelphia.

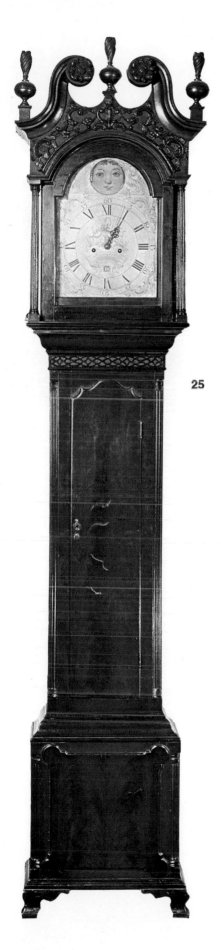

25

25 (right). Tall case clock. Mahogany case with applied carving. Brass 8-day, weight-driven movement with strike. Moon dial in the arch with eyes that wag with each swing of the pendulum. Made by Burrows Dowdney, Philadelphia, Pa., c.1770. H. 94″. The clock was formerly owned by Thomas Shields who became one of Philadelphia's best known silversmiths. Lent by The Dietrich Brothers Americana Corporation. (Diplomatic Rooms, Department of State)

25a (opposite). Close-up of the dial and hood of the Burrows Dowdney tall case clock showing the moon face with eyes that wag with each swing of the pendulum.

26

26a

26 (left). Tall case clock. Walnut case. Brass 8-day, weight-driven movement with strike, seconds dial, and calendar aperture. Brass dial with moon dial in the lunette. Made by David Rittenhouse, Norristown, Pa., 1769. H. 96″. Clock was made one year before Rittenhouse moved to Philadelphia and the year of the transit of the planet Venus. (Frank S. Schwarz and Son)

26a (above). Close-up of the dial of the David Rittenhouse clock.

27 (opposite, left). Tall case clock. Mahogany case, probably by John Townsend or John Goddard of Newport, R.I. Spirally fluted corner columns with bone or ivory insets. Door front and base decorated with double shell motif. Face engraved: ABISNAI WOODWARD/HARLAND/NORWICH. Brass 8-day movement with strike. Made by Thomas Harland, Norwich, Conn., c.1780. H. 87½″. (The Detroit Institute of Arts: Gift of Mrs. Alger Sheldon, Mrs. Susan K. Jellberg, Mrs. Lyman White, Alexander Muir Duffield, and Mrs. Oliver Pendar in memory of Helen Pitts Parker)

28 (right). Tall case clock. Mahogany case with inlaid eagle in the pediment. Brass 8-day, weight-driven movement with strike and musical attachment. Made by Effingham Embree, New York, N.Y., 1790–1800. H. 96". (The White House Collection)

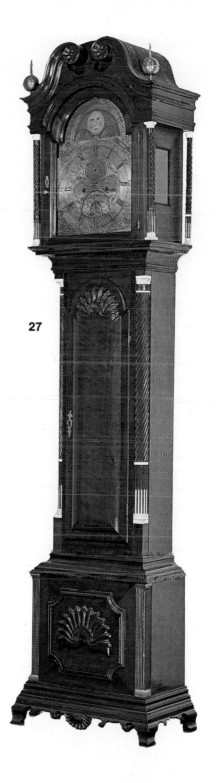

27

28

30a

29

29 (left). Tall case clock. Mahogany, chestnut, pine, and aspen case. Brass 8-day, weight-driven movement with strike and seconds dial. Made by William Claggett, Newport, R.I., c.1748. H. 100¼″. (The Colonial Williamsburg Foundation)

30 (opposite, left). Tall case clock. Walnut case. Brass 8-day, weight-driven movement with strike, seconds dial, and calendar. Brass dial. Made by Daniel Balch, Newburyport, Mass., dated 1756 on dial. H. 84″. Image Studios, David Towne, Photographer. (Herschel B. Burt Collection)

30a (above). Close-up of the dial of the tall case clock by Daniel Balch.

30

31 (right). Tall case clock. Walnut case with unusual double hood. Case is from the school of Job Townsend. Brass 8-day, weight-driven movement with seconds hand, calendar, and moon dial. Brass dial. Made by James Wady, Newport, R.I., 1745–1755. H. 98¼". Formerly owned by the Noyes Family. (The Henry Francis du Pont Winterthur Museum)

31a (below). Close-up of the hood and dial of the James Wady clock.

31a

31

25

32 (below, left). Tall case clock. Walnut case. Brass 8-day, weight-driven movement with strike, seconds hand, and calendar. Made by Isaac Pearson, Burlington, N.J., c.1723. H. 80⅝″. Tradition of original ownership by Elisha Lawrence. (The Henry Francis du Pont Winterthur Museum)

33 (right). Tall case clock. Soft wood case, probably pine with some walnut. Brass 8-day, weight-driven movement with quarter-hour strike. Aperture above center post shows the phases of the moon. Made by Christopher Sauer, Germantown, Pa., 1700–1725. H. 80″. Sauer was the well-known Germantown printer of almanacs. (The Library Company of Philadelphia)

35 (opposite, above left). Tall case clock. Pine case. Bull's-eye in center of door. Brass 8-day, weight-driven movement with strike. Seconds dial and calendar aperture. Made by William Claggett, Newport, R.I., c.1720. H. 92¼″. (Museum of Fine Arts, Boston: Gift of George W. Brown)

33

32

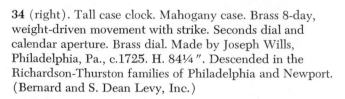

34

34 (right). Tall case clock. Mahogany case. Brass 8-day, weight-driven movement with strike. Seconds dial and calendar aperture. Brass dial. Made by Joseph Wills, Philadelphia, Pa., c.1725. H. 84¼″. Descended in the Richardson-Thurston families of Philadelphia and Newport. (Bernard and S. Dean Levy, Inc.)

34a (opposite, below left). Close-up of the brass dial in the tall case clock by Joseph Wills.

35

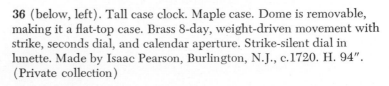

36 (below, left). Tall case clock. Maple case. Dome is removable, making it a flat-top case. Brass 8-day, weight-driven movement with strike, seconds dial, and calendar aperture. Strike-silent dial in lunette. Made by Isaac Pearson, Burlington, N.J., c.1720. H. 94″. (Private collection)

37 (below, right). Tall case clock. Walnut case. Brass 8-day, weight-driven movement with strike and date slot. Brass dial. Made by Thomas Stretch, Philadelphia, Pa., c.1755. H. 91″. Was in the family of the original owner until 1947. (Mark A. Shanaberger)

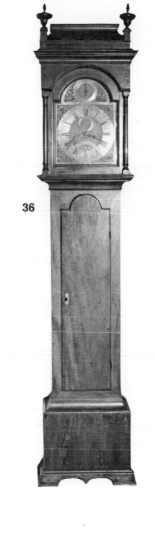

36

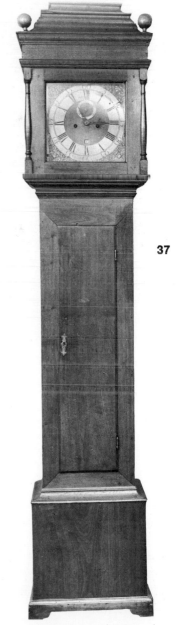

37

34a

39 (left). Tall case clock. Walnut case. Brass 8-day, weight-driven movement with strike and calendar aperture. Brass dial. Made by John Fisher, York Town, Pa., 1760–1800. H. 90½″. (The Colonial Williamsburg Foundation)

40 (below, right). Tall case clock. Mahogany case. Brass 8-day movement with hour strike and calendar aperture. Moon phase in arch. Flat-top hood. Made by James Lane, Philadelphia, Pa., c.1814. H. 91″. Believed to have been purchased by The Atheneum of Philadelphia from Lane in 1814. (The Atheneum of Philadelphia)

38 (left). Tall case clock. Walnut and tulip wood case. Brass 30-hour, weight-driven movement with alarm and calendar aperture. Square brass dial. Made by Augustin Neisser, Germantown, Pa., 1740–1770. H. 82⅜″. "J. Dyer" stamped three times on backboard. (The Colonial Williamsburg Foundation)

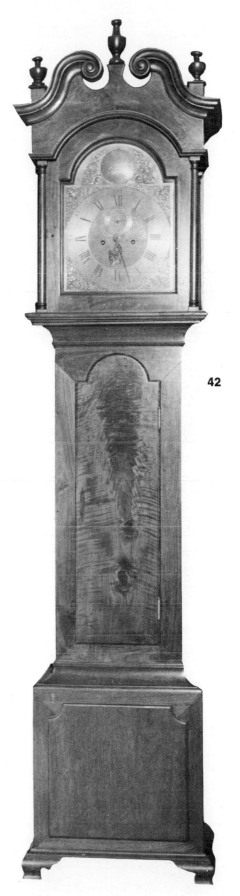

42 (below). Tall case clock. Red walnut case. Brass 8-day, weight-driven movement with strike, seconds dial, and calendar aperture. Brass dial. Made by Edward Duffield, Philadelphia, Pa., c.1745. H. 94″. (Private collection)

41

42

41 (above). Tall case clock. Mahogany case with applied carving. Brass 8-day, weight-driven movement, strike, seconds dial, and calendar. Made by Robert Shearman, Philadelphia, Pa., c.1800. Case attributed to Thomas Affleck, c.1765. H. 105″. (Greenfield Village and Henry Ford Museum)

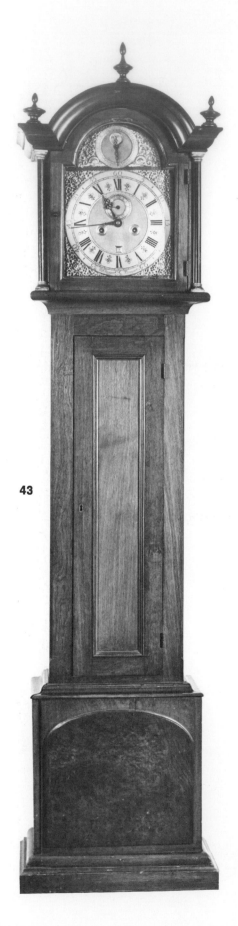

44 (left). Tall case clock. Mahogany case with round-top hood. Brass 8-day, weight-driven movement with strike, seconds dial, and calendar aperture. Strike and silent dial in lunette. Made by Samuel Bagnal, Boston, Mass., c.1750. H. 82″. (The Metropolitan Museum of Art: Kennedy Fund, 1918)

45 (right). Tall case clock. Mahogany case. Brass 8-day, weight-driven movement with strike, seconds dial, and calendar aperture. Made by Gawen Brown, Boston, Mass., c.1760, for Isaac Smith, Boston, Mass. Listed in his will of 1787 and valued at 13 pounds. Although marked "Gawen Brown/London" in the lunette, it was undoubtedly made in Boston. H. 94″. (John H. Distin)

43 (left). Tall case clock. Mahogany case. Brass 8-day, weight-driven movement with strike, seconds dial, and calendar aperture. Brass dial with moon phase in lunette. Made by William Claggett, Newport, R.I., c.1740. H. 88″. (The Preservation Society of Newport County)

46a

46

46 (right). Tall case clock. Walnut case. Brass 8-day, weight-driven movement with strike, seconds dial, and calendar. Brass dial. Made by George Crow, Wilmington, Del., c.1760. H. 91″. One of approximately six examples known. Photograph: Helga Photo Studio. (David Stockwell, Inc.)

46a (above). Close-up of the dial of the George Crow tall case clock.

47 (left). Tall case clock. Japanned oak case. Brass 8-day, weight-driven movement with strike, seconds hand, and calendar aperture. Brass dial. Made by Bartholomew Barwell, New York, N.Y., c.1750. H. 96″. (The Brooklyn Museum: Gift of Mrs. William Sterling Peters)

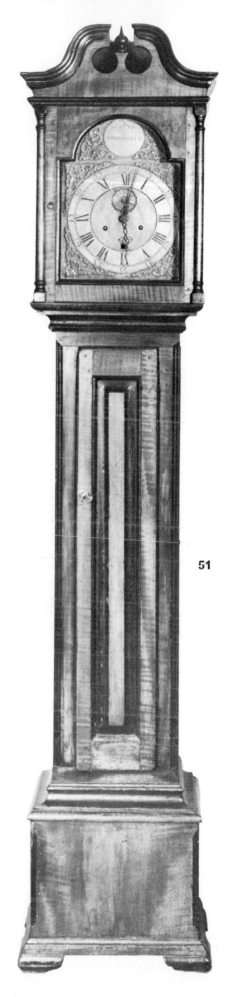

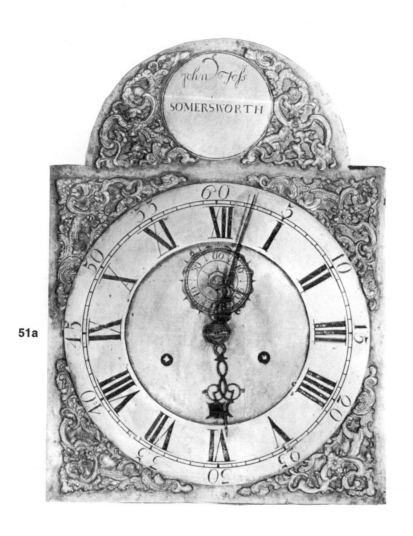

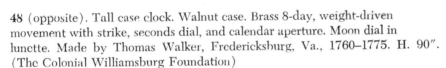

51a

51

48 (opposite). Tall case clock. Walnut case. Brass 8-day, weight-driven movement with strike, seconds dial, and calendar aperture. Moon dial in lunette. Made by Thomas Walker, Fredericksburg, Va., 1760–1775. H. 90". (The Colonial Williamsburg Foundation)

49 (opposite). Tall case clock. Mahogany case. Brass 8-day, weight-driven movement with strike, seconds hand, calendar, and moon dial. Brass dial. Made by John Wood, Philadelphia, Pa., 1755–1790. H. 100". Formerly owned by Major Trent, son of Chief Justice William Trent and founder of Trenton, N.J. Presented to Major Trent when he became a major in the Pennsylvania Militia. (The William Trent House Association)

50 (opposite). Tall case clock, Mahogany case. Brass 8-day, weight-driven movement with strike and seconds hand. Silvered dial. The case is from the Townsend-Goddard Workshop, Newport, R.I. Made by Caleb Wheaton, Providence, R.I., 1755–1795. H. 8' 3". (Museum of Art, Rhode Island School of Design: Bequest of Mrs. Allen Aldrich in memory of Allen Aldrich)

51 (right). Tall case clock. Curly maple case. Brass 8-day, weight-driven movement with strike, seconds dial, and calendar aperture. Made by John Foss, Somersworth, N.H., c.1760. H. 69½". (Private collection)

51a (above). Brass dial of the John Foss tall case clock.

52

52a

53

54

52 (opposite). Tall case clock. Carved walnut case. Brass
8 day, weight-driven movement with strike, seconds
dial, calendar aperture, and moon dial. Brass dial. Made by
Jacob Godshalk, Towamencin, Montgomery Co., Pa.,
1760–1770. H. 94". Photograph courtesy Israel Sack, Inc. (Stan
P. Sax Collection)

52a (center). Close-up of the hood and dial of the tall case
clock by Jacob Godshalk.

53 (above, left). Silhouette of John Bringhurst, original owner
of the Jacob Godshalk tall case clock. Photograph courtesy
Israel Sack, Inc. (Stan P. Sax Collection)

54 (above, right). Silhouette of Elizabeth Bringhurst, wife of
John Bringhurst, the original owner of the Jacob Godshalk
tall case clock. Photograph courtesy Israel Sack, Inc. (Stan
P. Sax Collection)

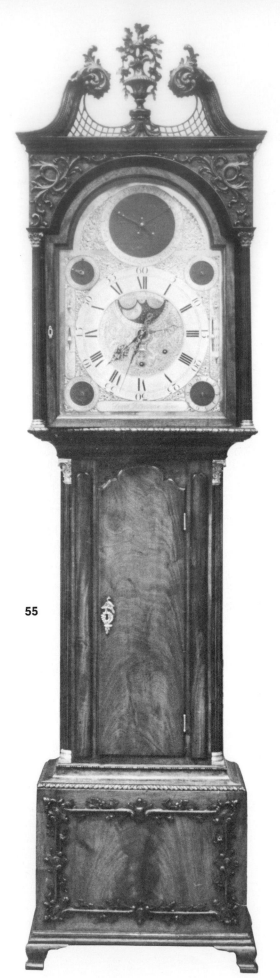

In Committee of Safety, 9th May, 1776.

PRESENT:

ROBERT MORRIS, Vice Presid't.

Dan'l Roberdeau,   John Nixon,
Tho's Wharton, jun'r,   Sam'l Morris, jun'r,
James Biddle,   David Rittenhouse,
George Clymer,   George Gray,
Michael Hillegas,   Joseph Parker.
Samuel Howell,

Resolved, That Capt. William Richards, be appointed Ships' Husband to the Naval armaments of this Province, and that he be allow'd —— ℔ annum for his services.

Resolved, That Mr. Rittenhouse be desired immediately to procure a quantity of Cartridge paper for large Canon.

Resolved, That Robert Towers, Commissary, deliver to Mr. Thomas Heinberger, or his order, twenty hundred pounds Salt Petre, to be manufactured into Gunpowder, taking a receipt for the same.

Upon application of Thomas Heinberger for a sum of Money to be advanced him to assist compleating the Powder Mill he is now building, and Jacob Antony appearing and offering to be bound with the said Heinberger for the repayment of the sum that may lent,

Resolved, That this Board lend the said Thomas Heinberger the sum of one hundred pounds, and that the Committee of Accounts pay him the same, they taking a Bond of the said Heinberger & Antony.

Resolved, That Mr. Rittenhouse & Mr. Owen Biddle be a committee to prepare Moulds for the casting of clock weights, and send them to some Iron Furnace, and order a sufficient number to be immediately made for the purpose of Exchanging them with the Inhabitants of this city for their Leaden Clock weights.

Resolved, That Mr. David Rittenhouse & Mr. Owen Biddle do engage immediately with proper Persons, to make the following quantities and qualities of shot, to be deliver'd to this Board with the greatest expedition, Vizt:

50 ton Round Shot, sorted to the different sized Canon now in use in this Province.
5 ton chain shot sorted.
5 ton Barr shot sorted.
10 ton Grape shot.

56

55 (left). Tall case clock. Mahogany case with applied carving. Brass 8-day movement. Made by David Rittenhouse, Philadelphia, Pa., 1773. H. 108″. The clock was made for Mr. Joseph Potts, who paid $640 for it. The clock tells the time of day in seconds, minutes, and hours, strikes on each quarter hour, and plays any one of ten tunes. It also indicates the day and date of each month, the phases of the moon, the orbit of the moon around the earth, the orbit of the earth around the sun, the signs of the zodiac, equation of time, and the then known planets, excluding Uranus and Pluto. (Drexel Museum Collection)

55a (opposite, above left). Movement of the tall case clock by David Rittenhouse.

55b (opposite, below). Back of the dial of the tall case clock made by David Rittenhouse.

56 (above). Page 561 from the Minutes of the Provincial Council of Pennsylvania, Council of Safety, dated 9th of May, 1776, authorizing Mr. Rittenhouse and Mr. Biddle to exchange iron clock weights for "Leaden Clock weights." It is very probable that many of the iron clock weights that we think are original may be replacements for the lead ones that were melted down and remolded into urgently needed ammunition during our War of Independence. (Lancaster Historical Society)

55

55a

55b

57 (below). Tall case clock. Tulip wood case. Brass and steel 30-hour, weight-driven striking movement with seconds hand. Brass dial. Made by David Rittenhouse, Norristown, Pa., c.1755. H. 78⅛". (The Henry Francis du Pont Winterthur Museum)

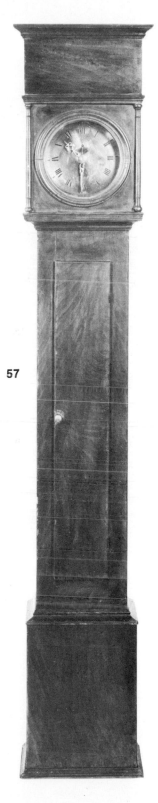

57

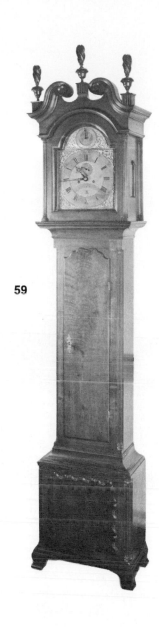

59

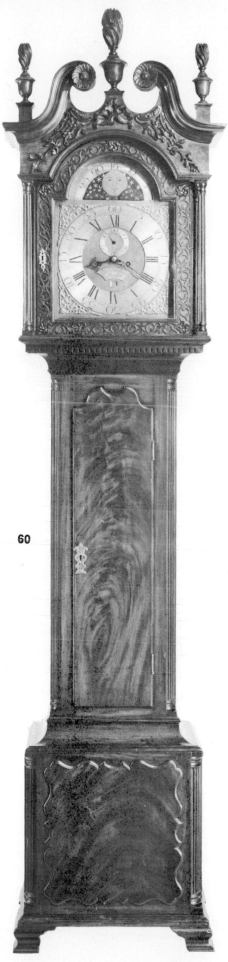

60

58 (opposite). Tall case clock. Solid mahogany, tulip, and poplar wood case. Brass 8-day, weight-driven striking movement with calendar aperture. Made by John Belsner, Fells Point and Baltimore, Md., c.1772. H. 95″. (The Baltimore Museum of Art)

59 (above). Tall case clock. Walnut case with flame finials. Brass 8-day, weight-driven movement with seconds dial and date aperture. Brass dial. Made by Frederick Dominick, Philadelphia, Pa., c.1770. H. 8′ 7″. (Independence National Historical Park Collection)

60 (right). Tall case clock. Carved red walnut case. Brass 8-day, weight-driven movement with strike, seconds hand, calendar, and moon dial. Brass dial. Made by Edward Duffield, Philadelphia, Pa., c. 1747. H. 102⅞″. The case for this handsome Chippendale clock clearly dates to 1765–1775, so it seems likely that a later owner decided to have the Duffield movement put into a case more in keeping with the fashion of the day. Duffield was a friend of Benjamin Franklin and executor of his estate. (The Henry Francis du Pont Winterthur Museum)

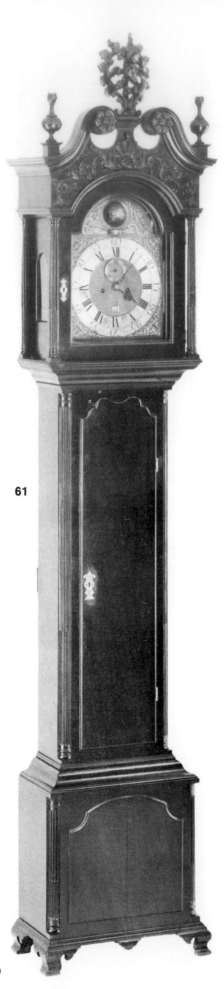

61

62

62a

61 (left). Tall case clock. Mahogany case. Brass 8-day, weight-driven movement with strike, seconds dial, and calendar aperture. Made by Edward Duffield, Philadelphia, Pa., c.1747. Case dates to 1760–1775. H. 113″. (The Colonial Williamsburg Foundation)

62 (above). Tall case clock. Mahogany case. Brass 8-day movement with strike, seconds dial, and moon dial. Rooster finial. Made by Frederick Maus, Philadelphia, Pa., c.1790. H. 8′ 4½″. (The Detroit Institute of Arts: Gibbs-Williams Fund)

62a (above). Detail of the rooster finial on the F. Maus tall case clock.

63 (left). Tall case clock. Painted and decorated yellow pine case. Brass 8-day, weight-driven movement with strike. Moon phase in lunette. Attributed to Johannes Spitler, Shenandoah Co., Va., c.1800. H. 85″. (Abby Aldrich Rockefeller Folk Art Collection)

64 (right). Tall case clock. Walnut case. Brass 8-day, weight driven movement with strike. Brass and pewter dial. Made by Jacob Graff, Lancaster, Pa., 1765–1775. H. 98″. (The Henry Francis du Pont Winterthur Museum)

64

65

65 (above). "Gosler, His Clock Case, Cutting it up." Watercolor by Lewis Miller, York, Pa. c.1825. Miller describes the situation as follows: "George Adam Gosler, Cabinetmaker, he made A fine clock case, for Baily—When it was done Mr. Baily he Scruplet About the price, it—was to high for the Gentleman. My work is good. A few words Said, Gosler took his hatchet and cut the Case all in Splinters—Sooner then let it go under his price out of his shop." (The Historical Society of York County)

66 (right). Tall case clock. Mahogany and mahogany veneer door and base panel. Brass 8-day, weight-driven movement with strike, seconds dial, and sweep-hand calendar. Moon phase in lunette. Made by Thomas Pearsall, New York, N.Y., c.1775. H. 102″. Image Studios, David Towne, Photographer. (Herschel B. Burt Collection)

66a (far right). Close-up of the dial of the tall case clock made by Thomas Pearsall.

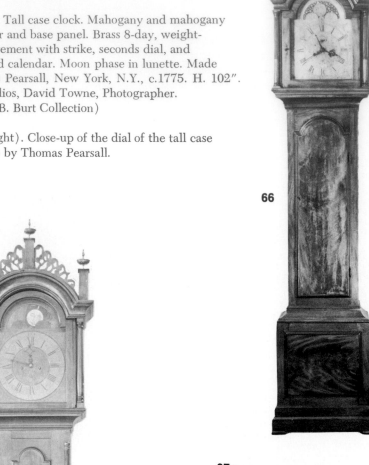

66

66a

67

67a

67 (far left). Tall case clock. Cherry case. Brass 8-day, weight-driven movement with strike, date and day of the week dials, and moon phase. Brass dial. Made by Stephen Hasham, Charlestown, N.H., c.1790. H. 95″. Hasham retired to operate a hotel. (New Hampshire Historical Society)

67a (left). Movement of the Stephen Hasham tall case clock.

69 (opposite, below right). Tall case clock. Pine case, stained mahogany. Wood 30-hour, weight-driven movement with strike, seconds dial, and calendar dial. Maker unknown. 1790–1813. H. 87″. (Gene L. Bagwell Collection)

69a (opposite, below left). Back view of the wood movement.

69b (opposite, below center). Front view of the wood movement.

68

68 (left). Tall case clock. Walnut case. Brass 8-day, weight-driven movement with strike and seconds dial. Brass dial. Made by Jonathan Purrington, Kensington, N.H., c.1750. H. 80″. Image Studios, David Towne, Photographer. (Herschel B. Burt Collection)

68a (below). Close-up of the dial of the tall case clock made by Jonathan Purrington.

68a

69a

69b

69

73 (right). Tall case clock. Cherry and pine case. Brass 8-day, weight-driven movement with strike and calendar aperture. Made by Nathan Howell, New Haven, Conn., c.1775. H. 91″. Photograph: Allen Mewbourn. (The Museum of Fine Arts, Houston: The Bayou Bend Collection)

71 (below). Tall case clock. Cherry case. Brass 8-day, weight-driven movement with strike, seconds hand, and calendar. Brass dial. Made by Daniel Burnap, East Windsor, Conn., 1785–1795. H. 89″. (The Henry Francis du Pont Winterthur Museum)

72 (right). Tall case clock. Mahogany case. Brass 8-day, weight-driven movement with strike, seconds dial, calendar, and moon phase. Made by Seril Dodge, Providence, R.I., c.1770. H. 94″. Case is of the Goddard-Townsend school of Newport, R.I. (Rhode Island Historical Society)

73

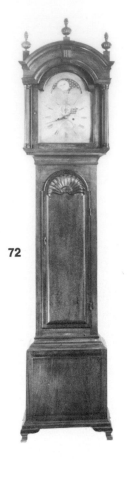

72

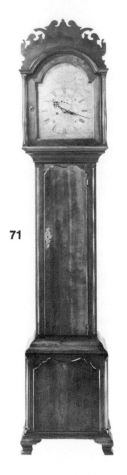

71

70

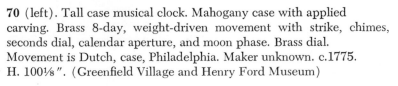

74

70 (left). Tall case musical clock. Mahogany case with applied carving. Brass 8-day, weight-driven movement with strike, chimes, seconds dial, calendar aperture, and moon phase. Brass dial. Movement is Dutch, case, Philadelphia. Maker unknown. c.1775. H. 100⅛″. (Greenfield Village and Henry Ford Museum)

74 (right). Tall case clock. Mahogany case. Brass 8-day, weight-driven movement with strike and musical attachment. Made by Benjamin Hanks, Norwich, Conn., c.1776. H. 92″. Hanks was apprenticed to Thomas Harland and made both the movement and case. The musical attachment plays six tunes. (Diplomatic Reception Rooms, Department of State)

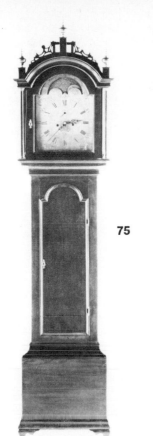

75 (left). Tall case clock. Mahogany case. Brass 8-day, weight-driven movement with strike, seconds dial, calendar, and moon phase. Silver dial. Over the arch, "Warranted for Mr. Benj'n Piper." Made by Benjamin Willard, Grafton, Mass., c.1771. H. 90″. (Greenfield Village and Henry Ford Museum)

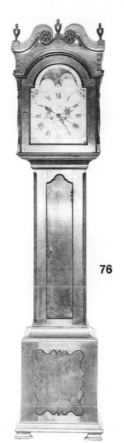

76 (left). Tall case clock. Walnut case. Brass 8-day, weight-driven movement with strike, date slot, and sweep-seconds hand. Made by Albert Browne, Sr., Yorktown, Pa., c.1785. H. 94″. Paper on the back of the dial reads: "Albert Browne Lived and Worked for a Short Time in Yorktowne, Pa. He Was A Farmer and Smithy and Made Several Clocks." (Mark A. Shanaberger)

77 (below). Tall case clock. Mahogany case. Brass 30-hour, weight-driven movement with strike and calendar aperture. Pull-up wind. Brass dial. Made by Thomas Norton, Rising Sun, Md., c.1795. H. 98″. (Greenfield Village and Henry Ford Museum)

79 (left). Tall case clock. Mahogany case. Brass 8-day, weight-driven movement with strike, seconds dial, and calendar. Case sits on a platform that increases the fall of the weights and also prevents dust from filtering up to the movement. Made by Isaac Brokaw, Bridgetown, N.J., c.1794. H. 93″. (Greenfield Village and Henry Ford Museum)

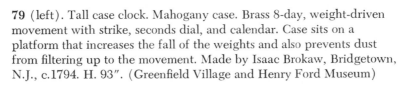

78 (right). Tall case clock. Walnut case. Brass 8-day, weight-driven movement with strike, sweep-seconds hands, and calendar hand. Made by Griffith Owen, Philadelphia, Pa., 1785–1795. H. 96⅞″. (Yale University Art Gallery: The Mabel Brady Garvan Collection)

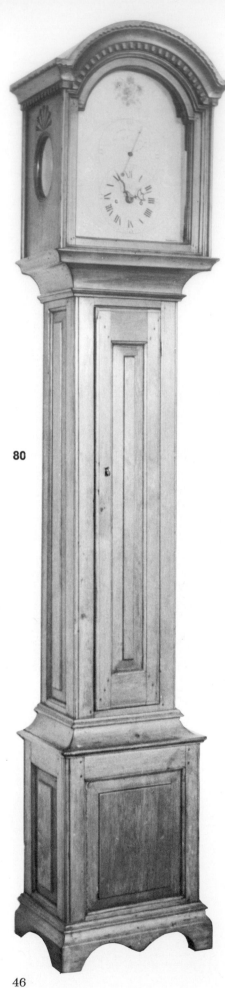

80

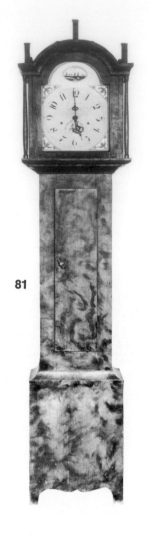

81

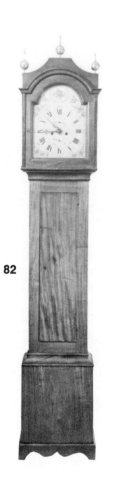

82

83

80 (far left). Tall case clock. Paneled pine case. Made by Abraham Edwards, Ashby, Mass., c.1795. H. 86½″. (Private collection)

81 (left). Tall case clock. Pine case, smoke-grained on ochre. Wood 30-hour, weight-driven movement with strike. Made by Silas Hoadley, Plymouth, Conn., 1825–1840. H. 85″. (Gary R. Davenport)

82 (above). Tall case clock. Brass 8-day, weight-driven movement with strike, seconds hand, and calendar. Made by Nathaniel Dominy IV, East Hampton, Long Island, N.Y., c.1799. Case made by Nathaniel Dominy V. H. 93¾″. Made for David Gardiner of Flushing, Long Island, N.Y. (The Henry Francis du Pont Winterthur Museum)

83 (right). Tall case clock. Pine case. Brass 8-day, weight-driven movement with strike and calendar. Case made by Erastus Rude, New Lebanon, Pa., signed and dated 1811. Movement made by Benjamin Youngs, Watervliet, N.Y., c.1800. H. 85¼″. Photograph: Lees Studio. (The Shaker Museum)

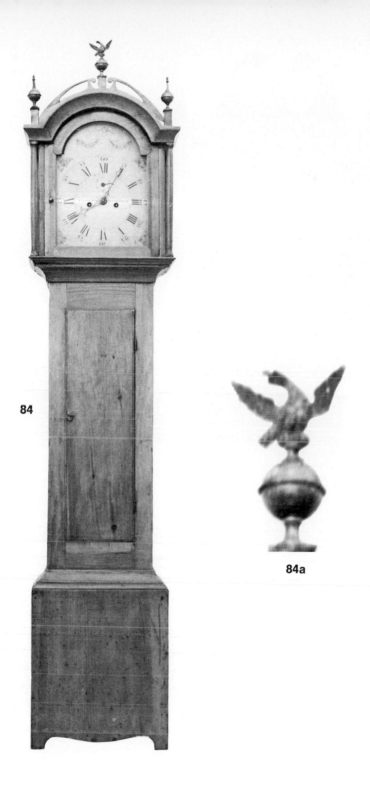

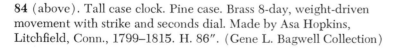

84a

84

85

84 (above). Tall case clock. Pine case. Brass 8-day, weight-driven movement with strike and seconds dial. Made by Asa Hopkins, Litchfield, Conn., 1799–1815. H. 86″. (Gene L. Bagwell Collection)

84a (above). Detail of the eagle finial on the tall case clock made by Asa Hopkins.

85 (right). Tall case clock. Pine case painted red, with gold eagle and leaf design. Brass 8-day, weight-driven movement with strike, seconds dial, calendar slot, and moon phase. Maker unknown. New Hampshire, c.1800. H. 92¾″. (Greenfield Village and Henry Ford Museum)

86 (below, left). Tall case clock. Cherry and mahogany case with satinwood inlay. Brass 8-day, weight-driven movement with strike. Seconds dial and calendar. Moon phase in lunette. Made by Samuel Hill, Harrisburg, Pa., c.1790. H. 108″. Made for Absalam Wells, Wellsburg, W.Va. Photograph: Harold McKeand. (The Huntington Galleries, Inc.)

87a

86

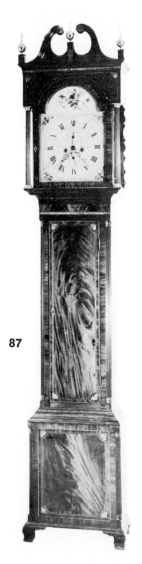

87

88

87 (near left). Tall case clock. Mahogany case. Brass 8-day, weight-driven movement with strike, seconds dial, and calendar dial. Made by Philip Garrett, Philadelphia, Pa., 1790–1802. H. 98¼″. Originally purchased by Joseph Gillingham of Philadelphia in 1802. (The White House Collection)

87a (above, left). Close-up of the hood and dial of the tall case clock made by Philip Garrett.

88 (above, right). Tall case clock. Mahogany case. Brass 8-day, weight-driven movement with strike, seconds dial, and calendar dial. Moon phase dial in lunette. Made by Ephraim Willard, Roxbury, Mass., c.1795. H. 93¼″. (Bernard and S. Dean Levy, Inc.)

89 (below, left). Tall case clock. Mahogany veneer case. Brass 8-day, weight-driven movement with strike, seconds hand, and calendar. Made by Simon Willard, Roxbury, Mass., 1790–1815. H. 88″. (The Henry Francis du Pont Winterthur Museum: Gift of Charles K. Davis)

91 (right). Tall case clock. Fruitwood case with inlay. Case attributed to the school of John Doggett, Roxbury, Mass. Brass 8-day, weight-driven movement with strike, seconds hand, calendar, and moon phase. Made by Joseph Mulliken, Concord, Mass., c.1795. H. 86⅝″. Photograph: Paul M. Macapia. (Seattle Art Museum: Gift of Mr. and Mrs. Bernard T. Poor)

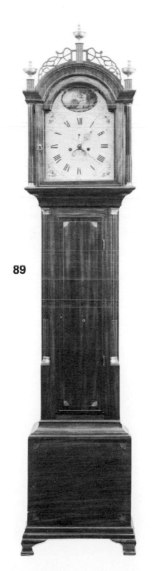

89

90

91

90 (near left). Tall case clock. Mahogany veneer case. Brass 8-day, weight-driven movement with strike, sweep-seconds hand, and calendar hand operating from the center post. Deadbeat escapement. Rocking ship in lunette. Brass pillars on the hood. Made by Walter Cornell, Newport, R.I., c.1800. H. 92″. (Greenfield Village and Henry Ford Museum)

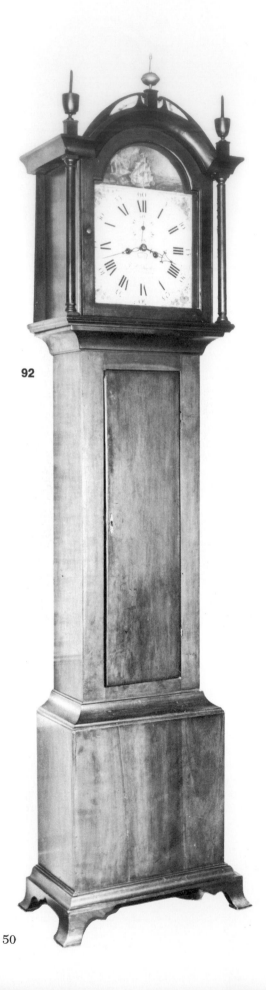

92 (left). Tall case clock. Cherry case. Brass 8-day, weight-driven striking movement with seconds dial, calendar, and rocking ship in lunette. Made by Edward Moulton, Rochester, N.H., c.1810. H. 90″. (Amos G. Avery Collection)

93 (center). Tall case clock. Cherry case. Brass 8-day, weight-driven movement with strike, seconds dial, calendar, and moon phase. Made by Timothy Chandler, Concord, N.H., c.1820. H. 94″. Very rare, small ball-and-claw feet. (Private collection)

94 (right). Tall case clock. Crotch mahogany veneer case. Brass 8-day, weight-driven movement with seconds and calendar dials. Made by Joshua Wilder, Hingham, Mass., c.1820. H. 84⅜″. (Rhode Island Historical Society)

95

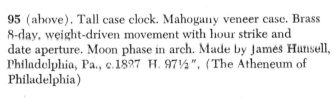

95a

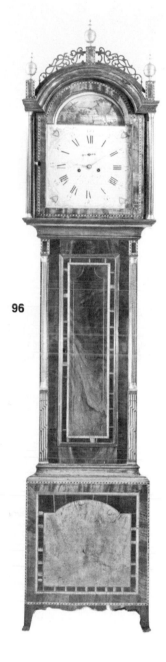

96

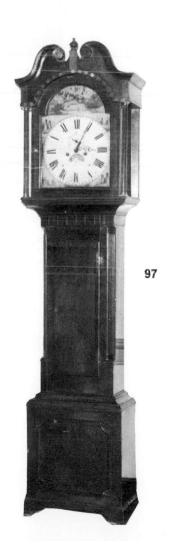

97

95 (above). Tall case clock. Mahogany veneer case. Brass 8-day, weight-driven movement with hour strike and date aperture. Moon phase in arch. Made by James Hansell, Philadelphia, Pa., c.1827 H. 97½". (The Atheneum of Philadelphia)

95a (above). Label of James Hansell, maker of the tall case clock, showing that it was sold January 6, 1827.

96 (far right). Tall case clock. Mahogany case with curly and bird's-eye maple veneer. Brass 8-day movement with strike. Made by Levi Hutchins, Concord, N.H., c.1810. H. 96". Photograph: Frank Kelly. (The Currier Gallery of Art)

97 (near right). Tall case clock. Solid mahogany case with inlay. Brass 8-day movement with strike and calendar aperture. Painted dial. Formerly owned by Senator Daniel Webster, Duxbury, Mass. Made by George Marsh, Wolcottville, Conn., c.1830. H. 84". (The Preservation of Virginia Antiques)

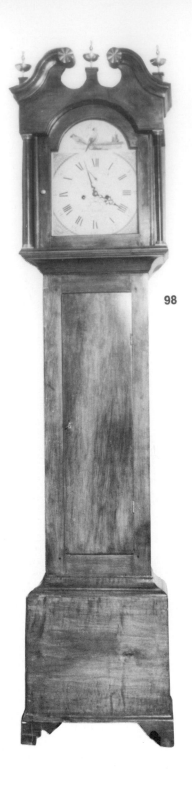

99a

98

99

99 (left). Tall case clock. Painted pine case. Wood 8-day, weight-driven movement with strike and seconds dial. Made by James Critchet, Candia, N.H., c.1820. H. 88¼″. Critchet made this clock for his personal use. It has a wood dial, wood hands, a movement of original design with three plates, four-blade fly, wire pinions, and pins for the snail, etc. (New Hampshire Historical Society)

99a (above). Close-up of the hood and dial of the tall case clock made by James Critchet.

99b (opposite). Detail of the wood movement of the tall case clock made by James Critchet.

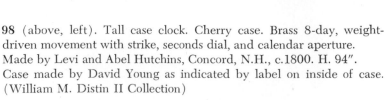

98 (above, left). Tall case clock. Cherry case. Brass 8-day, weight-driven movement with strike, seconds dial, and calendar aperture. Made by Levi and Abel Hutchins, Concord, N.H., c.1800. H. 94″. Case made by David Young as indicated by label on inside of case. (William M. Distin II Collection)

99b

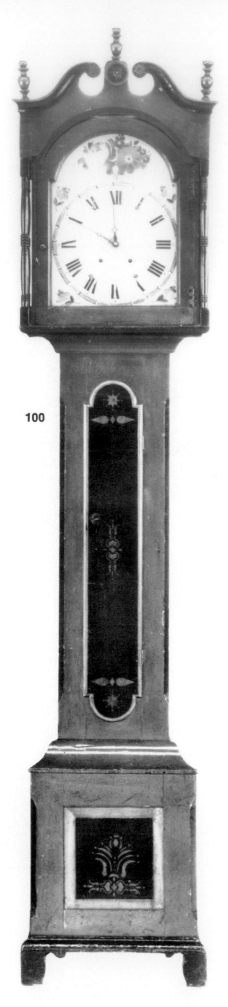

100

100 (left). Tall case clock. Painted pine case. Brass 8-day, weight-driven movement with strike. Case is painted red and black with gold-leaf trim. Maker unknown. Pennsylvania, c.1810. H. 100½″. (Greenfield Village and Henry Ford Museum)

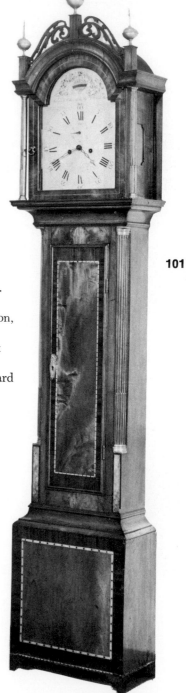

101

101 (right). Tall case clock. Inlaid mahogany case. Brass 8-day, weight-driven movement with strike and seconds hand. Made by Aaron Willard, Boston, Mass., 1806. H. 88″. Dial inscribed "Made for Mr. L. Seavern by A. Willard, 1806." (The Art Institute of Chicago: Gift of Mr. and Mrs. Frank H. Woods in memory of her mother Mrs. Edward Harris Brewer through the Antiquarian Society)

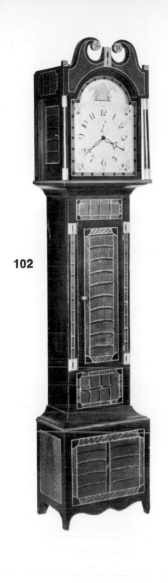

102

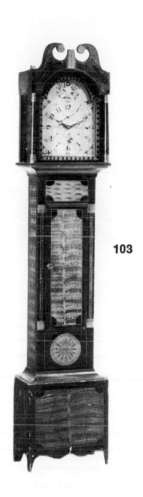

103

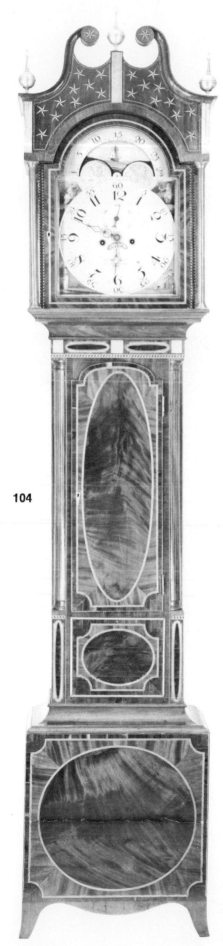

104

102 (above, left). Tall case clock. Painted and decorated case.
Brass 8-day, weight-driven movement with strike. Maker unknown.
c.1820. H. 82″. (Burton and Helaine Fendelman)

103 (above, right). Tall case clock. Painted and grained pine case.
Wood 30-hour, weight-driven movement with strike. Made by Riley
Whiting, Winchester, Conn., c.1820. H. 88″. (Greenfield Village and
Henry Ford Museum)

104 (right). Tall case clock. Mahogany veneer case with inlays.
Brass 8-day, weight-driven movement with strike, seconds dial, calendar, and moon phase. Made by George Jones, Jr., Wilmington, Del.,
1810–1820. H. 97⅜″. (The Henry Francis du Pont Winterthur
Museum)

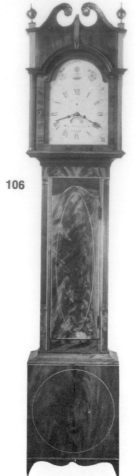

106

107

106 (above). Tall case clock. Mahogany case. Brass 8-day, weight-driven movement with strike, seconds hand, and calendar. Made by Asa Whitney, New York, N.Y., c.1800. H. 93″. (The New-York Historical Society)

107 (right). Tall case clock. Mahogany veneer case with maple and mahogany inlay. Brass 8-day, weight-driven movement with seconds dial, calendar, and moon phase. Made by Thomas Harland, Norwich, Conn., c.1800. H. 96″. The painted dial is unusual for Harland. (Greenfield Village and Henry Ford Museum)

105 (left). Tall case clock. Mahogany veneer case with inlays. Brass 8-day, weight-driven movement with strike, seconds hand, moon phase, and musical attachment. It has 11 bells, 22 hammers, and plays seven tunes, probably one for each day of the week. Made by either John or George Hoff, Jr., Lancaster, Pa., 1800–1816. H. 107″. (The Henry Francis du Pont Winterthur Museum)

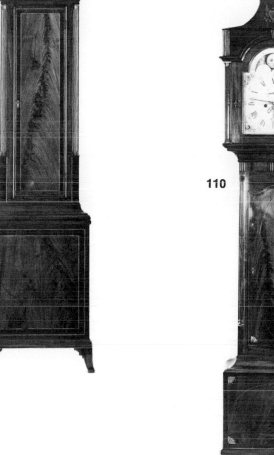

109 (left). Tall case clock. Mahogany case. Brass 8-day, weight-driven movement with strike, seconds dial, and calendar aperture. Moon phase in lunette. Made by Simon Willard, Roxbury, Mass., c.1809. H. 109″. Case attributed to Thomas Seymour, Boston. Clock was gift of Capt. John Goddard to Mary Goddard May on her wedding, July 19, 1809. (Museum of Fine Arts, Boston: Gift of Mr. and Mrs. Lawrence O. Paul)

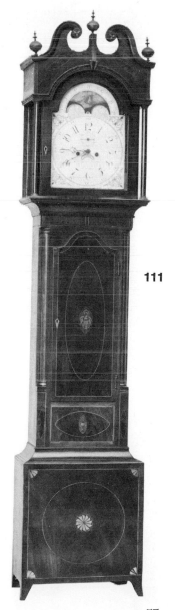

108 (left). Tall case clock. Walnut, maple, cherry, and mahogany case. Brass 8-day, weight-driven movement with strike. Moon phase in lunette. Inscribed on back of dial: "Made for Felix Bagley." Made by Johnston and Davis, Pittsburgh, Pa., c.1800. H. 95½″. (Museum of Art, Carnegie Institute)

110 (above, right). Tall case clock. Mahogany case with holly inlay. Brass 8-day, weight-driven movement and strike, seconds dial, and calendar aperture. Moon dial in lunette. Made by Leslie and Williams, New Brunswick, N.J., c.1790. Case by Matthew Egerton, Jr. H. 93¾″. (Bernard and S. Dean Levy, Inc.)

111 (right). Tall case clock. Mahogany case with satinwood inlays. Brass 8-day, weight-driven movement with strike, seconds dial, and calendar. Moon phase in lunette. Made by Joachim Hill, Flemington, N.J., 1815. H. 87″. (The Metropolitan Museum of Art: Gift of George Coe Graves, 1932)

112

113

114a

114

112 (left). Tall case clock. Cherry case with satinwood, mahogany, and walnut inlay. Brass 8-day, weight-driven movement with strike. Made by Abel Hutchins, Concord, N.H., c.1800. H. 91½". (Greenfield Village and Henry Ford Museum)

113 (above, left). Tall case clock. Mahogany case with inlays. Brass 8-day, weight-driven movement with strike, seconds and calendar dials, and moon phase. Made by Nehemiah Bassett, Albany, N.Y., 1795–1800. H. 98½". (Albany Institute of History and Art)

114 (right). Tall case clock. Mahogany case with unusual painted roses on the hood. Brass 8-day, weight-driven movement with strike, seconds dial, and calendar aperture. Case made in New York; movement made in Newcastle, England, 1800–1810. H. 96". (Israel Sack, Inc.)

114a (above, right). Close-up of the hood and dial of the New York clock with English works.

116

115

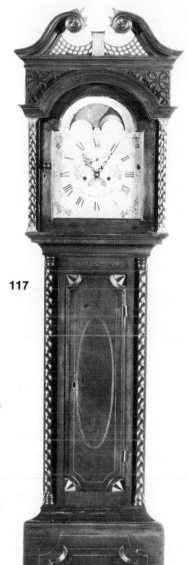

117

116 (above). Tall case clock. Walnut case with maple inlay. Brass 8-day, weight-driven movement with strike, seconds dial, calendar, and moon phase. Maker unknown. Pennsylvania, dated 1799. H. 91″. (Greenfield Village and Henry Ford Museum)

117 (right). Tall case clock. Mahogany case with twisted side pillars. Brass 8-day, weight-driven movement with strike, seconds dial, calendar, and moon phase. Made by Isaac Gere, Northampton, Mass., c.1795. H. 95½″. (Greenfield Village and Henry Ford Museum)

115a

115 (above, left). Tall case clock. Cherry case with inlay. Brass 8-day, weight-driven movement with strike and calendar aperture. Brass dial. Made by Jonathan Mulliken, Newburyport, Mass., c.1785. H. 88⅛″. Case made by Major John Dunlap of Goffstown and Bedford, N.H. (Amherst College)

115a (left). Detail of the hood and dial of the tall case clock made by Jonathan Mulliken.

118

118 (left). Tall case clock. Cherry case. Brass 8-day, weight-driven movement with strike, seconds dial, and musical attachment. Plays seven different tunes including a psalm on Sunday. One of two examples known. Made by Benjamin Willard, Grafton, Mass., c.1800. H. 94″. Image Studios, David Towne, Photographer. (Herschel B. Burt Collection)

118a (opposite). Side view of the movement showing the musical attachment of the tall case musical clock made by Benjamin Willard.

119 (right). Tall case clock. Country-style case. Brass 8-day, weight-driven movement with strike and rare perpetual calendar arrangement on the dial, sweep-seconds hand, and moon phase. Made by C. Cret, Orwigsburg (Philadelphia), Pa., c.1800. H. 94″. (Frank S. Schwarz and Son)

119a (below). Close-up of the hood and dial of the C. Cret tall case clock showing the rare calendar arrangement.

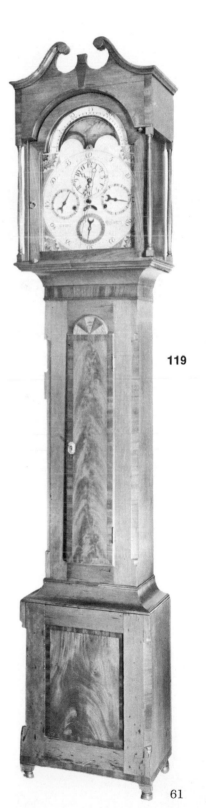

119

119a

121 (right). Tall case clock. Painted and grained case. Wood 30-hour movement. Marked on the great wheel: "September 18, 1821/John Perkins/No. 67/J.P. 73/Fitzwilliam, N.H." Made by John Perkins, Fitzwilliam, N.H., 1821. H. 69½". (Private collection)

121

120

120a

120 (left). Tall case clock. Maple case. Brass 8-day, weight-driven movement with strike, seconds dial, and calendar dial. Made by Timothy Chandler, Concord, N.H., c.1810. H. 89¾". Case made by David Young, Hopkinton, N.H. (Jennifer Parsons)

120a (above). Label of David Young who made the case for the Timothy Chandler tall case clock.

123 (right). Tall case clock. Mahogany case with inlay. Brass 8-day, weight-driven movement with strike, seconds dial, and calendar. Made by Jacob Alrichs, Wilmington, Del., c.1800. H. 101½″. (Frank S. Schwarz and Son)

123a (above). Close-up of the dial of the Alrichs tall case clock.

122 (left). Tall case clock. Mahogany case. Brass 8-day, weight-driven movement. Maker unknown. c.1800. Used by The Bank of New York for about 60 years. H. 124″. (The New-York Historical Society)

125 (opposite, above left). Tall case clock. Mahogany and mahogany veneer case. Brass 8-day, weight-driven movement with strike. Dish dial, glass, and hands are like those of a Massachusetts shelf clock. Case made by Henry Willard; movement by Aaron Willard, Jr., Boston, Mass., c.1830. H. 87″. (Private collection)

125a (right). Label on the back of the door of the tall case clock made by Aaron Willard, Jr.

125a

124

124 (left). Pennsylvania German *fraktur* showing tall case clock. c.1800. Pen and ink and watercolor. H. 12⅜″; W. 7⁷⁄₁₆″. (Greenfield Village and Henry Ford Museum)

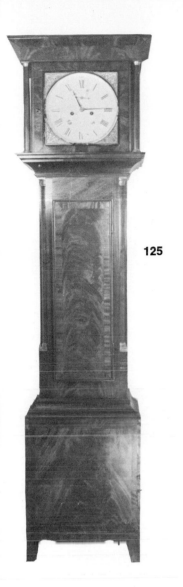

125

126

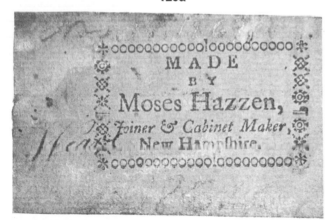

126a

126 (right). Tall case clock. Birch case with painted decoration. Brass 8-day, weight-driven movement with strike, seconds dial, calendar, and moon phase. Made by Timothy Chandler, Concord, N.H., c.1830. Die-stamped: "T. Chandler." H. 98″. Case made by Moses Hazen, Weare, N.H. (Weare Public Library)

126a (above). Label of Moses Hazen who made the case for the Timothy Chandler tall case clock.

127

127 (left). Tall case clock. Mahogany veneer case. Brass 8-day, weight-driven movement with strike, seconds dial, and rocking ship. Made by Nathaniel Munroe, Concord, Mass., c. 1810. H. 94″. Image Studios, David Towne, Photographer. (Herschel B. Burt Collection)

127a (below). Label pasted on the door of the tall case clock made by Nathaniel Munroe.

127a

128

128 (right). Tall case clock. Cherry case with stringing and banding. Brass 8-day, weight-driven movement with strike and seconds dial. Made by Philip Brown, Hopkinton, N.H., c.1810. H. 87½″. Brown was a clockmaker and silversmith until 1815, when he won a $25,000 lottery, after which he operated a clapboard mill and dealt in real estate. (Robin K. Ryan)

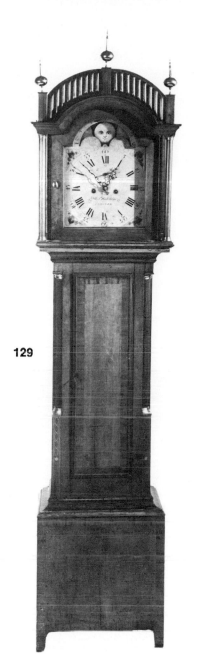

129

129 (left). Tall case clock. Cherry, walnut, and mahogany case with inlaid decoration. Brass 8-day, weight-driven movement with strike and moon phase. Made by Abel Hutchins, Concord, N.H., c.1810. H. 89½". Photograph: Bill Finney. (New Hampshire Historical Society)

130a

130

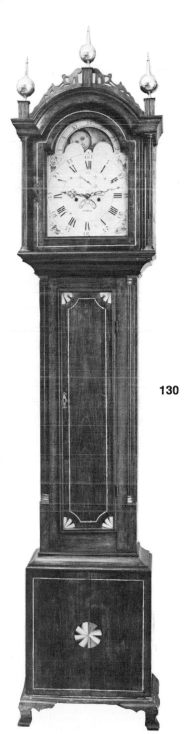

130 (right). Tall case clock. Maple and pine case. Brass 8-day, weight-driven movement with strike and calendar aperture. Moon phase in lunette. Case by David Young, Hopkinton, N.H. Movement by Aaron Willard, Boston, Mass., c.1810. H. 92½". Photograph: Allen Mewbourn. (The Museum of Fine Arts, Houston: The Bayou Bend Collection)

130a (above). Engraved label in the Aaron Willard tall case clock.

131 (below). Tall case clock. Painted pine case. Wood 30-hour, weight-driven movement with strike and seconds dial. Made by Simeon Cate, Sanbornton, N.H., c. 1830. H. 85¼″. Col. Simeon Cate was the proprietor of a clock factory and carried on the manufacture of chairs and cotton batting. Bought out the clock business of Timothy Gridley. (New Hampshire Historical Society)

131

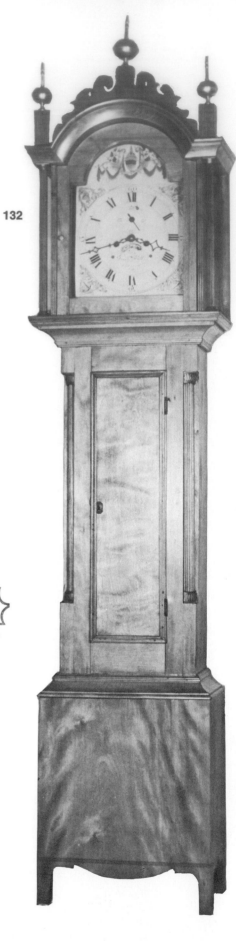

132

131a

131a (above). Wood movement of the Simeon Cate clock.

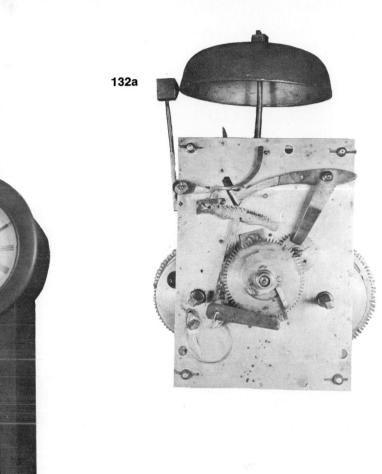

132a

133

134

132 (opposite, right). Tall case clock. Birch case with inlay. Brass 8-day, weight-driven movement with strike, seconds dial, and calendar. Made by Ivory Hall, Concord, N.H., c.1830. H. 97″. Hall was primarily a silversmith and jeweler. (New Hampshire Historical Society)

132a (above). Movement of the Ivory Hall tall case clock on opposite page.

133 (left). Tall case clock. Case is probably pine. Brass 8-day, weight-driven movement. Made by Isaac Youngs, New Lebanon, N.Y., c.1805. H. 72″. Image Studios, David Towne, Photographer. (Private collection)

134 (right). Tall case clock. Pine case, grain-painted to resemble mahogany. Wood 30-hour, weight-driven movement with strike and seconds dial. Made by Abraham Edwards, Ashby, Mass., c.1830. H. 86½″. (New Hampshire Historical Society)

136 (right). Astro-Regulator tall case clock. Mahogany case grained to look like rosewood. Brass 8-day, weight-driven movement. Made by Howard and Davis, Boston, Mass., c.1850. H. 87″. Two-glass mercury pendulum. Superb movement with gold-plated wheels. Later sold by Howard as Model #23. Photograph: Edward H. Goodrich. (American Clock and Watch Museum)

135

136

135 (left). Tall case clock. Probably pine, painted. Brass 8-day, weight-driven movement, originally fitted with an alarm that rang at sundown, the library's closing time. Made by John Child, Philadelphia, Pa., 1835. H. 92″. Purchased from Child in 1835 for $125. Peculiar shape is probably the result of the clock having been made to fit into a particular architectural space in The Library Company reading room. The pendulum bob weighs 15 pounds. (The Library Company of Philadelphia)

137 (opposite, left). Tall case clock. So-called Tramp Art case. Maker unknown. Probably upper New York State, c.1900. H. 71″. (Burton and Helaine Fendelman)

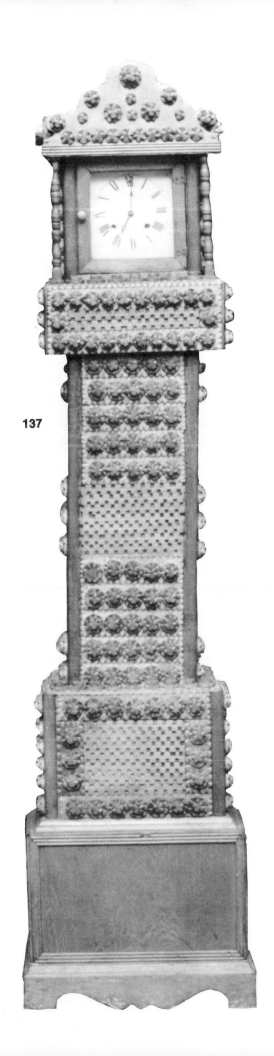

137

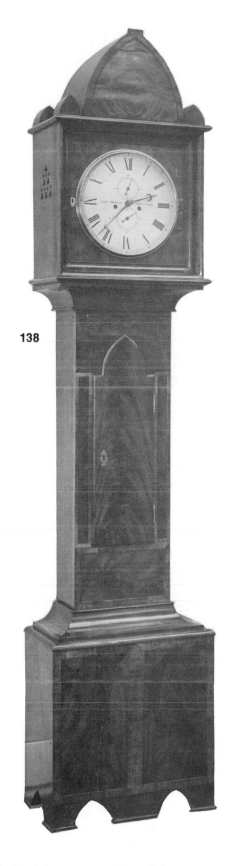

138

138 (above). Tall case clock. Mahogany case. Brass 8-day, weight-driven movement with strike, seconds hand, and calendar dial. Made by John Pringle, New York, N.Y., c.1834. (The New-York Historical Society)

139

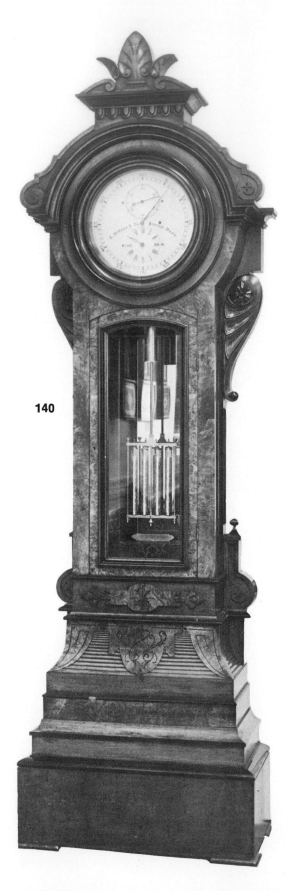

140

141

139 (left). Tall case regulator clock. Mahogany and mahogany veneer case. Brass 8-day, weight-driven movement. Made by E. Howard and Company, Boston, Mass., c.1857. H. 129″. (The Old Clock Museum)

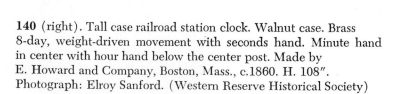

140 (right). Tall case railroad station clock. Walnut case. Brass 8-day, weight-driven movement with seconds hand. Minute hand in center with hour hand below the center post. Made by E. Howard and Company, Boston, Mass., c.1860. H. 108″. Photograph: Elroy Sanford. (Western Reserve Historical Society)

141 (opposite). Tall case clock. Solid mahogany case. Brass 8-day, weight-driven movement with strike. Made by Isaiah Lukens for the Philadelphia Bank c.1835. It was purchased by The Atheneum librarian, Henry Bird, in 1859 for $23.00. H. 176″. (The Atheneum of Philadelphia)

142

143

142 (left). Watchman's time clock. Walnut case. Brass 8-day, weight-driven movement. Made by E. Howard and Company, Boston, Mass., c.1860. H. 53¾″. Bottom dial is two-and-one-half days and is actuated by a wood rod from movement in back of time dial. Watchman, when making his rounds, pulled a chain that pushed in a pin around the periphery of lower dial. Originally was a wall clock. Base has been added. (The Clock Gallery)

143a

143 (opposite, right). Watchman's clock. Birch case. Brass 8-day, weight-driven movement. Made by Benjamin Morrill, Boscawen, N.H., c.1830. H. 54¼″. A warning bell announced the hour at which a watchman making rounds of five stations activated a cable. This raised a lever, depressing a pin on the drum. An inspection of the drum showed the stations visited. The plates are basically those of a tall case clock movement. (Private collection)

143a (above). Movement of the watchman's clock made by Benjamin Morrill.

DWARF TALL CASE CLOCKS

Dwarf tall case clocks, which are also called miniature tall case or grandmother clocks, are essentially scaled-down versions of tall case clocks. They are usually under five feet in height. These clocks were popular for a period of about twenty-five years, from roughly 1800 to 1825, and were fashioned by makers of full-scale tall case clocks. The movements were usually made of brass and ran for eight days; some included a strike train and a very few had alarm attachments. Among the most prolific makers were Joshua Wilder, Reuben Tower, the Baileys, and Nathaniel Hamlen.

144

144b

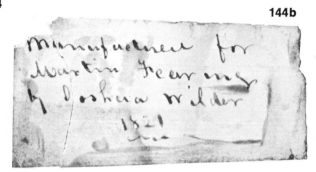

145 (below, left). Dwarf tall case clock. Mahogany case. Brass 8-day, weight driven movement with strike. Made by Reuben Tower, Hingham, Mass., 1810–1830. H. 48½". Photograph courtesy Israel Sack, Inc. (Stan P. Sax Collection)

145a (below, right). Close-up of the hood and dial of the dwarf tall case clock made by Reuben Tower.

145

144 (above, left). Dwarf tall case clock. Mahogany case. Brass 8-day, weight-driven movement with strike. Made by Joshua Wilder, Hingham, Mass., 1821. H. 50¾". Photograph courtesy Israel Sack, Inc. (Stan P. Sax Collection)

144a (opposite). Close-up of the dial of the dwarf tall case clock made by Joshua Wilder.

144b (above, right). Close-up of the contemporary inscription on the inside of the dwarf tall case clock made by Joshua Wilder. Inscription reads: "Manufactured for Martin Fearing, by Joshua Wilder 1821."

145a

146 (left). Box or coffin clock. Pine case. Brass 8-day, weight-driven movement. Attributed to the Shakers of Maine, c.1830. H. 32″. Has banjo-type movement. (Mark A. Shanaberger)

146

147 (left). Dwarf tall case or grandmother clock. Cherry case. Brass 8-day, weight-driven movement with alarm. Made by Benjamin Youngs, Watervliet, N.Y., c.1770. H. 43″. Photograph: Elroy Sanford. (Western Reserve Historical Society)

147

148

148a

148 (above). Miniature tall case clock. Butternut case. Bell metal 8-day, weight-driven movement with strike. Attributed to Joseph Chadwick, Boscawen, N.H., c.1810. H. 38¾″. (Private collection)

148a (left). Movement of the miniature tall case clock attributed to Joseph Chadwick.

149 (left). Dwarf tall case clock. Walnut case with banding and french feet. Brass 8-day, weight-driven movement with strike. Made by Nathaniel Hamlen, Augusta, Me., c.1810. H. 43″. (Greenfield Village and Henry Ford Museum)

150 (below, left). Dwarf tall case or grandmother clock. Cherry case. Brass 8-day, weight-driven movement. Made by Silas Parsons, Swanzey, N.H., c.1810. H. 39¼″. Strikes once on the hour. (Private collection)

151 (below, right). Dwarf tall case clock. Cherry and pine case with mahogany stain. Brass 8-day, weight-driven movement with strike. Probably made by Joshua Wilder, Hingham, Mass., c.1820. H. 44½″. Lent by Mrs. Louise Egbert Sailer. (The Brooklyn Museum)

152 (right). Dwarf tall case clock. Pine case. Wood 30-hour, weight-driven movement. The dial is painted on the back of the glass panel, leaving the hands exposed. Made by Jonathan Winslow, Massachusetts, c.1810. H. 48″. (New York State Historical Association)

149

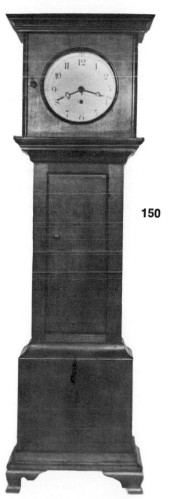

150

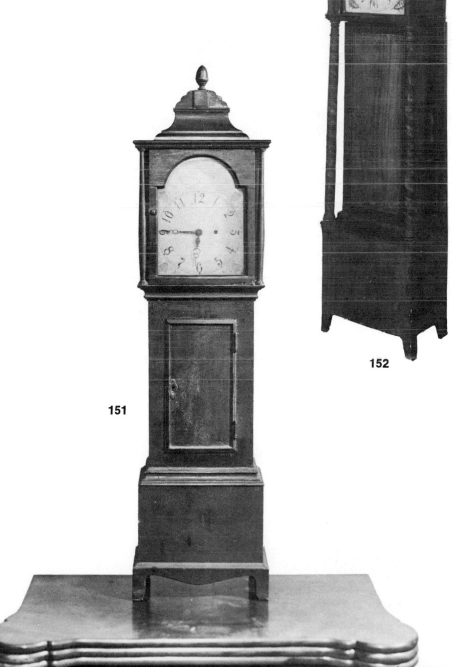

151

152

157 (below). Dwarf tall case clock. Cherry case. Brass 30-hour, weight-driven movement. Silvered dial. Made by John Winkley, Canterbury, N.H., c.1790. H. 37¼″. (Private collection)

153 (above, left). Dwarf tall case or grandmother clock. Mahogany case. Brass 8-day, weight-driven movement. Made by John Bailey, Jr., Hanover, Mass., c.1785. H. 40″. Photograph: Elroy Sanford. (Western Reserve Historical Society)

154 (above, center). Miniature tall case clock. Mahogany case. Brass 8-day, weight-driven movement with strike, seconds dial, and calendar dial. Made by Caleb Leach, Plymouth, Mass., c. 1780. H. 47½″. (The Metropolitan Museum of Art: Gift of George Coe Graves, 1930)

155 (above, right). Miniature tall case clock. Mahogany case. Brass 8-day, weight-driven movement with strike. Made by Joshua Wilder, Hingham, Mass., c.1810. H. 49″. (Greenfield Village and Henry Ford Museum)

156 (left). Dwarf tall case clock. Cherry case. Brass 2-day, weight-driven movement. Made by Timothy Chandler, Concord, N.H., c.1810. H. 34½″. Movement has iron plates, pendulum in front of front plate, solid wheels, cast fretwork. One of two examples known. (Private collection)

158 (left). Miniature tall case or grandmother clock. Solid mahogany case. Brass 8-day, weight-driven striking movement. Made by Joshua Wilder, Hingham, Mass., c.1810. H. 45″. Wilder is well known for this type of clock and was one of its most prolific makers. (Historic Deerfield, Inc.)

158

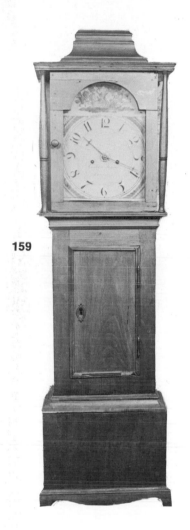

159

160

161

162

162a

159 (above). Miniature tall case clock. Pine case. Brass 8-day, weight-driven movement with an unusual alarm attachment. Made by Reuben Tower, Kingston, Mass., c.1815. H. 41″. Image Studios, David Towne, Photographer. (Private collection)

160 (right). Miniature tall case clock. Mahogany case. Brass 8-day, weight-driven movement with calendar aperture. Made by Thomas Claggett, Newport, R.I., 1730–1749. H. 61″. (The Metropolitan Museum of Art: Kennedy Fund, 1918)

161 (far right, above). Miniature tall case clock. Mahogany and mahogany veneer case. Brass 8-day, weight-driven movement. Made by Joshua Wilder, Hingham, Mass., 1810–1815. H. 51″. Image Studios, David Towne, Photographer. (Private collection)

162 (far right, below). Dwarf tall case or grandmother clock. Pine case. Brass 8-day, weight-driven movement with strike. Made by Noah Ranlet, Gilmanton, N.H., c.1800. H. 49⅛″. Four grandmother clocks are known to have been made by Ranlet. Eagle stencil appears to be original. (Private collection)

162a (near right). Movement of the Ranlet dwarf tall case. It is a reduced size of a regular tall case movement.

165

164 (right). Dwarf tall case clock. Painted pine case. Brass 30-hour, weight-driven movement with seconds dial and alarm. Made by B. S. Youngs, Schenectady, N.Y., c.1800. H. 36¼″. (Greenfield Village and Henry Ford Museum)

164

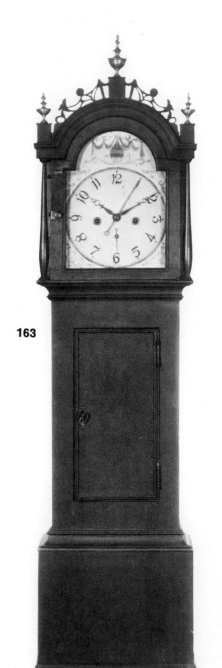

163

165 (above, right). Miniature tall case clock. Painted and stenciled case. Wood 30-hour movement. Handwritten label on inside of door reads: "This clock was made by/Jonathan Winslow born in/ Hardwick, Mass. on Aug. 15, 1765/Apprenticed to Cheney, Benjamin/and Timothy of East Hartford, Ct.,/where he carried on his/trade but lived in Warren,/New Salem, Worcester and Springfield, Mass. Died in/Springfield, July 20, 1847." The pewter hands are outside of the glass. The finials have been replaced. H. 48″. (Private collection)

163 (left). Dwarf tall case clock. Mahogany case. Brass 8-day, weight-driven movement with seconds dial, strike, and alarm. Made by Reuben Tower, Plymouth, Mass., c.1820. H. 47½″. (Greenfield Village and Henry Ford Museum)

166 (above). Portrait of John Thomas Avery by unknown artist, 1839. Watercolor. (Samuel and Esther Schwartz)

167 (above, left). Tall case clock. Mahogany case. Brass 8-day, weight-driven movement with strike. Moon phase in lunette. Made by James Doull, Charlestown, Mass., c.1810. Case made by John and/or Thomas Seymour, Boston, Mass. H. 96½″. (The White House Collection)

168 (above, center). Tall case clock. Inlaid cherry case. Brass 8-day, weight-driven movement with strike, seconds dial, calendar dial, and moon phase in lunette. Made by Abner Burnham, Litchfield Co., Conn., c.1800. H. 91½″. (Frank S. Schwarz and Son)

169 (above, right). Tall case clock. Cherry case. Brass 8-day, weight-driven movement with strike, seconds dial, and calendar aperture. Brass dial with strike and silent dial in lunette. Made by Benjamin Willard, Grafton, Mass., c.1760. H. 88″. (T. H. Eurich Company)

170 (opposite, below left). Tall case clock. Maple case. Brass 8-day, weight-driven movement with strike, seconds dial, and calendar aperture. Brass dial. Made by Edward Duffield, Philadelphia, Pa., c.1747. H. 102½″. Use of maple in a Philadelphia clock is rare, if not unique. (Frank S. Schwarz and Son)

171 (opposite, below right). Tall case clock. Mahogany case. Brass 8-day, weight-driven movement with strike. Rare round brass dial with sweep-seconds hand. Made by William Noyes, Boston, Massachusetts, area, c.1870. H. 91″. (Frank S. Schwarz and Son)

172 (right). Tall case clock. Mahogany veneer case with inlay. Brass 8-day, weight-driven movement with strike, seconds dial, calendar, and moon phase. Maker unknown. Case attributed to Matthew Egerton, Jr., New Brunswick, N.J., c.1790. H. 94″. (Diplomatic Reception Rooms, Department of State: Gift of Mr. and Mrs. Joseph H. Hennage)

172

172a

172a (above). Detail of the eagle inlay on the Egerton tall case clock.

173

173 (left). Tall case clock. Mahogany case with Near Eastern and Indian influence. Brass 8-day, weight-driven movement with strike. Lower dial shows the signs of the zodiac, phases of the moon and sun, day, day of the week, year, and month. Made by Tiffany & Co., New York, N.Y., c.1882. H. 105″. One of two clocks known in this style. (The Metropolitan Museum of Art: Gift of Mary J. Kingsband, 1906)

173a (below). Close-up of the dials on the Tiffany clock.

173a

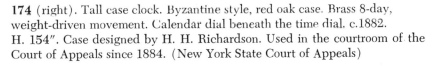

174a

174

174 (right). Tall case clock. Byzantine style, red oak case. Brass 8-day, weight-driven movement. Calendar dial beneath the time dial. c.1882. H. 154″. Case designed by H. H. Richardson. Used in the courtroom of the Court of Appeals since 1884. (New York State Court of Appeals)

174a (above). Detail of the calendar dial of the H. H. Richardson tall case clock.

175 (right). Bracket clock. Mahogany veneer case. Brass 8-day, spring-driven movement with strike, calendar, and strike and silent dial in lunette. Silvered dial with eagle. Made by Pearsall & Embree, New York, N.Y., 1785–1795. H. 21″. (The White House Collection)

176 (below). Bracket clock. Mahogany and pine case. Brass 8-day, two-train, spring-driven fusee-type movement with strike and calendar aperture. Brass dial with strike and silent dial in lunette. Made by Thomas Walker, Fredericksburg, Va., 1760–1775. H. 19¾″. (The Colonial Williamsburg Foundation)

175

176

BRACKET CLOCKS

The bracket clock was developed in England about 1650 or 1660. It was so named because it was generally set on a bracket that was attached to the wall. In some cases, however, because of its compact size, it was carried from room to room. The first cases were made in an architectural style, but they later evolved into the more usual bell or bracket top.

There is much controversy regarding bracket clocks in the United States. Some maintain that most of them were made in England and imported by American clockmakers who put their names on the dials. Others insist that the clocks were made here. Until some indisputable fact is discovered, the controversy will probably never be settled. However, no good reason has yet been given why American clockmakers could not have made them. An outstanding bracket clock is the one made by Aaron Willard illustrated in figure 177.

177

177 (left). Bracket clock. Mahogany veneer case. Brass 8-day, spring-driven movement with strike and calendar. Made by Aaron Willard, Roxbury, Mass., c.1780. H. 22″. Extremely rare clock by this maker. Probably unique. (The Henry Francis du Pont Winterthur Museum)

178 (below). Bracket clock. Mahogany case with satinwood inlay. Brass 8-day, spring-driven movement with strike, calendar, and moon phase. Silvered dial. Made by Andrew Billings, Poughkeepsie, N.Y., c.1795. H. 24¾". Made for Cadwalader Colden, former mayor of New York. Case made by Slover and Kortwright. (Greenfield Village and Henry Ford Museum)

179

179 (left). Bracket clock. Mahogany veneer case. Brass 8-day, spring-driven movement with seconds dial, strike, and calendar hand. Made by Stephen Van Wyck, New York, N.Y., 1797–1799. H. 16½″. (The Henry Francis du Pont Winterthur Museum)

180 (below, right). Bracket clock. Mahogany case. Brass 8-day, spring-driven movement with strike, fusee, and moon phase. Made by Abraham Stein, Philadelphia, Pa., c.1800. H. 20″. (Greenfield Village and Henry Ford Museum)

181 (below, left). Bracket clock. Walnut veneer case. Brass 8-day, spring-driven movement with strike and calendar aperture. Brass dial. Made by Charles Geddes, New York, N.Y., c.1775. H. 18″. (Greenfield Village and Henry Ford Museum)

180

181

182 (opposite, above left). Bracket clock. Painted case. Brass 8-day, spring-driven movement with strike. Made by Richard H. Jones, Baltimore, Md., c.1815. H. 15½″. (Greenfield Village and Henry Ford Museum)

183 (opposite, above right). Bracket clock. Mahogany veneer case. Brass 8-day, spring-driven movement with fusee. Made by Thomas Parker, Philadelphia, Pa., c.1790. H. 15¼″. (Private collection)

182

183

184 (below). Bracket clock. Mahogany veneer case with brass mounts. Brass 48-hour, spring-driven movement with strike. Movement signed: "Stephenson, London." Enameled face signed: "Thomas Parker Philad." Pierced fretted panels on either side backed with red silk, 1790–1800. H. 15½″. (Independence National Historical Park Collection)

184

185

185 (right). Bracket clock. Mahogany case with inlay. Brass 8-day, spring-driven movement with fusee, strike, and calendar dial. Painted blue dial with gilded spandrels. Made by Caleb Wheaton, Providence, R.I., c.1795. H. 21″. (Rhode Island Historical Society)

The introduction of the Massachusetts shelf clock about 1760–1770 probably was the result of the need for a clock that was less expensive than the tall case clock, which relatively few families could afford. Because of its much smaller size (avg. h. 24″–30″), less brass was used in the movement and considerably less wood was needed for the case. The movements for these clocks were very similar to those of the banjo clock, which was still to be invented. Running time varied from thirty hours to three or eight days. Some movements included a strike train and a few also had alarms. They enjoyed a great popularity and were made from 1760 to 1830 by the Willards, Daniel Balch, Seril Dodge, David Wood, and Levi Hutchins, among others.

MASSACHUSETTS SHELF CLOCKS

186 (left). Massachusetts shelf clock. Stained pine case. Brass 8-day, weight-driven movement. Brass dial. Made by John Winkley, Canterbury, N.H., c.1760. H. 26″. (Greenfield Village and Henry Ford Museum)

187 (above, center). Massachusetts shelf clock. Mahogany case. Brass 50-hour, weight-driven movement with strike. Brass dial. Made by Daniel Balch, Sr., Newburyport, Mass., dated 1783. H. 22¾″. Photograph: Donald F. Eaton. (Old Sturbridge Village)

188 (above, right). Massachusetts shelf clock. Mahogany veneer case with brass paw feet. Brass 36-hour, weight-driven movement with alarm. Made by Benjamin Willard, Roxbury, Mass., c.1774. H. 27″. (The Clock Gallery)

189

189 (left). Massachusetts shelf clock. Mahogany veneer case. Brass 8-day, weight-driven movement. Made by Aaron Willard, Boston, Mass., c.1790. H. 25¼″. (American Clock and Watch Museum)

190

191

190 (above, center). Massachusetts shelf clock. Mahogany case. Brass 8-day, weight-driven movement with strike and moon phase. Made by Seril Dodge, Providence, R.I., c.1790. H. 36¼″. Silvered dial with engraved floral motifs. Rare type of case for Rhode Island. (Rhode Island Historical Society)

191 (right). Massachusetts shelf clock. Mahogany case. Brass 8-day, weight-driven movement with strike. Strike-silent dial at top, seconds dial, and calendar dial. Made by Simon Willard, Roxbury, Mass., c.1785. H. 44″. Photograph: Donald F. Eaton. (Old Sturbridge Village)

93

193 (above). Case-on-case shelf clock. Cherry case. Brass 2-day, weight-driven movement with strike. Brass dial. Made by William Fitz, Portsmouth, N.H., 1760–1780. H. 29″. (Private collection)

192 (left). Massachusetts shelf clock. Mahogany case. Brass movement. Made by David Wood, Newburyport, Mass., 1766–1824. H. 32¾″. An outstanding example of this type of clock. (The Metropolitan Museum of Art: Gift of George Coe Graves, 1930)

194

195

194 (left). Case-on-case shelf clock. Cherry case. Brass 2-day movement with strike. Brass dial. Made by William Fitz, Portsmouth, N.H., 1760–1780. H. 28⅞″. (Private collection)

195 (above). Massachusetts shelf clock. Cherry and maple case. Brass 8-day, weight-driven movement with seconds hand. The hours are engraved on the main wheel and are seen through a semicircular opening on the brass dial. Made by Levi Hutchins, Concord, N.H., c.1790. H. 19⅞″. Photograph: Donald F. Eaton. (Old Sturbridge Village)

196

196 (above). Massachusetts shelf clock. Mahogany veneer case. Probably a brass 30-hour, weight-driven movement with calendar. Made by Simon Willard, Roxbury, Mass., 1790–1800. H. 28¾". Movement is an intermediate development between early Massachusetts wall clock and banjo type. (The Henry Francis du Pont Winterthur Museum)

197

198a

197a

198

197 (above, left). Case-on-case shelf clock. Case is probably pine. Brass 2-day, weight-driven movement. Round brass dial. Made by Levi Hutchins, Concord, N.H., c.1790. H. 20½″. Unique movement. Dial in front plate with cutout to show hours engraved on winding drum. Large hand shows the minutes, small hand shows the seconds. (Old Sturbridge Village)

197a (above). Close-up of the dial of the shelf clock made by Levi Hutchins.

198 (right). Massachusetts shelf clock. Butternut case. Brass 2-day, weight-driven movement. Brass kidney-shaped dial. Made by Levi Hutchins, Concord, N.H., c.1790. H. 21″. Case bears a slight resemblance to some early Simon Willard shelf clocks. (Private collection)

198a (above, right). Movement of the Hutchins shelf clock.

199 (below, left). Massachusetts shelf clock. Mahogany case with inlay. Brass 8-day, weight-driven movement. Case made by John Seymour, Boston, Mass. Movement made by James Doull, Charlestown, Mass., c.1815. H. 36″. (Mark A. Shanaberger)

200 (below, center). Massachusetts shelf clock. Mahogany case. Brass 8-day, weight-driven movement. Made by Aaron Willard, Boston, Mass., c.1805. H. 35″. (The Metropolitan Museum of Art: Gift of George Coe Graves, 1930)

201 (right). Massachusetts shelf clock. Mahogany case. Brass 8-day, weight-driven movement with strike. Brass dial. Probably made by Simeon Jocelin, New Haven, Conn., c.1798. H. 29″. Note round mirror on lower portion of case. (New Haven Colony Historical Society)

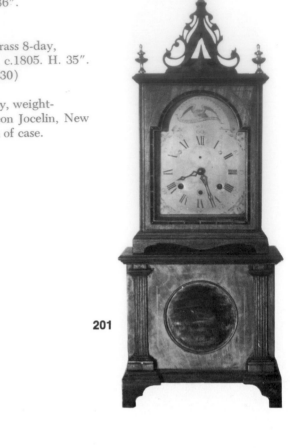

201

200

199

202 (right). Massachusetts shelf clock. Mahogany case. Brass 8-day, weight-driven movement. Brass dial. Made by Simon Willard, Roxbury, Mass., c.1800. H. 29½″. Photograph courtesy Israel Sack, Inc. (Eric M. Wunsch)

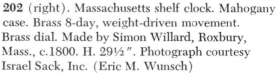

202

203 (below, left). Massachusetts shelf clock. Mahogany case. Brass 8-day, weight-driven movement. Made by Gardiner Parker, Westborough, Mass., c.1809. H. 35½″. Image Studios, David Towne, Photographer. (Private collection)

204 (below, center). Massachusetts shelf clock. Solid and veneered crotch mahogany case inlaid with satinwood. Brass 8-day, weight-driven movement. Made by Nathaniel Munroe, Concord, Mass., c.1810. H. 41″. Painted kidney-shaped dial with floral swag. (Museum of Art, Carnegie Institute)

205 (right). Massachusetts shelf clock. Mahogany case with pine, rose, and satinwood inlays. Brass 8-day, weight-driven movement. Made by Elnathan Taber, Roxbury, Mass., c.1805. H. 40″. (Museum of Fine Arts, Boston: M. and M. Karolik Collection)

205

204

203

206 (right). Massachusetts shelf clock. Mahogany case with satinwood banding. Brass 60-hour, weight-driven movement. Seconds bit marked with 45 shows in aperture under 12. Made by David Wood, Newburyport, Mass., c.1815. H. 34″. Image Studios, David Towne, Photographer. (Private collection)

206

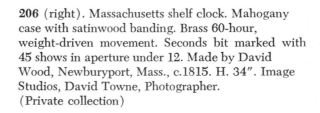

207 (above, left). Massachusetts shelf clock. Mahogany case. Brass 8-day movement. Made by Levi Hutchins, Concord, N.H., c.1830. H. 34⅝″. (The Currier Gallery of Art: Gift of Mr. and Mrs. Paul A. Sargeant in memory of Frank M. Sargeant)

208 (left). Massachusetts shelf clock. Case is painted black; however, white paint appears at right bottom of hood. Brass 8-day, weight-driven movement. Made by Daniel Hubbard, Medfield, Mass., c.1820. H. 32½″. (Mark A. Shanaberger)

209 (above). Massachusetts shelf clock. Mahogany case. Brass 8-day, weight-driven movement with strike. Panel is original and shows "The Escape of the Constitution." Made by Aaron Willard, Boston, Mass., c.1815. H. 35″. Image Studios, David Towne, Photographer. (Private collection)

209a

209a (above). Detail of the Aaron Willard signature on the dial door of the shelf clock.

209b (below). Detail of the painting on the Aaron Willard shelf clock showing "The Escape of the Constitution."

209b

LIGHTHOUSE CLOCKS

The lighthouse clock was the invention of Simon Willard, who patented it in 1822. The first ones made were alarm clocks that had the hammer striking the case instead of a bell, but most lighthouse clocks were made to tell time only. The movements were exposed and covered with a glass dome; some of these domes were made by the Sandwich Glass Company of Sandwich, Massachusetts. This type of clock is also often referred to as an Eddystone Lighthouse clock, taking its name from the Eddystone Lighthouse at Plymouth, England.

The lighthouse style, in spite of its pleasing appearance, was not popular and as far as is known, only about twenty or twenty-five examples were made, hence they are very rare today. The reader should note what is probably a unique painted example illustrated in figure 3. Sales agents were T. B. Jones of Boston and Thomas Richards of New York City.

210 (left). Lighthouse clock. Mahogany case with glass dome and brass ornaments. Brass 8-day, weight-driven movement with strike. Made by Simon Willard, Roxbury, Mass., c.1826. H. 29″. Photograph: Donald F. Eaton. (Old Sturbridge Village)

211 (above). Lighthouse clock. Mahogany case. Brass 8-day, weight-driven movement with alarm. Made by Simon Willard, Roxbury, Mass., c.1822. H. 31½″. (Mark A. Shanaberger)

213 (center, left). Eddystone Lighthouse clock. Cylindrical mahogany case. Brass 8-day, weight-driven movement with strike. Made by Simon Willard, Roxbury, Mass., c.1822. H. 23″. (Museum of Fine Arts, Boston: Bequest of Miss Belle Hunt)

214 (center, right). Eddystone Lighthouse clock. Mahogany case. Brass 8-day, weight-driven movement with alarm. Made by Simon Willard, Roxbury, Mass., c.1822. H. 28½″. (The Metropolitan Museum of Art: Gift of Mrs. Richard M. Lederer, 1957, in memory of Richard M. Lederer)

215 (right). Lighthouse clock. Rectangular mahogany case with black metal drum above. Brass 8-day, weight-driven movement with alarm. Made by Simon Willard, Roxbury, Mass., c.1822. H. 25″. (Museum of Fine Arts, Boston: Gift of Philip Spaulding, Oakes Ames Spaulding, and Robert Amos Spaulding)

212 (left). Lighthouse shelf clock. Mahogany case with original glass dome. Brass 8-day, weight-driven movement with strike (once on the hour). Made by Simon Willard and Son, Roxbury, Mass., c.1825. H. 30″. Photograph courtesy Israel Sack, Inc. (Stan P. Sax Collection)

103

216 (right). Massachusetts shelf clock. Mahogany case. Brass 30-hour, weight-driven movement with drop-off striking. Brass dial. Made by Aaron Willard, Roxbury, Mass., c.1780. H. 17″. Because of its size, this clock is unique. (Herschel B. Burt Collection)

217 (below, left). Massachusetts shelf clock. The case is mahogany, painted white with gilded pine frame and stenciled base. Brass 8-day, weight-driven movement. Dished dial. Made by Aaron Willard, Boston, Mass., c.1820. H. 34″. This rare clock is commonly called a Bride's or Presentation clock. (Herschel B. Burt Collection)

218 (below, right). Massachusetts shelf clock. Mahogany case. Brass 8-day, weight-driven movement with drop-off strike and calendar. Silver kidney-shaped dial. Made by Simon Willard, Roxbury, Mass., 1780. H. 32″. (Herschel B. Burt Collection)

216

217

218

SHELF CLOCKS

Shelf clocks were one of the most important types of clocks manufactured. They could be made inexpensively, and thus most people could afford to have them in their homes.

The Massachusetts shelf clock (see pages 92–101) as made by the Willards and others is considered by many to be the most beautiful type of shelf clock made in this country. The inventor's name is lost to us, although many people attribute it to Simon Willard. The designs of the earliest examples are reminiscent of tall case clocks (see fig. 194). The movements were brass and ran anywhere from thirty hours to three days. Later, a movement similar to the banjo movement was used, enabling the clock to run for eight days. The case style also changed, and many of them resembled a bracket clock set on a base (fig. 205). Some of the bases had scenes painted on the glass doors, others had a solid wood door, and still others did not have a door at all, but a wooden panel. Some of the later movements had a strike train added and some even had alarms.

The mass production of shelf clocks started in Connecticut when Eli Terry accepted an order in 1807 for approximately four thousand wood movements. The order was completed about 1810. Later, Terry developed the wood movement that was used in the popular pillar-and-scroll clock, which was copied by so many makers. Various types of movements were made: the visible escapement, the off-center escapement, the outside escapement, and the standard escapement that was between the front plate and the wood dial. A great many case styles evolved from the pillar-and-scroll design (fig. 235), namely the triple deck (fig. 309), the Empire style with carved pillars and splat (fig. 305), and the flat tops. Other styles developed were the steeple (fig. 329), steeple-on-steeple (fig. 268), beehive (fig. 346), and half octagons (fig. 392). Both brass and wood movements were used. Some were weight driven while others utilized either brass or steel springs for power.

Around 1840 the ogee case, with its S curves, was introduced and was still being made during the early 1900s. It was a very popular style and was made in different sizes from the miniature to the standard. Both wood and brass movements were used by the various makers and these ogee clocks ran for either thirty hours or eight days, with the thirty-hour clock being the most popular.

Another very popular clock was the steeple clock, invented by Elias Ingraham. Variations of this style, such as the double steeple, beehive, ripple front, and others, were developed by the many Connecticut clockmakers. All of them were exceedingly successful and many of them survive today.

From this time on, many varieties of shelf clocks were developed and made. This is evident from the appearance of the so-called kitchen clocks (fig. 447), mantel clocks (with either marble or wood cases painted and grained to simulate marble), cast-iron (fig. 430) and white-metal cases, cases made of papier-mâché (fig. 405), china cases (fig. 437), and others that reflect French influence.

Calendar clocks are another important type of shelf clock. The addition of a calendar to a clock mechanism is not indigenous to American clocks. The calendar movement first appeared on English tall case clocks about 1660. However, the American clockmaker did invent the many variations of the calendar that began to proliferate around 1860. These refinements included dials and indicator hands that gave the month, date, day of the week, phases of the moon, the time of the rising and setting of the sun, signs of the zodiac, etc. Some calendars even took leap year into account and so did not have to be adjusted manually. The many fascinating varieties of calendar shelf clocks can be found on pages 166 to 171. Calendar wall clocks were also made and are illustrated on pages 264 to 271.

219

219 (right). Miniature pillar-and-scroll shelf clock. Mahogany and mahogany veneer case. Wood 30-hour, weight-driven movement with strike. Made by Mark Leavenworth, Waterbury, Conn., c.1825. H. 25″. (Private collection)

220

220 (left). Pillar-and-scroll shelf clock. Mahogany and mahogany veneer case. Wood 30-hour, weight-driven movement with strike. Made by E. Terry and Sons, Plymouth, Conn., c.1825. H. 31½″. (William J. Haggerty Collection)

221 (below, left). Shelf clock. Mahogany veneer case with stenciled side columns and splat. Wood 30-hour, weight-driven movement with strike. Made by Marsh, Gilbert & Co., Bristol, Conn., c.1830. H. 33″. (Private collection)

222 (below, right). Shelf clock. Mahogany veneer case. Brass 8-day, weight-driven movement with strike, sweep-seconds hand, calendar, and moon phase. Made by Henry Ober, Elizabethtown, Pa., c.1820. H. 47½″. (Private collection)

221

222

223

224

225

223 (above, left). Pillar-and-scroll shelf clock. Mahogany and mahogany veneer case. Wood 30-hour, weight-driven movement with strike. Offcenter, inside-outside escapement. Compound lead weights. One of the very last of the prestandard Seth Thomas pillar-and-scroll clocks. Made by Seth Thomas, Plymouth, Conn., c.1820. H. 28¾″. (William J. Haggerty Collection)

224 (above, right). Shelf clock. Mahogany veneer case. Brass 8-day, weight-driven movement with strike, seconds dial, and moon phase. Brass dial. Made by Nathan Adams, Danvers, Mass., c.1790. H. 38¾″. (Private collection)

225 (right). Pillar-and-scroll shelf clock. Mahogany and mahogany veneer case. Wood 30-hour, weight-driven movement with strike. Made by Seth Thomas, Plymouth, Conn., c.1820. H. 31½″. (Greenfield Village and Henry Ford Museum)

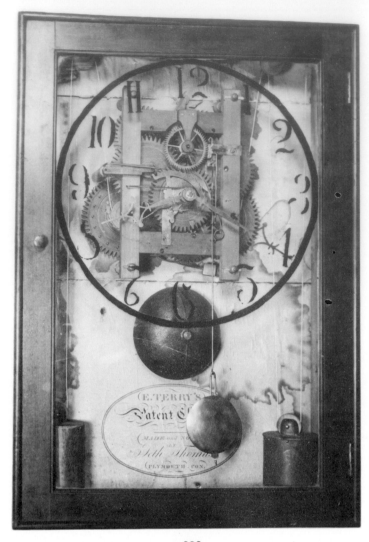

226

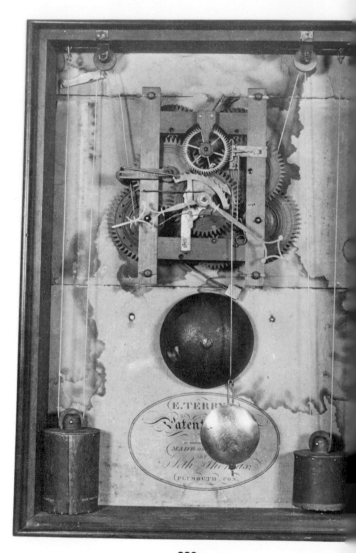

226a

226 (left). Box shelf clock. Cherry case. Wood 30-hour, weight-driven movement. Made by Seth Thomas, Plymouth, Conn., c.1816. H. 20″. The box clock was the first production model of the wood-movement shelf clock. Developed and patented by Eli Terry, and usually sold by Seth Thomas. Note the offcenter pendulum. (American Clock and Watch Museum)

226a (below). Box clock made by Seth Thomas with the door open showing the movement and label.

227

227 (left). Pillar-and-scroll shelf clock. Mahogany case. Wood 30-hour movement with outside escapement and strike. Unusual scrollwork top. Made by Eli Terry, Plymouth, Conn., 1810–1815. H. 32″. Tablet shows Monticello. (The New-York Historical Society)

228 (left). Box clock. Mahogany and mahogany veneer case. Wood 30-hour, weight-driven movement with strike and alarm. Made by Eli Terry & Sons, Plymouth, Conn., c.1820. H. 20″. The time train is also used for the alarm. (Amos G. Avery Collection)

228

229 (below). *Intelligence Office* by William H. Burr, 1840. Oil on canvas. Notice the shelf clock at the left side of the room. (The New-York Historical Society)

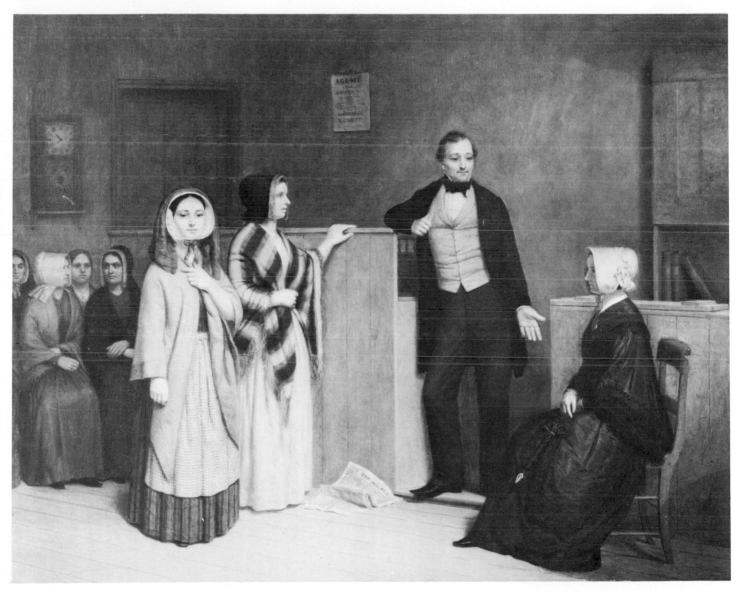

229

230a

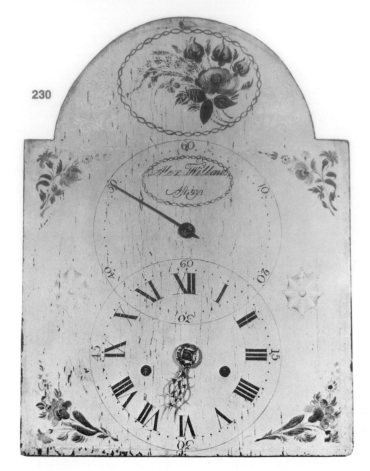

230 (above). Wood dial from a tall case clock made by Alexander T. Willard, Ashby, Mass., c.1820. (Amos G. Avery Collection)

230a (left). Side view of the Alexander T. Willard wood movement.

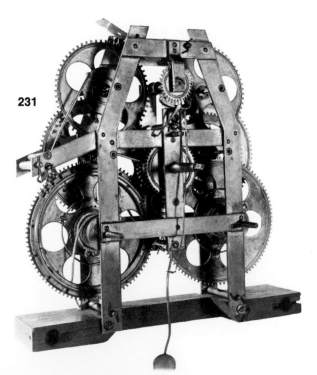

231 (above). Movement developed by Joseph Ives. Strap-brass frames and rolling pinions. Found in Empire cases by various makers in the 1830s. Made by Joseph Ives, Bristol, Conn., c.1830s. H. 8½ ". (American Clock and Watch Museum)

232 (opposite, below right). Another wood clock movement made by Alexander T. Willard showing back plate with count wheel. 1820–1825. H. 10″. (Amos G. Avery Collection)

233 (right). Eli Terry & Sons pillar-and-scroll shelf clock with door open and dial removed showing the movement and the "roller" type alarm. c. 1825. H. 32″. (Amos C. Avery Collection)

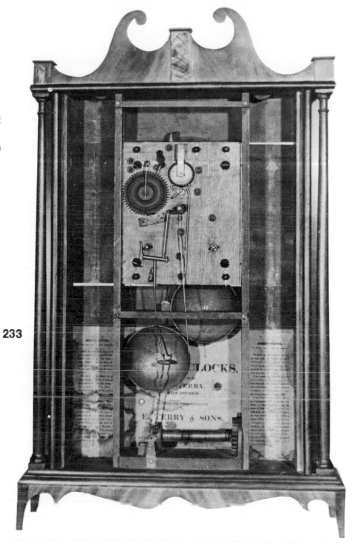

233

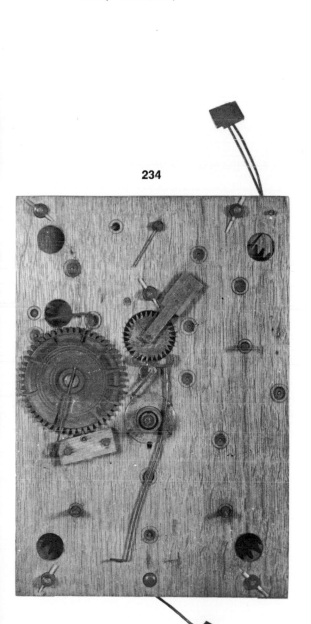

234

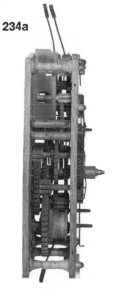

234a

234b

234 (above). Three photographs showing an unusual wood movement with double hammers. Maker unknown. Probably made in the Bristol, Conn., area, c.1830. H. 9½″. Photograph: Edward H. Goodrich. (American Clock and Watch Museum)

234a (above, right). Side view of the wood movement.

234b (right). Three-quarter view of the wood movement.

235

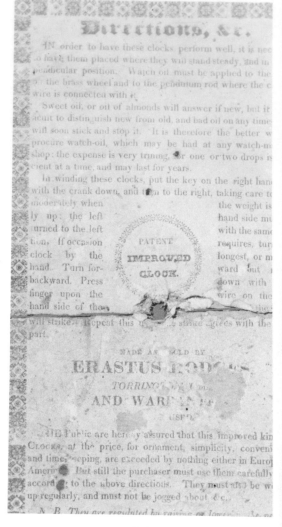

235a

235 (left). Miniature pillar-and-scroll shelf clock. Mahogany veneer case. Torrington-type wood 30-hour, weight-driven movement with strike. Made by Erastus Hodges, Torrington, Conn., c.1830. H. 28½″. (Private collection)

235a (above). Label of the Erastus Hodges miniature pillar-and-scroll shelf clock.

236

237

236 (left). Pillar-and-scroll shelf clock. Mahogany and mahogany veneer case. Wood 30-hour, weight-driven Torrington-type movement with strike. Made by Ethel North, Wolcottville, Conn., c.1820. H. 31½″. (Amos G. Avery Collection)

237 (above). Miniature pillar-and-scroll shelf clock. Mahogany case. Wood 30-hour, weight-driven Torrington-type movement with strike. Made by Erastus Hodges, Torrington; Conn., c. 1820. H. 28¼″. (Greenfield Village and Henry Ford Museum)

238a

238b

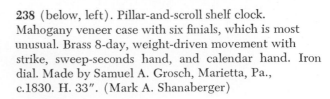

238 (below, left). Pillar-and-scroll shelf clock. Mahogany veneer case with six finials, which is most unusual. Brass 8-day, weight-driven movement with strike, sweep-seconds hand, and calendar hand. Iron dial. Made by Samuel A. Grosch, Marietta, Pa., c.1830. H. 33". (Mark A. Shanaberger)

238a (opposite). Grosch pillar-and-scroll clock with door open showing wood covers over the space where the weights drop.

238b (left). Grosch pillar-and-scroll clock with dial removed showing the movement.

239

238

239 (above). Pillar-and-scroll shelf clock. Mahogany and mahogany veneer case. Wood 30-hour, weight-driven movement with strike. Made by E. Terry and Sons, Plymouth, Conn. Label marked: "Movement made by Ephraim Downes of Bristol for the patentee," c.1840. H. 27". (J. Alford Jones)

240

241

242

240 (left). Reeded pillar-and-scroll shelf clock. Mahogany and maple case. Wood 30-hour, weight-driven movement with strike. Made by Ives and Lewis, Bristol, Conn., 1819–1823. H. 35½". Movement has roller pinions invented by Ives. (Gene L. Bagwell Collection)

243 (opposite, above left). Pillar-and-scroll shelf clock. Mahogany veneer case. Wood 30-hour, weight-driven movement with strike. Made by Bunnel and Scovill, Owego, Tioga Co., N.Y., c.1835. H. 28½". (The Clock Gallery)

243a (opposite, below left). Bunnel and Scovill pillar-and-scroll clock with door open showing the label.

241 (above, left). Pillar-and-scroll shelf clock. Cherry case with fluted columns. Brass 8-day, weight-driven banjo-type movement with seconds dial. Made by Asa Munger, Auburn, N.Y., c.1830. H. 38". Cases for Munger clocks are thought to have been made in the Auburn penitentiary. Wallpaper lined the backs of his cases. (Mark A. Shanaberger)

242 (right). Massachusetts pillar-and-scroll shelf clock. Maple case. Wood 30-hour, weight-driven movement with strike. Made by William Sherwin, Buckland, Mass., c. 1830. H. 29½". (Private collection)

244 (right). Pennsylvania pillar-and-scroll shelf clock. Mahogany veneer case. Brass 8-day, weight-driven movement with strike and moon phase beneath the center post. Unusual "dumbbell" striking system. Made by Jacob Custer, Norristown, Pa., c. 1835. H. 34¼". (Private collection)

244

243

243a

245

245 (right). Pennsylvania pillar-and-scroll shelf clock. Mahogany case with cherry veneered door. Wood, brass, and iron 30-hour, weight-driven movement with strike. Dial and bottom tablet are painted iron. Marked on back of movement: "Made by Joseph Holtzinger, Northampton or Norristown, Penn., Apr. 29, 1830, Clock No. 10." H. 32½". Feet have been replaced. (Mark A. Shanaberger)

246

247a

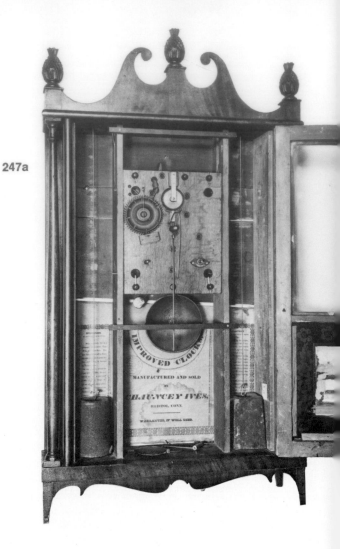

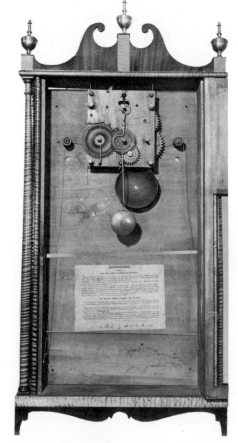

246b

246a

246a (above). Close-up of the label in the Ives & Lewis pillar-and-scroll clock above showing the maker's name penned at the bottom.

246b (right). Ives & Lewis pillar-and-scroll shelf clock with door open to show movement and label.

248a (right). Door open showing tablet of pillar-and-scroll shelf clock made by Silas Hoadley. Glass tablet has ribbed indentations and seems to have been opaqued by accidental heavy liming.

248a

247

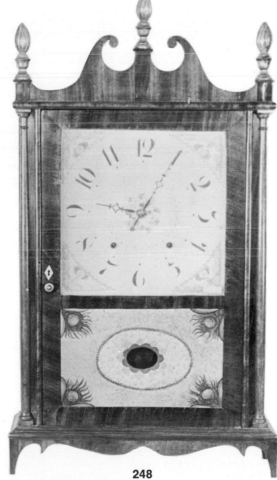

248

246 (opposite, far left). Pillar-and-scroll shelf clock. Mahogany and tiger maple veneer case. Wood 30-hour, weight-driven movement with strike. Made by Ives & Lewis, Bristol, Conn., c.1820. H. 37⅟₁₆″. Unusual mahogany plate movement with rolling pinions. (American Clock and Watch Museum)

247 (above). Pillar-and-scroll shelf clock. Mahogany veneer case with carved pineapple finials. Wood 30-hour, weight-driven movement with strike. Made by Chauncey Ives, Bristol, Conn., 1825–1830. H. 30¼″. (American Clock and Watch Museum)

247a (opposite, above right). Ives pillar-and-scroll shelf clock with door open showing the movement and label.

248 (right). Pillar-and-scroll shelf clock. Mahogany veneer case with carved wood finials. Upside-down, 30-hour wood movement. Made by Silas Hoadley, Plymouth, Conn., c.1825. H. 32″. Tablet is most unusual for a Connecticut pillar-and-scroll in that it is painted tin with a small opening to sight the pendulum bob. Hoadley's name is misspelled Hoadly. (Irving Cooperman Collection)

249

249 (opposite). Brass mantel clock. Brass 8-day, weight-driven movement with strike. Made by Dubec, Rue Michelle-Comte, No. 33 à Paris. Made in France 1800–1810 for the American trade. A number of variations of this clock are known. H. 19½″. Photograph courtesy Israel Sack, Inc. (Stan P. Sax Collection)

250

250a

250 (above, left). Shelf clock. Mahogany veneer case. Brass 30-hour, spring-driven movement with single fusee. Made by S.B. Terry and Co., Terryville, Conn., c.1840. H. 11″. Image Studios, David Towne, Photographer. (Private collection)

250a (above, right). Close-up of the movement with single fusee made by S.B. Terry and Co.

251a

251

251 (right). Shelf clock. Mahogany and mahogany veneer case. Brass 3½-day, weight-driven movement with alarm. Made by John Sawin, Boston, Mass., c.1835. H. 14″. A very unusual clock with a small Massachusetts shelf clock movement. Image Studios, David Towne, Photographer. (Herschel B. Burt Collection)

251a (above). Movement of the John Sawin shelf clock showing the alarm.

253 (right). Close-up of a triple-deck shelf clock made by C. and L. C. Ives showing the movement and wagon spring. Bristol, Conn., c.1850. H. 36″. Image Studios, David Towne, Photographer. (Private collection)

252 (above). Shelf clock. Mahogany and mahogany veneer case. Brass and iron 8-day, wagon-spring movement with strike. Made by Joseph Ives, New York, N.Y., c.1830. H. 28¾″. (Mark A. Shanaberger)

254 (right). Close-up of a wood 8-day, wagon-spring movement with strike. Made by Olmstead and Barnes, Brooklyn, N.Y., c.1828. H. 27″. Image Studios, David Towne, Photographer. (Private collection)

256 (right). Shelf clock. Cast-iron case grained to simulate oak. Brass 30-day, wagon-spring movement. Made by Joseph Ives, Bristol, Conn., c.1850. H. 15″. Image Studios, David Towne, Photographer. (Private collection)

256

255

255 (above). Shelf clock. Mahogany veneer case. Brass 8-day, wagon-spring movement with strike. Made by Joseph Ives, Brooklyn, N.Y., c.1825. H. 22″. Early style movement used in these cases and apparently the earliest production-model clock using Ives wagon spring. (American Clock and Watch Museum)

257 (right). Shelf clock. Mahogany veneer case. Brass 30-hour, wagon-spring movement with strike. Single-leaf wagon spring is attached to the top of the case and bends around the movement when wound. Made by Joseph Ives, Plainville and Farmington, Conn., c.1841. H. 23½″. (American Clock and Watch Museum)

257

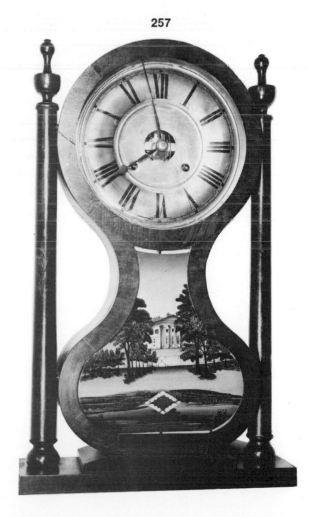

258 (below, left). Acorn shelf clock. Laminated case. Brass 8-day, fusee-type spring-driven movement. Forestville Manufacturing Co. on dial and J. C. Brown on label. Forestville, Conn., c.1845. H. 24¾ ". (Mark A. Shanaberger)

259 (below, right). Lyre shelf clock. Mahogany and bird's-eye maple case with some veneer. Brass 8-day, weight-driven movement with strike. Attributed to Benjamin Willard the Younger, Boston, Mass., c.1835. H. 29½ ". (Mark A. Shanaberger)

259a (right). Inside of the Willard lyre shelf clock showing the movement, with rack-and-snail strike.

259a

258

259

124

260 (above). *Lady at a Piano* by Amasa Hewens (1795–1855). Oil on panel. Signed and dated 1836 on the reverse. Notice mantel clock on the fireplace. (Childs Gallery)

261

262

261 (opposite). Shelf clock. Mahogany veneer case. Wood 30-hour, weight-driven movement with strike. Made by Rodney Brace, North Bridgewater, Mass., 1831–1835. H. 37¾″. Torrington-type movement made in the shops of Erastus Hodges of Torrington, Conn. Brace was probably a case maker. Photograph: Edward H. Goodrich. (Chris H. Bailey)

262 (left). Shelf clock. Mahogany veneer case with unusual reverse scrolls. Wood 30-hour, weight-driven movement with strike. Made by Jeromes and Darrow, Bristol, Conn., c.1820. H. 29½″. Photograph: Edward H. Goodrich. (American Clock and Watch Museum)

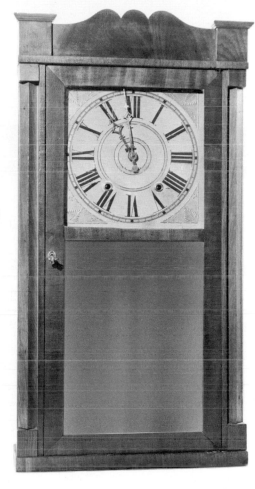

264

263

263 (left). Shelf clock. Mahogany veneer case with carved splat and paw feet. Brass 8-day, weight-driven movement with seconds dial. Made by Spencer, Hotchkiss & Co., Salem Bridge, Mass., c.1830. H. 31½″. (Private collection)

264 (above). Mirror shelf clock. Walnut veneer case. Wood 30-hour, weight-driven movement with strike. Made by David Dutton, Mount Vernon, N.H., c.1830. H. 31″. (William J. Haggerty Collection)

265 (above, left). Steeple-type shelf clock. Mahogany veneer case. Brass 8-day, wagon-spring movement with strike. Made by A. Walls, Bristol, Conn., c.1840. H. 26″. (Private collection)

266 (above, center). Double-steeple shelf clock. Mahogany veneer case with four candles. Brass 8-day, wagon-spring movement with strike. Made by Birge & Fuller, Bristol, Conn., c. 1846. H. 25″. (Private collection)

267 (above, right). Steeple-on-steeple or double-steeple shelf clock. Mahogany veneer case. Brass 8-day, wagon-spring movement with strike. Made by Birge & Fuller, Bristol, Conn., c.1845. H. 27½″. (William J. Haggerty Collection)

268a

268 (left). Double-steeple shelf clock. Mahogany veneer case. Brass 8-day, spring-driven, fusee movement with strike. Made by Elisha Manross, Bristol, Conn., c.1850. H. 23¾″. (Private collection)

268a (above). Close-up of the glass beneath the dial of the Manross clock.

269 (right). Shelf clock. Painted and stenciled pine case. Wood 30-hour, weight-driven movement with strike. Made by Luman Watson, Cincinnati, Ohio, c.1838. H. 30¼". (Private collection)

269

270 (below, left). Beehive shelf clock. Pine case with gesso and gold leaf. Brass 8-day, spring-driven movement with strike and alarm. Made by Brewster and Ingrahams, Bristol, Conn., c. 1850. H. 19¼". (Private collection)

271 (below, center). Acorn shelf clock. Rosewood veneer case made without side arms. Probably the last type made. Brass 8-day, spring-driven movement with fusee. Made by Jonathan C. Brown, Bristol, Conn., c.1850. H. 19¼". (Private collection)

272

270

271

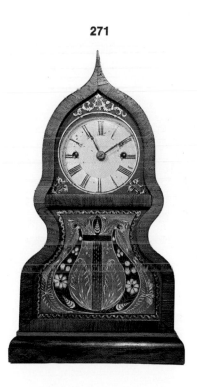

272 (right). Shelf clock. Stenciled mahogany veneer case. Wood 30-hour, weight-driven movement with strike. Made by Eli Terry, Jr., Plymouth, Conn., c. 1845. H. 24½". (J. Alford Jones)

129

273

273 (opposite). Shelf clock. Mahogany veneer case with hollow columns for the weights. Brass 8-day, weight-driven movement with strike. Made by George Marsh, Farmington, Conn., c.1830. H. 37″. (Private collection)

274 (right). Shelf clock. Mahogany and mahogany veneer case with fluted columns. Wood 30-hour, weight-driven movement with strike. Made by Henry Loomis, Bristol, Conn., c.1830. H. 29½″. (Private collection)

275 (below, left). Miniature triple-deck shelf clock. Walnut veneer case. Brass 30-hour, weight-driven movement with strike. Decalcomania on center glass, reverse painting on lower glass. Marbleized half columns, gilded gesso splat. Made by Birge & Mallory, Bristol, Conn., c.1845. H. 26″. (William J. Haggerty Collection)

276 (below, right). Shelf clock. Mahogany veneer case with carved half columns and splat. Wood 30-hour, weight-driven movement with strike. Made by Seth Thomas, Plymouth, Conn., c.1830. H. 28¾″. (Private collection)

274

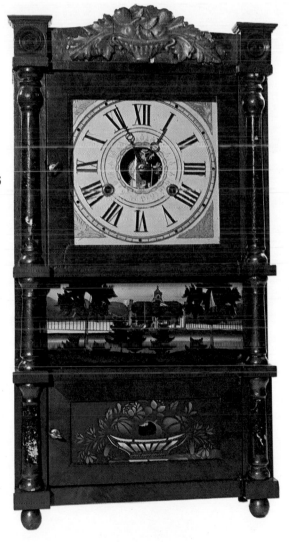

275

276

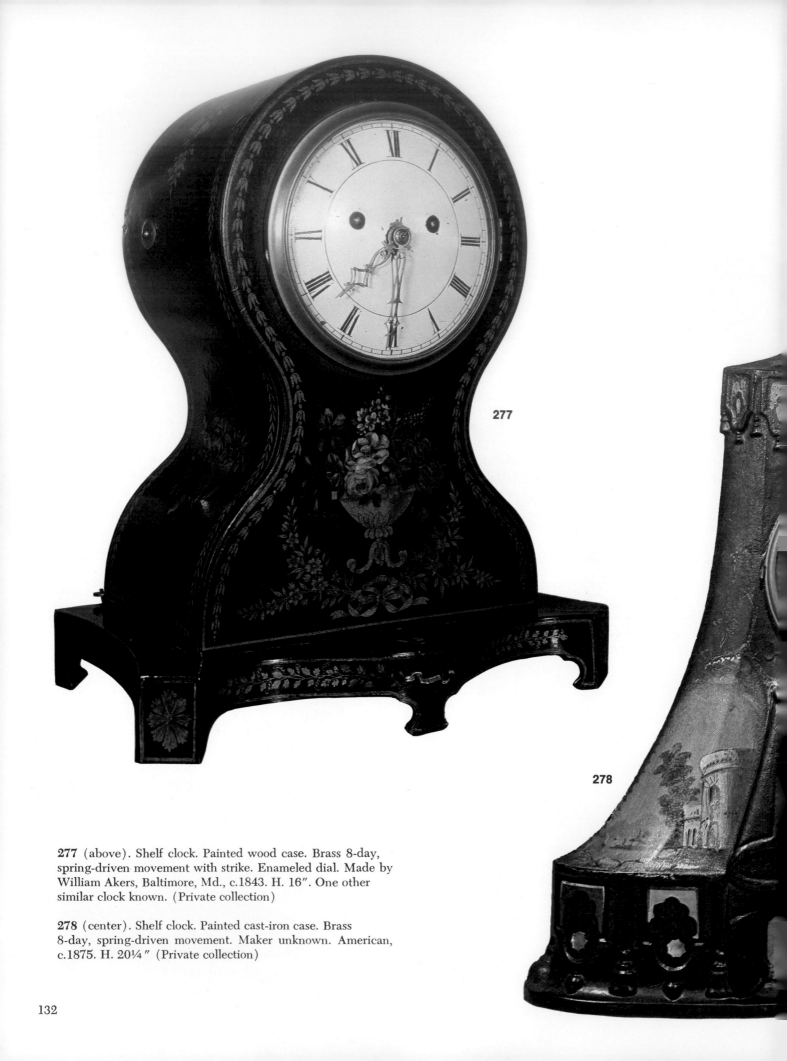

277 (above). Shelf clock. Painted wood case. Brass 8-day, spring-driven movement with strike. Enameled dial. Made by William Akers, Baltimore, Md., c.1843. H. 16″. One other similar clock known. (Private collection)

278 (center). Shelf clock. Painted cast-iron case. Brass 8-day, spring-driven movement. Maker unknown. American, c.1875. H. 20¼″ (Private collection)

279 (right). Shelf clock. Pine case with gold-leaf decoration. Brass 8-day, spring-driven movement with strike. Made by Brewster Manufacturing Co., Bristol, Conn., c.1854. H. 17″. (Private collection)

280 (below, right). Shelf clock. Cast-iron case with mother-of-pearl inlay and painted decoration. Brass 8-day, spring-driven movement with strike. Made by Sperry & Bryant, Williamsburg, L.I., N.Y., c.1850. H. 14″. (Private collection)

279

280

281 (right). Shelf clock. Painted papier-mâché case with mother-of-pearl inlay. Brass 8-day, spring-driven movement with strike. Made by Jonathan C. Brown, Bristol, Conn., c.1850. H. 17½". (Private collection)

281

282

282 (left). Miniature ogee shelf clock. Rosewood veneer case. Brass 30-hour, spring-driven movement with strike. Seth Thomas hands: minute hand shaped like an **S**; hour hand shaped like a **T**. Made by Seth Thomas, Plymouth Hollow, Conn., c.1850. H. 16¼". (William J. Haggerty Collection)

282a (above). Close-up of the painting on the Seth Thomas clock.

283 (right). Ogee shelf clock. Mahogany veneer case. Brass 30-hour, weight-driven movement with strike. Brass dial. Made by Chauncey Jerome, New Haven, Conn., c.1855. H. 26″. (David C. Foust Collection)

284 (below). Ogee shelf clock. Mahogany veneer case. Brass 30-hour, weight-driven movement with strike. Made by Daniel Pratt, Jr., Reading, Mass., c.1865. H. 25½″. (David C. Foust Collection)

284a (below, right). Close-up of the painting on the Daniel Pratt, Jr., clock.

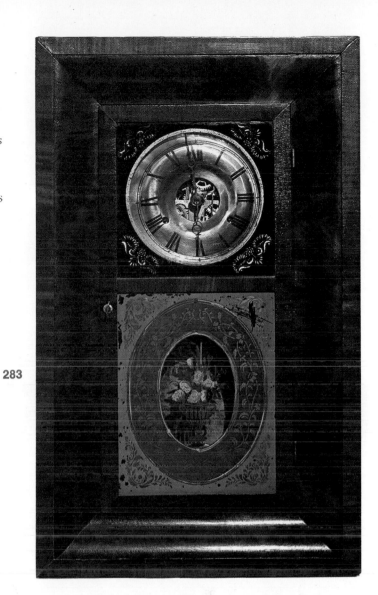

283

284

284a

285a

285

286

285 (left). Shelf clock. Mahogany veneer two-deck case. Brass 8-day, weight-driven movement with strike. Made by Forestville Manufacturing Co., Bristol, Conn., 1835–1839. H. 36½″. Top tablet shows the residence of J. C. Brown. (American Clock and Watch Museum)

285a (above, left). Two-deck shelf clock with doors open to show movement and label of the Forestville Manufacturing Co.

286 (above). Hollow-column shelf clock. Mahogany veneer case. Wood 30-hour, weight-driven movement. The weights fall inside the hollow columns. Made by E. and G. W. Bartholomew, Bristol, Conn., c.1830. H. 32⅛″. (American Clock and Watch Museum)

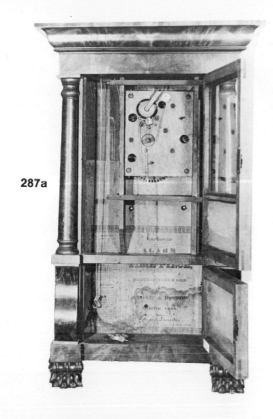

287a

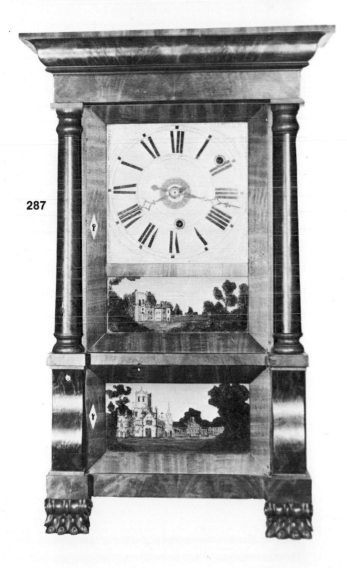

287

288

287 (left). Shelf clock. Mahogany and mahogany veneer case. Wood 30-hour, weight-driven movement with alarm only. Made by Jeromes and Darrow, Bristol, Conn., c.1835. H. 36¼". (Amos G. Avery Collection)

287a (above, left). Jeromes and Darrow shelf clock with door open and dial removed showing the arrangement of the movement in the case.

288 (above). Shelf clock. Mahogany veneer case. Brass 8-day, weight-driven movement with strike. Made by Richard Ward, Salem Bridge, Conn., c.1840. H. 28⅝". This clock contains a so-called Salem Bridge movement, but of an elongated type that was adapted by Ward. (American Clock and Watch Museum)

289

289a

PATENT
EIGHT DAY REPEATING
MUSICAL
BRASS CLOCKS.
MANUFACTURED AND SOLD BY
KIRKE AND TODD,
WOLCOTT, CONN.

289b

289 (above). Musical shelf clock. Mahogany veneer case. Brass 8-day, spring-driven movement with strike and musical attachment. Made by Kirke & Todd, Wolcott, Conn., c.1850. H. 40¾″. "Whistle" pipe organ, which played several tunes, was activated by the clock to play once a day at twelve o'clock noon. Pipes are decorative only. (American Clock and Watch Museum)

289a (above, right). Label of the Kirke & Todd musical shelf clock.

289b (right). Kirke & Todd musical shelf clock with back removed to show mechanism.

291

290

292

290 (above). Shelf clock. Mahogany veneer case with full columns and carved splat. Brass 8-day, weight-driven movement with strike. Made by Elisha Manross, Bristol, Conn., c.1854. H. 37″. Lower glass replaced. (David C. Foust Collection)

291 (above, right). Two-door shelf clock. Victorian-style case with rosewood veneer. Brass 30-hour, weight-driven movement with strike. Hollow half columns. Made by Seth Thomas, Plymouth Hollow, Conn., c.1860. H. 32½″. (The Clock Gallery)

292 (right). Shelf clock. Rosewood veneer case with shell columns. Brass 8-day, weight-driven movement with strike. Made by The Seth Thomas Clock Co., Thomaston, Conn., c.1885. H. 32″. (T. H. Eurich Company)

293 (below). Stovepipe shelf clock. Walnut veneer case. Brass 8-day, weight-driven movement with strike. One column removed to show how the weight travels down the pipe. Cast bell hammer marked "Auburn/1835." Made by Asa Munger, Auburn, N.Y., 1835. H. 40″. Munger's clocks all had heavy cast movements. (Irving Cooperman Collection)

294 (right). Shelf clock. Mahogany case. Brass 8-day, weight-driven movement with strike and seconds dial. Made by Asa Munger, Auburn, N.Y., c.1830. H. 39″. (J. Alford Jones)

294

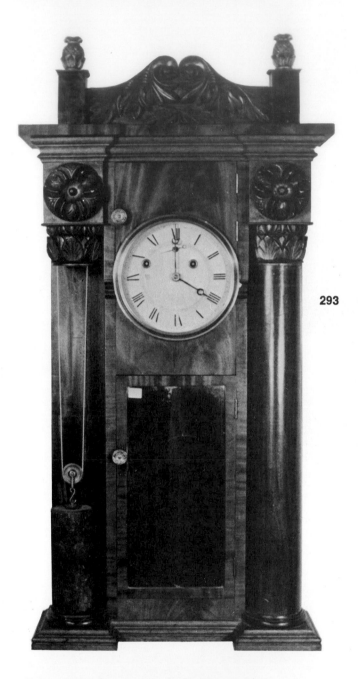

293

295

295 (right). Hollow-column shelf clock. Mahogany veneer case with acorn finials. Brass 30-hour, weight-driven movement with strike. Made by Austin Chittenden, Lexington, Mass., c.1836. H. 23¾″. Hollow columns contain the weights. (Private collection)

296 (opposite). Presentation shelf clock. Gold-leaf case with gesso decoration. Brass 8-day, spring-driven movement with fusee. Made by Atkins Clock Company, Bristol, Conn., c.1860. H. 18¾″. Photograph: Edward H. Goodrich. (American Clock and Watch Museum)

296

141

298

297 (below). Shelf clock. Mahogany and mahogany veneer case. Wood 30-hour, weight-driven movement with strike. Unusual small wood finials. Made by Seth Thomas, Plymouth, Conn., c.1828. H. 31″. (Mark A. Shanaberger)

297

298 (above). Shelf clock. Mahogany and mahogany veneer case. Stenciled half columns. Painted iron dial. Brass 8-day, weight-driven movement with strike. Made by Lucius Bradley, Watertown, Conn., c.1825. H. 31″. Salem Bridge movement. (Mark A. Shanaberger)

299 (below). Miniature shelf clock. Mahogany and mahogany veneer case, with stenciled side columns and carved eagle splat. Made by E. & G.W. Bartholomew, Bristol, Conn., c.1830. H. 29″. (Mark A. Shanaberger)

299

300 (above). Miniature shelf clock. Mahogany and mahogany veneer case with stenciled side columns and splat. Wood 30-hour, weight-driven movement with strike. Made by Jeromes and Darrow, Bristol, Conn., c.1825. H. 27½″. (Mark A. Shanaberger)

301 (left). Inside of a shelf clock showing original wallpaper lining and label. Made by Hotchkiss & Benedict, Auburn, N.Y., c. 1830. H. 31″. (Mark A. Shanaberger)

302 (below). Shelf clock. Butternut and mahogany and butternut veneer case. Note the carved rooster on splat instead of an eagle. Wood 30-hour, weight-driven movement with alarm. Made by Putnam Bailey, North Goshen, Conn., c.1835. H. 24¾″. (American Clock and Watch Museum)

302a (below, left). Bailey shelf clock with door open showing the wood movement and label.

301

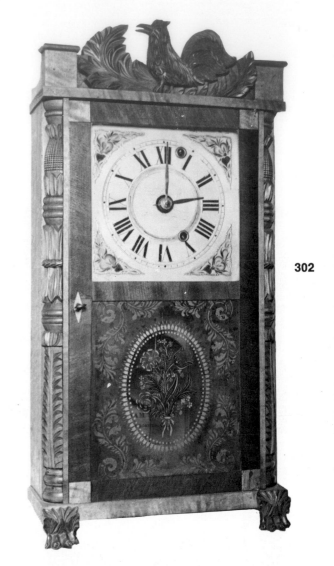

302

302a

303 (opposite, above). Shelf clock. Mahogany and mahogany veneer case. Carved half columns and splat. Wood 8-day, weight-driven movement with strike. Made by Henry Terry, Plymouth, Conn., c.1828. H. 37″. Tablet has been replaced. (Mark A. Shanaberger)

304 (opposite, below). Shelf clock. Mahogany veneer case with carved half columns and splat. Wood 30-hour, weight-driven movement with strike. Eagle hands. Made by Hart and Sons, Goshen, Conn., c.1830. H. 35½″. (David C. Foust Collection)

303

305 (below). Shelf clock. Mahogany veneer case with carved half columns. Carved eagle splat and two doors. Wood 8-day, weight-driven movement with strike. Made by Henry Terry at the "manufactory" of E. Terry and Sons, Plymouth, Conn., c.1850. H. 37″. (Private collection)

304

305

307

308

306 (above). Three-deck shelf clock. Mahogany and maple case. Tiger maple side columns with carved lion-and-unicorn splat. Maker unknown. Bristol, Conn., c.1840. H. 39½". Probably made for the Canadian trade. (Mark A. Shanaberger)

309

310

307 (opposite, above right). Shelf clock. Mahogany veneer case. Brass 2½-day, weight-driven movement. Made by Lucius Bradley, Watertown, Conn., c.1825. H. 20″. Image Studios, David Towne, Photographer. (Private collection)

308 (opposite, below right). Transitional shelf clock. Mahogany veneer case with stenciled half columns and splat. Wood 30-hour, weight-driven movement with strike. Made by Seth Thomas, Plymouth, Conn., c.1835. H. 29″. (David C. Foust Collection)

309 (left). Triple-deck shelf clock. Mahogany and mahogany veneer case with gilt columns and splat. Brass 8-day, weight-driven movement with strike. Made by Birge, Mallory & Co., Bristol, Conn., c.1843. H. 38″. (J. Alford Jones)

310 (above). Shelf clock. Mahogany case with stenciled half columns and splat. Wood 30-hour, weight-driven movement with strike. Made by D. N. and R. Day, Westfield, Mass., c.1830. (Amos G. Avery Collection)

311 (left). Ogee shelf clock with door open showing label of Chauncey Jerome of Bristol, Conn., c.1830. H. 26″. (David C. Foust Collection)

311

312

312 (above, right). Inside of an ogee clock showing the movement. Made by James Collins, Goffstown, N.H., c.1830. H. 28½″. (Mark A. Shanaberger)

313 (below). Ogee shelf clock. Mahogany veneer case. Brass 8-day, weight-driven movement with strike. Made by Hills, Goodrich and Co., Plainville, Conn., c.1850. H. 31″. (Private collection)

314 (below, right). Ogee shelf clock by Chauncey Jerome of Bristol, Conn., with the door open showing the single weight. Dial marked New Haven. Movement marked Bristol. c.1844. H. 25¾″. (Irving Cooperman Collection)

313

314

316

315 (below). Ogee shelf clock. Mahogany veneer case. Brass 30-hour, weight-driven movement with strike. Made by George Marsh, Winsted, Conn., c.1830. H. 25¼″. (The Clock Gallery)

316 (right). Ogee shelf clock. Mahogany veneer case. Brass 30-hour, weight-driven movement with strike. Made by S.B. Terry and Co., Terryville, Conn., c.1840. H. 19¾″. Image Studios, David Towne, Photographer. (Private collection)

315

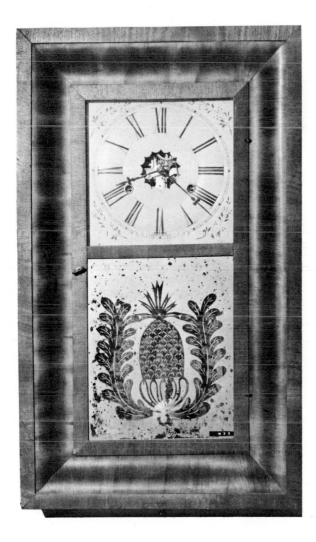

317

317 (right). Ogee shelf clock. Mahogany and mahogany veneer case. Brass 30-hour, weight-driven movement with strike. Round brass dial. Tablet shows the Public Square, New Haven, Conn. Made by Jeromes, Gilbert, Grant and Co., Bristol, Conn., c.1840. H. 25¹⁵⁄₁₆″. (Yale University Art Gallery)

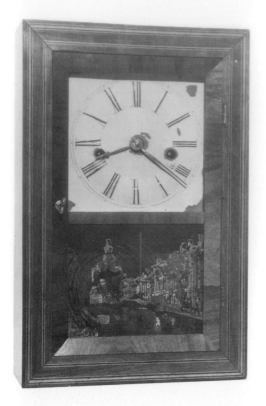

318

322 (opposite, above left). Miniature ogee shelf clock. Burl walnut veneer case. Brass 30-hour, weight-driven movement with strike. Made by Waterbury Clock Company, Waterbury, Conn., c.1860. H. 18½ ". (R. A. Romeo Collection)

323 (opposite, above center). Miniature reverse ogee shelf clock. Mahogany veneer case. Brass 30-hour, spring-driven movement with fusee. Made by Smith & Goodrich, Bristol, Conn., c.1850. H. 14¾ ". (Private collection)

324 (opposite, above right). Miniature ogee shelf clock. Mahogany veneer case. Brass 30-hour, weight-driven movement with strike. Made by Henry Terry, Plymouth, Conn., c.1835. H. 19½ ". (Private collection)

325 (opposite, below). *Taking the Census* by Francis William Edmonds, 1854. Oil on canvas. An ogee shelf clock sits on the fireplace mantel. Photograph courtesy The Brooklyn Museum. (Private collection)

318 (above). Miniature shelf clock. Mahogany veneer, banded case. Brass 30-hour, spring-driven movement with strike. Brass springs. Made by Elisha Manross, Bristol, Conn., c.1853. H. 13″. (David C. Foust Collection)

319 (below, left). Miniature ogee shelf clock. Rosewood veneer case. Brass 8-day, spring-driven movement with strike. Made by Seth Thomas Clock Co., Thomaston, Conn., c.1870. H. 16¼ ". (David C. Foust Collection)

321

320

319

320 (above, left). Miniature ogee shelf clock. Mahogany veneer case. Brass 30-hour, spring-driven movement with strike. Made by E.N. Welch Manufacturing Co., Bristol, Conn., c.1855. H. 18¼ ". (David C. Foust Collection)

321 (above, right). Miniature ogee shelf clock. Mahogany veneer case. Brass 8-day, spring-driven movement with strike and alarm. Made by Ansonia Clock Company, Ansonia, Conn., c.1855. H. 18½ ". (J. Alford Jones)

322

323

324

325

326

327

326 (left). Ogee shelf clock. Mahogany veneer double-door case. Brass 8-day, weight-driven movement with strike. Made by Forestville Manufacturing Co., Bristol, Conn., c.1849. H. 30¾″. Photograph: Edward H. Goodrich. (American Clock and Watch Museum)

327 (right). Ogee shelf clock. Mahogany veneer case. Brass 8-day, weight-driven movement with strike and alarm. J.J. & W. Beals label. Could have been made by Hills, Goodrich and Co., Plainville, Conn., c. 1850. H. 31″. (Private collection)

327a (opposite). Close-up of the dial and label of the J.J. & W. Beals ogee shelf clock.

328

328 (left). Steeple shelf clock. Mahogany veneer case. Brass 30-hour, weight-driven movement with strike. Made by Seth Thomas, Plymouth Hollow, Conn., c.1825. H. 28¾″. A glass tablet fills the triangular space above the dial. (Private collection)

329 (right). Steeple shelf clock. Mahogany veneer case. Brass 30-hour, spring-driven movement with double fusee. Made by Smith & Goodrich, Bristol, Conn., c.1844. H. 22″. Has ogee movement with pulleys in top of case for cords. Image Studios, David Towne, Photographer. (Private collection)

329

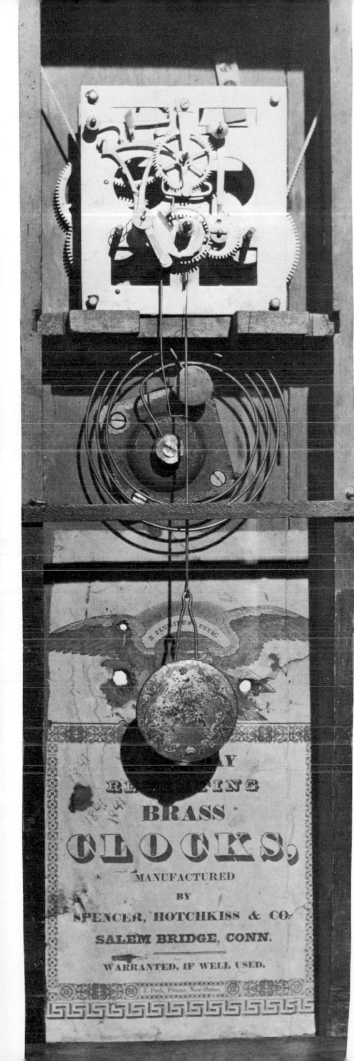

330 (above). Steeple shelf clock. Mahogany veneer case. Brass 8-day, weight-driven movement with strike and seconds dial. Compound pulleys, rack-and-snail strike. Made by Spencer, Hotchkiss & Co., Salem Bridge, Conn., c.1830. H. 41″. (David C. Foust Collection)

330a (left). Spencer, Hotchkiss steeple shelf clock with door open to show movement and label.

331 (left). Steeple shelf clock. Mahogany veneer case. Brass 8-day, spring-driven movement with strike. Made by The Connecticut Clock Company, New York, N.Y., c.1872. H. 20″. (David C. Foust Collection)

332 (below, left). Steeple shelf clock. Mahogany veneer case. Brass 8-day, spring-driven movement with strike. Made by Chauncey Jerome, Bristol, Conn., c.1845. H. 20″. (Private collection)

334 (opposite, below left). Steeple shelf clock. Mahogany veneer case. Brass 30-hour, spring-driven movement with fusee, balance wheel, and strike. Attributed to Silas B. Terry, Plymouth, Conn., c.1845. H. 22¾″. Hands have been replaced. (American Clock and Watch Museum)

334a (opposite, above left). Steeple shelf clock with door open showing movement.

331

333

333a

332

333 (above, center). Twin-steeple shelf clock. Mahogany veneer case. Brass 30-hour, spring-driven movement with strike. Made by Silas B. Terry, Terryville, Conn., c.1850. H. 19½″. Image Studios, David Towne, Photographer. (Private collection)

333a (right). Close-up of the Terry movement in 333 showing one spring that runs both the time and the strike.

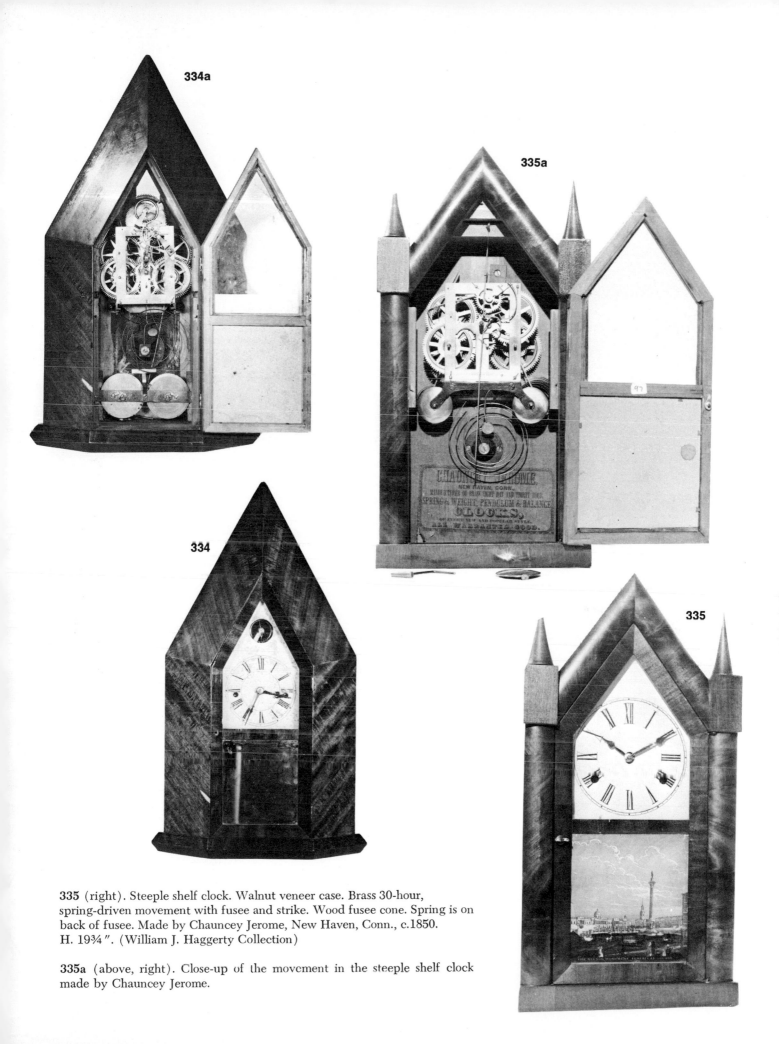

335 (right). Steeple shelf clock. Walnut veneer case. Brass 30-hour, spring-driven movement with fusee and strike. Wood fusee cone. Spring is on back of fusee. Made by Chauncey Jerome, New Haven, Conn., c.1850. H. 19¾". (William J. Haggerty Collection)

335a (above, right). Close-up of the movement in the steeple shelf clock made by Chauncey Jerome.

336 (right). Steeple shelf clock. Rosewood veneer case with applied decorative ripple molding on the front. Brass 8-day, spring-driven movement with strike. Made by J. C. Brown, Forestville, Conn., 1850–1855. H. 20″. Photograph: Edward H. Goodrich. (American Clock and Watch Museum)

337 (below). Steeple shelf clock. Rosewood veneer case with applied ripple front. Brass 8-day, spring-driven movement with strike. Made by Forestville Manufacturing Co., Bristol, Conn., 1850–1855. H. 19¾″. (American Clock and Watch Museum)

336

337

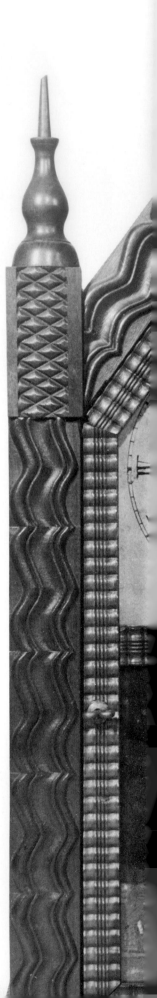

338

339

338 (center). Steeple shelf clock with variation of the ripple front. Mahogany veneer case. Made by J. C. Brown, Bristol, Conn., c.1848. H. 19¾″. (Private collection)

339 (above). Steeple shelf clock. Rosewood veneer case with ripple front. Brass 30-hour, spring-driven movement with strike and alarm. Made by Terry & Andrews, Bristol, Conn., c.1847. H. 19¾″. Movement has brass springs. (Gene L. Bagwell Collection)

341 (above). Round Gothic shelf clock. Rosewood veneer case. Brass 8-day, spring-driven movement with strike. Original brass springs. Made by Brewster and Ingrahams, Bristol, Conn., c.1845. H. 20″. (William J. Haggerty Collection)

340 (above). Round Gothic shelf clock with ripple front. Mahogany veneer case. Brass 8-day, spring-driven movement with strike. Made by J. C. Brown, Bristol, Conn., c.1848. H. 20″. (Private collection)

342 (right). Shelf clock with door open to show movement and label. Brewster and Ingrahams, Bristol, Conn., c.1845. H. 20″. Photograph: Edward H. Goodrich. (American Clock and Watch Museum)

343 (right). Beehive shelf clock with ripple front. Mahogany veneer case. Brass 8-day, spring-driven movement with strike. Made by E.N. Welch Manufacturing Co., Bristol, Conn., c.1860. H. 18¾″. (Private collection)

344 (above, center). Beehive shelf clock. Mahogany veneer case. Brass 8-day, spring-driven movement with strike. Made by the Ansonia Clock Company, Ansonia, Conn., c.1850. H. 18½″. (David C. Foust Collection)

345 (above). Beehive shelf clock. Mahogany veneer case. Brass 8-day, spring-driven movement with strike. Made by Jerome & Company, New Haven, Conn., c.1857. H. 18¾″. (R. A. Romeo Collection)

346 (right). Beehive shelf clock with ripple front. Mahogany veneer case. Brass 8-day, spring-driven movement with strike. Made by J. C. Brown, Bristol, Conn., c.1848. H. 18¾″. (Private collection)

347 (right). Round-top shelf clock. Rosewood
veneer case. Brass 8-day movement with strike.
Made by E.N. Welch Manufacturing Co., Bristol,
Conn., c.1865. H. 16″. (T. H. Eurich Company)

348 (below). Round-top shelf clock. Rosewood
veneer case. Brass 30-hour movement with strike.
Made by Bradley & Hubbard, West Meriden,
Conn., c.1860. H. 17¾″. (T.H. Eurich Company)

347

348

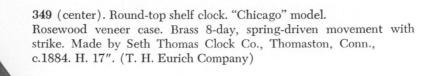

349

349 (center). Round-top shelf clock. "Chicago" model. Rosewood veneer case. Brass 8-day, spring-driven movement with strike. Made by Seth Thomas Clock Co., Thomaston, Conn., c.1884. H. 17″. (T. H. Eurich Company)

350

350 (above). Round-top shelf clock. Rosewood veneer case. Brass 8-day movement with strike. Made by Noah Pomeroy & Company, Bristol, Conn., c.1851. H. 16½″. (T. H. Eurich Company)

351 (right). Shelf clock. Mahogany veneer case with rounded sides. Brass 30-hour, weight-driven movement with strike. Attributed to Eli Terry, Jr., Terryville, Conn., c.1840. H. 22″. (T. H. Eurich Company)

351

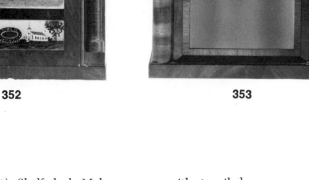

352

353

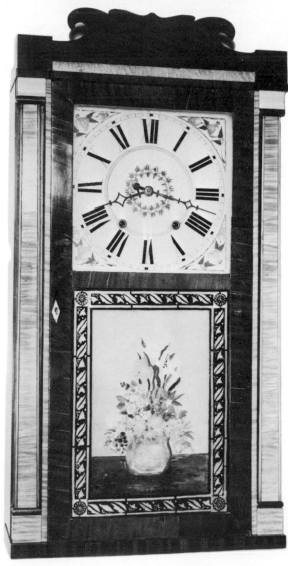

354

352 (above, left). Shelf clock. Mahogany case with stenciled half columns and splat. Wood 30-hour, weight-driven "upside-down" movement with strike and alarm. Ivory bushings. Made by Silas Hoadley, Plymouth, Conn., c.1835. H. 36″. (Gene L. Bagwell Collection)

353 (above, right). Shelf clock. Mahogany veneer case. Brass 48-hour, spring-driven movement with strike and fusee. Brass dial. Made by James Weston, Boston, Mass., c.1850. H. 23½″. (Greenfield Village and Henry Ford Museum)

354 (right). Shelf clock. Mahogany, tiger and bird's-eye maple veneer case. Wood 30-hour, weight-driven movement with strike. Made by Putnam Bailey, North Goshen, Conn., c.1835. H. 35⅝″. Bailey purchased movements from several sources and cased them. Tablet has been replaced. (American Clock and Watch Museum)

356

355

357

358

355 (above). Shelf clock. Tiger maple and veneer case. Wood 30-hour, weight-driven movement with strike. Note patriotic tablet. Made by Daniel M. Tuthill, Saxtons River, Vt., 1842. H. 26¹⁄₁₆″. (American Clock and Watch Museum)

356 (above, right). Shelf clock. Walnut case. Brass 8-day, spring-driven movement with strike. Made by Forestville Manufacturing Co., Bristol, Conn., c.1849. H. 31⅝″. (Old Economy Village)

357 (near right). Shelf clock. Rosewood veneer case. Brass 8-day, weight-driven movement with strike. Made by E. C. Brewster & Son, Bristol, Conn., c.1855. H. 31″. (William J. Haggerty Collection)

358 (far right). Shelf clock. Mahogany veneer case with reverse bevel. Wood 30-hour, weight-driven movement with alarm. Made by Silas Hoadley, Plymouth, Conn., c.1835. H. 21⅛″. (American Clock and Watch Museum)

359

359 (left). Double-dial calendar shelf clock. Oak case. Brass 8-day movement with strike. Lower dial indicates day of the month. Made by The Monarch Calendar Clock Company, Knoxville, Tenn., c.1875. H. 31¾″. (T. H. Eurich Company)

360

360 (right). Double-dial calendar shelf clock. Walnut case. Brass 8-day, spring-driven movement with strike. B. B. Lewis calendar mechanism. Made by The E. Ingraham and Company, Bristol, Conn., c.1885. H. 21″. Listed in the 1884 catalogue at $8.40. (American Clock and Watch Museum)

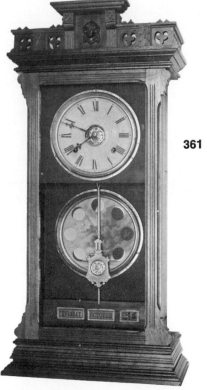

361

361a

362

361 (opposite, center). Double-dial calendar shelf clock. Walnut case. Brass 8-day, spring-driven movement with strike, moon phase dial in center, day, month, and date calendar at the bottom. Calendar and moon phase change at twelve midnight. Movement was probably made by E.N. Welch Manufacturing Co., Bristol, Conn. Front plate of movement stamped: "Macomb Calendar Clock Co., Macomb, Ill." c.1892. H. 29½". Probably the rarest of the calendars. (Robert G. Mindrup Collection)

361a (opposite, below left). Movement, moon phase, and calendar of the Macomb calendar clock.

362 (opposite, below right). Shelf clock with twisted side columns. Walnut case. Brass 8-day movement with strike and calendar hand. White cameo pendulum bob. Made by Waterbury Clock Company, Waterbury, Conn., c.1875. H. 26¾". (T. H. Eurich Company)

363

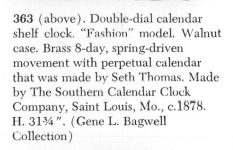

364

365

363 (above). Double-dial calendar shelf clock. "Fashion" model. Walnut case. Brass 8-day, spring-driven movement with perpetual calendar that was made by Seth Thomas. Made by The Southern Calendar Clock Company, Saint Louis, Mo., c.1878. H. 31¾". (Gene L. Bagwell Collection)

366

364 (above, center). Double-dial perpetual calendar shelf clock. Walnut case. Brass 8-day, spring-driven movement with strike. Made by Ithaca Calendar Clock Co., Ithaca, N.Y., c.1880. H. 21". (R. A. Romeo Collection)

365 (above, left). Double-dial calendar shelf clock. "Italian" model. Rosewood case with gilt columns. Brass 8-day, spring-driven movement with strike. Made by Welch, Spring and Company, Forestville, Conn., c.1880. H. 20". (O. Harry Burt Collection)

366 (right). Double-dial calendar shelf clock. Walnut case. Brass 8-day, spring-driven movement with strike. Perpetual calendar. Made by Waterbury Clock Company, Waterbury, Conn., c.1889. H. 28¼". (Robert G. Mindrup Collection)

367

367 (left). Double-dial calendar shelf clock. No. 1 Regulator. Walnut case. Brass 8-day, two-weight movement. Made by Ithaca Calendar Clock Co., Ithaca, N.Y., c.1865. H. 43″. (Private collection)

367a (below). Detail of splat and carved head on the Ithaca calendar clock.

369 (opposite, left). Ithaca box skeleton calendar clock. Walnut case with ebony trim. Brass 8-day, spring-driven movement with strike and calendar. Movement made by Samuel E. Root, calendar made by Ithaca Calendar Clock Co., Ithaca, New York, c.1869. H. 22¾″. Rare, probably a salesman's model. (Joe Brincat Collection)

370 (opposite, right). Double-dial calendar shelf clock. Rosewood veneer case. Brass 8-day, weight-driven movement with strike. Made by Seth Thomas, Plymouth Hollow, Conn., c.1858. H. 30″. (Private collection)

367a

368

369

370

368 (left). Double-dial calendar shelf clock. "Cottage" model. Brass 8-day, spring-driven movement with strike and calendar. Made by Ithaca Calendar Clock Co., Ithaca, N.Y., 1860–1870. H. 24¼″. (J. Alford Jones)

371

371 (left). Double-dial calendar shelf clock. "Fashion No. 9." Walnut case. Brass 8-day, spring-driven movement with strike. Made by the New Haven Clock Co., New Haven, Conn., for the National Calendar Clock Company, c.1880. H. 32″. (Private collection)

372

373

372 (above). Flat-top shelf clock. Rosewood veneer case. Brass 30-hour, spring-driven movement with strike. Made by the William L. Gilbert Co., Winsted, Conn., c.1870. H. 14¾″. (David C. Foust Collection)

373 (left). Double-dial calendar shelf clock. "Fashion No. 3." Walnut case. Brass 8-day, spring-driven movement with strike on bell. Lyre-type movement. Short, Star of Texas pendulum. Made by the Seth Thomas Clock Co., Thomaston, Conn., c.1880. H. 30″. (Private collection)

374

375

376

374 (above, left). Double-dial calendar shelf clock. "Fashion No. 6." Walnut case. Brass 8-day, spring-driven movement with strike on gong. Seth Thomas lyre-type movement. Long pendulum. Made by the Seth Thomas Clock Co., Thomaston, Conn., c.1876. H. 33″. (Private collection)

375 (above). Ithaca parlor, double-dial calendar shelf clock. Walnut case. Brass 8-day, spring-driven movement with strike and calendar. Made by the Ithaca Calendar Clock Co., Ithaca, N.Y., c.1870. H. 20¾″. (J. Alford Jones)

376 (left). Round-top shelf clock. "Venetian" model. Rosewood veneer case with gilt columns. Tin-plated brass 8-day, spring-driven movement with strike. Made by The E. Ingraham and Company, Bristol, Conn., c.1860. H. 18¼″. Tin plate. (Private collection)

377

378

379

380

377 (above, left). Miniature Empire-style shelf clock. Rosewood veneer case. Brass 30-hour, weight-driven movement with strike. Made by Chauncey Jerome, New Haven, Conn., c.1850. H. 27″. (David C. Foust Collection)

378 (above, center). Shelf clock. Mahogany case with black and gilt pillars. Brass 8-day movement with strike. Made by Seth Thomas, Thomaston, Conn., c.1875. H. 16⅛″. (T. H. Eurich Company)

379 (above, right). Shelf clock. "Huron" model. Rosewood veneer case. Brass 8-day movement with hour strike. Made by The E. Ingraham and Company, Bristol, Conn., c.1884. H. 16″. (T. H. Eurich Company)

381

380 (above). Shelf clock. Painted case. Brass 6-ball, spring-driven movement with strike and torsion suspension. Made by Boston Clock Co., Chelsea, Mass., under the patents of A. D. Crane, c.1890. H. 21¼″. Clock runs for one year. (Private collection)

381 (left). Miniature shelf clock. Rosewood veneer case. Brass 8-day, spring-driven movement with strike. Made by Seth Thomas, Thomaston, Conn., c. 1860. H. 16½″. (J. Alford Jones)

382

383

384

385

382 (above, left). Shelf clock. Rosewood and bird's-eye maple case. Brass 30-hour, spring-driven movement with strike. Made by The E. Ingraham and Company, Bristol, Conn., c.1890. H. 15¼". (Greenfield Village and Henry Ford Museum)

383 (above, center). Shelf clock. "Grecian" model. Rosewood veneer case. Brass 8-day, spring-driven movement with strike and alarm. Made by The E. Ingraham and Company, Bristol, Conn., c.1860. H. 14½". (J. Alford Jones)

384 (above, right). Miniature Empire-style shelf clock. Mahogany veneer case. Brass 8-day, spring-driven movement. Made by E. B. Goodrich, Bristol, Conn., c.1854. H. 20½". Goodrich made cases and purchased the movements elsewhere. (Private collection)

386

385 (above). Empire shelf clock. Mahogany veneer case. Brass 8-day, weight-driven movement with strike. Made by Birge & Co., Bristol, Conn., c.1848. H. 32½". (David C. Foust Collection)

386 (right). Skeletonized, torsion pendulum shelf clock. Brass 8-day, weight-driven movement with strike. Made by Aaron Dodd Crane, Belleville, N.J., c.1842. H. 20¾". Made for the 15th Annual Fair of the American Institute in New York City, 1842. (New Jersey State Museum Collection: Gift of James R. Seibert)

387 (left). Shelf clock. Walnut base and pillars. Glass dome. Brass 8-day, spring-driven movement with strike. Made by the Ansonia Clock Company, Ansonia, Conn., c.1875. H. 17¾″. Davies Pat. on pendulum. (R. A. Romeo Collection)

388 (below). Group of three shelf clocks made by Welch, Spring and Company, Forestville, Conn.: (left to right) 1. "Gerster V. P." model. c.1875. H. 18¾″; 2. "Patti No. 2" model. c.1875. H. 10½″; 3. "Patti No. 1" model. c.1875. H. 18¾″. (O. Harry Burt Collection)

389 (right). Shelf clock. Rosewood veneer case. Brass 30-hour movement. Companion piece to the "Duchess" model. Made by New Haven Clock Co., New Haven, Conn., c.1860. H.14¼″. Label reads: "Jerome and Co., New Haven, Conn." Movement made by the New Haven Clock Co. (William J. Haggerty Collection)

390 (below, center). Shelf clock. Walnut veneer case. Brass 8-day, spring-driven movement. Made by E.N. Welch Manufacturing Co., Bristol, Conn., c.1870. H. 9″. (O. Harry Burt Collection)

389

390

391

392

391 (above). Shelf clock. "Italian No. 3." Rosewood veneer case. Brass 8-day, spring-driven movement with strike. Made by Welch, Spring and Company, Forestville, Conn., c.1875. H. 13½″. (O. Harry Burt Collection)

392 (left). Shelf clock. "Duchess" model. Rosewood veneer case. Brass 8-day, spring-driven movement with strike. Made by New Haven Clock Co., New Haven, Conn., c.1860. H. 18¼″. This is probably an export model. Label reads: "Jerome and Company, New Haven, Conn." Movement made by The New Haven Clock Co. (William J. Haggerty Collection)

393. Series of four shelf clocks. Cast-iron cases with gilt decoration. Made by Terry Clock Co., Waterbury, Conn., c.1870: (left to right) 1. Brass 8-day, spring-driven movement with simple calendar. H. 11″; 2. Brass 8-day, spring-driven movement with strike. H. 8¾″; 3. Brass 8-day, spring-driven movement with alarm. H. 8¾″; 4. Brass 30-hour, spring-driven movement with alarm. H. 6″. (William J. Haggerty Collection)

395

394

394a

394 (above, left). Shelf clock. Mahogany veneer case. Brass 30-hour, spring-driven movement using Ives rolling pinion on rolling verge. Made by Atkins, Whiting & Co., Bristol, Conn., 1847–1857. H. 16″. Image Studios, David Towne, Photographer. (Private collection)

394a (above, right). Close-up of the Atkins, Whiting & Co., brass movement.

395 (right, above). Shelf clock with flat top. Mahogany veneer case with gilt side columns. Brass 8-day movement with hour strike and alarm. Made by Seth Thomas, Thomaston, Conn., c.1880. H. 16″. (T. H. Eurich Company)

395a (right). Seth Thomas shelf clock with door open to show the alarm.

395a

396 (right). Cottage clock. Pine case painted black with gilt decoration. Brass 30-hour, spring-driven movement. Made by Chauncey Jerome, New Haven, Conn., c.1850. H. 12″. Has "upside-down" verge and escape wheel, wood dial. (William J. Haggerty Collection)

396a (right, below). Chauncey Jerome cottage clock with back removed showing "upside-down" verge and escape wheel.

397 (below, left). Shelf clock. Mahogany veneer case. Brass 30-hour, spring-driven movement with strike. Made by S.B. Terry and Co., Terryville, Conn., c.1840. H. 15″. Image Studios, David Towne, Photographer. (Private collection)

396

397

396a

398 (below). Collection of cottage clocks: (left to right) 1. Made by the Terry Clock Co., Winsted, Conn. Iron case. Brass 8-day, spring-driven movement with alarm, c.1860. H. 9″. 2. Made by Seth Thomas, Thomaston, Conn., c.1870. Mahogany veneer case. Brass 30-hour, spring-driven movement. H. 9½″. 3. Made by Seth Thomas, Thomaston, Conn., c. 1870. Pine case with veneered door. Brass 30-hour, spring-driven movement with alarm. H. 9″. 4. Made by The Teutonia Manufactory, c.1870. Pine case. Brass 30-hour, spring-driven movement with alarm. H. 9″. (J. Alford Jones Collection)

398

399 (right). Shelf clock. Painted metal case with mother-of-pearl inlay. Brass 8-day, spring-driven movement. Made by C. Goodrich, Forestville, Conn., c.1857. H. 21¾″. (Gene L. Bagwell Collection)

400 (below). Iron-front shelf clock. Iron case painted to resemble rosewood. Brass 8-day, spring-driven movement with strike. Made by Bristol Clock Co., Bristol, Conn., c.1860. H. 18″. (Gene L. Bagwell Collection)

400

399

402 (right). Shelf clock. Painted metal case with mother-of-pearl inlay. Brass 8-day, spring-driven movement with strike. Made by Terry & Andrews, Bristol, Conn., 1846–1850. H. 15⅝″. Metal dial. (Gene L. Bagwell Collection)

401

402

403

401 (above). Shelf clock. Rosewood veneer case. Glass door is backed with pressed gold foil and black velvet. Brass 8-day, spring-driven movement with strike. Made by Chauncey Jerome, Bristol, Conn., c.1845. H. 16″. (American Clock and Watch Museum)

403 (left). Shelf clock. Cast-iron case with mother-of-pearl inlay and painted decoration. Brass 8-day, spring-driven movement with strike. Made by Terry & Andrews, Bristol, Conn., c.1851. H. 14″. Embossed metal dial marked "Ansonia Clock Company." Theodore Terry of Terry & Andrews was employed by Ansonia and apparently took movements with him from the old Terry & Andrews plant. Photograph: Edward H. Goodrich. (American Clock and Watch Museum)

404 (right). Shelf clock. Painted case with mother-of-pearl inlay. Brass 30-hour, spring-driven movement with alarm. Made by E. and A. Ingraham, Bristol, Conn., c.1854. H. 17″. (Gene L. Bagwell Collection)

404

405 (right). Shelf clock. Papier-mâché case with mother-of-pearl inlay and painted decoration. Made by Chauncey Jerome, New Haven, Conn. Case was probably made by Litchfield Manufacturing Co., 1851–1854. H. 20⁷⁄₁₆″. Photograph: Edward H. Goodrich. (American Clock and Watch Museum)

405

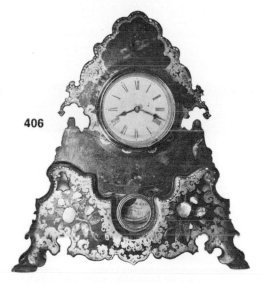

406

406 (above). Shelf clock. Cast-iron case with mother-of-pearl inlay and painted decoration. Brass 8-day, spring-driven movement with strike. Made by Terry, Downs and Co., Bristol, Conn., c.1855. H. 20³⁄₁₆″. (American Clock and Watch Museum)

407 (right). Shelf clock. Painted cast-iron case with mother-of-pearl inlay. Brass 8-day, spring-driven movement. Made by William J. Hill, Bristol, Conn., c. 1850. H. 10½″. (Gene L. Bagwell Collection)

407

408

408 (left). Shelf clock. Stenciled pine case. Brass 30-hour, spring-driven movement with strike. Made by E. C. Brewster & Son, Bristol, Conn., c.1855. H. 17″. (J. Alford Jones)

409 (right). Shelf clock. Painted cast-iron case. Brass 30-hour, spring-driven movement. Made by Waterbury Clock Company, Waterbury, Conn., c.1890. H. 11½″. (The Clock Gallery)

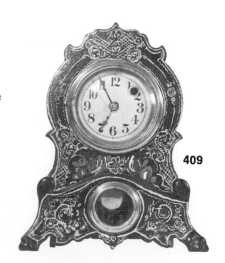

409

410 (right). Shelf clock. "Italian No. 2." Rosewood veneer case. Brass 8-day, spring-driven movement with strike. Made by Welch, Spring and Company, Forestville, Conn., c.1875. H. 17½". (O. Harry Burt Collection)

411 (below). Shelf clock. "Lucca V.P." model. Rosewood case. Brass 8-day, spring-driven movement with strike. Made by Welch, Spring and Company, Forestville, Conn., c.1875. H. 23½". (O. Harry Burt Collection)

410

411

412

412 (right). Shelf clock. "Patti No. 1." Rosewood case with glass sides. Brass 8-day, spring-driven movement with strike. Made by Welch, Spring and Company, Forestville, Conn., c.1875. H. 18¾". (O. Harry Burt Collection)

413 (left). Shelf clock. "Cary" model. Rosewood case with glass sides. Brass 8-day, spring-driven "Patti" movement with strike. Made by Welch, Spring and Company, Forestville, Conn., c.1884. H. 19¾″. (O. Harry Burt Collection)

414 (below, center). Shelf clock. "Titiens" model. Rosewood case. Brass 30-day, spring-driven, nickel-plated movement, porcelain dial. Made by Welch, Spring and Company, Forestville, Conn., c.1875. H. 23″. (O. Harry Burt Collection)

415 (below, right). Shelf clock. "Gerster V.P." model. Rosewood case. Brass 8-day, spring-driven "Patti" movement. Made by Welch, Spring and Company, Forestville, Conn., c. 1875. H. 18¾″. (O. Harry Burt Collection)

413

414

415

416

416 (left). Shelf clock. "Patti No. 2." Rosewood case. Chrome-plated brass 8-day, spring-driven movement with strike. 3″ dial. Made by Welch, Spring and Company, Forestville, Conn., c.1875. H. 10½″. (O. Harry Burt Collection)

417 (above). *The Mother's Watch* by James Goodwin Clonney, 1852–1856. Oil on canvas. A China case clock is sitting on a shelf in the upper right corner of the painting. Photograph courtesy Hirschl & Adler Galleries, Inc. (Westmoreland County Museum of Art)

419

420

418

418a

418 (opposite, below left). Shelf clock. "Erie" model. Walnut case. Brass 8-day movement with strike and alarm. Made by Seth Thomas Clock Co., Thomaston, Conn., c.1884. H. 19″. (T. H. Eurich Company)

418a (opposite, below right). Lyre-type movement used in the "Erie" model shelf clock.

419 (opposite, above right). Shelf clock. "Oriental" model. Rosewood veneer case. Brass 8-day movement with strike. Made by The E. Ingraham Company, Bristol, Conn., c.1884. H. 18″. (T. H. Eurich Company)

420 (opposite, right). Shelf clock. Rosewood veneer case. Brass 8-day movement with strike. Extra-weighted pendulum bob. Made by the Waterbury Clock Company, Waterbury, Conn., c.1880. H. 17½″. (T. H. Eurich Company)

421 (right). Globe clock. Walnut case. Movement made by Theodore R. Timby in Baldwinsville, N.Y., c. 1864. H. 27″. Globe made by Gilman Joslin, a Boston map maker. All clocks were numbered. (T. H. Eurich Company)

422 (below, center). Shelf clock. Rosewood veneer case. Brass 8-day, spring-driven movement with strike and alarm. Made by Atkins Clock Mfg. Co., Bristol, Conn., c.1855. H. 16¾″. (William J. Haggerty Collection)

421

422

23

424

423 (above, left). Shelf clock. Mahogany and rosewood case. Brass 8-day weight-driven, 3-ball movement with torsion suspension and strike. Made by Aaron D. Crane, Newark, N.J., c.1860. H. 20½″. (Private collection)

424 (right). Shelf clock with gallery. Walnut case. Brass 8-day movement with strike. Made by Ansonia Clock Company, Ansonia, Conn., c. 1880. H. 18″. (T. H. Eurich Company)

425

425 (right). Shelf clock. Cast-iron painted case. Brass 8-day, spring-driven movement with strike. Made by Gilbert and Hubbard, Meriden, Conn., c.1864. H. 20″. (The Old Clock Museum)

426 (below). Shelf clock. "Cupid" model. Cast metal case. Brass 8-day, spring-driven movement with strike. Made by Jerome Manufacturing Company, New Haven, Conn., c.1854. Case made by N. Mueller. H. 19″. (The Old Clock Museum),

426

427 (opposite). Shelf clock. Cast metal case. Brass 8-day, spring-driven movement with strike. Made by Seth Thomas Clock Co., Plymouth, Conn., c.1858. H. 22″. (The Old Clock Museum)

427

428 (below). Shelf clock. "Domino" model. Black-painted wood case. Brass 8-day, spring-driven movement with strike. Made by The E. Ingraham and Company, Bristol, Conn., 1886–1892. H. 16″. Introduced in 1886 and last sold in the 1891/92 catalogue; cost was $11. Photograph: Edward H. Goodrich. (American Clock and Watch Museum)

428

429 (below). Shelf clock. Cathedral-style cast-iron case. Brass 8-day, spring-driven movement. Made by E.N. Welch Manufacturing Co., Bristol, Conn., c.1875. H. 18″. (The Old Clock Museum)

429

430

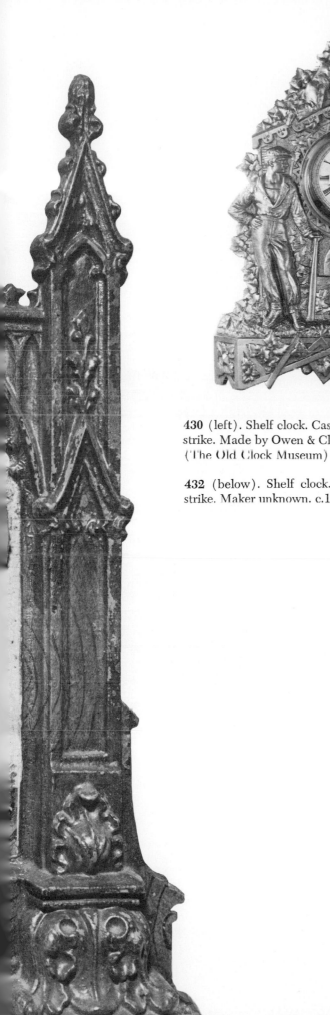

431 (left). Shelf clock. "Ball Players" model. Cast metal case. Brass 8-day, spring-driven movement with strike. Made by the American Clock Company, New York, N.Y., c.1870. H. 17″. (The Old Clock Museum)

431

430 (left). Shelf clock. Cast-iron case. Brass 8-day, spring-driven movement with strike. Made by Owen & Clark, New York, N.Y., c.1850. H. 18″. (The Old Clock Museum)

432 (below). Shelf clock. Cast-iron case. Brass 8-day, spring-driven movement with strike. Maker unknown. c.1885. H. 18½″. (Burton and Helaine Fendelman)

432

433 (above, left). Shelf clock. Pine case, stained. Brass 8-day movement with strike. Maker unknown. c. 1885. H. 24¼″.
(T. H. Eurich Company)

434 (above, right). Shelf clock. Pearwood case. Brass 8-day movement with strike. Made by The E. Ingraham and Company, Bristol, Conn., c.1880. H. 22″. (T. H. Eurich Company)

435 (left). Kitchen shelf clock. Solid pine case. Brass 8-day movement with strike. Made by The E. Ingraham and Company, Bristol, Conn., c.1884. H. 20½″. (T. H. Eurich Company)

436 (right). Shelf clock. Pine case. Brass 30-hour movement with strike. Made by F. Kroeber and Company, New York, N.Y., c.1878. H. 15″. Paper marked "One Day Despatch." (T. H. Eurich Company)

436

437

437 (above, left). Mantel clock. Painted china case. Brass 8-day spring movement with strike. Outside escapement. Movement made by Seth Thomas Clock Co., Thomaston, Conn. Case made in Bonn, Germany, c.1900. H. 12″. (T. H. Eurich Company)

438 (left). Miniature teardrop shelf clock. Walnut case. Brass 30-hour, spring-driven movement. Made by the Barnes Brothers Clock Co., Bristol, Conn., c.1881. H. 13½″. (B. A. Romeo Collection)

438

439

439 (right). Mantel clock. Painted china case. Brass 8-day, movement with strike. Made by the Ansonia Clock Company, New York, N.Y., c. 1900. H. 12″. (T. H. Eurich Company)

440

442

440 (above). Shelf clock. Walnut case with drawer in bottom. Level, compass, barometer, and hygrometer, with metal dial. Brass 8-day movement with strike. Made by William L. Gilbert Co., Winsted, Conn. Patented 1881. H. 20″. (T. H. Eurich Company)

441 (below). Shelf clock. Walnut case. Brass 8-day movement with strike. Made by Seth Thomas, Thomaston, Conn., c.1895. H. 24¼″. (T. H. Eurich Company)

441

443 (right). Shelf clock. Kidney-shaped dial opening. Walnut case. Brass 8-day movement with strike. Probably made by George Owen, Winsted, Conn., c.1875. H. 23″. (T. H. Eurich Company)

443

444

444 (above). Shelf clock. Walnut fish-scale case. Brass 8-day movement with strike and alarm. Made by E.N. Welch Manufacturing Co., Bristol, Conn., c.1885. H. 23¼″. (T. H. Eurich Company)

442 (left). Shelf clock. Walnut case. Brass 8-day movement with strike. Made by William L. Gilbert Co., Winsted, Conn., c.1865. H. 22¼″. (T. H. Eurich Company)

445 (right). Shelf clock. Walnut case. Brass 8-day movement with strike and alarm. Made by F. Kroeber, New York, N.Y., c. 1875. H. 21¾″. (T. H. Eurich Company)

445

446

446 (opposite). Shelf clock. Pressed oak case. Brass 8-day, spring-driven movement with strike and alarm. Made by The E. Ingraham and Company, Bristol, Conn., c.1880. H. 21″. (Chicago Historical Society)

447 (right). Shelf clock. Oak case. Brass 8-day, spring-driven movement with strike. Made by the Ansonia Clock Company, Ansonia, Conn., c.1875. H. 22¾″. (T. H. Eurich Company)

448 (below, center). Shelf clock. Oak case. Brass 8-day movement with strike and alarm. Made by Seth Thomas, Thomaston, Conn., c.1880. H. 23½″. (T. H. Eurich Company)

447

448

450

449

449 (left). Shelf clock. Oak case with twisted columns. Brass 8-day movement with strike. Made by William L. Gilbert Co., Winsted, Conn., c.1875. H. 28½″. (T. H. Eurich Company)

450 (above). Shelf clock. Pressed oak case with painted green leaf and red grape design. Brass 8-day movement with strike. Made by William L. Gilbert Co., Winsted, Conn., c.1890. H. 23″. (T. H. Eurich Company)

451 (right). Shelf clock. Oak case with impressed portrait of Admiral George Dewey. Brass 8-day, spring-driven movement with strike. Made by E. N. Welch, Bristol, Conn., c.1899. H. 24½". (Gene L. Bagwell Collection)

451a (below). Detail showing the portrait of Admiral Dewey on the E. N. Welch shelf clock.

452 (opposite, left). Shelf clock. Pressed oak case with portrait of Admiral Dewey, flags, and cannon balls. Brass 8-day movement with strike. Made by The E. Ingraham Company, Bristol, Conn., c.1900. H. 32". (T. H. Eurich Company)

452a (opposite, above right). Detail showing the portrait of Admiral Dewey on the E. Ingraham shelf clock.

452b (above). Detail showing design of anchors and stars on the base of the E. Ingraham shelf clock.

451

451a

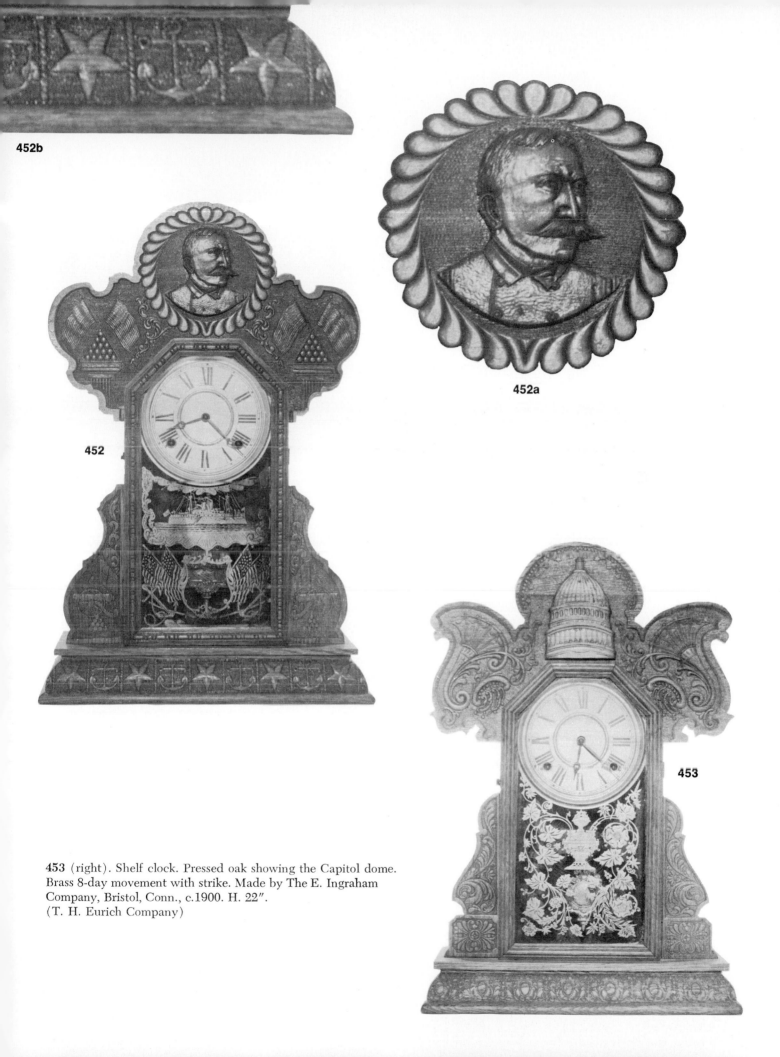

452b

452a

452

453

453 (right). Shelf clock. Pressed oak showing the Capitol dome. Brass 8-day movement with strike. Made by The E. Ingraham Company, Bristol, Conn., c.1900. H. 22″. (T. H. Eurich Company)

454 (right). Mantel clock. Walnut case with painted Chinese motifs and dragon feet. Brass 8-day movement with strike. Made by The E. Ingraham Company, Bristol, Conn., c.1900. H. 10″. (T. H. Eurich Company)

454

455

455 (left). Shelf clock. Black metal case. Brass 8-day, spring-driven movement with strike. Outside escapement made by Ansonia Clock Company, Brooklyn, N.Y., c.1885. H. 11″. (Fond du Lac Historical Society)

456

457

456 (above). Shelf clock. Black enameled case. Brass 8-day, spring-driven movement with strike. Outside escapement. Made by Ansonia Clock Company, Brooklyn, N.Y., c.1884. H. 10½″. (Fond du Lac Historical Society)

457 (right). Shelf clock. Cast-iron and brass case. Brass 8-day, spring-driven movement with strike. Made by Seth Thomas and Sons, Thomaston, Conn., c.1890. H. 11¾″. (Greenfield Village and Henry Ford Museum)

458 (right, above). Shelf clock. "Black Prince" model. Ebonized wood case. Brass 8-day, spring-driven movement with strike. Made by The E. Ingraham Company, Bristol, Conn., c.1884. H. 13½". This model was carried in the 1881–1884 trade catalogues and sold for $6.50. Photograph: Edward H. Goodrich. (American Clock and Watch Museum)

459 (right, below). Shelf clock. Black metal case. Brass 8-day, spring-driven movement with strike. Made by Ansonia Clock Company, Brooklyn, N.Y., c.1887. H. 9". (Fond du Lac Historical Society)

460 (below). Shelf clock. Marble and bronze case. Brass 8-day, spring-driven movement with strike, visible escapement. Seated figure of a man on top of case. Maker unknown. c.1880. H. 21". (Chicago Historical Society)

NOVELTY CLOCKS

Novelty clocks have been placed in a section by themselves because of their often peculiar styles. They do not fit into any one category because of their movements, case designs, or how the clock performed—such as the illuminated alarm clock that lights a wick or a candle instead of sounding an alarm. Such clocks were made by various companies throughout the country chiefly during the last quarter of the nineteenth century.

461

462

463

461 (above). Violin shelf clock. Walnut case. Brass 8-day, spring-driven movement with strike. Lyre-type movement. Made by Seth Thomas Clock Co., Thomaston, Conn., c.1885. H. 29″. (Joe Brincat Collection)

462 (above, right) and **463** (right). Two "Old/Mr. Boston"/"Fine Liquors" advertising bottles. Clocks were made by William L. Gilbert Co., Winsted, Conn., and ran for eight days. c.1900. Figure 462 is 10⅜″ high; 463 is 22½″ high. (Gene L. Bagwell Collection)

464 (above). Time globe. Brass 8-day movement. Made by The Chicago Globe Chronometer Co., Chicago, Ill., c.1900. H. 20″ with 12″ globe. Invented by George W. Ramage. It shows the hours, minutes, and seconds on two time wheels. The chronometric balance was made by The Chelsea Clock Company. Only two are known to be in existence today. (Irving Cooperman Collection)

465 (right). Swinging shelf clock. Brass 8-day, spring-driven movement. Made by Ansonia Clock Company, New York, N.Y., c.1890. H. 31″. (The Old Clock Museum)

466 (above). Various types of cast-iron cases used for blinking-eye clocks. c.1860. (The Old Clock Museum)

468 (opposite, left). Blinking-eye clock. "Sambo" model. Cast-iron case. Maker unknown. c.1860. H. 16″. (Western Reserve Historical Society)

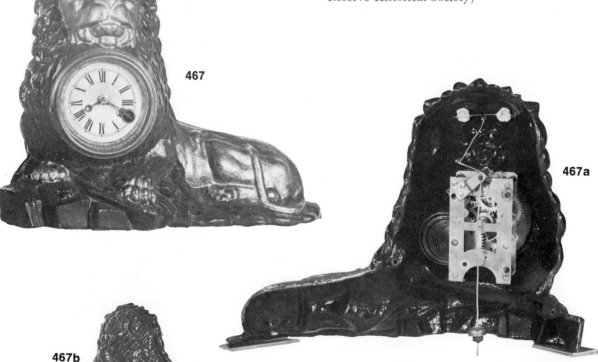

467 (above, left). Blinking-eye shelf clock. Cast-iron case in the form of a lion. Brass 30-hour, spring-driven movement. Maker not known. Case made by Bradley & Hubbard, West Meriden, Conn., c.1860. H. 16″. (American Clock and Watch Museum)

467a (above). Movement of blinking-eye shelf clock.

467b (left). Back of blinking-eye shelf clock.

469 (right). Blinking-eye shelf clock. "Continental" model. Brass
marine spring-driven, 30-hour movement. Cast-iron case made by
Bradley & Hubbard, West Meriden, Conn., c. 1865. H. 16¾".
This model was marketed by The Waterbury Clock Company, The
American Clock Company, and others during the 1860s.
(American Clock and Watch Museum)

469

468

470

470 (right). Blinking-eye clock. "Squire" model. Cast-iron case. Maker
unknown. c. 1860. H. 16". (Western Reserve Historical Society)

471

471 (left). So-called nursery clock. Made by The Waltham Watch Company, Waltham, Mass., c.1880. H. 9″. Milk-glass dial that is made to fit in front of a gas jet for seeing the time at night. Clock can be removed from the jet. (Valentine Museum)

472

473

475a

474

202

472 (opposite, above center). Alarm clock. Made by The Parker Clock Company, Meriden, Conn., c.1893. H. 4½". (Irving Cooperman Collection)

473 (opposite, above right). Alarm clock. Made by Waterbury Clock Company, Waterbury, Conn., c.1877. H. 7¼". (Irving Cooperman Collection)

474 (opposite, below left). Briggs rotary shelf clock. Brass 30-hour, spring-driven movement. Made by E. N. Welch Manufacturing Co., Bristol, Conn., c.1880. H. 7¾". Invented by John C. Briggs, a civil engineer of Concord, N.H. Patented in 1855 and 1858. (New Hampshire Historical Society)

475 (below). Illuminated alarm clock. Walnut veneer case. Brass 30-hour, spring-driven movement. Made by the Ansonia Brass and Copper Company, New York, N.Y., c.1875. H. 16". Illuminated portion made by H. J. Davies. A cam was added to the alarm portion of the movement, which would activate the illuminated portion of the clock. Photograph shows the alarm has set off the action, with the match igniting the wick. (Irving Cooperman Collection)

475a (opposite, below right). Illuminated alarm clock. Clock dial removed, exposing brass 30-hour movement and alarm mechanism.

475

476 (above). Flying pendulum or "Ignatz" clock. Oak case. Brass 30-hour, spring-driven movement. Made by the New Haven Clock Co., New Haven, Conn., under Jerome and Company name, c.1884. H. 10¼". Movement was invented and patented by Alder Christian Clausen, Oct. 9, 1883. (Irving Cooperman Collection)

476a

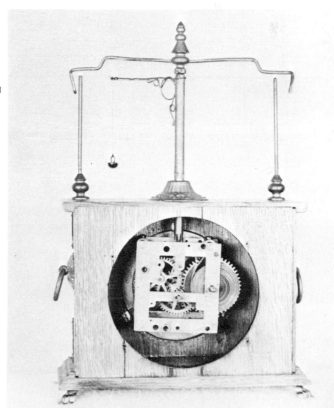

476a (right). Flying pendulum clock. Back removed showing the 30-hour movement.

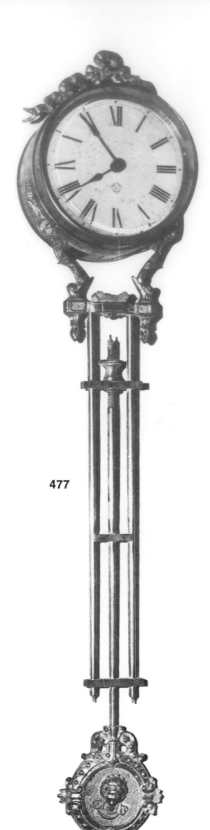

477 (left). Wall clock. Brass 8-day, spring-driven movement. Winds from the back. Pendulumlike appendage is stationary. Made by Ansonia Clock Company, Ansonia, Conn., c.1870. H. 14″. (Fond du Lac Historical Society)

478 (below, left). Yale pendulet clock. Wood case. Brass 30-hour, spring-driven movement. Made by the Yale Clock Co., New Haven, Conn., c.1882. H. 4¾″. (Irving Cooperman Collection)

479 (below, right). Yale pendulet clock. Nickel-plated case. Brass 30-hour, spring-driven movement. Made by the Yale Clock Co., New Haven, Conn., c.1882. H. 3¼″. (Irving Cooperman Collection)

479

477

478

480

480 (right). Candlestand clock. Brass 30-hour, spring-driven movement. Bell glass covering clock on stand. Made by Seth Thomas and Sons, New York, N.Y., c.1870. H. 9½″. (Chicago Historical Society)

482 (right). Year clock. Brass movement. Made by the Year Clock Co., New York, N.Y., c.1900. H. 11″. Spring barrel is 6″ in diameter and 2¼″ deep. Probably a salesman's sample. (Irving Cooperman Collection)

482

483

481

481 (above, left). Candlestand shelf clock. White marble base. Brass 30-hour, spring-driven movement. Made by the Terryville Manufacturing Co., Terryville, Conn., c.1852. H. 10″. (Private collection)

483 (right). Columbus wall clock. Wood 30-hour, weight-driven movement with torsion-bar escapement. Made by Bostwick & Burgess Mfg. Co., Norwalk, Ohio. H. 14″. Made for sale at the World's Columbian Exposition, Chicago, Ill., 1892–1893. (Greenfield Village and Henry Ford Museum)

484 (right). Postal scale. Made by Howard and Davis, Boston, Mass., c.1865. H. 4½″. Few people know that besides clocks Howard and Davis also made fire engines, scales, and other miscellaneous items. They produced the first scales used by the U.S. Post Office Department. (Irving Cooperman Collection)

484a (below). Detail of postal scale showing the mark of Howard and Davis.

484

484a

485

485 (left). Roasting jack. This jack dates back to the 18th century and could very well have been made by a clockmaker. (Gene L. Bagwell Collection)

486 (right). Group of English and European gauges and measuring devices used by clockmakers, c.1800. (Ted Crom)

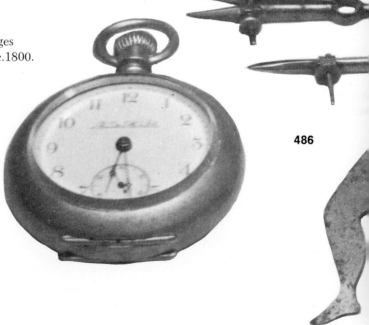

486

TOOLS

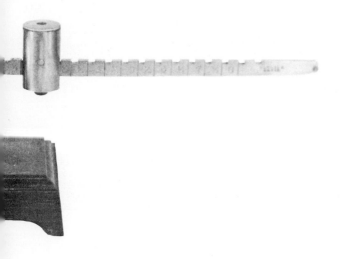

Clockmakers' tools were much alike in the United States, England, and Europe. Those shown on the following pages are mostly English, but they will give a good idea of the types of tools used by American clockmakers. Such tools have not changed a great deal over the years except that they have become mechanized rather than being operated by hand.

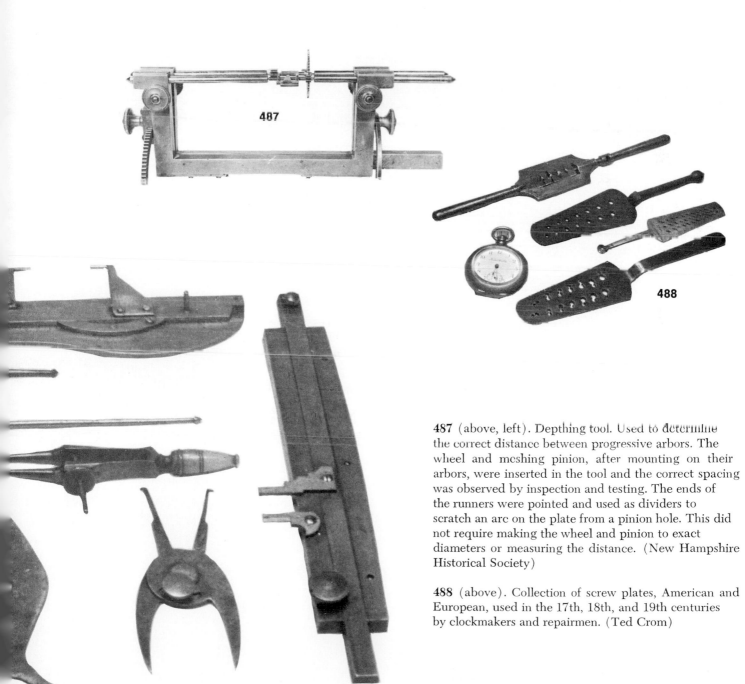

487 (above, left). Depthing tool. Used to determine the correct distance between progressive arbors. The wheel and meshing pinion, after mounting on their arbors, were inserted in the tool and the correct spacing was observed by inspection and testing. The ends of the runners were pointed and used as dividers to scratch an arc on the plate from a pinion hole. This did not require making the wheel and pinion to exact diameters or measuring the distance. (New Hampshire Historical Society)

488 (above). Collection of screw plates, American and European, used in the 17th, 18th, and 19th centuries by clockmakers and repairmen. (Ted Crom)

489 (right). Wheel-cutting engine. Cherry base. New Hampshire origin, c.1780. 13½″ x 21⅜″. Large, circular horizontal wheel disk is the index plate to regulate spacing of teeth. Wheel to be cut is in a horizontal position above. A wheel of 60 teeth could be cut in about ten minutes. (New Hampshire Historical Society)

490 (below). Small bench and hand vises of English and European manufacture, used by all clockmakers and repairmen of the 18th and 19th centuries. (Ted Crom)

491 (bottom). Roller pinion automated drill. American, date unknown. (Ted Crom)

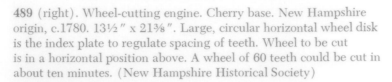

489

490

491

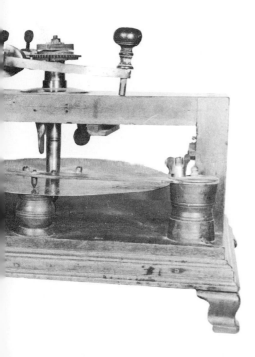

492 (below). Gear-cutting engine. (Amos G. Avery Collection)

493 (bottom). Mainspring winder. American, 1800–1850. 8″ x 5½″.
(Ted Crom)

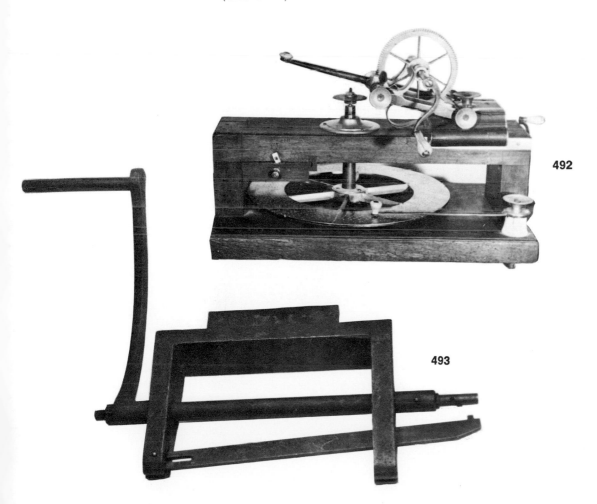

492

493

494 (above). Gear-cutter, gear-cutting table, and original
box, used in cutting gears for the Columbus clock. (David C.
Foust Collection)

495 (right). Gear-cutter used to cut gears for the Columbus
clock. (David C. Foust Collection)

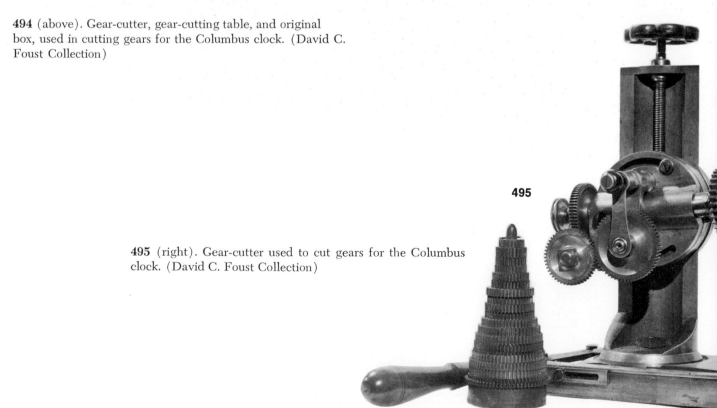

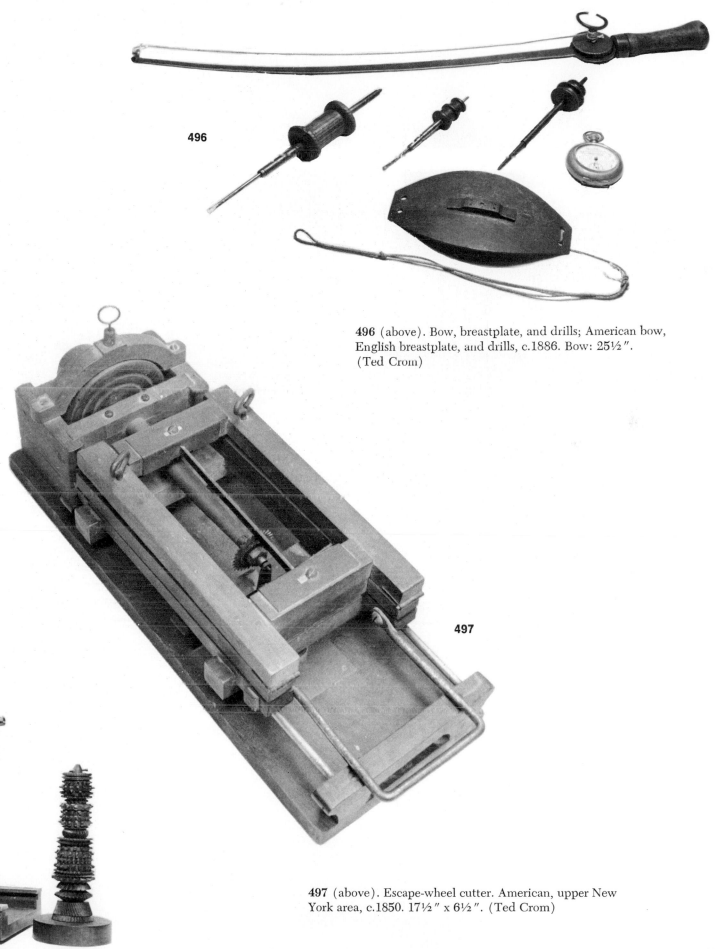

496 (above). Bow, breastplate, and drills; American bow, English breastplate, and drills, c.1886. Bow: 25½″. (Ted Crom)

497 (above). Escape-wheel cutter. American, upper New York area, c.1850. 17½″ x 6½″. (Ted Crom)

498

499

498 (above, left). Turning lathe. Made by J. M. Bottum,
New York, c.1870. 11″ x 11½″. (Ted Crom)

499 (above, right). Collection of miscellaneous tweezers used
in the 18th and 19th centuries. (Ted Crom)

500 (below). Wheel-cutting engine. American, New England,
c.1800. Wood base, brass index plate. 24½″ x 11″.
(Ted Crom)

500

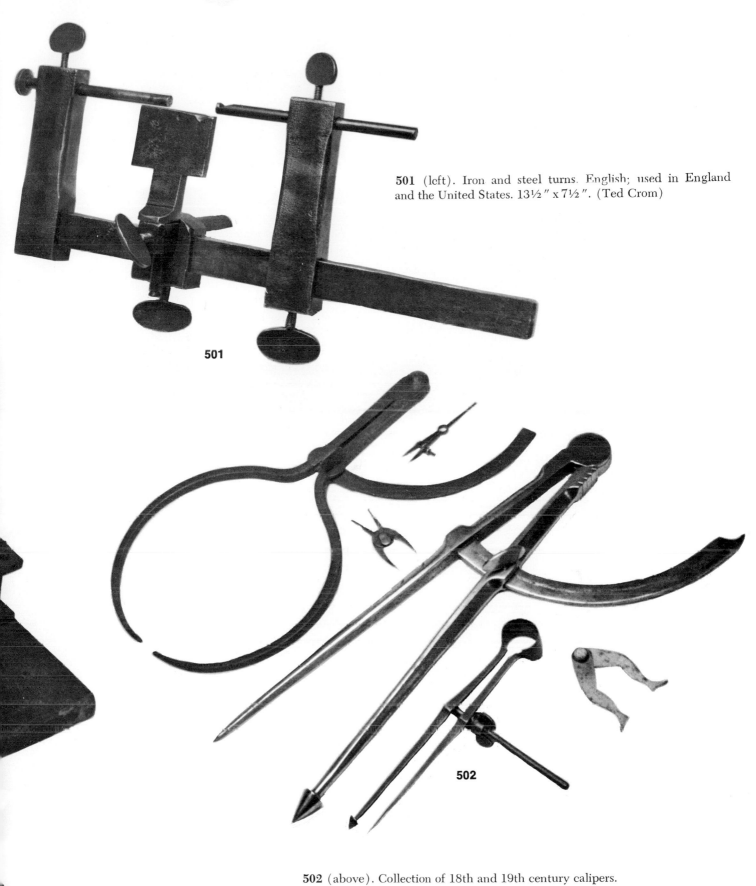

501 (left). Iron and steel turns. English; used in England and the United States. 13½″ x 7½″. (Ted Crom)

501

502

502 (above). Collection of 18th and 19th century calipers. European; similar to the types used by American clockmakers. (Ted Crom)

503

The banjos were made by the Willards and other important makers of the early nineteenth-century. Most of them were timepieces only—that is, they did not strike. Others had a strike train added and still others had alarm attachments. During the middle of the nineteenth-century the Howard and Davis banjos made their appearance. Compared to the earlier banjos, which usually had beautifully painted glass tablets on the body and door, they were very plain in design, lacking the side arms, finials, and other ornamentation. The movements were of excellent quality, and they were much used in offices, public buildings, and railroad stations. The lyres and girandoles were a variation of the banjo. As previously stated, the invention of the lyre has been attributed to Aaron Willard, Jr., but was made by others including Lemuel Curtis, John Sawin, and Joseph Dyer.

The New Hampshire mirror clocks were generally made in New Hampshire, although a few examples are known to have been made in other New England states and New York State. Some of the movements were scaled-down versions of the tall case, some were of the banjo type, and other examples used the so-called wheelbarrow movement.

The gallery clock was another type of wall clock used in public buildings such as churches and federal, state, and city offices. The early ones, produced by the Willards and others, were ornately gilded and had eight-day, weight-driven movements. A notable example made by Simon Willard is in Statuary Hall in Washington, D.C. Others can be seen in many of the churches in Massachusetts. Subsequently, the case design gradually evolved into a simple round case with a spring-driven movement.

WALL CLOCKS

The design of wall clocks very probably evolved from the English lantern clock or the wag-on-wall clock. There are many sizes and designs. The most popular wall clocks have been the "Improved Patent Timepiece," better known as the banjo clock, which was patented by Simon Willard in 1802, and the familiar schoolhouse clocks of the 1850s and 1860s, which came in many varieties and styles. In between were the New Hampshire mirror clock, the invention of which has been attributed to Benjamin Morrill of New Hampshire; the lyre clock, often attributed to Aaron Willard, Jr., wall regulators, calendar clocks, and others.

503 (above). Wall clock. Wood case. Made by Thomas Bennett in 1727, for which he was paid twelve shillings. Brass 8-day, weight-driven movement. Made by John Avery, Boston, Mass., c.1726. H. 60″. Installed in the Old North Church in 1726 and used to time sermons. Still in use. Cleaned by Simon Willard and Sons in 1823 and 1829. Photograph: Anastasi of Boston Studio. (Old North Church)

504 (opposite). Wall clock. Brass 7-day, weight-driven movement with strike. Made by Peter Sprunk, Philadelphia, Pa., c.1790. H. 38″. Designed by Thomas Jefferson and installed in the front hall of Monticello, Jefferson's home near Charlottesville, Virginia, the clock is powered by eight cannon balls, each weighing 18 pounds, that drive the strike side and six cannon balls that drive the time side. The weights hang in the corners of the room and also serve to show the days of the week as they pass labeled markers affixed to the wall. Holes cut into the floor allow the weights to descend into the basement. Photograph: Ed Roseberry. (Thomas Jefferson Memorial Foundation)

505

505 (left). Wall clock. Mahogany case. Brass 30-hour movement. Strikes once every hour. Brass dial. Made by Simon Willard, Grafton, Mass., c.1775. H. 28¼″. (The Metropolitan Museum of Art: Gift of George Coe Graves, 1930)

506 (above). Wall clock. Two part mahogany case. Brass 2-day, weight-driven movement with strike and moon phase. Clock strikes once each hour. Made by Simon Willard, Grafton, Mass., c. 1777. H. 26½″. Photograph: Donald F. Eaton. (Old Sturbridge Village)

507 (below). Wall clock. Crotch mahogany case.
Brass 30-hour, weight-driven movement with strike and
seconds dial. Steel dial with brass rim. Made by
Simon Willard, Grafton, Mass., 1780–1790. H. 24½″.
(Museum of Fine Arts, Boston: Gift of Mr. and Mrs.
Walter Stephen Barker)

508 (right). Wall clock. Mahogany case. Brass 30-hour
movement. Strikes once on the hour. Brass dial.
Made by Aaron Willard, Boston, Mass., 1757–1844.
H. 23″. (The Metropolitan Museum of Art: Gift of
George Coe Graves, 1930)

507

508

509 (right). Gallery clock in the Supreme Court, Washington, D.C. Made and installed by Simon Willard, c.1837. H. 42″. (Architect of the Capitol)

509a (below). Movement of the Simon Willard gallery clock in the Supreme Court.

509b (opposite). Bill of sale for the Willard clock in Supreme Court. Signed by Simon Willard, Washington, Oct. 31, 1837. (Architect of the Capitol)

510 (opposite). Close-up of the movement of the Franzoni clock in the U.S. Capitol. Movement made by Simon Willard and Son, Boston, Mass., c.1800. (Architect of the Capitol)

510

Washington Oct 31 - '37

Supreme Court of the United States

To Simon Willard Dr

To One large Clock for Court Room.
Putting up and regulating the Same ✓ $180:00
Washington 31st Oct 1837 Received of Alexander
Hunter marshal One hundred and Eighty
Dollars in full of the above account —

Simon Willard

509b

511

511 (left). Gallery clock. Gilt case with spread eagle above. Brass 8-day, weight-driven movement. Made by Simon Willard, Roxbury, Mass., c.1800. H. 22″. (Museum of Fine Arts, Boston: Gift of S. Richard Fuller)

513

513 (below). Gallery wall clock. Gilded pine case. Brass 8-day, weight-driven movement. Pendulum ball stamped "Willard-Boston." Painted mahogany dial. Name and date on dial are for a later presentation. Made by Aaron Willard, Jr., Boston, Mass., c.1830. Diam. 35″. Image Studios, David Towne, Photographer. (Herschel B. Burt Collection)

512

512 (above). Gallery clock. Gilt case with eagle at top. Brass 8-day, weight-driven movement. Made by Simon Willard, Roxbury, Mass., c.1800. H. 50″. Diam. of dial: 27″. (Greenfield Village and Henry Ford Museum)

514 (below). Gallery clock. Corrugated chestnut case. Brass 8-day, spring-driven movement. Made by The E. Ingraham and Company, Bristol, Conn., c.1880. Diam. 18″. Produced from 1875 to 1886 in 10-, 12-, 14-, and 18-inch sizes, and was available in walnut, chestnut, or gilt. 18-inch size retailed for $20 in 1880. Photograph: Edward H. Goodrich. (American Clock and Watch Museum)

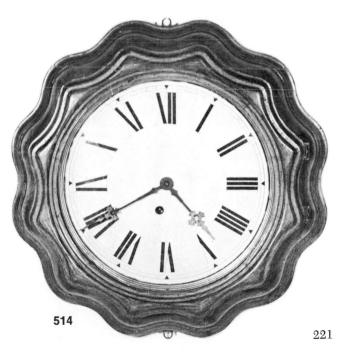

514

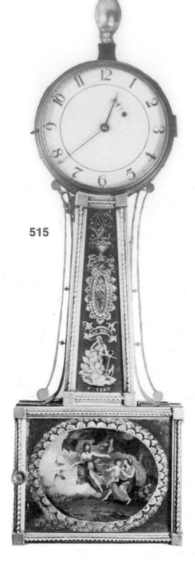

515 (left). Banjo clock. Mahogany and pine case. Brass 8-day, weight-driven movement. Made by Lemuel Curtis, Concord, Mass., c.1815. H. 29½". Movement is touch-marked "L. Curtis #2." T-bridge escapement. Image Studios, David Towne, Photographer. (Private collection)

515

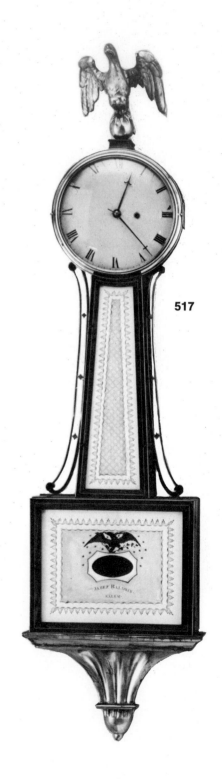

517

516

516 (left). Banjo clock. Mahogany and gilt case. Brass 8-day, weight-driven movement. Attributed to Aaron Willard, Boston, Mass., 1810–1820. H. 35⅜". Formerly belonged to Hart Woodcock, a well-known painter who spent his winters in Nassau, B.W.I., and his summers on an old farm near Belfast, Me., called Woodbine. Tablet shows the Stonebridge Tavern. (Gene L. Bagwell Collection)

517 (right). Banjo clock. Mahogany case. Brass 8-day, weight-driven movement. "Upside-down" verge escapement. Glass panels signed Willard and Nolen. Made by Jabez Baldwin, Salem, Mass., 1805–1809. H. 45¼". (Yale University Art Gallery: The Mabel Brady Garvan Collection)

518 (right). Banjo clock.
Mahogany veneer case. Brass
8-day, weight-driven movement.
Made by Abel Stowell, Worcester,
Mass., c.1820. H. 31¼″.
(J. Alford Jones)

520 (below). Banjo clock. Mahogany and
mahogany veneer case. Brass 8-day, weight-
driven movement. Dial inscribed: "Presented
to/J.L. Dunning/ by Simon Willard." The
design of this clock is so unusual for Willard
that it prompts the question: Did Willard
invent this case style, or did he work with
Dunning on the design? Roxbury, Mass.,
c.1815. H. 34½″. (Mark A. Shanaberger)

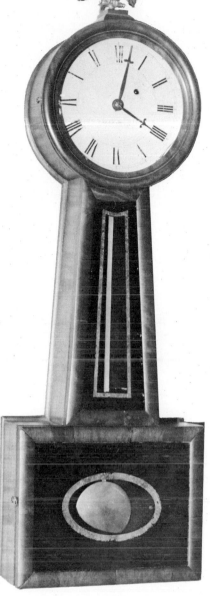

518

519

520

519 (above). Banjo clock. Mahogany case with satinwood
inlay. Brass 8-day, weight-driven movement. Made by Simon
Willard, Roxbury, Mass., c.1805. H. 34″. The banjo clock
was patented by Willard under the label of "Improved
Patent Timepiece." (Museum of Fine Arts, Boston: Gift of
Miss Theodora Willard)

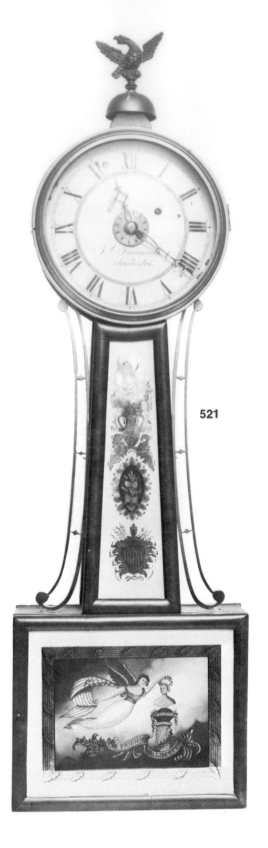

521

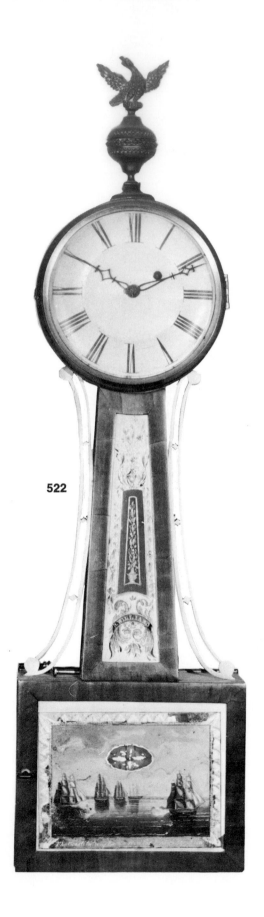

522 (below). Banjo clock. Mahogany veneer case. Brass 8-day, weight-driven movement. Made by David Williams, Newport, R.I., c.1815. H. 35¼". (Private collection)

522

521 (above). Banjo clock. Mahogany case. Brass 8-day, weight-driven movement with alarm. Maker unknown. Dial marked "I. Farnsworth/ Charleston." c.1820. H. 33". Farnsworth was probably the owner of the clock. (Mark A. Shanaberger)

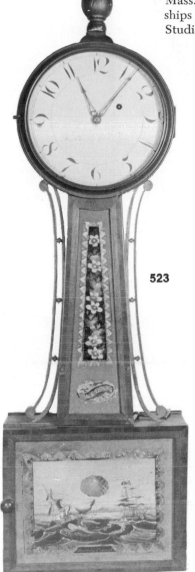

523 (left). Banjo clock. Mahogany case. Brass 8-day, weight-driven movement. Made by Elnathan Taber, Roxbury, Mass., c.1810. H. 33″. The painted tablet, depicting the ships *Hornet* and *Peacock,* is of exceptional quality. Image Studios, David Towne, Photographer. (Private collection)

523

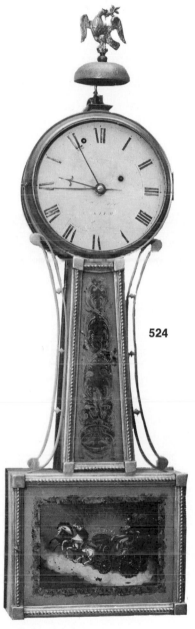

524

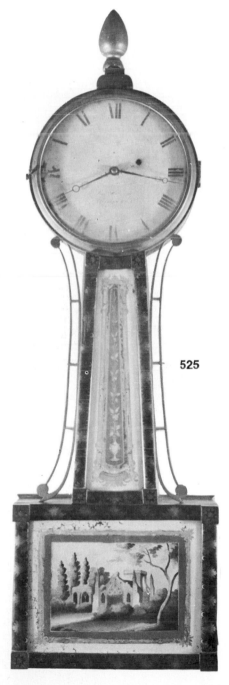

525

524 (above). Banjo clock. Mahogany and gilt case. Brass 8-day, weight-driven movement with alarm. Alarm bell on top of case. Made by Aaron Willard, Boston, c.1809. H. 34½″. (The Metropolitan Museum of Art: Gift of George Coe Graves, 1930)

525 (right). Banjo clock. Stenciled mahogany case. Brass 8-day, weight-driven movement. Made by Levi Hutchins, Concord, N.H., c.1810. H. 32⅞″. Banjos made by Levi Hutchins are rare, as is the stenciled case. The plates have arch cutouts on the base. Case is numbered 1101 and may have been made in Boston. (Herschel B. Burt Collection)

526 (right). Banjo clock. Mahogany and pine case. Brass 8-day, weight-driven movement. Made by Leonard W. Noyes, Nashua, N.H., c.1825. H. 39″. New Hampshire-style side rails. Image Studios, David Towne, Photographer. (Herschel B. Burt Collection)

527 (below, left). Banjo clock. Mahogany veneer and gilded case. Brass 8-day, weight-driven movement with strike. Made by James Collins, Goffstown, N.H., c.1820. H. 40″. The Collins house in Goffstown is still standing. Hands may be replacements. (Mark A. Shanaberger)

527a (below, center). Movement of the James Collins banjo clock. This same type of movement was used in several styles of clocks.

528 (below, right). Banjo clock. Mahogany veneer case. Brass 8-day, weight-driven movement. Made by John Sawin, Boston, Mass., c.1825. H. 41″. (Private collection)

526

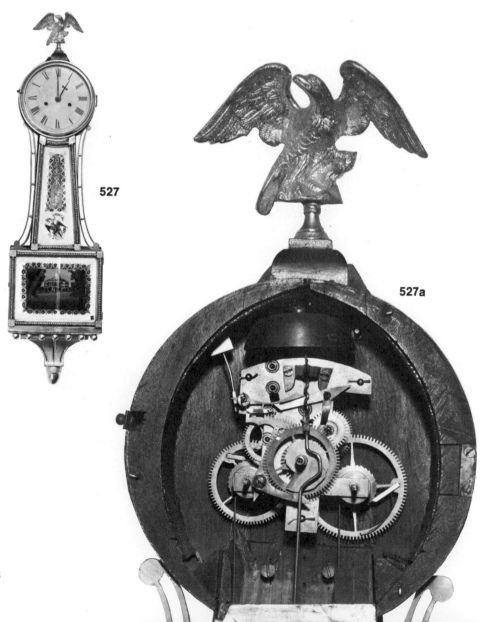

527

527a

528

531 (right). Banjo clock. No. 95. Mahogany case. Brass 8-day, weight-driven movement. Made by E. Howard and Company, Boston, Mass., c.1857. H.39½". (R. A. Romeo Collection)

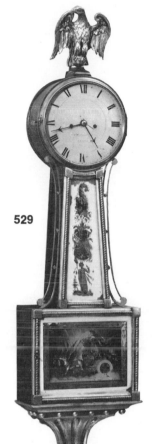

529

531

529 (left). Banjo clock. Mahogany and pine case. Brass 8-day, weight-driven movement with strike. Made by Aaron Willard, Jr., Boston, Mass., c.1820. H. 42⅜". No. 499 on rear of dial and No. 500 on inside of back and top rear side of door. (The Colonial Williamsburg Foundation)

530

532

530 (above, center). Banjo clock. Mahogany and pine case. Brass 8-day, weight-driven movement. Tablet shows Nahant Hotel. The same view is found on Staffordshire plates. Made by Sawin and Dyer, Boston, Mass., c.1825. H. 33". Image Studios, David Towne, Photographer. (Private collection)

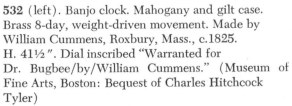

532 (left). Banjo clock. Mahogany and gilt case. Brass 8-day, weight-driven movement. Made by William Cummens, Roxbury, Mass., c.1825. H. 41½". Dial inscribed "Warranted for Dr. Bugbee/by/William Cummens." (Museum of Fine Arts, Boston: Bequest of Charles Hitchcock Tyler)

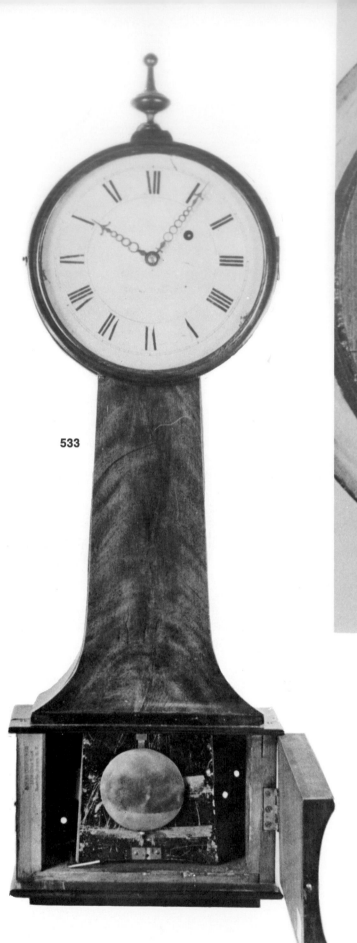

533

533a

533 (left). Banjo shelf clock with the door open. Made by Curtis and Dunning, Concord, Mass., c.1840. H. 29½". (Irving Cooperman Collection)

533a (above). Movement of the Curtis and Dunning banjo shelf clock.

535 (opposite, center). Banjo clock. Gilded mahogany and pine case. Brass 8-day, weight-driven movement. Made by Abiel Chandler, Concord, N.H., c.1830. H. 39¼". Photograph: Bill Finney. (New Hampshire Historical Society)

536 (opposite, left). Banjo clock. Mahogany case. Brass 8-day, weight-driven movement. Made by Edmund Currier, Salem, Mass., c.1828. H. 41". Image Studios, David Towne, Photographer. (Private collection)

534 (right). Banjo clock. Mahogany veneer case. Brass 8-day, weight-driven movement. Made by James Doull, Philadelphia, Pa., c.1835. H. 23½″. Doull is actually James McDoull who went to Philadelphia from Massachusetts around 1830. This is the first recorded Philadelphia banjo. Photograph: Patrick Radebaugh. (Frank S. Schwarz and Son)

534

536

535

537

537 (right). Banjo clock. Mahogany veneer case. Wood 30-hour, weight-driven movement with strike. Attributed to either Eli Terry & Sons or Eli Terry, Jr., Plymouth, Conn., c.1830. H. 36″. (Harold Klock Collection)

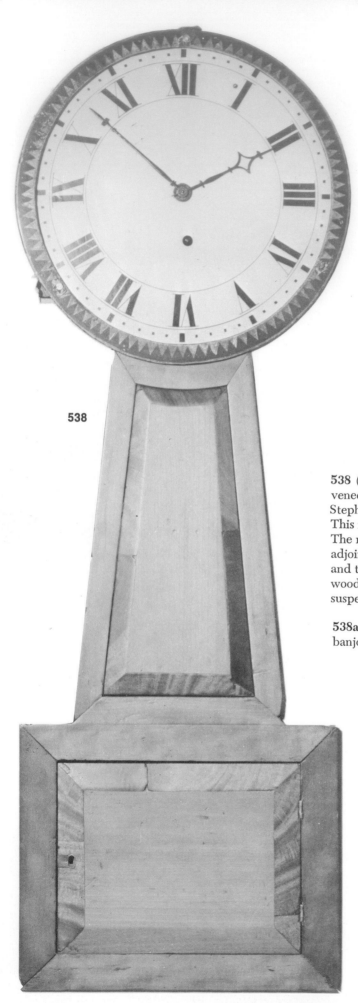

538

538 (left). Between-the-wall banjo clock. Maple and veneer case. Brass 8-day, weight-driven movement. Made by Stephen Hasham, Charlestown, N.H., c.1830. H. 36″. This is one of two clocks Hasham made for his home. The movement was placed between the walls with dials in adjoining rooms. One side had an imitation banjo front and the other was only a bezel. Movement was placed in a wood frame. Pendulum adjustment was from the point of suspension. (New Hampshire Historical Society)

538a (opposite). Movement of the Hasham between-the-wall banjo clock.

538a

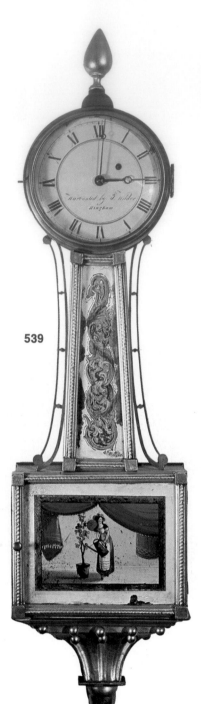

539

540 (below, center). Lyre wall clock. Mahogany case. Brass 8-day, weight-driven movement. Made by Walter H. Durfee, Providence, R.I., c. 1890. H. 42½". (T. H. Eurich Company)

541 (below, right). Banjo clock. No. 4. Cherry case with rosewood graining. Brass 8-day, weight-driven movement. Made by Howard and Davis, Boston, Mass., 1845–1850. H. 32". (William J. Haggerty Collection)

539 (left). Banjo clock. Mahogany veneer and gilt case with bracket. Brass 8-day, weight-driven movement. Made by Joshua Wilder, Hingham, Mass., 1810–1812. H. 39½". (Private collection)

541

540

543

544

542 (above, left). Lyre wall clock. Mahogany case. Brass 8-day, weight-driven movement that strikes once on the hour. Made by John Sawin, Boston, Mass., c.1830. H. 32¼". Glasses have been replaced. (Dr. Paul H. Ernest Collection)

543 (above, right). Banjo clock. Mahogany and gilt case. Brass 8-day, weight-driven movement with strike and seconds dial. Made by Aaron Willard, Boston, Mass., c.1810. H. 35". (Private collection)

544 (right). Banjo clock. Mahogany case. Brass 8-day, weight-driven movement. Made by Horace Tifft, North Attleboro, Mass., c.1820. H. 35". (William J. Haggerty Collection)

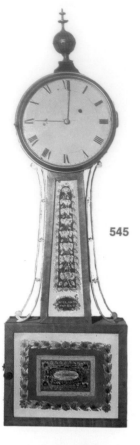

545 (above, left). Banjo clock. Mahogany and mahogany veneer case. Brass 8-day, weight-driven movement. Made by Simon Willard, Roxbury, Mass., c.1810. H. 34½″. (T. H. Eurich Company)

546 (above, center). Banjo clock. Mahogany veneer case with stenciling. Brass 8-day, weight-driven movement. Made by Levi Hutchins, Concord, N.H., c.1815. (Private collection)

547 (above, right). Banjo clock. Mahogany and gilt case. Brass 8-day, weight-driven movement. Unusual tablet with biblical scene: "Lot leaving Sodom and Gomorrah." Made by David Williams, Providence, R.I., c. 1810. H. 34″. (T. H. Eurich Company)

548 (left). Wall clock. Mahogany veneer case. Brass 8-day, weight-driven movement with repeat striking. Made by Timothy Chandler, Concord, N.H., c.1825. H. 37½″. (Private collection)

549 (above). Banjo clock. Mahogany and mahogany veneer case. Brass 8-day, weight-driven movement. Made by Joshua Seward, Boston, Mass., c.1830. H. 29″. (William J. Haggerty Collection)

550

550 (left). Banjo clock. Mahogany veneer case. Excellent tablets. Brass 8-day, weight-driven movement. Made by Simon Willard, Roxbury, Mass., c.1806. H. 32¾″. (Private collection)

551 (right). Banjo clock. Mahogany crossbanded case. Brass 8-day, weight-driven movement. Made by Aaron Willard, Jr., Boston, Mass., c.1815. H. 33¾″. Movement is signed: "Aaron Willard, Jr., Boston." (Dr. Paul H. Ernest Collection)

551a (below, right). Banjo clock by Aaron Willard, Jr., with the dial removed showing the signed movement.

552 (below, left). Banjo clock. Mahogany case. Unusual blue dial. Brass 8-day, weight-driven movement. Made by Simon Willard, Roxbury, Mass., c.1805. H. 34″. Photograph courtesy Israel Sack, Inc. (Private collection)

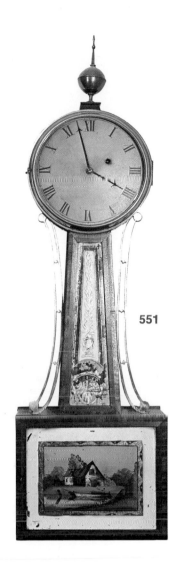

551

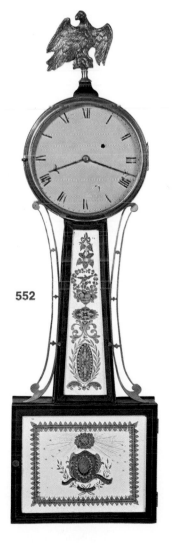

552

551a

553

553 (left). Presentation banjo clock. Gilded case. Brass 8-day, weight-driven movement. Made by Abiel Chandler, Concord, N.H., c.1820. H. 39¼″. Movement has cutout arch on plates. Large keystone on pendulum. (New Hampshire Historical Society)

554 (right). Wall regulator. Mahogany veneer case. Brass 8-day, weight-driven movement with seconds dial. Made by Simon Willard, Roxbury, Mass., c.1820. H. 44″. Charles Coleman was probably the owner. (Private collection)

554

555

555 (right). Banjo clock. Mahogany case. Brass 8-day, weight-driven movement. Made by Enoch H. Nutter, Dover, N.H., c.1825. H. 41½″. Movement stamped "E.H.N." (Mark A. Shanaberger)

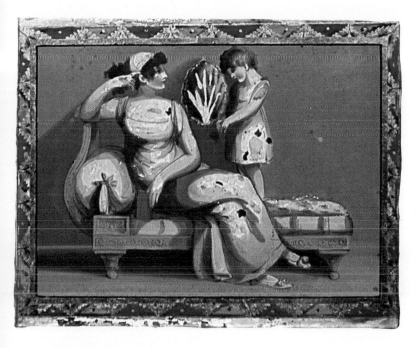

556a (above). Detail of the tablet painting on the Benjamin F. Willard, Jr., wall clock.

556

556 (right). Wall clock. Mahogany veneer case with columns. Brass 8-day, weight-driven movement. Made by Benjamin F. Willard, Jr., Lexington, Mass., c.1835. H. 39¼". (Private collection)

557

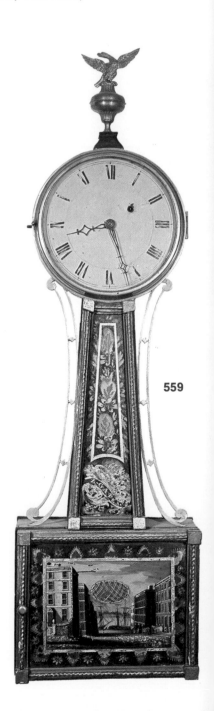

559

557 (left). Banjo clock. Mahogany and gilt case. Brass 8-day, weight-driven movement. Made by Aaron Willard, Boston, Mass., c.1815. H. 39″. (T. H. Eurich Company)

558 (far left). Banjo clock. No. 5. Cherry case with rosewood graining. Brass 8-day, weight-driven movement. Made by Howard and Davis, Boston, Mass., 1845–1850. H. 29″. (William J. Haggerty Collection)

558

559 (right). Banjo clock. Mahogany and gilt case. Brass 8-day, weight-driven movement. Made by Zacheus Gates, Charlestown, Mass., c.1820. H. 34″. (Private collection)

560 (opposite). Lyre wall clock. Gilt wood case. Brass 8-day, weight-driven movement with strike. Made by Joseph Ives, New York, N.Y., c.1840. H. 38¼″. (Private collection)

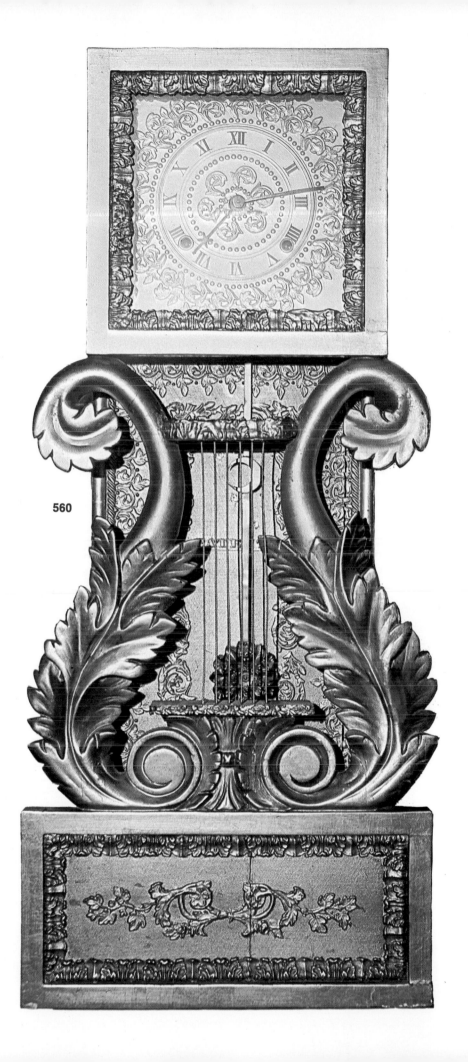

560

561a

561

561 (right). Striking banjo clock. Mahogany veneer case. Brass 8-day, weight-driven, skeletonized movement with strike and seconds dial. Made by Jonathan Billings, Acton, Mass., 1839. H. 38½″.
(Stan P. Sax Collection)

561a (above). Close-up of the label of the striking banjo clock made by Jonathan Billings.

561b (below). Close-up of the movement from the striking banjo clock made by Jonathan Billings.

561b

564a

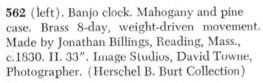

562 (left). Banjo clock. Mahogany and pine case. Brass 8-day, weight-driven movement. Made by Jonathan Billings, Reading, Mass., c.1830. H. 33″. Image Studios, David Towne, Photographer. (Herschel B. Burt Collection)

563 (right). Banjo clock. Mahogany veneer case with stenciling. Brass 8-day, weight-driven movement. Made by Enoch H. Nutter, Dover, N.H., c.1830. H. 40″. (Herschel B. Burt Collection)

564 (far right). Presentation banjo clock. Mahogany and gilt case with bracket. Brass 8-day, weight-driven movement. Made by Daniel Pratt and Sons, Reading, Mass., c. 1850. H. 41½″. (The Clock Gallery)

564a (above). Detail of the tablet on the Daniel Pratt and Sons banjo clock.

562

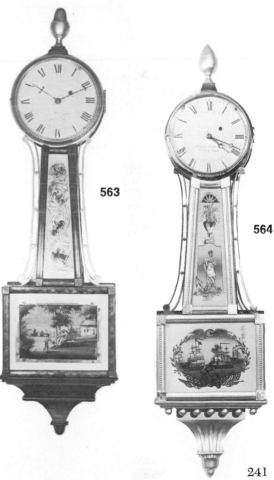

563

564

565 (below, left). Banjo clock. Mahogany and mahogany veneer case. Brass 8-day, weight-driven movement. Attributed to Aaron Willard, Jr., Boston, Mass., c.1830. H. 40½″. (Mark A. Shanaberger)

566 (below, center). Banjo clock. Mahogany and mahogany veneer case. Brass 8-day, weight-driven movement with flat brass pendulum rod. Made by John Sawin, Boston, Mass., c.1840. H. 32″. Image Studios, David Towne, Photographer. (Herschel B. Burt Collection)

567 (below, right). Banjo clock. Mahogany and mahogany veneer case. Brass 8-day, weight-driven movement. Made by Enoch H. Nutter, Dover, N.H., c.1830. H. 34″. Nutter also made silver spoons and operated a jewelry store. (New Hampshire Historical Society)

565

566

567

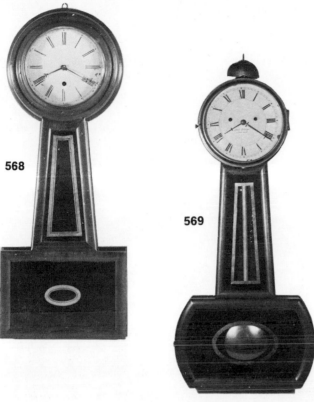

568

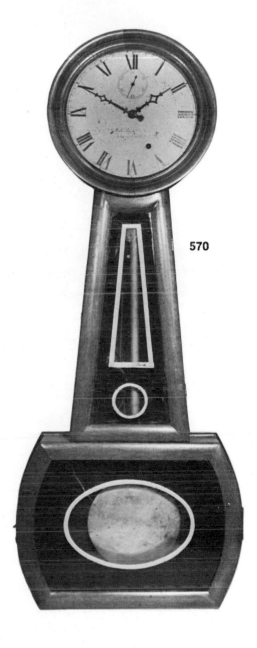

569

570

570a

568 (far left). Banjo clock. Walnut case. Brass 8-day, spring-driven movement. Made by E. and A. Ingraham, Bristol, Conn., c. 1855. H. 31″. This is the earliest style of Connecticut spring-driven banjo. They were originally pendulum gallery clocks; throat and box sections were added. Some still have gallery labels in them. Photograph: Edward H. Goodrich. (American Clock and Watch Museum)

569 (above, center). Banjo clock. Mahogany case. Brass 8-day, weight-driven movement with strike. The case is very similar to the style adopted by Howard and Davis. Made by Sona Billings, Acton, Mass., c.1840. Photograph: Edward H. Goodrich. (American Clock and Watch Museum)

570 (above, right). Banjo clock. Rosewood veneer case. Wood 8-day, weight-driven movement with seconds dial. Made by Harvey Ball, Nashua, N.H., c.1850. H. 48¾″. Unique wood movement in a case of Howard design. Ball was a violin maker as well as a locksmith and clock repairer. (Private collection)

570a (left). Close-up of the wood movement in the Harvey Ball banjo clock.

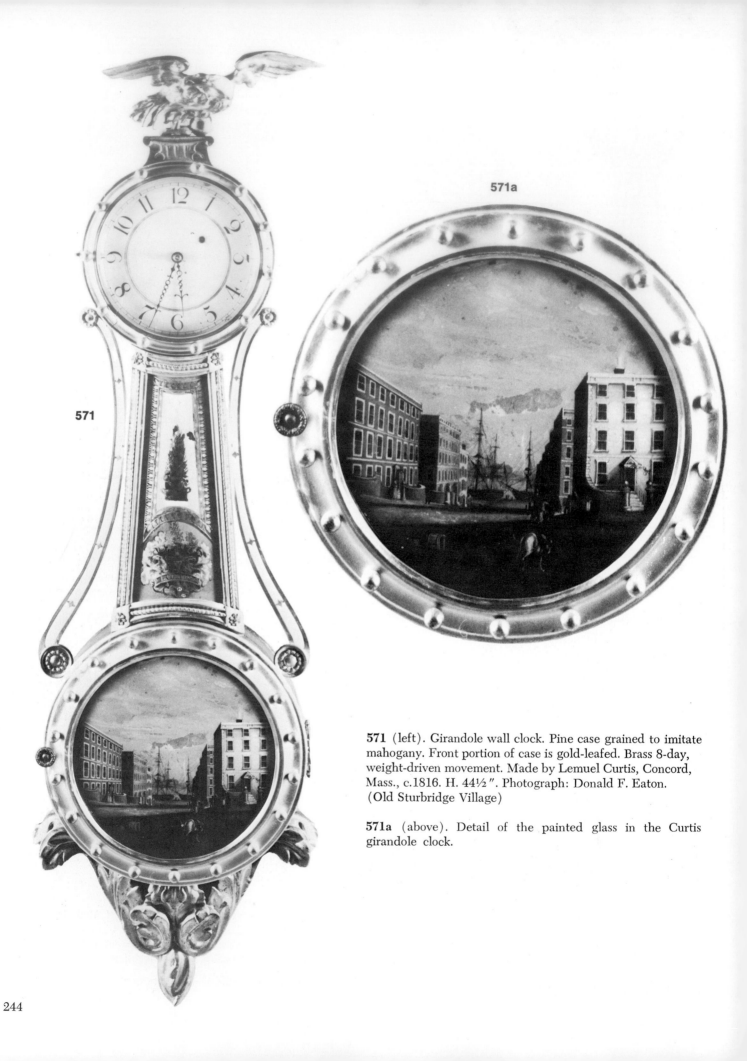

571a

571

571 (left). Girandole wall clock. Pine case grained to imitate mahogany. Front portion of case is gold-leafed. Brass 8-day, weight-driven movement. Made by Lemuel Curtis, Concord, Mass., c.1816. H. 44½". Photograph: Donald F. Eaton. (Old Sturbridge Village)

571a (above). Detail of the painted glass in the Curtis girandole clock.

244

GIRANDOLE CLOCKS

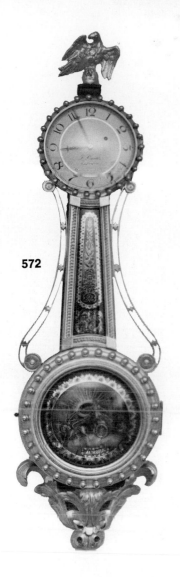

572

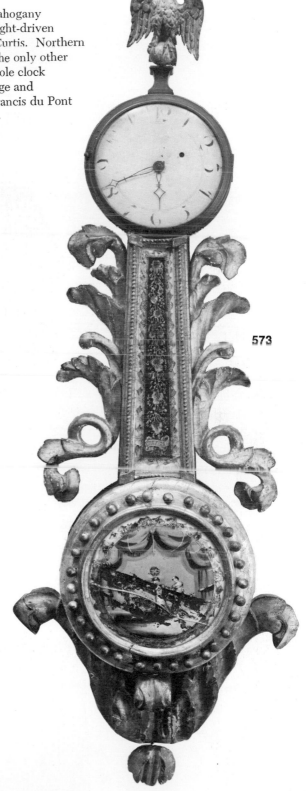

573 (right). Girandole wall clock. Mahogany veneer and gilt case. Brass 8-day, weight-driven movement. Attributed to Lemuel Curtis. Northern New England, 1820–1825. H. 44″. The only other known example of this style of girandole clock is in the collection of Greenfield Village and Henry Ford Museum. (The Henry Francis du Pont Winterthur Museum)

573

572 (above). Girandole wall clock. Gilded case. Brass 8-day, weight-driven movement. Made by Lemuel Curtis, Burlington, Vt., c.1830. H. 45½″. Some regilding and repairs. (Mark A. Shanaberger)

The girandole clocks illustrated on these two pages are a variation of Simon Willard's banjo clock. Developed by Lemuel Curtis about 1815 and apparently made only by him, girandole clocks are very beautiful timepieces with exquisite paintings on the convex glasses (similar in style to girandole looking glasses from which they get their name), exceedingly fine carving on the bracket below the glass, and with the entire surface finished in gold leaf. The balls on the round bezels are found in two different sizes —usually there are twenty-six of the larger and thirty-seven of the smaller. A variation of this style had flamelike arms (see fig. 573) instead of the more usual brass side arms illustrated in figures 571 and 572.

574 (below). Lyre wall clock. Mahogany case with brass overlay. Brass 8-day, weight-driven movement. Attributed to Samuel Abbott, Boston, Mass., c.1810. H. 78½". Brass fretwork on top of case. Finial and glass are replacements. (Mark A. Shanaberger)

574a (right). Movement of the lyre wall clock.

574a

574

575

575 (left). Lyre wall clock. Mahogany and mahogany veneer case. Wood bezel. Brass 8-day, weight-driven movement. Made by John Sawin, Boston, Mass., c.1822. H. 41½". (Private collection)

575a (below). Detail showing original bill of sale for the lyre wall clock by John Sawin. "Mr. Nath. R. Thorndike bought of/John Lemon one Mahogany timepiece/valued at twenty-five dollars/Andover April 9th 1830/received payment/John Lemon." Lemon was a wood-carver. (Private collection)

575a

576 (below, center). Lyre wall clock. Mahogany and mahogany veneer case. Brass 8-day, weight-driven movement with alarm. Made by Abiel Chandler, Concord, N.H., c.1820. H. 43″. Chandler apparently made more lyres than banjos. The alarm attachment is most unusual. (Herschel B. Burt Collection)

576a (right). Movement and alarm of the Abiel Chandler lyre wall clock.

576a

577a

576

577

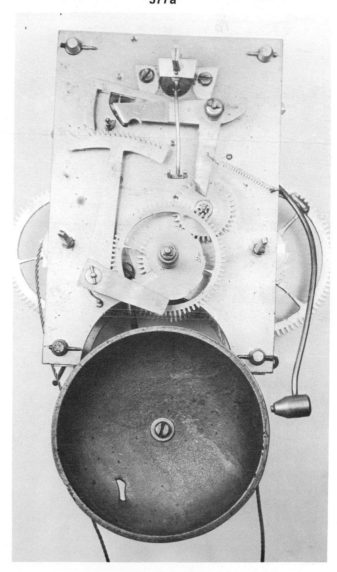

577 (left). Lyre wall clock. Mahogany and mahogany veneer case. Brass 8-day, weight-driven movement with strike. Made by Abiel Chandler, Concord, N.H., c.1820. H. 43½″. (Private collection)

577a (right). Movement of the Abiel Chandler lyre wall clock. Note rack striking with the hammer on the right side.

578 (below). Figure-8 wall clock. No. 9. Walnut case. Brass 8-day, weight-driven movement. Made by E. Howard and Co., Boston, Mass., c.1857. H. 37¼".
(R. A. Romeo Collection)

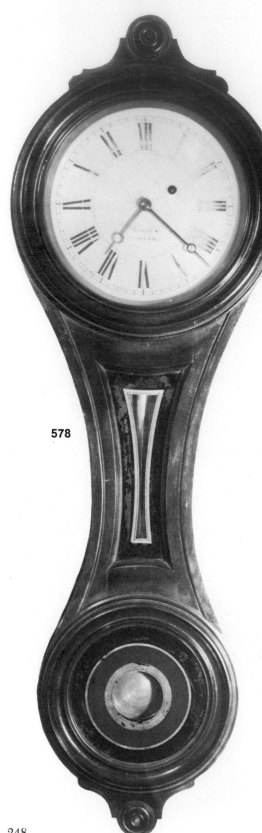

578

579

580

579 (above, left). Banjo clock. No. 1. Cherry case with rosewood grain. Brass 8-day, weight-driven movement with seconds dial. Made by E. Howard and Co., Boston, Mass., c.1857. H. 50".
(R. A. Romeo Collection)

580 (above, right). Banjo-type wall regulator. Mahogany and mahogany veneer case. Brass 8-day, weight-driven movement with seconds dial. Attributed to Abiel Chandler, Concord, N.H., c.1830. H. 51". Similar to clocks made by Simon and Aaron Willard.
(Mark A. Shanaberger)

582 (below, right). Shelf or wall clock. Red painted case. Brass 8-day, weight-driven movement. Case made by T. G. Furber, Hewington, N.H.; movement made by George G. Brewster, Portsmouth, N.H., c.1834. H. 36″. Besides being a clockmaker, Brewster was also a dental surgeon. (Private collection)

583 (below, left). Banjo-type wall regulator. Mahogany veneer case. Brass 8-day, weight-driven movement with seconds dial. Made by Simon Willard, Roxbury, Mass., c.1808. H. 54″. Note the unusual hands. (Private collection)

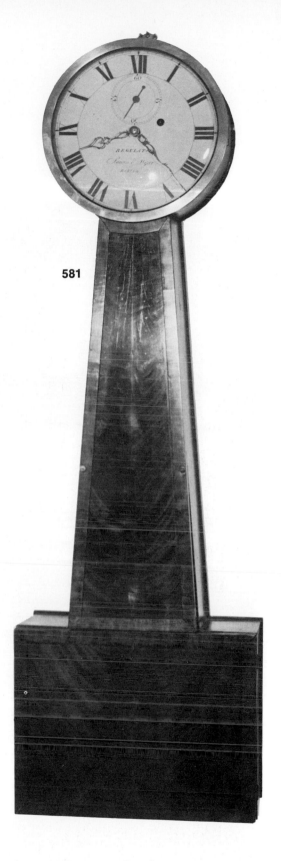

581 (above). Banjo regulator. Mahogany and mahogany veneer case. Brass 8-day, weight-driven movement with seconds dial. Made by Sawin and Dyer, Boston, Mass., c.1824. H. 48½″. (Private collection)

584

585

585 (above). Lyre wall clock. Gilded case with shell bracket. Brass 8-day, weight-driven movement. Made by John Sawin, Boston, Mass., c.1835. H. 42¼″. The all-gilt case is very rare. (Mark A. Shanaberger)

588 (opposite, left). Lyre wall clock. Mahogany and mahogany veneer case. Brass 8-day, weight-driven movement. Made by Joshua Seward, Boston, Mass., c.1830. H. 38″. Image Studios, David Towne, Photographer. (Hershel B. Burt Collection)

584 (above, left). Wall or shelf lyre-type banjo clock. Mahogany and gilded case. Brass 8-day, weight-driven movement with strike. Made by Abner Rogers, Berwick, Me., c.1815. H. 35½″. Finial and throat glass have been replaced. (Mark A. Shanaberger)

586 (right). Lyre wall clock. Mahogany and mahogany veneer carved case. Brass 8-day, weight-driven movement. Maker unknown. c.1835. H. 39″. (Private collection)

587 (far right). Lyre wall clock. Mahogany and mahogany veneer case. Brass 8-day, weight-driven movement. Maker unknown. c.1835. H. 41″. (Private collection)

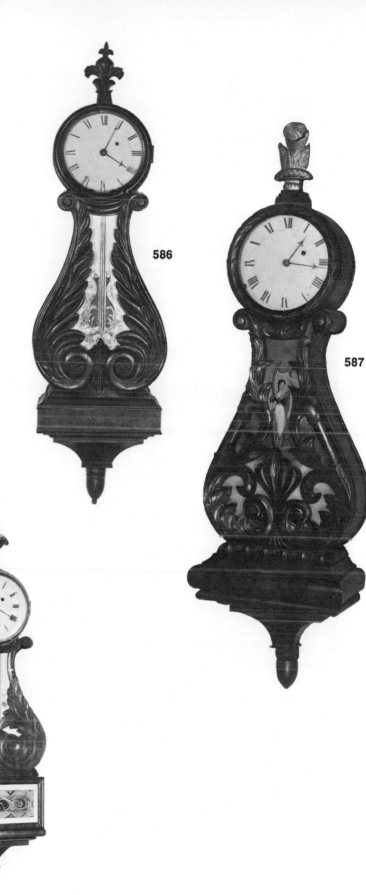

586

587

588

589

589 (above). Lyre wall clock. Carved mahogany case. Brass 8-day, weight-driven movement. Made by Abiel Chandler, Concord, N.H., c.1832. H. 38″. Photograph: Elroy Sanford. (Western Reserve Historical Society)

590 (below). Connecticut mirror wall clock. Mahogany case. Brass 8-day, weight-driven movement with strike. Iron plates designed by Joseph Ives. Made by Merriman and Ives, Bristol, Conn., 1818–1819. H. 57¼". (Dr. Paul H. Ernest Collection)

591 (right). New Hampshire-type mirror clock. Gilded case. Brass 8-day, weight-driven movement with alarm. Made by J. F. Felt, Portland, Me., c.1825. H. 47½". Case has been regilded, and dial has been repainted. (Mark A. Shanaberger)

591

590

592

592 (right). New Hampshire-type mirror clock with door open showing weight and pendulum. Made by I. Randall and Company, New York, N.Y., c.1850. H. 31½". (Irving Cooperman Collection)

252

593

593 (right). New Hampshire mirror clock.
Gilt pine case with carved eagle splat. Brass
8-day, weight-driven movement. Maker unknown.
New Hampshire, 1825–1830. H. 48″.
(Amos G. Avery Collection)

593a

593a (above). Wheelbarrow movement of the New Hampshire mirror clock.

594

594 (left). New Hampshire-type mirror clock. Gilded case.
Brass 8-day, weight-driven movement. Made by Samuel
Abbott, Boston, Mass., 1810–1832. H. 34½″. Case has been
regilded. (Mark A. Shanaberger)

595 (right). New Hampshire mirror clock. Painted pine case. Brass 8-day, weight-driven movement. Made by James C. Cole, Rochester, N.H., c. 1820. H. 29¼". Dish dial, conventional banjo movement with wood weight guides. (New Hampshire Historical Society)

595a (below, right). Banjo-type movement in the New Hampshire mirror clock made by James C. Cole.

596 (below, left). New Hampshire mirror clock. Pine gilt case. Brass 8-day, weight-driven movement. Attributed to Joseph Chadwick, Boscawen, N.H., c.1825. H. 29½". Chadwick, together with his brother-in-law Benjamin Morrill, may have introduced the New Hampshire mirror clock design. (New Hampshire Historical Society)

595

596

595a

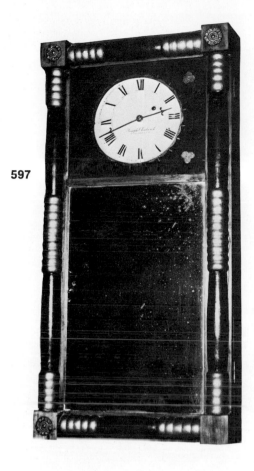

597

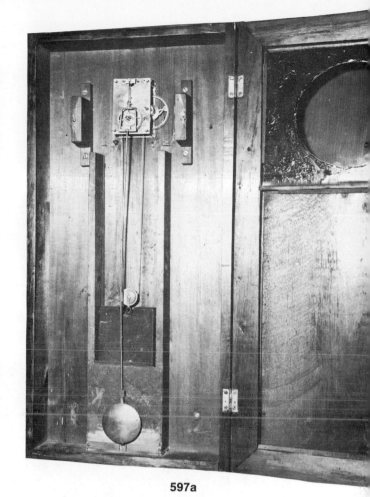

598

597a

599

597 (above, left). New Hampshire mirror clock. Pine case painted and gilded. Brass 8-day, weight-driven movement. Made by Joseph Chadwick, Boscawen, N.H., 1825–1830. H. 30″. (Amos G. Avery Collection)

597a (above, right). New Hampshire mirror clock made by Joseph Chadwick with the door open.

598 (above). Movement of a Joseph Chadwick New Hampshire mirror clock. c.1830. H. 4″. (New Hampshire Historical Society)

599 (right). New Hampshire-type mirror clock. Pine and mahogany veneer case. Brass 30-hour, weight-driven movement with strike. Made by George Marsh, Winchester, Conn., c.1825. H. 26″. Wallpaper lining on inside of case. (Mark A. Shanaberger)

600a

600 (opposite, above left). New Hampshire mirror clock. Painted and gilded case. Brass 8-day, weight-driven movement with strike, calendar, alarm, and seconds dial. Made by David French, New Ipswich, N.H., c.1825. H. 28½". French died at 28 and this is his only known clock. Cornice of the case is that used on early mirrors before split columns. This is the only known New Hampshire mirror clock with time, strike, alarm, day of week, and date. (New Hampshire Historical Society)

600a (above). Movement of the New Hampshire mirror clock made by David French.

601 (opposite, above right). New Hampshire mirror clock. Birch case. Brass 8-day, weight-driven movement. Made by Benjamin Morrill, Boscawen, N.H., c.1820. H. 32½". Morrill used various means of identification of his clocks: name on dial, paper label, and "Morrill" cast in the iron weights. (New Hampshire Historical Society)

601a (opposite, below). Movement of the Benjamin Morrill New Hampshire mirror clock. The "wheelbarrow"-type movement was developed to conserve on brass, and Morrill is the only maker known to have used plates of this type. (New Hampshire Historical Society)

600

601

601a

602 (right). New Hampshire-type mirror clock with the door ope[n] showing the alarm. Made by Abner Rogers, Berwick, Me., c.1830. H. 29¾″. (J. Alford Jones)

602

603

603 (above). New Hampshire mirror clock. Brass 8-day, weight-driven movement with strike. Maker unknown. New Hampshire, c.1830. H. 32½″. Striking is of the "rattrap" type. (Amos G. Avery Collection)

603a (right). Close-up of the movement of the New Hampshire mirror clock, showing the rattrap striking arrangement.

603a

604 (above). "Rattrap" movement in a New Hampshire mirror clock made by Abiel Chandler, Concord, N.H., c.1820. H. 32″. When the pointer drops in the rim hole of the wheel, it starts a trap that stops the striking. (New Hampshire Historical Society)

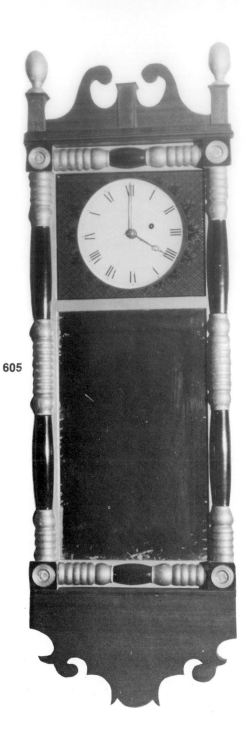

605

606

606a

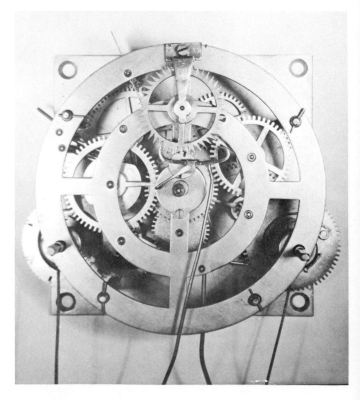

605 (above, left). New Hampshire mirror clock. Mahogany and gilt case. Brass 8-day, weight-driven movement with silent tick. Maker unknown. c.1830. H. 43″. Pallets have a spring on the face. (J. Alford Jones)

606 (above, right). New Hampshire mirror clock. Mahogany veneer case. Brass 8-day, weight-driven movement with strike. "David Dutton/Mount Vernon/ N.H." on label. Movement was made by Silas B. Terry. c.1835. H. 31″. (New Hampshire Historical Society)

606a (right). Silas B. Terry movement in the David Dutton New Hampshire mirror clock.

607a

607 (below, left). New Hampshire mirror clock. Birch and pine case. Brass 8-day, weight-driven movement with strike. Made by James Collins, Goffstown, N.H., c.1830. H. 30½″. Collins is the only maker known to have made this style of case. Weights are weighted tin cans. Collins left Goffstown about 1840 for the Midwest and died in Wolcottville, Ind., 1882. (New Hampshire Historical Society)

607a (left). Movement of the New Hampshire mirror clock made by James Collins.

608 (below, right). New Hampshire mirror clock. Mahogany and gilt case. Brass 8-day, weight-driven movement with alarm. Made by Abner Rogers, Berwick, Me., 1830. H. 29¾″. (J. Alford Jones)

607

608

609 (above, left). Wall clock. Mahogany case. Brass 8-day, weight-driven movement with alarm. Made by Elnathan Taber, Roxbury, Mass., 1790–1800. H. 35″. (Private collection)

610 (above, center). Wall clock. Mahogany veneer case. Brass 8-day, weight-driven movement. Made by J. L. Dunning, Burlington, Vt., c.1830. H. 35″. Image Studios, David Towne, Photographer. (Herschel B. Burt Collection)

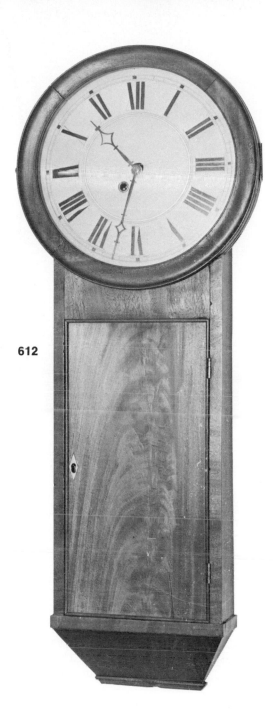

612

613

612 (left). Wall regulator clock. Mahogany veneer case. Brass 8-day, weight-driven movement. Brass panel slides up to expose the weight. Wood dial. Made by Silas B. Terry, Plymouth, Conn., c.1830. H. 34″. (Private collection)

612a (opposite, above right). Wall regulator by S. B. Terry with the door open to expose the movement, sliding panel, and label.

611 (opposite, below). Wall or shelf clock. Mahogany and mahogany veneer case. Brass 8-day, weight-driven movement. Made by J. L. Dunning, Burlington, Vt., c.1830. H. 30″. Image Studios, David Towne, Photographer. (Herschel B. Burt Collection)

613 (right). Wall clock. Walnut case. Brass 8-day, weight-driven movement. Made by Phineas Davis, York, Pa., c.1820. H. 23½″. Davis worked on the first coal-burning locomotive and sold it to the Baltimore and Ohio Railroad for the Baltimore–Washington run. Davis was killed on a trial run of the locomotive. (Mark A. Shanaberger)

614 (right). Ithaca double-dial wall calendar clock. No. 12 "Kildare" model. Mahogany case. Brass 30-day, spring-driven movement. Made by E. N. Welch Manufacturing Co., Forestville, Conn., for the Ithaca Calendar Clock Co., Ithaca, N.Y., c.1870. H. 32½″. A bracket on the bottom of the clock may be removed to convert it from a wall clock to a shelf clock. (Joe Brincat Collection)

615 (below, left). Wall calendar clock. Walnut and rosewood veneer case. Brass 8-day, weight-driven movement. Made by William L. Gilbert, Winsted, Conn., c.1868. H. 34″. Maranville calendar. (Private collection)

615

616

616 (right). Double-dial wall calendar clock. "Peanut" model. Rosewood veneer case. Brass 8-day, spring-driven movement with strike. Made by Seth Thomas, Plymouth Hollow, Conn., c.1859. H. 23½″. (Private collection)

617

618 (below). Wall calendar clock. Rosewood veneer case. Brass 8-day, spring-driven movement with Galusha Maranville calendar. Manual adjustment. Made by Gilbert Manufacturing Co., Winsted, Conn., for N. C. Hyde and Company, c.1865. H. 25″. (Robert G. Mindrup Collection)

618

619

617 (above). Double-dial wall calendar clock. "Steeple" model. Walnut case. Brass 8-day, spring-driven movement with strike. Movement made by E. N. Welch Manufacturing Co., Forestville, Conn., for the Ithaca Calendar Clock Co., Ithaca, N.Y., c.1870. H. 32″. Horton calendar. (Private collection)

619 (right). Double-dial wall calendar clock. Walnut case. Brass 8-day, spring-driven movement with strike. Made by L.F. and W. Carter, Bristol, Conn., c.1860. H. 30″. Pendulum movement. B. B. Lewis calendar. (Private collection)

621 (right). Double-dial wall calendar clock. Walnut case. Brass 8-day, spring-driven movement with strike. Made by Jerome & Company, New Haven, Conn., c.1850. H. 36″. Can be made into a shelf clock by removing the lower bracket. (Private collection)

621

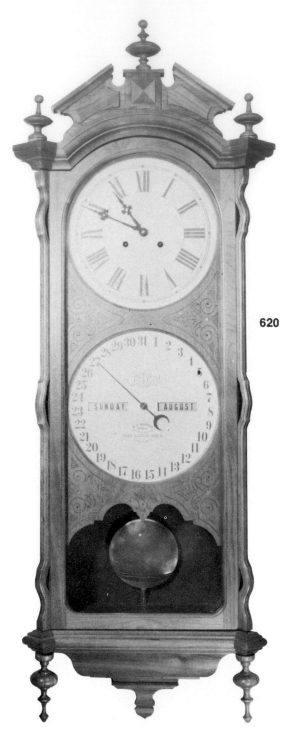

620

622

620 (above). Double-dial wall calendar clock. No. 2 Bank model. Walnut case. Brass 8-day, weight-driven movement. Made by the Ithaca Calendar Clock Co., Ithaca, N.Y., c.1880. H. 61″. (R. A. Romeo Collection)

622 (right). Double-dial wall calendar clock. Ash case. Brass 8-day, spring-driven movement with strike. B.B. Lewis calendar. Label reads: "Made expressly for L.F. & W. Carter." Made by The E. Ingraham and Company, Bristol, Conn., c. 1880. H. 22″. (Private collection)

623 (left). Double-dial wall calendar clock. "Library" model No. 6. Walnut case. Brass 8-day, spring-driven movement with strike. Made by the Ithaca Calendar Clock Co., Ithaca, N.Y., c.1875. H. 32″. (Private collection)

624 (below, right). Double-dial wall calendar clock. Oak case. Brass 30-day, double-spring-driven movement. Made by the New Haven Clock Co., New Haven, Conn., c.1870. H. 48″. (Private collection)

625 (below, left). Double-dial wall calendar clock. Regulator No. 2. Walnut case. Brass 8-day, weight-driven movement. Made by the Ithaca Calendar Clock Co., Ithaca, N.Y., c.1880. H. 48″. (R. A. Romeo Collection)

623

625

624

626 (left). Wall calendar clock. Mahogany case. Brass 60-day, spring-driven movement. Made by the Prentiss Calendar and Time Company, New York, N.Y., c.1890. H. 37″. Calendar is separate and has its own spring for winding. (Private collection)

627 (below, center). Double-dial wall calendar clock. Walnut case. Brass 8-day, spring-driven movement. Made by Waterbury Clock Company, Waterbury, Conn., c.1890. H. 29″. (Private collection)

626

627

628

628 (above). Wall astronomical clock. Rosewood veneer case. Brass 8-day, spring-driven movement with calendar and strike. Made by the E. N. Welch Manufacturing Co., Bristol, Conn. Calendar portion invented by D. J. Gale, c.1878. Diam. 17½″. Perpetual calendar indicating time, day of week, date, month, moon phase, and time of sunrise and sunset for the latitude of New England. (Robert G. Mindrup Collection)

628a (above). Movement of a Gale astronomical clock. c.1878. H. 8″. (Joe Brincat Collection)

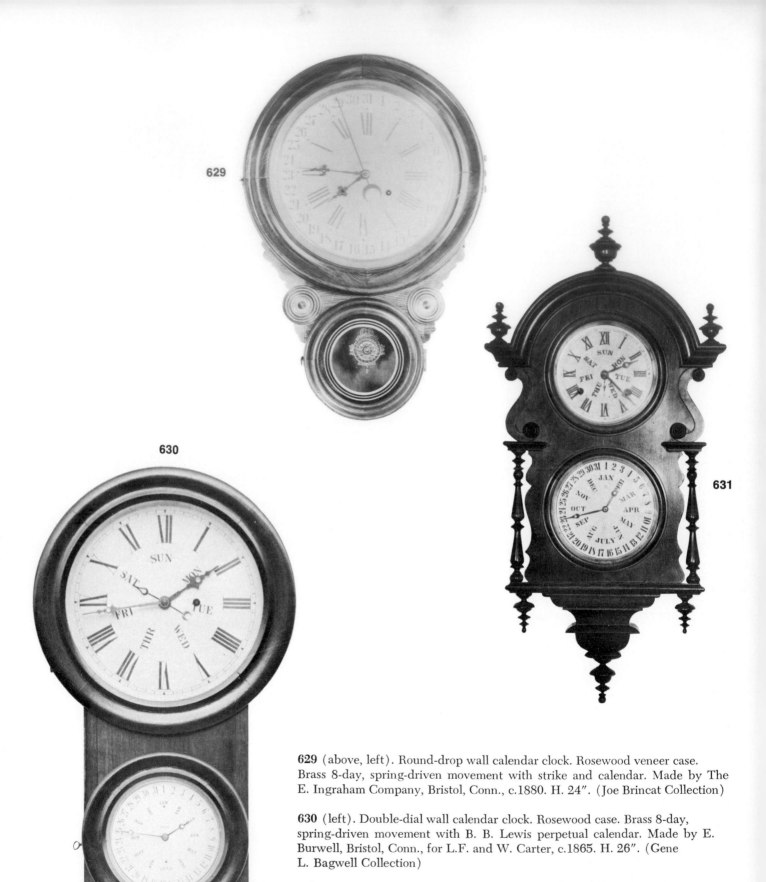

629 (above, left). Round-drop wall calendar clock. Rosewood veneer case. Brass 8-day, spring-driven movement with strike and calendar. Made by The E. Ingraham Company, Bristol, Conn., c.1880. H. 24″. (Joe Brincat Collection)

630 (left). Double-dial wall calendar clock. Rosewood case. Brass 8-day, spring-driven movement with B. B. Lewis perpetual calendar. Made by E. Burwell, Bristol, Conn., for L.F. and W. Carter, c.1865. H. 26″. (Gene L. Bagwell Collection)

631 (above, right). Double-dial wall calendar clock. "Wagner" model. Walnut case. Brass 8-day, spring-driven movement with strike. Made by Welch, Spring and Company, Forestville, Conn., c.1875. H. 32½″. (O. Harry Burt Collection)

633

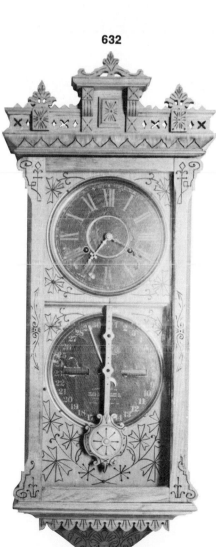

632

632 (left). Ithaca double-dial wall calendar clock. No. 5½ "Hanging Belgrade" model. Ash case. Brass 30-day, spring-driven movement with calendar. Made by the E. N. Welch Manufacturing Co., Forestville, Conn., for the Ithaca Calendar Clock Company, Ithaca, N.Y., c.1870. H. 37″. Wood pendulum, rod, and bob. (Joe Brincat Collection)

633 (above). Wall calendar clock. Oak case. Brass 8-day, spring-driven movement with strike and simple calendar. Made by The E. Ingraham and Company, Bristol, Conn., c.1880. H. 24¾″. (William J. Haggerty Collection)

634 (right). Wall regulator. Mahogany veneer case. Brass 8-day, weight-driven movement with seconds dial. Made by S.B. Terry and Co., Terryville, Conn., c.1852. H. 33½″. Pendulum in front of weight. This is the first of this type of clock that Terry is said to have made with his own label, and also made for Seth Thomas and others, using their labels. (The Clock Gallery)

634

635 (below). Wall clock. No. 1 "Special." Walnut veneer case. Brass 8-day, weight-driven movement with strike and seconds dial. Made by Seth Thomas, Plymouth Hollow, Conn., c.1865. H. 44″. (Private collection)

635a (below, right). Close-up of the pendulum and label of the wall clock made by Seth Thomas. Center of pendulum shows a view of the factory.

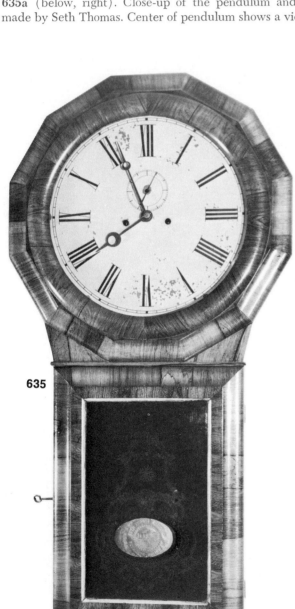

635

635a

636 (below, left). Wall regulator. Rosewood veneer case. Brass 8-day, weight-driven movement. Made by Gilbert Manufacturing Co., Winsted, Conn., c.1870. H. 33½″. (William J. Haggerty Collection)

637 (below, center). Wall clock. Mahogany case. Brass 8-day, weight-driven movement. Made by E. Howard and Company, Boston, Mass., c.1857. H. 31″. (J. Alford Jones)

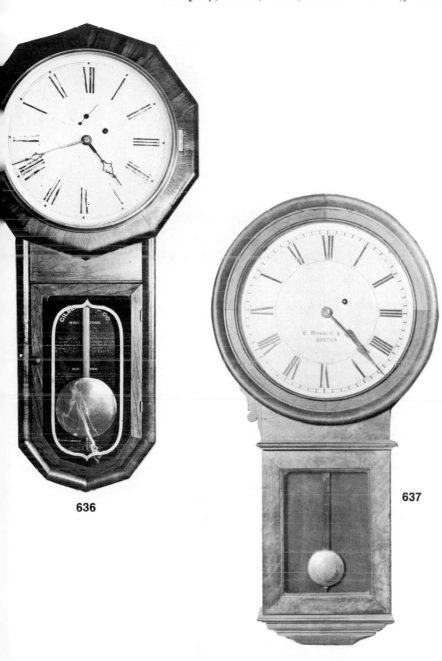

636

637

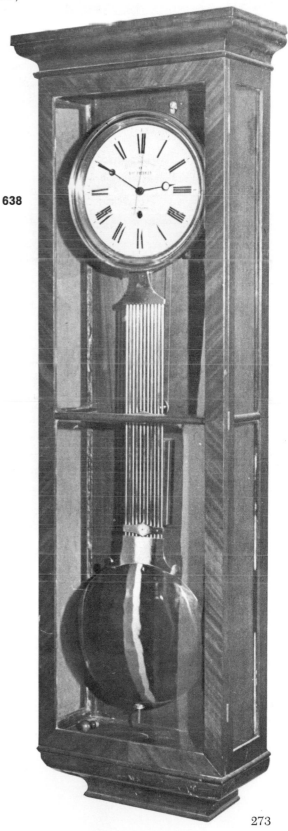

638

638 (right). Wall clock. Mahogany veneer case. Brass 8-day, weight-driven movement. Made by Stanislaus Fournier, New Orleans, La., c.1870. H. 69″. Case made by Prudence Mallard. The clock was made for the U.S. Customs House in New Orleans. Acquired from the grandnephew of A. Barbier, who was an apprentice of Fournier. Stanislaus Fournier was the only commercial clockmaker in New Orleans. (Frank L. Kemp Collection)

639

640

639 (left). Wall regulator. No. 2. Oak case. Brass 8-day, weight-driven movement. Made by Seth Thomas Clock Co., Thomaston, Conn., c.1853. H. 34″. (R. A. Romeo Collection)

641 (opposite, left). Wall clock. Marble case. Brass 8-day, weight-driven movement. Made by the E. Howard Watch and Clock Co., Boston, Mass., c.1875. H. 35″. Riggs and Brothers were Philadelphia merchants. The clock is essentially a Howard Model No. 27. Photograph: Edward H. Goodrich. (American Clock and Watch Museum)

640 (right). Wall clock. "Ionic" model. Rosewood veneer and gilt case. Brass 8-day, spring-driven movement with strike and alarm. Made by The E. Ingraham and Company, Bristol, Conn., c.1880. H. 22″. This model was carried from 1862 to 1924. Price in 1880 was $8.50. Photograph: Edward H. Goodrich. (American Clock and Watch Museum)

641

642

643

642 (above, center). Watchmaker's regulator. No. 13. Walnut case. Brass 8-day, weight-driven movement with seconds dial. Made by the E. Howard Watch and Clock Co., Boston, Mass., c.1874. H. 56″. (R. A. Romeo Collection)

643 (right). Wall regulator. Walnut case. Brass 8-day, weight-driven movement. Made by the E. Howard Watch and Clock Co., Boston, Mass., c.1881. Made on special order for the Charter Oak Life Insurance Company, Hartford, Conn., and delivered to them in February 1881. Has Graham deadbeat escapement with jeweled pallets and jeweled pivots on the verge and escape wheel. Photograph: Edward H. Goodrich. (American Clock and Watch Museum)

275

644 (right). Wall regulator. Mahogany case. Brass 8-day, weight-driven movement. Dished dial. Made by Abel Stowell, Jr., Boston, Mass., c.1850. H. 30¼″. (Private collection)

645 (below, left). Connecticut wall acorn or lyre clock. Mahogany veneer case. Brass 8-day, spring-driven movement with strike. Made by the Forestville Manufacturing Co., Bristol, Conn., c.1849. H. 26¾″. (Private collection)

644

645

646

646 (right). Wall clock. Walnut case. Brass 8-day movement. Made by Henry Sperry & Company, New York, N.Y., c.1859. H. 86″. Inscribed: "This Clock Stood For Many Years in the/ 'Amen Corner' of the Old Fifth Avenue Hotel./ Presented to the Bank by Our President/ Honorable John Whalen/ January 1st, 1925. Photograph: Helga Photo Studio, Inc. (Museum of the City of New York: Gift of The Bank of the Manhattan Company)

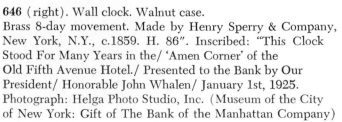

276

648 (right). Wall clock. Walnut and walnut veneer case. Brass 8-day, weight-driven movement with sweep-seconds hand and deadbeat escapement. Made by E. N. Welch Manufacturing Co., Bristol, Conn., c. 1885. H. 47″. Case is similar to the "Patti" model shelf clocks. Photograph: Edward H. Goodrich. (American Clock and Watch Museum)

648

647

647 (left). Wall regulator. No. 5. Walnut case with glass sides. Brass 8-day, weight-driven movement with seconds dial. Made by Welch, Spring and Company, Forestville, Conn., c.1875. H. 52″. (O. Harry Burt Collection)

649

650

649 (left). Wall regulator. No. 4. Walnut case. Brass 30-day, spring-driven movement. Made by Welch, Spring and Company, Forestville, Conn., c.1875. H. 41″. (O. Harry Burt Collection)

650 (below, center). Wall regulator. No. 7. Walnut case. Brass 8-day, spring-driven "Patti" movement. Made by Welch, Spring and Company, Forestville, Conn., c.1875. H. 47″. (O. Harry Burt Collection)

651

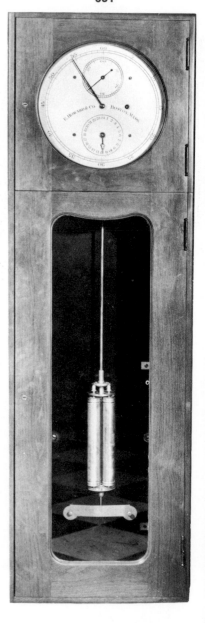

651 (right). Master timer wall clock. Walnut case. Brass 8-day, weight-driven movement with gravity escapement and four-jar mercury pendulum. Made by E. Howard Watch and Clock Co., Boston, Mass., c.1875. H. 58½″. This clock was used as a master timer at the Engineering Laboratory of The Ford Motor Company, Dearborn, Mich., for many years. (Greenfield Village and Henry Ford Museum)

652

653

652 (far left). Wall regulator. No. 75. Oak case. Brass 8-day, weight-driven movement. Made by E. Howard Watch and Clock Co., Boston, Mass., c.1889. H.34″. Movement signed: "HOWARD." Dial signed: "NELSON H. BROWN, BOSTON." (R. A. Romeo Collection)

653 (left). Wall regulator. No. 70. Oak case. Brass 8-day, weight-driven movement. Made by E. Howard Watch and Clock Co., Boston, Mass., c. 1889. H. 32″. (R. A. Romeo Collection)

654 (below, left). Wall clock. Walnut case. Brass 8-day, weight-driven movement. Seconds dial. Made by Seth Thomas Clock Co., Thomaston, Conn., c.1875. H. 34″. (Private collection)

655 (below, center). Wall clock. Keyhole type. Cherry case with rosewood graining. Brass 8-day, weight-driven movement. Made by E. Howard Watch and Clock Co., Boston, Mass., c.1880. H. 31″. (Joe Brincat Collection)

656 (below, right). Wall regulator clock Rosewood and rosewood veneer case. Brass 8-day, weight-driven movement. Maker unknown. c.1875. H. 35″. (Mark A. Shanaberger)

654

655

656

657

657 (left). Wall regulator. Stained pine case. Brass weight-driven movement wound with two large dry cells. Weights are about the size of a thick nickel. Made by the American Clock Company, New York, N.Y., c. 1890. H. 51". (J. Alford Jones)

658 (below, center). Wall regulator clock. Walnut case. Brass 8-day, weight-driven movement with seconds dial, and four-jar mercury pendulum. Made by E. Howard Watch and Clock Co., Boston, Mass., c.1890. H. 61". (Mark A. Shanaberger)

658

659

659 (right). Wall regulator. Walnut case. Brass 8-day, weight-driven movement with strike and seconds dial. Made by William L. Gilbert Clock Co., Winsted, Conn., c.1890. H. 69". (Greenfield Village and Henry Ford Museum)

660

660 (above). Wall regulator. "General"
model. Cherry case. Brass 8-day, weight-
driven movement with seconds dial.
Made by the Ansonia Clock Company,
New York, N.Y., c.1886. H. 68″. 18″ dial.
(R. A. Romeo Collection)

661

661 (right). Wall clock. Ebony case with gilt decoration.
Brass 8-day, spring-driven movement with strike. Made by
the Ansonia Clock Company, New York, N.Y., c.1900. H. 35″.
(Private collection)

LIST OF CLOCKMAKERS

Note: The dates cited in the following list of makers are generally working dates. In several cases birth and death dates have been included where it might prove helpful to the reader.

Abbets, James
Albany, N.Y., 1760

Abbey, David
Pittsburgh, Pa., 1830s

Abbott, George
Philadelphia, Pa., c. 1822

Abbott, John
Portsmouth, N.H., c. 1840

Abbott, Moses
Sutton, N.H., and Pomfret, Vt., c. 1820

Abbott, Samuel
Boston, Mass., 1810–1832. Made banjo, shelf, New Hampshire mirror, and tall clocks.

Abbott and Brother
Birmingham, Ala., c. 1901

Abel, Robert K.
Philadelphia, Pa. Listed in directories, 1840–1841.

Acker, Joseph D.
West Chester, Pa., c. 1850. Listed in directories.

Adams, Charles
Erie, Pa., c. 1860

Adams, E. W.
Seneca Falls, N.Y., 1820–1850. Made tower, regulators, and shelf clocks.

Adams, John
Newburyport, Mass., c. 1858

Adams, Jonas
Rochester, N. Y., c. 1839

Adams, Nathan
Danvers, Mass., 1780–1790; Boston, 1790–1820

Adams, Samuel
Boston, Mass., c. 1820

Adams, Smith
Bangor, Me., c. 1850

Adams, Thomas F.
Boston, Mass., c. 1810

Adams, Thomas F.
Baltimore, Md., n.d.; Petersburg, Va., 1804; Edenton, N.C., c. 1810

Adams, Walter
Bristol, Conn., c. 1810

Adams, William
Boston, Mass., c. 1810

Adams & Eaton
Boston, Mass., c. 1816. Listed in directories.

Adams, H. E. and Son
Burlington, Vt., n.d.

Adams and Harland
Boston, Mass., c. 1813

Adams and Trott
Boston, Mass., c. 1810. Listed in directories.

Adolph, Duff
Philadelphia, Pa., c. 1837

Agar, Edward
Beaver St., New York, N.Y., c. 1760

Aherns, Adolph
Philadelphia, Pa., c. 1837. Listed in directories.

Aiken, David S.
Yarmouth, Mass., n.d.

Aikinson, Peabody
Concord, Mass., c. 1790. An apprentice of Levi Hutchins.

Aitken, John
Philadelphia, Pa., c. 1785. Listed in directories, 1813; adv. 1785.

Akers, Edward
Baltimore, Md., 1843–1882

Akers, William
Baltimore, Md., c. 1840

Albee, Willard W.
Newburyport, Mass., c. 1860. Listed in directories.

Albert, John
Huntington Twp., York (now Adams) Co., Pa., c. 1816. Tall clocks known.

Albright, R. E.
Flushing, N.Y., c. 1860

Albright, Thomas F.
Philadelphia, Pa., c. 1835. Listed in directories.

Alcott, Obed
Plymouth, Conn., c. 1811

Alden & Eldridge
Bristol, Conn., c. 1820

Alder, Samuel
Philadelphia, Pa., 1785–1810

Alder, W. D.
New York, N.Y., c. 1860. Chronometer known.

Allebach, Henry
Reading, Pa., c. 1829

Allebach, Jacob
Philadelphia, Pa., 1825–1840

Allebach, M. B.
Philadelphia, Pa., 1770–1780

Allen, Alexander
Buffalo St., Rochester, N.Y., c. 1860

Allen, Isaac A.
Enfield, Conn., c. 1860

Allen, J. T.
Rochester, N.Y., c. 1840

Allen, James
Boston, Mass., 1680–1700

Allen, Jared T.
Batavia, N.Y., c. 1830

Allen, John
New York, N.Y., 1790–1800s

Allen, William
Adv. 1772

Allenbach, Henry
Reading, Pa., c. 1820. Adv. 1829.

Allenspachern, Joseph
Philadelphia, Pa., c. 1780

Allison, Gilbert
Pa., n.p.; n.d. Tall clocks known.

Alloway, William
Ithaca, N.Y., c. 1820. Adv. 1823.

Allyn, John
Hartford, Conn., c. 1650. Possibly a trader.

Allyn, Nathan
Hartford, Conn., c. 1800. Took over Enos Doolittle's business and sold it in 1808.

Almy, H. R.
New York, N.Y., c. 1875. Made cast-iron cases.

Almy, James I.
New Bedford, Mass., c. 1836

Almy, John C.
Exeter, N.H., c. 1830

Alrichs, Henry
Wilmington, Del., c. 1850. Son of Jacob Alrichs.

Alrichs, Jacob
Wilmington, Del., 1797–1855. Adv. for apprentice, 1797. Not many examples after c. 1810.

Alrichs, Jonas
Wilmington, Del., 1780–1793. Worked with his uncle 1793–1797.

Alrichs, Wessell
New Castle, Del., c. 1697. Moved to Salem, N.J.

Alrichs, Jacob and Jonas
Wilmington, Del. Uncle and nephew, worked together 1793–1797.

Alrichs and McClary
Wilmington, Del., 1793–1797. Established first machine shop in Wilmington.

Alsop, Thomas
Philadelphia, Pa., c. 1840. Listed in directories, 1842, 1849–1850.

Altmore, Marshall
Philadelphia, Pa., c. 1800

Alvord, Philo
Utica, N.Y., 1812–1878

Amana Clocks
Made by members of a European sectarian group at Buffalo, N.Y., 1843–1855; and at Iowa County, Iowa.

Amant, Peter (or Fester)
Philadelphia, Pa., c. 1790. Listed in directories.

Amberman, John
Brooklyn and New York, N.Y., c. 1850. Listed in directories.

American Clock Company
New York, N.Y. Organized in 1849 to succeed Connecticut Protective Clock Company. Had factory in Bristol, Conn. Took over New Haven Clock Company and E. N. Welch, later Seth Thomas and W. L. Gilbert. Offices in Philadelphia and San Francisco.

American Cuckoo Clock Comp.
Philadelphia, Pa., n.d.

American Manufacturing and Supply Company
New York, N.Y., n.d. Made electric battery clocks, shelf, tall, gallery, and regulator clocks.

Ames, Horace
New York, N.Y., c. 1860

Amidon, L.
Bellows Falls, Vt., c. 1860

Anderson, David D.
Marietta, Ohio, c. 1820

Anderson, David M.
Waynesboro, Pa., later to Honey Brook, Pa., c. 1820

Anderson, Henry C.
Charleston, Va., c. 1825

Anderson, Jesse
n.p.; n.d.

Anderson, John
Maryland, c. 1745. Probably case-maker.

Andre, John A.
Pottstown, Montgomery Co., Pa., c. 1860. Clockmaker, watchmaker, dentist, and politician.

Andreas, Abraham
Bethlehem, Pa., c. 1790. Originally a millwright but learned clockmaking.

Andreas, Henry
Bethlehem, Pa., c. 1790

Andrew, John
Salem, Mass., c. 1750

Andrews, D. B.
Cincinnati, Ohio, c. 1850

Andrews, Elon
Utica, N.Y., c. 1820

Andrews, Franklin C.
New York, N.Y., and Bristol, Conn., c. 1840. Listed in directories.

Andrews, Hu.
Washington, Pa., n.d. Known to have made tall case clocks.

Andrews, James
New York, N.Y., c. 1810

Andrews, Joseph
Lancaster Co., Pa., c. 1838

Andrews, William N.
Cheshire, Conn., c. 1850

Andrews, L. M. and F.
Bristol, Conn., c. 1835. Shelf clocks known.

Andrews, M. and T.
Meriden, Conn., c. 1830

Andrus & Beach
Watertown, Conn., n.d. Made shelf clocks with wood movements.

Angell, J. A.
Providence, R.I., n.d.

Angell, Otis N.
Johnston, R.I., c. 1830

Angelus Clock Co.
Philadelphia, incorporated 1874; Thomas E. Cahill, President, John Rogers, Secretary and Treasurer. Made 8-day striking clocks that sounded the Angelus bell at 6:00 A.M., noon, and 6:00 P.M. Clock cases in form of cathedral door with 4-inch spire finial.

Angstadt, Adam
Berks Co., Pa., c. 1790. Also a gun-smith of note.

Annin, M.
New York, N.Y., c. 1786

Anniston, Isaac
Philadelphia, Pa., 1780–1800

Ansonia Brass & Battery Co.
Ansonia, Conn., c. 1870. Alternate name for Ansonia Clock Company.

Ansonia Clock Company
Ansonia, Conn., 1851–1878; New York, N.Y., 1879–1930. Started by Anson G. Phelps in 1851 as subsidiary of Ansonia Brass Company. Became separate company c. 1859. For the most part made

spring-driven clocks. Manufacturing moved to Brooklyn, N.Y., 1878. Made gallery, shelf, china case, mantel, bobbing doll, and swinging doll clocks.

Anspeth, J. Rollin
Buffalo, N.Y., c. 1880

Antame, Joseph A.
Philadelphia, Pa., 1750–1800

Anthony, Isaac
Newport, R.I., c. 1730. Most likely dealer.

Anthony, Jacob, Sr.
Philadelphia, Pa., c. 1800

Anthony, Jacob, Jr.
Philadelphia, Pa., c. 1800

Anthony, L. D.
Providence, R.I., 1840–1850

Antrim, Charles
Philadelphia, Pa., 1844–1847

Antrim, Charles W.
n.p.; c. 1840

Appel, John E.
Dover, Pa., 1770–1780

Appleton, George B.
Salem, Mass., 1859–1865

Appleton, James
Marblehead, Mass., c. 1820

Applewhite, William
Columbia, S.C., c. 1820; Camden, S.C., c. 1830

Arbuckle, Joseph
Philadelphia, Pa., c. 1840

Archer, William
New York, N.Y., c. 1830

Archer, William, Jr.
Salem, Mass., c. 1850

Ardery, R.
Zanesville, Ohio, 1850–1870

Aris, Samuel
Portsmouth, N.H., c. 1780

Arkell, James
Canajoharie, N.Y. Partner of Louis Juvet, 1880–1886.

Armstrong, Thomas
Brooklyn, N.Y., 1830–1840

Arnold, Jacob
Philadelphia, Pa., c. 1840

Arnold, Jared
Amber, N.Y., 1825–1840

Arrison, John
Philadelphia, Pa., c. 1835. Listed in directory, 1837.

Arthur, H. G.
Boston, Mass., c. 1830

Arthur, James
New York, N.Y., last half 19th century

Arwin, William
Albany, N.Y., c. 1835

Ash, Lawrence
Philadelphia, Pa., 1762. Worked with Edward Duffield. Later moved to Baltimore, Md.; then to Boston, Mass.

Ashby, James
Boston, Mass., c. 1770. Adv. 1771, 1773.

Ashcroft, O.
New York, N.Y., c. 1840. Listed in directories.

Ashton, C.
Philadelphia, Pa., 1760–1800

Ashton, Isaac
Philadelphia, Pa., c. 1790

Ashton, Samuel
Philadelphia, Pa., c. 1790

Ashton, W.
Philadelphia, Pa., 1762–1797. Made clocks as well as watches.

Ashton, W. & C.
Philadelphia, Pa., n.d.

Ashwin & Co.
Pennsylvania, n.d.

Askew, James
Charleston, S.C., 1770–1790

Aspenwall, Samuel
Pittstown, Pa., n.d.

Aspinwall, Zalmon
Boston, Mass., c. 1810

Aston, Thomas
Newburyport, Mass., c. 1860

Atherton, Matthew
Philadelphia, Pa., 1835–1845

Atherton, Nathan, Jr.
Philadelphia, Pa., c. 1825

Atherton, Otis
New York, N. Y., c. 1798

Atkins, Alvin
Rochester, N.Y., 1840–1850

Atkins, Eldridge G.
Bristol, Conn., 1838–1842

Atkins, George
Bristol, Conn., n.d.

Atkins, Irenus
Bristol, Conn., 1830–1856

Atkins, Jearum
Joliet, Ill., c. 1840

Atkins, Joel
Middletown, Conn., c. 1770

Atkins, John
Chicago, Ill., n.d.

Atkins, Merritt W.
Bristol, Conn., 1856

Atkins, Rollin
Bristol, Conn., 1825

Atkins & Allen
Bristol, Conn., c. 1820

Atkins Clock Co.
Bristol, Conn., 1859–1879. After Atkins Clock Mfg. Co.

Atkins Clock Mfg. Co.
Bristol, Conn., 1855–1857

Atkins & Co., I.
Bristol, Conn., 1847–1857

Atkins & Downs
Bristol, Conn., 1831–1832

Atkins & Norton
Bristol, Conn., n.d.

Atkins & Porter
Bristol, Conn., 1840–1846

Atkins, R. & I.
Bristol, Conn., 1833–1837

Atkins & Son
Bristol, Conn., c. 1870

Atkins & Welton
Bristol, Conn., 1835–1836

Atkins, Whiting & Co.
Bristol, Conn., 1850–1854

Atkinson, Anna Maria LeRoy
Lady clockmaker, Lancaster, Pa., c. 1740. Married Wilmer Atkinson, cutler, 1749. Made clocks at Lancaster with name of husband on dial. Daughter of Abraham LeRoy (Swiss), clockmaker of Lancaster. Finally moved to Baltimore with husband.

Atkinson, James
Boston, Mass., 1745–1756

Atkinson, LeRoy
Baltimore, Md., 1820–1830

Atkinson, Nathaniel P.
Boscawen, N.H., c. 1805
Atkinson, M. & A.
Baltimore, Md., c. 1800
Atkinson, M. & W.
Baltimore, Md., 1780–1790
Atkinson, Wilmer
See Atkinson, Anna Maria LeRoy.
Worked at Lancaster, Pa., 1740s–
1750s. Clocks bearing his name made
by his wife.
Atlee, John S.
Columbia Boro, Pa., 1820
Atmar, Ralph
Charleston, S.C., 1790–1810
Attmore, Marshall
Philadelphia, Pa., 1820–1840. Listed in
directories.
Atwood, Anson L.
Bristol, Conn., c. 1835. Made parts for
such firms as Manross, Ingraham and
Brewster.
Atwood, B. W.
Plymouth, Mass., c. 1860
Atwood & Brackett
Littleton, N.H., 1850–1860
Austin, Benjamin
Kalamazoo, Mich., c. 1840
Austin, Isaac
Upper Delaware Ward, Pa., c. 1783
Austin, John
Philadelphia, Pa., c. 1830
Austin, Josiah
Salem, Mass., 1853–1855. Later to
Boston.
Austin, Orrin
Waterbury, Conn., c. 1820
Austin, Seymour
Hartford, Conn., c. 1800. Later to
Ohio.
Avery, John
Boston, Mass., 1726. Maker of clock in
Old North Church, Boston, Mass.
Avery, John, Jr.
Preston, Conn., 1732–1794
Avis, M.
Reading, Pa., c. 1820. Adv. in news-
papers, 1827.
Avisse, Charles
Baltimore, Md., 1812
Ayers, Alex
Lexington, Ky., 1790–1810
Ayers, E.
Louisville, Ky., 1816–1831
Ayers, Hamilton
New Holland, Lancaster Co., Pa.,
1820–1840
Ayers, Samuel
Lexington, Ky., 1790–1820
Ayers, T. R. J.
Keokuk, Iowa, 1860–1870
Ayers & Beard
Louisville, Ky., 1816–1831

Babbitt, H. W.
Providence, R.I., 1848
Babcock, Alvin
Boston, Mass., 1810–1813
Babcock, George W.
Providence, R.I., 1830–1840. Very
possibly dealer only.
Babcock & Co.
Philadelphia, Pa., 1832

Bach, Valentine
Hagerstown, Md., c. 1795. Adv. 1798.
Bachelder, Ezra
Danvers, Mass., 1793–1840
Bachelor, N.
n.p., 1830–1850
Bachman, Jacob
Lampeter, Pa., c. 1750. Father of John,
who later worked with him.
Bachman, John
Lampeter, Pa., c. 1820. Made cases for
clockmakers.
Bachman, Joseph
New York, N.Y. Listed in directory,
1855.
Backes, J. P.
Charleston, S.C., c. 1850
Bacon, John
Bristol, Conn., 1834–1835. Worked
with Chauncey Boardman.
Bacon, Samuel
Annapolis, Md., c. 1752
Badder, Isaac
Dayton, Ohio, c. 1830
Badely, Thomas
Boston, Mass., c. 1720
Badger, James
Brooklyn, N.Y., c. 1840
Badlam, Stephen
Boston, Lower Mills, and Dorchester,
Mass., 1751–1815. Cabinetmaker.
Badman, Joseph
Colebrookdale, Pa., c. 1780
Badollet, Paul
New York, N.Y., c. 1790
Baerr, William
Weaverville, Calif., late 1850s–1860s.
Watch and clockmaker.
Bagnall, Benjamin
Boston, Mass., 1710–1740. Believed to
have been Boston's first clockmaker.
Apprenticed to Peter Stretch.
Bagnall, Benjamin, Jr.
Boston, Mass. Son of Benjamin, Sr.
Also worked in Philadelphia, Pa., New-
port, and Providence, R.I. Had shop in
Cornhill, near Town House, 1770.
Bagnel, Samuel
Boston, Mass., 1740–1760. Brother of
Benjamin, Jr.
Bailey, Calvin
Hanover, Mass., 1800–1810
Bailey, E. S.
Abbeville, S.C., c. 1840; Newberry,
S.C., 1850–1860
Bailey, Emmor
London Grove (Chester Co.), Pa.,
c. 1790
Bailey, Gamaliel
New York, N.Y., c. 1820; Cincinnati,
Ohio, 1830–1840
Bailey, I. G.
Probably Connor, N.H., c. 1845
Bailey, J. T.
Philadelphia, Pa., c. 1825
Bailey, Joel
Bradford, Pa., 1775–1790
Bailey, John
Hanover, Mass., c. 1775. Son of
Colonel John Bailey.
Bailey, John, Jr.
New Bedford, Mass., 1770–1820. Also
worked in Hanover and Lynn, Mass.

Bailey, John III
New Bedford, Mass., c. 1800. Also
worked in Hingham, Mass.
Bailey, Joseph
New Bedford and Lynn, Mass., 1790–
1840
Bailey, Lebbeus
North Yarmouth, Me., c. 1800
Bailey, Parker
Rutland, Vt., c. 1860
Bailey, Putnam
North Goshen, Conn., c. 1830
Bailey, William
Philadelphia, Pa., 1816–1840
Bailey, Banks and Biddle
Philadelphia, Pa.; started out as Bailey
and Kitchen, 1832–1846; then Bailey
and Company; then Bailey, Banks and
Biddle.
Bailey & Brothers
Utica, N.Y., c. 1847
Bailey, G. S. & Co.
Danbury, Conn., c. 1860
Bailey & Kitchen
Philadelphia, Pa., c. 1840. Probably
dealers only but clocks with name
on dial are reported.
Bailey & Owen
Abbeville, S.C., 1840–1850
Bailey & Parker
Rutland, Vt., 1850–1860
Bailey & Ward
New York, N.Y., c. 1832
Baird Clock Co.
Plattsburgh, N.Y., c. 1892
Baird, R. A. and Alva
Ravenna, Ohio, c. 1850
Baker, Alexander
New York, N.Y., c. 1854
Baker, Benjamin H.
Philadelphia, Pa., c. 1820
Baker, David
New Bedford, Mass., 1840–1850
Baker, Eleazer
Ashford, Conn., 1780–1830
Baker, Elias
New Brunswick, N.J., c. 1840
Baker, George
Providence, R.I., and Ipswich, Mass.,
1820–1830
Baker, George
New York, N.Y., c. 1865
Baker, James
Philadelphia, Pa., c. 1840
Baker, Joseph
Philadelphia, Pa., c. 1775
Baker, Samuel
New Brunswick, N.J., 1810–1850
Baker, Thomas
Concord, N.H., c. 1815. Continued
Abel Hutchins's business.
Baker, Thomas, Jr.
Haverhill and Salem, Mass., c. 1800
Baker, William
Boston, Mass., c. 1820
Bakewell, John P.
Pittsburgh, Pa., n.d.
Balch, Benjamin
Salem, Mass., 1790–1800; Boston,
Mass., 1810–1830
Balch, Charles H.
Newburyport, Mass., c. 1810
Balch, Daniel
Newbury, Mass., 1760–1780

Balch, Daniel, Jr.
Newbury and Newburyport, Mass., 1780–1820
Balch, Ebenezer
Wethersfield and Hartford, Conn., 1740–1790
Balch, James
Salem, Mass., 1820–1860
Balch, Joseph
Wethersfield, Conn., 1782–1794. Also worked in Williamstown, Mass., and Johnstown, N.Y.
Balch, Moses
Lowell, Mass., c. 1830. Moved to Lynn, Mass., c. 1844.
Balch, Thomas H.
Newburyport and Salem, Mass., 1820–1830
Balch, Benjamin & Son
Salem, Mass., 1837. Also Boston, Mass.
Balch (James), & Son
Salem, Mass., c. 1830
Balch & Lamson
Salem, Mass., c. 1840
Baldwin, Anthony W.
Lampeter Sq., Lancaster Co., Pa., c. 1810
Baldwin, Ebenezer
Nashua, N.H., 1810–1830
Baldwin, Edgar
Troy, N.Y., c. 1840
Baldwin, Ezra
Winsted, Conn., c. 1840
Baldwin, George W.
Sadsburyville, Chester Co., Pa., 1810–1820. Brother of Anthony.
Baldwin, Harlan
Sadsburyville, Chester Co., Pa., c. 1800. Brother of George and Anthony.
Baldwin, Jabez
Salem and Boston, Mass., c. 1800
Baldwin, Jedidiah
Hanover, N.H., 1790–1800; Rochester, N.Y., c. 1830. Brother of Jabez.
Baldwin, Matthias W.: 1795–1866
Elizabethtown, N.J., c. 1830. Later turned to building locomotives.
Baldwin, Oliver
Coatesville, Pa., c. 1860
Baldwin, Robert
Coatesville, Pa., c. 1860
Baldwin, Thomas F. H.
Downingtown and Coatesville, Pa., 1830–1859
Baldwin & Jones
Boston, Mass., c. 1812
Baldwin, S. S. & Son
New York, N.Y., 1820–1830
Baler, John
Northampton, Pa., n.d.
Ball, Albert
Poughkeepsie, N.Y., 1840–1850
Ball, B.
New Haven, Conn., c. 1860
Ball, Charles
Poughkeepsie, N.Y., 1840–1850
Ball, H.
Nashua, N.H., c. 1850. Made banjo clocks with wood movements.
Ball, S.
Black Rock, N.Y., c. 1820
Ball, William
Philadelphia, Pa., 1730–1800

Ball, Webb Clock Co.
Cleveland, Ohio, c. 1880
Ballard, Bartholomew
Antrim, N.H., c. 1800. Later to Columbus, Ohio.
Ballard, S.
Antrim, N.H., n.d.
Bancroft, G. P.
Granville, Ohio, c. 1830
Bandell & Co.
St. Albans, Vt., n.d.
Banfield, Forristall & Co.
Boston, Mass., 1860s
Banks, Edward
Portland, Me., c. 1830
Banks, Joseph
Philadelphia, Pa., c. 1820
Bannaker, Benjamin
Ellicott's Mills and Baltimore, Md., from c. 1781. One of the very few black clockmakers. Later distinguished himself in the field of astronomy.
Banstein, John
Philadelphia, Pa., 1791
Banta, W. C.
Springfield, Ohio, c. 1865
Bantel, Philip
New York, N.Y., 1840–1860. Patented 100-day clock, 1858.
Barbeck, C. G.
Philadelphia, Pa., c. 1830
Barber, C. W.
Middlebury, Ohio, c. 1840
Barber, Ephraim
Marlborough, Mass., n.d.
Barber, George
Unionville, Conn., c. 1830
Barber, James
Philadelphia, Pa., 1840–1850
Barber, William
Philadelphia, Pa., 1840–1850
Barbes & Welch
Bristol, Conn., n.d.
Barborka, J.
Iowa City, Iowa, 1870–1900
Barger, George
Philadelphia, Pa., 1844
Barker, B. B.
New York, N.Y., 1780–1800
Barker, James F.
Palmyra, N.Y., 1820s
Barker, Jonathan
Worcester, Mass., 1780s
Barker, William
Boston, Mass., c. 1825
Barker and Mumford
Newport, R.I., n.d.
Barker and Taylor
Worcester, Mass., c. 1790
Barklay, J.
Baltimore, Md., 1820s
Barklay, J. & S.
Baltimore, Md., 1812–1816
Barnard, Samuel
Utica, N.Y., c. 1840
Barnes, Alphonso
Bristol, Conn., 1805–1875
Barnes, B. D.
Oswego, N.Y., 1850–1860
Barnes, Carlyle F.
Bristol, Conn., c. 1880
Barnes, Edward M.
Bristol, Conn., 1834–1845

Barnes, Harry
Bristol, Conn., c. 1880
Barnes, John
Philadelphia, Pa., c. 1750
Barnes, Stephen
Bristol, Conn., 1790–1810
Barnes, Stephen
New Haven, Conn., 1840–1850
Barnes, Thomas, Jr.
Bristol, Conn., 1811–1840. Also banker, in real estate, etc.
Barnes, Timothy
Litchfield, Conn., 1790–1825
Barnes, Wallace
Bristol, Conn., 1825–1890. Son of Alphonso. Also worked as farmer, druggist, and in real estate.
Barnes, William H.
New Haven, Conn., 1840s–1850s
Barnes & Bacon
Bristol, Conn., c. 1840
Barnes & Bailey
Berlin, Conn., c. 1831
Barnes, Bartholomew, & Co.
Bristol, Conn., c. 1830
Barnes Brothers Clock Co.
Bristol, Conn., c. 1880
Barnes & Co. (Thomas, Jr., Wm. Johnson, and Willys Roberts, a son of Gideon)
Bristol, Conn., 1819–1823
Barnes, Darrow & Co.
Bristol, Conn., 1838–1840
Barnes & Jerome
Bristol, Conn., 1833
Barnes and Johnson
Bristol, Conn., c. 1820
Barnes, L. M. & Co.
North Adams, Mass., 1850–1860
Barnes, Thomas and Company
Bristol, Conn., 1800–1825
Barnes & Waterman
Bristol, Conn., 1811–1812
Barnhart, Simon
Kingston, Ross Co., Ohio, 1840–1850
Barnhill, Robert
Philadelphia, Pa., c. 1775
Barninger, Daniel
Conestoga, Pa., c. 1850
Barnitz, A. E.
York, Pa., c. 1850
Barns, John
Ann Arundel Co., Md., c. 1756
Barr, John
Port Glasgow, Wayne Co., N.Y., prior to c. 1840
Barr Mfg. Co.
Weedsport, N.Y., late 1800s
Barragant, Peter
Philadelphia, Pa., 1820–1830
Barrell, Colborn
Boston, Mass., 1770–1790. Adv. 1772
Barrett & Sherwood
San Francisco, Calif., 1850–1860. Made clocks and chronometers.
Barrington, Joseph
Dumfries, Va., 1790–1839; then Salisbury, N.C.
Barrow, Samuel
Philadelphia, Pa., c. 1771. Adv. 1770 that he makes all kinds of watches and clocks.
Barrows, James M.
Tolland, Conn., c. 1830

Barry, Standish
Baltimore, Md., 1784–1810
Bartberger, Ben
Pittsburgh, Pa., n.d.
Bartels, Franz
Jersey City, N.J., 1860–1870
Bartens & Rice
New York, N.Y., c. 1878
Bartholomew, George W.
Bristol, Conn., 1833–1845
Bartholomew, Harry
Bristol, Conn., 1850s
Bartholomew, W. J.
Brooklyn, N.Y., 1850–1860
Bartholomew, William G.
Bristol, Conn., c. 1850. Helped to
found Forestville Manufacturing Co.
Bartholomew & Barnes
Bristol, Conn., c. 1830
Bartholomew, Brown & Co.
Bristol, Conn., 1833–1834
Bartholomew, E. & G.
Bristol, Conn., c. 1820
Bartholomew, Eli and Co.
Bristol, Conn., 1810–1820
Barton, Benjamin
Alexandria, Va., c. 1830
Barton, John
Salem, Mass., 1840–1850; Newbury-
port, Mass., 1849–1850
Barton, Joseph
Stockbridge, Mass., late 1700s; Utica,
N.Y., 1804–1832
Barton, O. G.
Fort Edward, N.Y., c. 1830
Barton, William C.
Salem, Mass., 1830s
Bartow, John
Haverhill, Mass., 1840–1850
Barwell, Bartholomew
New York, N.Y., 1749–1760
Bascom & North
Torrington, Conn., 1800–1830
Basil
Baltimore, Md., n.d.; Albany, N.Y.,
c. 1773
Bassett, Charles
Probably Vermont or New York, n.d.
Bassett, Geo. Francis
Philadelphia, Pa., 1790s
Bassett, Nehemiah
Albany, N.Y., c. 1800
Bassett & Gibbs
Litchfield, Conn., c. 1830
Bassett, J. & W.H.
Cortland, N.H., 1810–1820; Albany,
N.Y., after 1820
Batchelder, Andrew
Danvers, Mass., 1800–1840
Batchelder, Charles
New York, N.Y., 1840–1850
Batchelder, Ezra, Jr.
Danvers, Mass., 1780–1820
Batchelder, K. L.
Concord, N.H., n.d.
Batchelor, N.
New York, N.Y., 1840s
Batchelow & Bensel
New York, N.Y., c. 1840
Bateman, Joseph
Norristown, Pa., n.d.
Bateman, Valentine
Reading, Pa., n.d.

Bates, Amos
New Bedford, Mass., 1830–1850.
Chronometer maker.
Bates, James C.
Haverhill, Mass., 1860–1880
Bateson, John
Boston, Mass., 1720
Bath, Barten
New York, N.Y., c. 1840
Battell, George E.
Newburyport, Mass., c. 1860
Batterson, James
Philadelphia, Pa., 1705; Boston, Mass.,
1707–1710; Charleston, S.C., 1711–
1727
Batterson, John
Annapolis, Md., c. 1723. Could be
watchmaker only.
Batting, Joseph
Philadelphia, Pa., c. 1840
Battles, A. B.
Utica, N.Y., c. 1840
Bauer, John
Northampton, Pa., n.d.
Bauer, John N.
New York, N.Y., 1820–1840
Baugh, Valentine
Abingdon, Va., c. 1820
Baumann, George
Columbus, Ohio, c. 1840
Bawd & Dotter
New York, N.Y., c. 1805
Bayley, Calvin
Hanover, Mass., c. 1800
Bayley, John
Hanover, Mass., 1770–1810
Bayley, John
Hingham, Mass., 1815–1820. Son of
John, 1st.
Bayley, Joseph
Hingham, Mass., c. 1800
Bayley, Lebbens
Maine, c. 1800
Bayley, Simeon C.
Philadelphia, Pa., 1794
Baynes, B. B.
Lowell, Mass., c. 1830. Adv. 1835.
Beach, Charles
Bristol, Conn., c. 1840
Beach, Edmund
Brooklyn, N.Y., n.d.
Beach, Miles
Litchfield, Conn., 1760–1785; Hart-
ford, Conn., 1788–1790 and 1797–1810
Beach, Nathan
Connecticut, c. 1825. Dial painter.
Beach, William
Hartford, Conn., 1820–1830
Beach & Byington
Plymouth, Conn., late 1840s
Beach & Hubbel
Bristol, Conn., c. 1860
Beach, J. J. & W.
Boston, Mass., c. 1840. Clock dealers.
Beach, Miles & Son
Hartford, Conn., 1813–1825
Beach & Sanford
Hartford, Conn., 1785–1788
Beach & Ward
Hartford, Conn., 1790–1798
Beals, J. J.
Boston, Mass., c. 1870

Beals, William
Boston, Mass., c. 1853
Beals, J. J., Clock Establishment
Boston, Mass., c. 1820. Clock dealer.
Beals, J. J. & Company
Boston, Mass., c. 1845
Beals, J. J. and Son
Boston, Mass., c. 1850
Beals, J. J. and W.
Boston, Mass., c. 1845
Bear, J.
Lexington, Va., c. 1800
Beard, Duncan
Appoquinemonk, Del., 1755–1797
Beard, Evan
Louisville, Ky., c. 1820
Beard, Robert
Maryland, c. 1775
Beard & Co., E.C.
Louisville, Ky., 1830–1870
Beard & Weaver
Appoquinemonk, Del., 1770–1790
Beardsley, H.P.
Coronna, Mich., c. 1870
Beasley, John M.
Fayetteville, N.C., c. 1830
Beath, John
Boston, Mass., c. 1805
Beath & Ellery
Boston, Mass., c. 1810
Beatley, Ralph
Chelsea, Mass., c. 1840
Beattie, George
Columbus, Ohio, c. 1850
Beatty, Albert L.
Philadelphia, Pa., 1833
Beatty, Charles A.
c. 1810
Beatty, George
Harrisburg, Pa., c. 1810
Bechel, Charles
Bethlehem, Pa., c. 1850
Bechtel, Henry
Philadelphia, Pa., c. 1817
Bechtel, Nazareth
Bethlehem, Pa., n.d.
Bechtler, Christopher, Jr.
New York, N.Y., 1829, from Europe;
Rutherford, N.C., 1831; later Spartan-
burg, S.C.
Bechtler, Christopher, Sr.
Philadelphia, Pa., 1830–1831; New
York, N.Y., 1829; to Rutherford, N.C.,
1831
Bechtler, C., & Son
Spartanburg, S.C., c. 1857
Beck, Henry
Philadelphia, Pa., 1837–1839
Beck, Jacob
Hanover, Pa., c. 1820
Beck, Thomas
Philadelphia, Pa., c. 1775; to Trenton,
N.J., c. 1784
Beckel, Charles F.
Bethlehem, Pa., c. 1820
Becker, Charles
Cleveland, Ohio, c. 1830
Becker, Jacob
Hanover, Pa., c. 1820
Beckwith, Dana
Bristol, Conn., 1818–1823
Beckwith, Jabez
Newport, N.H., c. 1875

Bedford, E.
Batavia, N.Y., c. 1816
Beebe, William
New York, N.Y., c. 1820
Beecher, William
Southbridge, Mass., n.d.
Beer, Alfred
Versailles, Ind., 1850–1880
Beer, Robert
Olean, Ind., 1820–1825; Versailles, Ind., after 1825
Behn, M. H.
New York, N.Y., c. 1860
Beidt, Julius
Philadelphia, Pa., c. 1848
Beigel, Henry
Philadelphia, Pa., c. 1810
Beirderman, John
Hamburg, Pa., c. 1820
Beitel, Joseph O.
Nazareth, Pa., n.d.
Beith and Ellery
Boston, Mass., c. 1800
Belk, William
Philadelphia, Pa., 1790–1800
Belknap, Ebenezer
Boston, Mass., 1820–1830
Belknap, Jeremiah
n.d.; n.p.
Belknap, William
Boston, Mass., c. 1820
Bell, James
New York, N.Y., 1800–1820
Bell, John
New York, N.Y., c. 1730
Bell, M.
Manteo, N.C., late 1880s
Bell, S. W.
Philadelphia, Pa., c. 1837
Bell, Samuel
Boston, Mass., c. 1813
Bell, Thomas W.
Philadelphia, Pa., c. 1837
Bell, William
Philadelphia, Pa., c. 1800
Bell, William M.
Probably Delaware, n.d.
Bell Brothers
San Antonio, Tex., from 1850s. Could be dealers only.
Belsner, Johann
Cocalico, Pa., 1785
Belsner, John
Fells Point and Baltimore, Md., c. 1760
Bemis, Augustus
Paris, Me., c. 1810
Bemis, Jonathan
Paris Hill, Me., n.d. Apprentice to Enoch Burnham.
Bemis, Merrick
n.p.; n.d.
Bemis, Samuel
Boston, Mass., and Keene, N.H., c. 1800
Benedict, A.
Syracuse, N.Y., c. 1830
Benedict, Albert
Lewisburg, Pa., c. 1860
Benedict, Andrew C.
New York, N.Y., 1810–1830
Benedict, Martin
New York, N.Y., c. 1830
Benedict, Philip
Lancaster, Pa., c. 1800s

Benedict, S. W.
New York, N.Y., c. 1840
Benedict, Samuel
New York, N.Y., c. 1840
Benedict and Brothers
New York, N.Y., c. 1835
Benedict & Burnham
Waterbury, Conn., c. 1850; became Waterbury Clock Co.
Benedict & Scudder
New York, N.Y., 1820–1830
Benham, Augustus
New Haven, Conn., 1840–1850
Benham, John H.
New Haven, Conn., c. 1835
Benjamin, Barzillaic
New Haven, Conn., c. 1820
Benjamin, Everard
New Haven, Conn., 1840–1860
Benjamin, John
Stratford, Conn., 1750–1790
Benjamin and Company
New Haven, Conn., c. 1846
Benjamin and Ford
New Haven, Conn., c. 1848
Bennett, Alfred
New York, N.Y., 1830–1840
Bennett, James
New York, N.Y., 1765–1785
Bennett, R. Jones
Easton, Md., c. 1820
Bennett, T. N.
Canandaigua, N.Y., 1850–1860
Bennett, W. O.
Philadelphia, Pa., c. 1840
Bennett & Caldwell
Philadelphia, Pa., 1820–1830
Bennett & Thomas
Petersburg, Va., c. 1820
Benny, James
Easton, Md., c. 1820
Benrus, Peter C.
New York, N.Y., c. 1870s
Bensel, Leonard J.
New York, N.Y., c. 1880
Bentley, Caleb
York, Pa., n.d.
Bentley, Eli
West Whiteland, Pa., c. 1770; later to Taneytown, Md.
Bentley, George
Taneytown, Md., c. 1810 and later. Son of Eli Bentley. A clock with "G. Bentley, Taneytown," on dial is owned in this village.
Bentley, Thomas
Gloucester and Boston, Mass., c. 1770
Berault, John
New York, N.Y., c. 1850
Berke, August
Louisville, Ky., c. 1860
Berkly, J.
Lewisburg, Pa., 1800–1820
Bernhard, Louis
Bloomsburg, Pa., c. 1850
Berrgant, Peter
Philadelphia, Pa., 1829–1833
Berringer, A. J.
Albany, N.Y., c. 1830
Berringer, Jacob
Albany, N.Y., c. 1840
Berry, James
New York, N.Y., 1780–1792

Berryhill, Stephen
Donegal, Pa., 1815
Berwick, Abner
Brunswick, Me., c. 1820
Bessonet, John
New York, N.Y., c. 1790
Best, Daniel
Cincinnati, Ohio, c. 1804
Best, Samuel
Cincinnati, Ohio, c. 1800
Best, Thomas
Lebanon, Ohio, c. 1820. Made clocks as well as watches.
Best, Robert and Samuel
Cincinnati, Ohio, c. 1810
Bevans, William
Norristown, Pa., 1790–1810
Bevins, William
Philadelphia, Pa., c. 1815
Bichault, James
Boston, Mass., 1729
Bickford, D.
n.p.; 1840–1850
Biddle, Owen
Philadelphia, Pa., 1760–1770. Worked with David Rittenhouse on astronomical observations.
Biegel, Henry
Philadelphia, Pa., c. 1810
Biernsen, Thomas
Philadelphia, Pa., c. 1820s
Biershing, Henry
Hagerstown, Md., 1815–1843
Bigelow, John B.
Boston, Mass., c. 1840
Bigelow & Brothers
Boston, Mass., c. 1840
Bigelow and Kennard
Boston, Mass., n.d.
Bigger, Gilbert
Baltimore, Md., 1784–1800
Bigger, William
Baltimore, Md., c. 1802
Bigger & Clarke
Baltimore, Md., c. 1784
Biggins, H.
n.p.; c. 1840s
Biggs, Thomas
Philadelphia, Pa., c. 1820
Bill, Joseph
Middletown, Conn., c. 1840
Billings, Andrew
Poughkeepsie, N.Y., 1790–1820
Billings, I.
Acton, Mass., c. 1810
Billings, Jonathan
Reading and Acton, Mass., c. 1830
Billings, Joseph
Reading, Pa., 1770–1780
Billings, L.
Northampton, Mass., c. 1830
Billings, Sona
Acton, Mass., c. 1840
Billon, Charles
Philadelphia, Pa., c. 1810; Saint Louis, Mo., c. 1820
Billon, A. C. & Co.
Davenport, Iowa, c. 1850
Billow, Charles, & Co.
Boston, Mass., c. 1796
Bills, Elijah
Colebrook and Plymouth, Conn., 1820–1840

Bills, Rodger
   Colebrook River, Conn., n.d.
Bills, E. and E. A.
   Colebrook River, Conn., c. 1840
Billy Bros.
   St. Lucas, Iowa, n.d.
Bind, William
   Philadelphia, Pa., c. 1830. Dial maker.
Bingham, B. D.
   Nashua, N.H., 1830–1840
Bingham, P. L.
   Nashua, N.H., n.d.
Bingham & Bricerly
   Philadelphia, Pa., 1770–1800
Binney, Horace
   Philadelphia, Pa., 1800–1840
Birce, J.
   Brattleboro, Vt., 1820–1830
Birdsley, E. C. & Co.
   Meriden, Conn., c. 1830. Also made
   combs.
Birge, J.
   Brattleboro, Vt., c. 1800
Birge, John
   Bristol, Conn., 1830–1860. Partner in
   many clock enterprises; moved to New
   York; later back to Bristol.
Birge & Co.
   Bristol, Conn., c. 1848
Birge, Case & Co.
   Bristol, Conn., 1833–1834
Birge & Fuller
   Bristol, Conn., 1844–1847. Noted for
   wagon-spring movements and double
   steeple clocks.
Birge and Gilbert
   Bristol, Conn., c. 1837
Birge, Gilbert & Co.
   Bristol, Conn., 1835–1837
Birge and Hale
   Bristol, Conn., c. 1820
Birge, Hayden & Co.
   Saint Louis, Mo., c. 1850
Birge & Ives
   Bristol, Conn., 1832–1833
Birge, Mallory & Co.
   Bristol, Conn., 1838–1843
Birge, Peck & Co.
   Bristol, Conn., 1849–1859
Birge and Tuttle
   n.p.; c. 1820
Birnie, Lawrence
   Philadelphia, Pa., 1774–1777
Bisbee, J.
   Brunswick, Me., 1790–1820
Bishop, Dan F.
   Bristol, Conn., 1853–1855
Bishop, Daniel E.
   Bristol, Conn., 1853–1855
Bishop, Henry D.
   Bethlehem, Pa., c. 1830s
Bishop, Homer
   Bristol, Conn., late 1830s or early
   1840s
Bishop, J.
   Allentown, Pa., c. 1810
Bishop, James
   Watertown, Conn., 1825–1830
Bishop, Joseph
   Wilmington, N.C., 1817–1825
Bishop, Joseph
   Philadelphia, Pa., 1829–1833
Bishop, Moritz
   Easton, Pa., 1786–1788

Bishop, Rufus
   Mount Joy, Pa., c. 1850
Bishop & Bradley
   Watertown and Plymouth, Conn.,
   1820–1830
Bishop & Norton
   Bristol, Conn., 1853–1855
Bispham, Samuel
   Philadelphia, Pa., and New Jersey;
   working in Philadelphia as early as
   1696.
Bissell, David
   East Windsor, Conn., c. 1832
Bixler, Arthur B.
   Easton, Pa., c. 1900
Bixler, C. Willis
   Easton, Pa., n.d. Son of Daniel Bixler.
Bixler, Christian
   Reading, Pa., 1750–1790
Bixler, Christian, Jr.
   Easton, Pa., 1780–1825
Bixler, Daniel
   Easton, Pa., c. 1830s
Black, John
   Philadelphia, Pa., c. 1840
Blackford, Edward
   New York, N.Y., c. 1830
Blackman, J. N.
   New Milford, Conn., c. 1880
Blackman, John S.
   Danbury, Conn., c. 1790
Blackner, John L.
   Cleveland, Ohio, c. 1830
Blacksley, Richard
   Dayton, Ohio, c. 1825
Blair, Elisha
   Brooklyn, N.Y., c. 1840
Blaisdell, Abner
   Chester, N.H., c. 1775. Son of Isaac.
Blaisdell, Charles
   Ossipee, N.H., c. 1860
Blaisdell, David
   Amesbury, Mass., 1712–1756
Blaisdell, David II
   Chester, N.H., 1736–1794. Son of
   David.
Blaisdell, David III
   Chester and Peachum, N.H., 1767–
   1807. Son of Isaac.
Blaisdell, Ebenezer
   Chester, N.H., 1778–1813. Son of
   Isaac. Apprentice of T. Chandler.
Blaisdell, Isaac: 1738–1781
   Chester, N.H., c. 1760
Blaisdell, Isaac, Jr.
   Chester, N.H., c. 1790
Blaisdell, Isaac II
   Chester, N.H., 1760–1797. Son of
   Isaac.
Blaisdell, Jonathan
   Amesbury, Mass., 1678–1748. Father
   of David.
Blaisdell, Nicholas
   Amesbury, Mass., and Portland, Me.,
   1743–1800. Son of David.
Blaisdell, Richard
   Chester, N.H., 1762–1790. Son of
   Isaac.
Blake, E. G.
   Farmington, Me., c. 1850
Blakeslee, Edward K.
   Cincinnati, Ohio, 1840–1850
Blakeslee, Jeremiah
   Plymouth, Conn., c. 1840

Blakeslee, Milo
   Plymouth, Conn., c. 1824. Worked for
   Eli Terry, Jr.
Blakeslee, R.
   New York, N.Y., c. 1848
Blakeslee, William
   Newtown, Conn., c. 1820
Blakeslee, Ziba
   Newtown, Conn., c. 1800. Made turret
   and church clocks, tall clocks and
   watches. Father of William.
Blakeslee, M. and Co.
   Terryville, Conn., n.d.
Blakeslee, M. E. & Co.
   Heathenville, Conn., c. 1830
Blakeslee, Marvin and Edward
   Plymouth, Conn., c. 1830
Blakesly, Harper
   Cincinnati, Ohio, c. 1830
Blakewell, John P.
   Pittsburgh, Pa., c. 1830s. Was issued a
   patent for glass wheels.
Blanc, Lewis
   Philadelphia, Pa., c. 1810
Blanchard, Asa
   Lexington, Ky., 1808–1838. Also a
   noted silversmith.
Blanchard, Joshua
   Cincinnati, Ohio, 1820–1830
Bland, Samuel
   Philadelphia, Pa., 1837–1850
Blankford, William
   Chicago, Ill., c. 1880
Blatt, John
   Philadelphia, Pa., c. 1840s. Probably
   dealer only.
Blaus, Samuel
   n.p.; n.d.
Bliss, H. A.
   Bennington, Vt., n.d.
Bliss, John
   Zanesville, Ohio, c. 1815
Bliss, William
   Cleveland, Ohio, c. 1810
Bliss and Co.
   New York, N.Y., c. 1890. Chronometer
   maker.
Bliss and Creighton
   Brooklyn, N.Y., n.d.
Bloomer, George
   Northampton, Pa., n.d.
Bloomer, William
   Mount Victory, Ohio, c. 1860
Bloomer & Sperry
   New York, N.Y., c. 1840
Blowe, George
   Philadelphia, Pa., 1830–1860
Blummer, Jacob
   Allentown, Pa., c. 1700
Blummer, Joseph
   Allentown, Pa., c. 1700
Blummer and Graff
   Allentown, Pa., c. 1700
Blundy, Charles
   Charleston, S.C., c. 1750
Blunt and Co.
   New York, N.Y., c. 1869
Blunt, E. and G. W.
   New York, N.Y., c. 1850
Blydenburg, Samuel
   New York, N.Y., c. 1830
Boardman, Chauncey
   Bristol, Conn., 1811–1850. Made move-
   ments for other makers.

Boardman, Chester
Plymouth, Conn., c. 1842
Boardman, George
Bristol, Conn., n.d.
Boardman and Dunbar
Bristol, Conn., c. 1805
Boardman and Smith
Bristol, Conn., c. 1832
Boardman and Wells
Bristol, Conn., 1832–1843. Prolific makers of wood- and brass-movement clocks of all types.
Bochemsde, Frederick
Boston, Mass., 1810–1825
Bode, W.
Philadelphia, Pa., c. 1790
Bodeley, Thomas
Boston, Mass., c. 1720
Boehme, Charles L.
Baltimore, Md., 1799–1812
Boehner, John
Bethlehem, Pa., c. 1745
Boemper, Abraham: 1705–1793
Bethlehem, Pa., c. 1730s
Bofenschen, Charles
Camden, S.C., 1854–1857
Bogardus, Everardus
New York, N.Y., c. 1675
Bogardus, James
New York and Henrietta, N.Y., c. 1820. Also worked as engraver and die maker.
Boifeuillet, John P.
Savannah, Ga., 1850–1860
Boikman, Ebenezer
Attleboro, Mass., c. 1750s
Bois-de-Chesne, John Francis
Charleston, S.C., c. 1750s
Bolles, Thomas N.
n.p.; 1790–1810
Bollman, William
Atlanta, Ga., c. 1870
Boloquet, Marcel
New Bern, N.C., 1750–1760
Bolte, H. N.
Atlantic City, N.J., c. 1860
Bond, Charles
Boston, Mass., c. 1825
Bond, William
Boston, Mass., 1800–1810
Bond and Son
Boston, Mass., n.d.
Bond, William & Son
Boston, Mass., 1815–1840
Bonfanti, Joseph
New York, N.Y., c. 1823. Probably dealer and importer.
Bonnard, M.
Philadelphia, Pa., 1799
Bonnet, Jacob
Zanesville, Ohio., c. 1850
Bonnet, John M.
Zanesville, Ohio, 1850–1860
Booth, H. B.
Rochester, N.Y., n.d.
Booth, Hiram N.
New York, N.Y., c. 1840
Borhek, Edward
Philadelphia, Pa., c. 1825
Borneman, Henry H.
Boyertown, Berks Co., Pa., 1840–1880s
Borneman, Joseph H.
Boyertown, Berks Co., Pa., c. 1855

Boss & Peterman
Rochester, N.Y. Adv. c. 1841
Boston Clock Co.
Chelsea, Mass., 1888–1897. Was Eastman Clock Co.; then Chelsea Clock Co.
Bostwick & Burgess Mfg. Co.
Norwalk, Ohio, 1892–1893. Makers of some 20,000 famous wood-movement Columbus Clocks. Made for the World's Columbian Exposition, 1892–1893.
Botsford, J. S.
Troy, N.Y., c. 1840
Botsford, L. F.
Albany, N.Y., 1830–1831
Botsford, Patrick
New Haven, Conn., 1840–1850
Botsford, S. N.
Whitneyville, Conn., c. 1850
Bottomley, T.
Boston, Mass., 1784
Boughell, Joseph
New York, N.Y., c. 1780
Bouju, Joseph
Saint Louis, Mo., c. 1820
Boult & Johnson
Hagerstown, Md., n.d.
Bouston, John
Philadelphia, Pa., c. 1790
Boute, Lewis Charles
Philadelphia, Pa., c. 1830
Bouvrier, Daniel
Zanesville, Ohio, c. 1816
Bouvrier, M.
Baltimore, Md., Pittsburgh, Pa., and Zanesville, Ohio, 1800–1827
Bowen, George A.
Boston, Mass., c. 1840
Bowen, J. B.
Waltham, Mass., c. 1820
Bower, Henry
Philadelphia, Pa., 1800–1825
Bower, Michael
Philadelphia, Pa., c. 1790
Bower, William
Charleston, S.C., 1772–1773
Bowers, George
Philadelphia, Pa., c. 1850
Bowman, George
Columbus, Ohio, c. 1840
Bowman, John
New Holland, Lancaster Co., Pa., c. 1810
Bowman, Joseph
New Holland and Elliott's Corner, Pa., c. 1800
Bowman, Joseph
Strasburg, Pa., 1820–1844
Bowman and Baldwin
Lampeter, Pa., n.d.
Bowne, Samuel
New York, N.Y., c. 1750
Boyce, Benjamin M.
Boston, Mass., 1880–1895
Boyd, H.
Blairsville, Pa., c. 1830
Boyd, John
Sadsburyville, Pa., 1830–1860
Boyd, John
Lowell, Mass., c. 1860
Boyd, Thomas
Philadelphia, Pa., c. 1805

Boyd and Richards
Philadelphia, Pa., c. 1808
Boyer, Jacob
Boyertown, Berks Co., Pa., c. 1775
Boynton, Calvin
Buffalo, N.Y., 1850–1860
Boynton, John
Massachusetts, c. 1825. Exact location unknown. Kentucky rifles by him are known.
Boynton, John E.
Manchester, Iowa, c. 1860
Boyter, Daniel
Boston, Mass., 1800; Poughkeepsie, N.Y., 1803
Brabner, William A.
Boston, Mass., c. 1825
Brace, Jared
Newtown, Conn., n.d.
Brace, Rodney
Torrington, Conn., c. 1790; North Bridgewater, Mass., after 1800. With Isaac Packard.
Brace, William H.
Saint Albans and Greenville, Ohio, c. 1820s
Brace & Packard
Brockton, Mass., c. 1825
Brackett, Jeffrey
Boston, Mass., 1830–1850
Brackett, O.
Vassalborough, Me., n.d.
Brackett, R.
Vassalborough, Me., n.d.
Bradbury, Jacob
New York, N.Y., c. 1840
Bradford, O. C.
Binghamton, N.Y., c. 1841
Bradier, John
Philadelphia, Pa., 1800–1810
Bradley, Abner
Watertown, Conn., c. 1800s
Bradley, D. W.
New York, N.Y., c. 1850
Bradley, Dimon
n.p.; 1810–1825
Bradley, Frederick
New York, N.Y., n.d.
Bradley, G. C.
Binghamton, N.Y., c. 1840
Bradley, H.
Marietta, Ohio, c. 1810
Bradley, Horace
Rochester, N.Y., c. 1830
Bradley, Lucius
Watertown, Conn., c. 1800s
Bradley, Nelson
Plymouth, Conn., c. 1840
Bradley, Richard
Hartford, Conn., c. 1825
Bradley, B. and Co.
Boston, Mass., c. 1850
Bradley & Barnes
Boston, Mass., c. 1850
Bradley & Hubbard
West Meriden, Conn., c. 1850. Cast-iron clocks.
Bradley, Z. & Son
New Haven, Conn., c. 1840
Brady, John
Philadelphia, Pa., c. 1835
Bradycamp, Lewis
Lancaster, Pa., 1836–1870. Apprenticed to Martin Schreiner.

Brainard, O. T.
Tama City, Iowa, c. 1860
Brake, Frederick
Albany, N.Y., 1840–1844
Bramble, G. A.
n.p.; c. 1858
Brand, James
Boston, Mass., c. 1711
Brand, John
Boston, Mass., 1711–1712
Brandegee, Elishana
Berlin, Conn., c. 1832
Brands & Matthey
Philadelphia, Pa., c. 1799
Brandt, Adam
New Hanover (now Hanover), Pa.,
1750–1760
Brandt, Aimé
Philadelphia, Pa., c. 1820
Brandt, Jacob
New Hanover, Montgomery Co., Pa.,
1790–1810
Brandt, A. and Co.
Philadelphia, Pa., c. 1803
Brandt, Aimé & Charles
Philadelphia, Pa., 1802–1813; Aimé
alone, 1817–1825
Brandt, Brown & Lewis
Philadelphia, Pa., c. 1790
Brandt, Charles and Co.
Philadelphia, Pa., c. 1815
Brannan, G.
Columbus, Ohio, c. 1850
Brasher, Abraham
New York, N.Y., 1757
Brasier, Amable
Philadelphia, Pa., 1795–1820
Brassington, John
Alexandria, Va., c. 1820
Brastow, A. and Co.
Lowell, Mass., n.d.
Brastow, Adison & Co.
Lowell, Mass., c. 1830s
Bready, C. L.
Philadelphia, Pa., c. 1800
Brearly, James
Philadelphia, Pa., 1790–1810
Breckel, Richard
New York, N.Y., c. 1775
Breckenridge, J. M.
Meriden, Conn., c. 1830; New Haven,
Conn., 1840–1870
Breckwell, John
Pikeland, Chester Co., Pa., c. 1830
Breese, Lyman
Wellsburg, Va., c. 1830
Breidenbach, L.
Philadelphia, Pa., c. 1805
Breitinger & Kunz
Philadelphia, Pa., n.d.
Breneiser, George
Adamstown, Pa., c. 1800
Brener, William
Yeadon, Pa., n.d.
Brenfter, Walter
Canterbury, Conn., c. 1810
Brenkelaer, Jan
New York (?) or Hudson Valley, N.Y.,
n.d. Tradition dates this maker from
1660–1750s.
Brennan, Barnabas
Philadelphia, Pa., c. 1840

Brenneiser, George
Womelsdorf, Berks Co., Pa., 1810–
1850. Brother of Samuel Brenneiser.
Brenneiser, Samuel
Reading and Adamstown, Lancaster
Co., Pa., 1810–1850
Brenneiser, Samuel II
Reamstown, Pa., 1830–1860
Brenneiser, William
Reamstown, Lancaster Co., Pa., 1780–
1830
Brent, Adam
New Hanover, Pa., n.d.
Brewer, C.
Middletown, Conn., c. 1800
Brewer, Isaac
Philadelphia, Pa., 1810–1820
Brewer, Thomas A.
Philadelphia, Pa., 1830–1850
Brewer, William
Philadelphia, Pa., 1770–1790
Brewster, Abel
Canterbury, Conn., 1775–1807. Did an
extensive business on credit. Sold out
to Hart and Wilcox c. 1807.
Brewster, Charles E.
Portsmouth, N.H., c. 1840
Brewster, George G.
Portsmouth, N.H., c. 1850
Brewster, W.
Middlebury, Vt., c. 1785
Brewster & Brown
Bristol, Conn., 1839–1840
Brewster & Co.
Bristol, Conn., c. 1840. Company was
among first to use coil springs in move-
ments.
Brewster, E. C. and Co.
Bristol, Conn., c. 1861
Brewster and Ingrahams
Bristol, Conn., 1840–1850. Company
was one of the most outstanding in the
production of shelf clocks. Did large
export business.
Brewster and Ives
Bristol, Conn., c. 1840
Brewster Manufacturing Co.
Bristol, Conn., c. 1850. Succeeded
Brewster and Ingrahams.
Brewster & Son, E. C.
Bristol, Conn., c. 1855
Brewster & Willard
Portsmouth, N.H., 1830–1840
Brice, James
Cincinnati, Ohio, n.d.
Brickard, H.
Bainbridge, Pa., c. 1860
Brickerhoof, C.
New York, N.Y., 1790–1800. Bell
maker.
Brickett, William
Boston, Mass., c. 1860
Brigdon, C. H.
Canton Junction, Mass., c. 1890
Brigdon, George S.
Norwich, Conn., 1810–1830
Briggs, John C.
Concord, N.H., 1840–1850. Invented
Briggs "Rotary" clock, pat. 1855 and
1856.
Briggs, Nathaniel
Boston, Mass., c. 1820
Bright, Jacob
Sunbury, Pa., 1790–1810

Brinckerhoff, Dirck
Dock Street, New York, N.Y., c. 1756
Brindle, G. B.
Norwich, Conn., n.d.
Bringhurst, Joseph
Philadelphia, Pa., c. 1813
Brinsmaid, Abram
Burlington, Vt., c. 1810
Brintzinghoffer, F.
Philadelphia, Pa., c. 1804
Bristol Brass Clock Manufactory, The
Bristol, Conn., 1818–1819
Bristol Brass & Clock Co.
Bristol, Conn., 1850–1903
Bristol Clock Case Co.
Bristol, Conn., 1854–1857
Bristol Clock Co.
Bristol, Conn., and New York, N.Y.,
c. 1843
Bristol Manufacturing Co.
Bristol, Conn., c. 1837
Brittain, Joseph
Bakerstown, Pa., c. 1830
Broadbridge, James
Newburgh, N.Y., 1805–1830
Brock, Ferdinand
Carondelet, Mo., c. 1860
Brockett, Jesse
New Haven, Conn., c. 1860
Broderson, Christian
Russellville, Ky., 1830–1885
Broderson, Emil
Cincinnati, Ohio, with Duhme & Co.,
c. 1860
Brogan, John
New York, N.Y., c. 1810
Brokaw, Aaron
Rahway and Elizabeth, N.J., 1780–
1840. Carried on his father, Isaac's,
business.
Brokaw, Isaac
Bridgetown and Elizabethtown, N.J.,
1770–1810
Brokaw, John
Woodbridge, N.J., 1770–1780. Son of
Isaac.
Brokesmield, Joseph
Cincinnati, Ohio, c. 1830
Bronson, Bennet
Waterbury, Conn., c. 1800
Bronson, I. W.
Buffalo, N.Y., 1825–1830
Bronson, Pharris
Waterbury, Conn., Cairo, N.Y., 1810–
1830
Brook, John
New York, N.Y., c. 1830
Brooker, John
Germantown, Pa., n.d.
Brooks, B. F.
Utica, N.Y., c. 1825
Brooks, Bernard
Salem Crossroads, Pa., c. 1830
Brooks, Charles
Utica, N.Y., c. 1835
Brooks, F. O.
Madison, Ind., c. 1860
Brooks, Hervey
Goshen, Conn., c. 1805. Probably not
a maker.
Brooks, John
Germantown, Pa., n.d.
Brooks, L. S.
n.p.; c. 1825

Brooks, Thomas
Mount Joy, Pa., c. 1805
Brooks, Watts
Goshen, Conn., c. 1820. Son of Hervey.
Brooks, William P.
Boston, Mass., c. 1850. Dealer only.
Brooks, B. F. & Co.
Utica, N.Y., c. 1830
Brooks and Griswold
Utica, N.Y., c. 1830
Broomall, Lewis R.
Philadelphia, Pa., 1846–1850
Broughham, George
Baltimore, Md., 1780–1800
Brower, S. Douglas
Troy, N.Y., 1841–1842
Brown, Albert
Columbia, Lancaster Co., Pa., c. 1850
Brown, David
Providence, R.I., 1834–1850
Brown, Edward L.
Newburyport, Mass., c. 1860
Brown, F.
Savannah, Ga., c. 1850
Brown, Gawen
Boston, Mass., 1750–1776. Made tower clocks, tall case clocks, watches.
Brown, George
Bristol, Conn., 1856–1862
Brown, J. H.
Des Moines, Iowa, c. 1856
Brown, John
Lancaster Boro, Pa., 1821–1850
Brown, John J.
Andover, Mass., c. 1840
Brown, John R.
Probably Connecticut, c. 1850
Brown, John W.
Newburyport, Mass., c. 1825
Brown, Jonathan C.
Bristol, Conn., 1833–1855. One of the principals of Forestville Manufacturing Co., Forestville, Conn., 1842–1849. Used his name as well as Forestville Manufacturing Co. on labels. Used coil springs and fuzee. Developed the acorn clock. His home in Bristol, pictured on many tablets, is still standing.
Brown, Joseph R.
Providence, R.I., c. 1847
Brown, Laurent
Rochester, N.Y., 1841
Brown, Philip
Hopkinton, N.H., c. 1810. Cabinet-maker.
Brown, Robert
Baltimore, Md., c. 1829. Also known as Robert Brown and Son.
Brown, S.
Norristown, Pa., c. 1850
Brown, Samuel
New York, N.Y., c. 1810
Brown, Samuel A.
Lowell, Mass., c. 1830
Brown, Seth E.
Concord, N.H., c. 1830
Brown, Thomas
Zanesville, Ohio, c. 1830
Brown, Thomas W.
New York, N.Y., 1830–1870
Brown, William
Philadelphia, Pa., 1820–1830
Brown, William
York, Pa., 1840–1850

Brown and Anderson
Wilmington, N.C., 1850–1860
Brown & Bacon
Bristol, Conn., n.d.
Brown & Buck
Columbus, Ohio, 1840–1850. Could be dealers only.
Brown and Butler
Bristol, Conn., c. 1850
Brown & Co., Samuel
New York, N.Y., 1820–1830
Brown & Goodrich
Bristol, Conn., 1810–1830
Brown & Kirby
New Haven, Conn., 1840
Brown and Lewis
Bristol, Conn., 1830–1840
Brown and Marsters
New York, N.Y., n.d.
Brown, Robert and Son
Providence, R.I., c. 1833
Brown & Sharpe
Providence, R.I., 1840–1850. Makers of precision tools today.
Browne, Albert
Yorktown, Pa., c. 1780. Farmer and smith.
Browne, Liberty
Philadelphia, Pa., c. 1800
Browning, Samuel
Boston, Mass., c. 1815
Brownold, D.
Louisville, Ky., c. 1860
Brownson, I. W.
Buffalo, N.Y., 1820–1830
Bruckman, V. C.
Atlantic City, N.J., c. 1880
Bruff, Charles
New York, N.Y., 1770–1800
Bruff, James
New York, N.Y., c. 1760
Brughner, Jacob
Brooklyn, N.Y., 1840–1850
Bryant, E. D.
New York, N.Y., c. 1850
Bryant, Thomas
Rochester, N.Y., c. 1830
Buard, Charles W.
Philadelphia, Pa., c. 1850
Bucher, Jesse
Dayton, Ohio, 1825–1840
Buck, Solomon
Glens Falls, N.Y., c. 1820
Buckle, Jacob
Pittsburgh, Pa., c. 1830
Buckley, David
Litchfield, Conn., c. 1835. Cabinet-maker.
Buckley, Joseph
Fairfield, Conn., 1775–1815
Buckley, Samuel
Philadelphia, Pa., c. 1811
Buckman, George W.
Baltimore, Md., c. 1802
Budd, Joseph
Mount Holly and New Mills (now Pemberton), N.J., 1810–1820
Buel, David
East Hampton, Conn., c. 1830. Maker of clock bells.
Buell, Orlando
New Preston, Conn., and Staten Island, N.Y., n.d.

Buerk, J. E.
Boston, Mass., c. 1860. Maker of watchman's clocks.
Buffet, George Francis
Philadelphia, Pa., c. 1796
Bulkley, Joseph
Fairfield, Conn., 1775–1815
Bull, James P.
Newark, N.J., 1850–1857
Bull, John
York, Pa., 1800–1850
Bullard, Charles
Boston, Mass., c. 1810. Dial and tablet painter for Willards and others.
Bundy Manufacturing Co.
Binghamton, N.Y., 1875–1900. Made time-recording clocks.
Bung, Jacob
Lancaster, Pa., 1815–1819
Bunker, Benjamin
Nantucket, Mass., 1800–1830
Bunnel and Scovill
Owego, N.Y., n.d.
Bunnell, Edwin
Bristol, Conn., 1840–1850
Bunting, Daniel
Philadelphia, Pa., 1844
Burdick, M. H.
Bristol, Conn., 1840–1850. Clock dealer.
Burdict, S. P.
Philadelphia, Pa., c. 1880
Burg, Jacob
Lancaster Co., Pa., n.d.
Burger, Joseph
New York, N.Y., n.d. Dial maker.
Burgi, Frederick
Trenton, N.J., 1774–1775
Burgi, Jacob
Lancaster, Pa., c. 1750
Buritt, P.
Ithaca, N.Y., c. 1820
Burk, Charles
Philadelphia, Pa., c. 1848
Burkelow, Samuel
Philadelphia, Pa., 1791–1799
Burkhart, Trudpert
Philadelphia, Pa., c. 1840. Musical clockmaker.
Burkle, Jacob
Pittsburgh, Pa., c. 1830
Burkmar, Thomas
Boston, Mass., c. 1770
Burnap, Daniel
East Windsor and Andover, Conn., 1780–1800. Also silversmith.
Burnap, Ela
Boston, Mass., 1810–1820
Burnes Clock Co.
Connecticut, n.d.
Burnett, Smith
Newark, N.J., c. 1770–1830
Burnham, Abner
Litchfield, Conn., c. 1800
Burnham, E. B.
Salisbury, N.C., c. 1820
Burnham, Enoch
Paris, Rumford, and Portland, Me., 1806–1830
Burnham, J. W.
Salisbury, Conn., c. 1825
Burnham, P. B.
Greenville, S.C., c. 1850

Burnham, Daniel and Son
Sharon, Conn., c. 1790
Burns, Hugh
Philadelphia, Pa., c. 1811
Burr, C. A.
Rochester, N.Y., 1841–1842. Probably dealer.
Burr, Jonathan
Lexington, Mass., c. 1830; Chicago, Ill., c. 1840
Burr & Chittenden
Lexington, Mass., 1830
Burr, Ezekiel & William
Providence, R.I., c. 1790
Burrage, John
Baltimore, Md., c. 1769
Burritt, Joseph
Ithaca, N.Y., c. 1830. Probably dealer.
Burroughs, Thomas
Lowell, Mass., c. 1834
Burrowes, Isaac
Strasburg, Pa., 1796–1808
Burrowes, John
Strasburg, Pa., c. 1808
Burrowes, Thomas
Strasburg, Pa., 1790–1810
Burot, A.
Baltimore, Md., 1810–1827
Burt & Cady
Kansas City, Mo., c. 1860
Burton, Wolsey
Philadelphia, Pa., and Dover, Del., c. 1725
Burtt, Thomas F.
Stoneham, Mass., 1855–1890
Burut, Andrew
Baltimore, Md., 1819–1837
Burwell, Elias
Bristol, Conn., 1859–1867. Maker of calendar clocks.
Burwell & Carter
Bristol, Conn., 1859–1861
Bush, George
Easton, Pa., 1810–1830
Bush, Henry
Cincinnati, Ohio, c. 1830
Bush, Michael
Easton, Pa., n.d.
Butler, Franklin
Philadelphia, Pa., c. 1840
Butler, James
Boston, Mass., 1725–1750
Butler, Nathaniel
Utica, N.Y., c. 1800
Butler & Bartlett
West Chester, Pa., c. 1830
Butler, Henderson & Co.
Clement, Nova Scotia, n.d.
Butler, Roman & Co.
Annapolis, Md., and Nova Scotia, n.d.
Byan, C. C.
Amesbury, Mass., 1850–1860
Byington, Lawler
Bristol, Conn., Newark, N.J., and New York, N.Y., 1820–1850. Probably dealer only, although some labels have his name on them.
Byington & Co.
Bristol, Conn., 1843–1849
Byington & Graham
Bristol, Conn., 1852–1853
Byram, Ephraim
Sag Harbor, L.I., N.Y., c. 1850

Byrne, James
Philadelphia, Pa., New York, N.Y., and Elizabeth, N.J., 1780–1800

Cable, Stephen
New York, N.Y., 1840–1850
Cachot, Felix
Bardstown, Ky., 1813–1839. Was a former Trappist monk.
Cadwell, Edwin
New York, N.Y., c. 1840
Cain, C. W.
New York, N.Y., 1830
Cain, Michael
Albany, N.Y., c. 1830
Cairns, John
Providence, R.I., c. 1780
Cairns, John, Jr.
Providence, R.I., 1830–1840
Calame, Olivier
Frederick, Md., 1810–1820
Calderwood, Andrew
Philadelphia, Pa., 1800–1822. Listed in directories.
Caldwell, James E.
Philadelphia, Pa., 1840–1850
Caldwell, & Co.
Philadelphia, Pa., c. 1850. Imported foreign clocks.
Calendar & Auger
Meriden, Conn., c. 1860
Calendar Clock Co.
Glastonbury, Conn., c. 1856
Calhoun, W. H.
Nashville, Tenn., n.d.
Calor, C. H.
Plainville, N.J., 1888–1889
Camerden & Forster
New York, N.Y., late 1880s
Camp, Ephraim
Salem Bridge, Conn., 1800–1825
Camp, Hiram
Bristol, Conn., with Chauncey Jerome, 1829; New Haven, 1844. Founded New Haven Clock Co.
Campbell, Alexander
Philadelphia, Pa., c. 1798
Campbell, Alexander
Brooklyn, N.Y., 1840–1850
Campbell, Benjamin
Hagerstown, Md., 1775–1792; Uniontown, Pa., 1792–1830
Campbell, Charles
New York, N.Y., 1790–1810
Campbell, Charles
Philadelphia, Pa., 1795–1799
Campbell, Isaac
Philadelphia, Pa., 1813–1824
Campbell, James
Steubenville, Ohio, c. 1810
Campbell, John
Hagerstown, Md., c. 1770
Campbell, John
New York, N.Y., and Brooklyn, N.Y., c. 1840
Campbell, R. A.
Baltimore, Md., 1832
Campbell, Robert G.
Ravenna, Ohio, 1820–1830
Campbell, Thomas
New York, N.Y., c. 1810
Campbell, William
Carlisle, Pa., 1765; Philadelphia, Pa., 1799

Canby, Charles
Wilmington, Del., 1815–1850. Apprenticed to Ziba Ferris in 1808. Sold his business to George Elliott c. 1852.
Canby & Nielson
West Chester, Pa., c. 1810
Candee & McEwan
Edgefield, S.C., c. 1850
Canfield, Samuel
Middletown, Conn., 1780–1790; Lansingburgh, N.Y., 1790–1800
Canfield & Foote
Middletown, Conn., c. 1790
Cannon, William
Philadelphia, Pa., c. 1730
Capper, Michael
Philadelphia, Pa., 1799
Capron, J. B.
New Milford, Conn., n.d.
Carey, James
Brunswick, Me., 1800–1840
Carleton, Dudley
Bradford, Newbury, Vt., 1750–1780
Carleton, James H.
Haverhill, Mass., c. 1853
Carleton, John C.
Bradford, Vt., c. 1800
Carleton, Michael: 1757–1836
Bradford, Mass., 1780–1820. Also tinsmith.
Carman, Martin
Conestoga, Pa., 1847–1850
Carman, Samuel
Brooklyn, N.Y., 1840s
Carney, Hugh
Wolcottville, Conn., 1810–1830
Carpenter, A. W.
New Holland, Lancaster Co., Pa., 1830–1860. Succeeded his father, Anthony.
Carpenter, Anthony
New Holland, Lancaster Co., Pa., c. 1820
Carpenter, C. H.
Middleboro, Mass., c. 1860
Carpenter, James
Harrison (or Harrisontown), N.J., early 19th century
Carpenter, Joseph
Norwich, Conn., 1769–1804
Carpenter, Lumen
Oswego, N.Y., c. 1840
Carr, Frank B.
Fall River, Mass., c. 1860
Carr, J. P.
New York, N.Y., c. 1810
Carr, James
Ohio, c. 1830. Peddler of clocks.
Carr, James
Lowell, Mass., c. 1830. In business with William Moulton.
Carr, Lyman
Manchester, N.H., 1850–1860
Carr, Norman C.
Concord, N.H., n.d.
Carr, T. P.
New York, N.Y., c. 1810
Carrell, Daniel
Philadelphia, Pa., 1780s; Charleston, S.C., 1790–1800
Carrell, John
Philadelphia, Pa., 1791–1793. Adv. in directories.

Carrell, John & Daniel
Philadelphia, Pa., c. 1785
Carryl, Patrick
New York, N.Y., c. 1750
Carson, George
York, Pa., c. 1820
Carson, Thomas
Albany, N.Y., c. 1830
Carter, Jacob
Philadelphia, Pa., c. 1805
Carter, Jacob
Concord, N.H., c. 1840
Carter, Thomas
Philadelphia, Pa., 1823–1824
Carter, William
Philadelphia, Pa., c. 1683
Carter, L. F. and W.
Bristol, Conn., c. 1860
Carter, W. W. & L. F.
Bristol, Conn., 1863–1868. Manufactured calendar clocks under the patents of Lewis and Burwell.
Carter & Weller
Stockbridge, N.Y., c. 1830. Probably assembled movements.
Carvalks, D. N.
Philadelphia, Pa., c. 1846
Carvallo, N.
Charleston, S.C., c. 1780
Carver, Jacob
Philadelphia, Pa., 1785–1799
Carwithin, William
Charleston, S.C., c. 1733. Cabinet-maker.
Case, Erastus
Bristol, Conn., 1830–1837
Case, Harvey
Bristol, Conn., 1830–1837
Case & Birge
Bristol, Conn., c. 1830
Case, Dyer, Wadsworth & Co.
Augusta, Ga., 1835. Assembled clocks.
Case & Robinson
Bristol, Conn., 1845–1855. Also made toys and other items.
Case, Willard & Co.
Bristol, Conn., c. 1835
Cassal, Abraham
Philadelphia, Pa., c. 1835
Castan, Stephen
Philadelphia, Pa., c. 1810
Castan, Stephen and Company
Philadelphia, Pa., c. 1819
Castens, J. M.
Charleston, S.C., c. 1770
Caswell, A.
New York, N.Y., c. 1850
Cate, Simeon
Sanbornton, N.H., 1820–1830
Cater, Stephen
Charleston, S.C., 1744–1748. Also repaired clocks and watches.
Cathcart, A. H.
Marshall, Mich., c. 1860
Catherwood, John
Charleston, S.C., c. 1760
Catlin, Joel
Augusta, Ga., c. 1820
Cave, Joseph
West Goshen and West Chester, Pa., 1819–1835. Also Marshalltown and Philadelphia, Pa.
Cecil, Charles
Philadelphia, Pa., 1800–1810

Cellers, John
Chillicothe, Ohio, c. 1810
Chadwick, Joseph
Boscawen, N.H., 1810–1831. Brother-in-law of Benjamin Morrill. Apprenticed to Timothy Chadwick.
Chamberlain, Benj. M.
Salem, Mass., 1840–1870
Chamberlain, Charles
Philadelphia, Pa., c. 1830
Chamberlain, Cyrus
New Haven, Conn., 1840–1850
Chamberlain, John
Cincinnati, Ohio, c. 1810. Partner in Read, Watson and Chamberlain.
Chamberlain, Lewis
Elkton, Md., c. 1824; Philadelphia, Pa., 1830–1850
Chamberlin, William
Towanda, Pa., 1838–1850
Champlin, John
New London, Conn., c. 1770
Champney, L. C.
Troy, N.Y., c. 1830
Champney, Lewis
Philadelphia, Pa., c. 1840
Champney & Felton
Troy, N.Y., c. 1850. Could be dealers.
Chandlee, Benjamin
Philadelphia, Pa., 1715–1740. Son-in-law and apprentice of Abel Cottey.
Chandlee, Benjamin, Jr.
Nottingham, Pa., 1750–1790
Chandlee, Benjamin III
Baltimore, Md., 1814–1835. Son of Goldsmith Chandlee. Continued his father's business.
Chandlee, Ellis
Nottingham, Pa., 1775–1800. Son of Benjamin Chandlee, Jr. Worked with his father.
Chandlee, Goldsmith
Stephensburg and Winchester, Va., 1780–1815. Son of Benjamin Chandlee, Jr.
Chandlee, Goldsmith, Jr.
Winchester, Va., c. 1820. Son of Goldsmith Chandlee.
Chandlee, Isaac
Nottingham, Pa., c. 1800
Chandlee, John
Wilmington, Del., 1775–1805
Chandlee, Veazey
Maryland, c. 1845
Chandlee & Holloway
Baltimore, Md., 1810–1824
Chandlee & Sons
Nottingham, Pa., c. 1770
Chandler, Abiel
Concord, N.H., 1830–1860. Son of Timothy Chandler.
Chandler, John
Suffolk, Md., c. 1774
Chandler, Timothy, Major
Concord, N.H., 1783–1829. Besides clocks, he made wool cards. Built factory in Concord, 1809.
Chandler and Ward
Concord, N.H., c. 1840
Chapin, Aaron and Elliphalet
Windsor and Hartford, Conn., 1780–1800
Chapin, Edwin G.
Buffalo, N.Y., c. 1835

Chapin, Aaron and Son
Hartford, Conn., 1825–1830
Chapin, S. & A.
Northampton, Mass., c. 1835
Chapman, C. H.
Easthampton, Mass., c. 1860
Chapman, Charles
Troy, N.Y., 1838–1839
Chappel & Sartwell
Busti, near Jamestown, N.Y., and Chautauqua, N.Y., 1830–1840. Hang-up tall-case movements; wag-on-wall.
Charles, Lewis
Philadelphia, Pa., c. 1837
Chase, George
New York, N.Y., c. 1850
Chase, John F.
Newark, N.J., c. 1850
Chase, John W.
Hopkinton, N.H., c. 1810
Chase, Samuel
Newburyport, Mass., c. 1850
Chase, Timothy
Belfast, Me., 1820–1840
Chase, William H.
Salem, Mass., c. 1840
Chaudron, Edward
Philadelphia, Pa., c. 1816
Chaudron, J.
Philadelphia, Pa., c. 1795
Chaudron, P.
Philadelphia, Pa., c. 1795
Chaudron, Simon
Philadelphia, Pa., 1798–1815
Chaudron & Rasch
Philadelphia, Pa., c. 1810
Cheney, Ashel
East Hartford and Northfield, Conn., c. 1790. Son of Benjamin.
Cheney, Benjamin
Manchester, Conn., 1740–1800. To Hartford, Conn. Benjamin Willard was one of his apprentices. Made brass- and wood-movement clocks.
Cheney, Benjamin, Jr.
Berlin, Conn., 1793–1833. Vandalia, Ill., 1834–1840s. Son of Benjamin.
Cheney, Elisha
Berlin, Conn., 1793–1833. Vandalia, Ill., 1834–1840s. Son of Benjamin, Jr.
Cheney, Martin
Windsor, Vt., c. 1790. Son of Benjamin, Sr.
Cheney, Olcott
Middletown and Berlin, Conn., 1810–1840. Son of Elisha.
Cheney, Russel
Putney and Thetford, Vt., 1790–1800. Son of Benjamin, Sr.
Cheney, Silas
East Hartford, Conn., c. 1750
Cheney, Timothy
East Hartford, Conn., 1750–1790. Brother of Benjamin, Sr.
Cheeseman, James L.
New York, N.Y., c. 1830
Chelsea Clock Co.
Chelsea, Mass., 1897
Cherry, James
Philadelphia, Pa., c. 1840. Listed in directories.
Cheshire Clock Co.
Cheshire, Conn., c. 1880

Chester, George
  New York, N.Y., c. 1740
Chester, Richard: 1770?–1816
  York, Pa., c. 1800
Child, Henry T.
  Philadelphia, Pa., c. 1840
Child, John
  Philadelphia, Pa., 1810–1830
Child, S. J.
  Lyons, N.Y., c. 1830
Child, Samuel T.
  Philadelphia, Pa., c. 1840
Child, Thomas T.
  Philadelphia, Pa., c. 1840
Child, True W.
  Boston, Mass., c. 1823
Child, S. & T.
  Philadelphia, Pa., c. 1850
Childs, Ezekiel
  Philadelphia, Pa., 1830–1835
Childs, John
  Philadelphia, Pa., c. 1835
Chipperfield, N. W.
  New York, N.Y., c. 1850
Chipperfield, N. W. & Co.
  New York, N.Y., c. 1850
Chittenden, Austin
  Lexington, Mass., 1831–1837
Chittenden and Burr
  Lexington, Mass., c. 1830. Probably a
  casing shop.
Choate, George W.
  New Bedford, Mass., 1840–1850
Chollot, John B.
  Philadelphia, Pa., c. 1815
Christ, Daniel
  Kutztown, Pa., early 19th century
Chrystler, William
  Philadelphia, Pa., c. 1820
Church, Edward
  New Haven, Conn., 1840–1850
Church, Joseph
  Hartford, Conn., 1820–1830
Church, Lorenzo
  Hartford, Conn., c. 1840
Church, William F.
  Skowhegan, Me., c. 1830
Churchill, Joel
  Bristol, Conn., c. 1835
Cincinnati Time Recorder Co.
  Cincinnati, Ohio, c. 1936
Cito, J. C.
  Boston, Mass., 1810 or 1820. Probably
  a dealer.
Clackner, John
  Troy, N.Y., c. 1830
Claggett, H.
  Newport, R.I., 1720–1740
Claggett, Thomas
  Newport, R.I., 1740–1790
Claggett, William
  Boston, Mass., 1714–1716; Newport,
  R.I., 1716–1749. Also an engraver;
  engraved plates for paper money of
  R.I.
Clapp, John
  Roxbury, Mass., 1764–1840. Cabinet-
  maker.
Clapp, Preserved
  Amherst, Mass., c. 1750
Clapp & Brothers
  Rutland, Vt., c. 1830
Clapp & Co.
  Augusta, Ga., c. 1820

Clapp, Cook & Co.
  Waterbury, Conn., c. 1815
Clapp & Cowles
  Plainville, Conn., 1870–1889
Clapp & Engle
  Hazelton, Pa., n.d.
Clapp, Ephraim & Charles
  Philadelphia, Pa., 1806–1811
Clapp, Gilbert & Brown
  New York, N.Y., c. 1840
Clapp, Jesse W. & Co.
  Philadelphia, Pa., 1809–1814
Clapp & Latham
  Charleston, S.C., c. 1780
Clark, A. J.
  Circleville, Ohio, n.d.
Clark, A. N.
  Plainville, Conn., c. 1888
Clark, Amos
  Lewisberry, York Co., Pa., 1790–1810
Clark, B. H.
  Newcomerstown, Ohio, c. 1840
Clark, Benjamin
  Philadelphia, Pa., c. 1790
Clark, Benjamin S.
  Wilmington, Del., 1837–1850
Clark, Benjamin W.
  Philadelphia, Pa., c. 1830
Clark, Charles
  Philadelphia, Pa., c. 1810
Clark, Charles
  Fayetteville, N.C., c. 1820
Clark, Daniel
  Waterbury, Conn., 1815–1820
Clark, David
  Charleston, S.C., 1760–1780
Clark, Edward
  Philadelphia, Pa., 1797
Clark, Elias
  Philadelphia, Pa., c. 1800
Clark, Ellis
  Philadelphia, Pa., 1810–1840
Clark, Ellis, Jr.
  Philadelphia, Pa., c. 1840
Clark, Ephraim
  Philadelphia, Pa., 1780–1800
Clark, Gabriel
  Baltimore, Md., c. 1830
Clark, George D.
  Coosade, Ala., c. 1875
Clark, Heman
  Plymouth Hollow, Conn., c. 1807.
  Prolific maker of shelf clocks.
Clark, Horace G.
  Weston, Vt., c. 1830
Clark, Horatio
  Vermont, c. 1800
Clark, Jesse
  Philadelphia, Pa., c. 1810
Clark, Joseph
  New York, N.Y., c. 1768
Clark, Joseph
  Danbury, Conn., c. 1800
Clark, Levi
  Norwalk, Conn., n.d.
Clark, Lucius
  Winsted, Conn., c. 1841
Clark, Philip
  Albany, N.Y., c. 1835
Clark, Richard
  Charleston, S.C., c. 1765
Clark, Robert
  Charleston, S.C., c. 1780

Clark, Russell,
  Woodstock, Vt., c. 1840
Clark, Thomas
  Boston, Mass., c. 1765
Clark, Thomas W.
  Philadelphia, Pa., 1830–1850
Clark, William H.
  Palmer, Mass., 1850–1860
Clark, Benjamin & Edward
  Philadelphia, Pa., 1790–1810
Clark, Benjamin & Ellis
  Philadelphia, Pa., c. 1820s
Clark & Co., F.
  Augusta, Ga., c. 1820
Clark, Ephraim & Charles
  Philadelphia, Pa., c. 1800
Clark, Gilbert & Brown
  New York, N.Y., c. 1840
Clark, Gilbert & Co.
  Winchester, Conn., 1800–1850
Clark and Hartley
  Philadelphia, Pa., c. 1835
Clark, Jesse, W. & C.
  Philadelphia, Pa., c. 1811
Clark & Latham
  Charleston, S.C., 1770–1790
Clark & Turner
  Fayetteville, N.C., c. 1820
Clarke, Ambrose
  Baltimore, Md., c. 1780
Clarke, C. W.
  Philadelphia, Pa., n.d.
Clarke, Charles
  Philadelphia, Pa., 1806–1811
Clarke, E. M.
  Lowell, Mass., n.d.
Clarke, George G.
  Providence, R.I., 1824
Clarke, George H.
  New York, N.Y., n.d.
Clarke, George R.
  Utica, N.Y., c. 1820
Clarke, John
  New York, N.Y., 1770–1790; Phila-
  delphia, Pa., 1790–1800
Clarke, Lucius
  Winsted, Conn., c. 1841
Clarke, Sylvester
  Salem Bridge, Conn., c. 1830
Clarke and Brown
  Manchester, N.H., c. 1880
Clarke and Dixon
  Manchester, N.H., c. 1880
Clarke & Ellis
  Philadelphia, Pa., 1811–1845
Clarke, Gilbert & Co.
  Winsted, Conn., 1842
Clarke & Hutchinson
  Philadelphia, Pa., 1810–1815
Claton, C.
  Philadelphia, Pa., n.d.
Claton, Elias B.
  Philadelphia, Pa., c. 1848
Claude, Abraham
  Annapolis, Md., c. 1780
Claude & French
  Annapolis, Md., c. 1780
Claudon, J. G.
  Charleston, S.C., c. 1760
Clausen, A. C.
  Pat. Oct. 9, 1883, for "Ignatz" clock.
Claymore, Robert
  Germantown, Pa., 1765–1780. Slave of
  Dr. Christopher Witt.

Clayton, C.
Philadelphia, Pa., n.d.
Clayton, John
Charleston, S.C., c. 1743
Clayton, Richard
Cincinnati, Ohio, c. 1830
Clayton, Samuel
Brooklyn, N.Y., 1840–1850
Clein, John
Philadelphia, Pa., 1830–1833
Clemens, Moses
New York, N.Y., c. 1740
Clerc, Henry
New York, N.Y., c. 1810
Cleveland, Benjamin N.
New York, N.Y., and Newark, N.J.,
1790–1830
Cleveland, Francis
Zanesville, Ohio, c. 1810
Cleveland, William
Salem, Mass., 1778–1800. Probably
uncle of William Cleveland.
Cleveland, William
New London, Norwich, and Salem,
Conn.; working 1792–1820. Grand-
father of President Grover Cleveland.
Apprenticed to Thomas Harland.
Clifford, Ebenezer
Kensington, Exeter, N.H., c. 1780
Coad, Frank A. M., Rev.
Hillsboro, N.H., c. 1800
Coates, Isaac
Philadelphia, Pa., 1835–1839
Coates, William
Buffalo, N.Y., 1835–1839
Cobb, J. L.
Winchester, Conn., n.d.
Cobb, Z. B.
Cincinnati, Ohio, c. 1850
Cochran, George
West Chester, Pa., 1799–1807
Cochran, L.
Northfield Centre, Vt., c. 1850
Cochrane, A. Thomas
New York, N.Y., c. 1810
Cockrell, James
Philadelphia, Pa., c. 1843
Cocks, James
New York, N.Y., c. 1810
Coe, Benjamin
Alexander, N.Y., 1850–1860
Coe, Russell
New York, N.Y., c. 1840
Coe, Russell
Meriden, Conn., 1850s
Coe and Company
New York, N.Y., c. 1850
Coffin, Henry T.
Nobleboro, Me., c. 1850
Coffin, Simeon
Yarmouth, Me., 1820–1840. Casemaker.
Coggeshall, G.
Bristol, Conn., c. 1810
Cogswell, Henry
Salem, Mass., c. 1854
Cogswell, John Cleveland
Salem, Mass., c. 1820
Cogswell, Joseph
Norwich, Conn., 1780–1800
Cogswell, Robert: 1791–1862
Possible dry goods business, c. 1837.

Cohen, Thomas
Chillicothe, Ohio, 1800, 1810; Saint
Louis, Mo., 1840–1850
Cole, David
New York, N.Y., c. 1840
Cole, James C.
Rochester, N.H., 1810–1820. Watch
and clockmaker.
Cole, R. P.
Ludlow, Vt., c. 1830
Cole, Shubael
Great Falls, N.H., 1830–1850
Colebrook
Connecticut, c. 1840
Coleman, James
Philadelphia, Pa., c. 1833
Coleman, John
Philadelphia, Pa., c. 1848
Coleman, Nathaniel: 1765–1842
Burlington, N.J., 1787–1835
Coleman, Samuel
Trenton, N.J., after 1842
Coles, John
Boston, Mass., c. 1810. Dial painter.
Collins, James: 1802–1844
Goffstown, N.H., c. 1820
Collins, O.
Prospect, Conn., c. 1830
Collins, Stephen
Goffstown, N.H., 1847
Collins, W. A.
Troy, N.Y. Listed in directories 1840–
1841.
Collins, William
New York, N.Y., c. 1850
Collins & Co.
Cranston, R. I., 1830–1850
Collom, David W.
Philadelphia, Pa., c. 1846
Colonial Clock Co.
New York, N.Y., n.d.
Colonial Mfg. Co.
Zeeland, Mich., 1929
Colt, John
Paterson, N.J., c. 1825
Colvin, Walter
Trenton, N.J., c. 1785
Compton, William,
Rochester, N.Y., c. 1845
Comstock, L. F.
Plymouth, Conn., c. 1830
Comstock and Minor
Plymouth, Conn., c. 1830
Conant, Elias
Bridgewater, Mass., 1770–1810; Lynn,
Mass., c. 1811
Conant, H.
New York, N.Y., 1889. Inventor of
isochronal clock.
Conant, Nathaniel Peabody
Danvers, Mass., c. 1850
Conant, W. S.
New York, N.Y., c. 1820
Conant & Sperry
New York, N.Y., c. 1840
Conger, John
Bristol, Conn., c. 1830
Coning, Richard
Boston, Mass., c. 1795
Conklin & Ritchey
Clinton, Ill., 1850–1860. Probably
dealers.

Conlyn, Thomas
Carlisle, Cumberland Co., Pa., c. 1835.
Probably dealer only.
Connecticut Clock Company
New York, N.Y., c. 1870
Conn. Protective Clock Co.
Bristol, Conn., c. 1849. Conglomerate
of eleven makers including the In-
grahams, Brewsters, Birge, Manross,
Brown, T. Terry, Smith, Goodrich,
Gilbert, and Jerome.
Conover, David F.
Philadelphia, Pa., n.d.
Conrad, Osborne
Philadelphia, Pa., c. 1841
Conrad, Osborne & Co.
Philadelphia, Pa., c. 1850
Constant, Francis
Kingston, N.Y., c. 1850
Converse, Pascal
New Haven, Conn., 1840–1850
Converse and Crane
Boston, Mass., c. 1865
Conway, Thomas A.
Baltimore, Md., c. 1820
Cook, Alex
n.p.; n.d.
Cook, Benjamin E.
Northampton, Mass., 1840–1850
Cook, Erastus
Rochester, N.Y., c. 1820
Cook, Frederick B.
Columbia, Lancaster Co., Pa., 1828–
1832; York, Pa., 1832–1842
Cook, Harry
Poughkeepsie, N.Y., c. 1815
Cook, Samuel
Waterbury, Conn., 1820–1830
Cook, William G.
Baltimore, Md., 1810–1820
Cook, Zenas
Waterbury, Conn., 1815–1820
Cook and Jacques
Trenton, N.J., c. 1880
Cook & Stillwell
Rochester, N.Y., 1840–1850
Cooke, Benjamin
Philadelphia, Pa., c. 1860. Probably
dealer.
Cooke, Samuel
Waterbury, Conn., c. 1830
Cooke's Sons, B. G.
Philadelphia, Pa., c. 1853. Clock whole-
salers.
Cooley, Henry P.
Cooperstown and Troy, N.Y., c. 1830
Coolidge, Henry J.
New Haven, Conn. Adv. 1787.
Cooper, Charles
Lebanon, Pa., 1800–1820
Cooper, John
New York, N.Y., c. 1840
Cooper, Joseph
Columbia, S.C., c. 1840
Cooper, Joseph B.
Philadelphia, Pa., c. 1840
Cooper, Robert
Philadelphia, Pa., c. 1850
Cooper, Samuel B.
Philadelphia, Pa., c. 1840
Cooper, T.
Olneyville, R.I., c. 1849

Cope, Jacob
Watsontown, Pa., c. 1800
Cope, John
Lancaster, Pa., c. 1800
Copeland, Robert
Baltimore, Md., 1790–1800
Coppert, T.
Olneyville, R.I., c. 1840
Coppuck, George
Mount Holly, N.J., 1824–1860
Corbett, Thomas
Canterbury, N.H., c. 1810. Shaker clockmaker.
Corey, P.
Providence, R.I., c. 1848
Corgee, Arthur
Philadelphia, Pa., c. 1820
Corl, Abraham
East Nantmeal Twp. "Coventry," Chester Co., Pa., c. 1800
Corliss, A. G.
Portland, Me., c. 1860
Corliss, James
Weare, N.H., c. 1800
Cornell, Walter
Newport, R.I., 1790–1820
Cornwell, Nathan
Darien, Ga., c. 1820
Cortelyou, Jacques: 1781–1822
n.p.; c. 1805
Corvazier, Edward
Philadelphia, Pa., c. 1846
Corwin, Eben M.
n.p.; c. 1860
Cory, Lewis
Rahway, N.J., 1820–1840
Coryton, Josiah
Alexandria, Va., 1780–1800
Cotley, Abel
Philadelphia, Pa., 1690–1705. Probably earliest American clockmaker.
Couch, Stow and Co.
Rock Springs, Tenn., n.d. Probably dealer.
Couper, Robert
Philadelphia, Pa., n.d.
Covell, Gray & Co.
New York, N.Y., c. 1872
Cowan, William
Richmond, Va., c. 1819
Cowbery, S.
Westmoreland, N.H., c. 1815
Cowles, Deeming
Farmington, Conn., n.d.
Cowles, Irwin
n.p.; c. 1865
Cowley, L. D.
Lagrange, Ind., c. 1860
Cowper, John
Philadelphia, Pa., 1710–1720
Cox, Benjamin
Philadelphia, Pa., 1810–1815
Cox, James
New York, N.Y., c. 1810
Cox & Clark
New York, N.Y., c. 1832
Cozens, J. B.
Philadelphia, Pa., 1815–1825
Cozens, Josiah B.
Philadelphia, Pa., 1815–1830
Crafte, Jacob
Shepherdstown, Va., 1790–1820

Craig, James
Williamsburg, Va., c. 1772
Craig, John B.
Pittsburgh, Pa., c. 1845
Cranch, Richard
Boston and Braintree, Mass., 1765–1775
Cranch, William
Boston, Mass., n.d.
Crane, Aaron D.
Newark and Belleville, N.J., 1830–1850. Torsion pendulum clocks.
Crane, John E.
Lowell, Mass., 1840–1850
Crane, Jonas
Newark, N.J., c. 1850
Crane, Simeon
Canton, Mass., c. 1810
Crane, William
Canton, Mass., c. 1780
Craven, Alfred
Philadelphia, Pa., c. 1843
Crawford, William
Oakham, Mass., c. 1770
Crawley, Abraham
Boston, Mass., c. 1816
Crawley, C.
Philadelphia, Pa., c. 1820
Crawley, John
Philadelphia, Pa., c. 1800
Crehore, Charles Crane: 1793–1879
Boston, Mass., c. 1825. Cases for Willards and others.
Cret, C.
Orwigsburg, Pa., c. 1800
Creuse, Benjamin
Philadelphia, Pa., c. 1772
Crisswell, Isaac
Philadelphia, Pa., 1840–1850
Critcher, James
Candia, N.H., c. 1800
Crittenden, Charles
Tallmadge, Ohio, c. 1830
Crittenden, Simeon
Guilford, Conn., 1820–1850
Crocker, J. R.
Valley Falls, R.I., c. 1860
Crocker, Orasmus
East Meriden, Conn., c. 1830
Crocker, William
Philadelphia, Pa., c. 1830; New York, N.Y., c. 1840
Cromwell, Wm.
New York, N.Y., c. 1820
Crooke and Phelps
Northampton, Mass., n.d.
Crosby, C. A.
Boston, Mass., c. 1875
Crosby, Charles
Albany, N.Y., c. 1830
Crosby, D. S.
New York, N.Y., c. 1850
Crosby & Vosburg
New York, N.Y., c. 1850
Cross, James
Rochester, N.H., n.d.
Cross, Theodore
Boston, Mass., c. 1775
Crouchley, Thomas W. H.
New York, N.Y., c. 1840
Crow, George
Wilmington, Del., 1740–1770. Clocks and surveyors' instruments.

Crow, George, Jr.
Wilmington, Del., c. 1800
Crow, John
Wilmington, Del., c. 1790. Probably dealer.
Crow, Thomas
Wilmington, Del., c. 1770; Philadelphia, Pa., c. 1790; West Chester, Pa., 1800
Crowley, John
Philadelphia, Pa., c. 1813
Crowley & Farr
Philadelphia, Pa., c. 1820
Crowther, William
New York, N.Y., c. 1820
Crum & Barber
Unionville, Conn., 1830–1840
Cummens, William
Roxbury, Mass., 1788-1834. Maker of long case, shelf clocks, and timepieces. Usually put on his clocks, "Warranted by William Cummens, Roxbury." Apprenticed to Simon Willard.
Cummens, William, Jr.
Roxbury, Mass., c. 1816. Apprentice of his father, William, Sr.
Cummings, John
Catskill and Albany, N.Y., c. 1780
Cummings, S.
Concord, N.H., c. 1790. Worked for Timothy Chandler.
Cure, Jule F.
Philadelphia, Pa., 1839–1840
Cure, Louis
Philadelphia, Pa., 1811–1819; Brooklyn, N.Y., c. 1830
Currier, E.
Hopkinton, N.H., n.d.
Currier, Edmund
Salem, Mass., 1820–1830
Currier, John
Salem, Mass., c. 1830
Currier, T. D.
Waldoboro, Me., c. 1820
Currier & Foster
Salem, Mass., 1790–1820
Currier and Trott
Boston, Mass., c. 1830
Curtis, Benjamin
Boston, Mass., c. 1805. Brother of Samuel and Lemuel.
Curtis, Charles
Roxbury, Mass., n.d. Dial maker.
Curtis, Joel
Waterbury, Conn., c. 1814. Worked with Dimon Bradley.
Curtis, Lemuel
Concord, Mass., 1810–1818; Burlington, Vt., c. 1819. One of the great clockmakers. Made banjos, lyres, shelf lyres, and girandoles.
Curtis, Lewis
Farmington, Conn., 1795–1820; Saint Charles, Md., 1820–1835; Hazel Green, Wis., 1836–1840s
Curtis, Samuel
Boston, Mass., c. 1815. Dial maker and painter. Worked with Spencer Nolen.
Curtis, Solomon
Philadelphia, Pa., c. 1790
Curtis, Thomas
Lowell, Mass., c. 1860

Curtis, W.
Newburyport, Mass., c. 1800
Curtis & Clark
Plymouth, Conn., c. 1825
Curtis & Dunning
Concord, Mass., 1813–1815; Burlington, Vt., c. 1819
Curtis, H., & Co.
Meriden, Conn., c. 1830
Curtis, J., & Co.
Cairo, N.Y., c. 1830
Curtis & Marsh
Farmington, Conn., c. 1830
Cushing, George D.
Braintree, Mass., 1800–1810
Cushing, Peter H.
Braintree, Mass., n.d.
Cushing, Theodore
Hingham, Mass., c. 1808
Cushman Manufacturing Co.
New Haven, Conn., c. 1910
Custer, Daniel
Reading, Pa., 1810–1820
Custer, Isaac
Norristown, Montgomery Co., Pa., c. 1820. Brother of Jacob.
Custer, Jacob D.
Norristown, Pa., c. 1830
Cutler, John N.
Albany, N.Y., 1829–1850
Cutler, John N., Jr.
Albany, N.Y., c. 1842
Cutley, Able
Philadelphia, Pa., c. 1720
Cyclo Clock Company
New York, N.Y., c. 1890

Dadin, Louis
Charleston, S.C., c. 1840
Daft, Thomas
Philadelphia, Pa., 1775–1780; New York, N.Y., 1786–1790
Daggett, Gilbert
Providence, R.I., c. 1860. Son of T. Daggett.
Daggett, James
Saint Louis, Mo., c. 1820
Daggett, T.
Providence, R.I., c. 1840
Dakin, James
Boston, Mass., 1790–1810. Listed in directories.
Dalziel, John
New York, N.Y., c. 1790
Dana, Daniel
Providence, R.I., 1800–1840
Dana, George
Providence, R.I., 1800–1824
Dana, Payton
Providence, R.I., c. 1849
Dana, Payton & Nathaniel
Providence, R.I., c. 1800
Dana & Whittaker
Providence, R.I., 1805–1825
Daniel, G.
Cincinnati, Ohio, c. 1820. Worked for Luman Watson.
Daniel, G. I.
Rome, N.Y., c. 1840
Daniel, George C.
Elizabeth City, N.C., c. 1830. Adv. opening of shop in 1829. Later moved to Halifax.

Daniel, Henry H.
White River Village, Vt., n.d.
Danner, Alexander
Lancaster, Pa., 1785–1840. Made cases for Lancaster clockmakers.
Danner, Jacob
Lancaster, Pa., c. 1820
Darby & Harder
New York, N.Y., c. 1840
Darlington, Benedict
Westtown, Chester Co., Pa., 1800–1840. Probably casemaker only. No clocks known.
Darrow, Elijah
Bristol, Conn., 1810–1850. Painted dials and tablets, made some clocks, with Jeromes and Darrow.
Darrow, Franklin C.
Bristol, Conn., 1850–1865. Made clock tablets.
Darrow & Matthews
Bristol, Conn., 1824–1826
Darrow, William, & Co.
Bristol, Conn., 1834–1836
Dart, Lewis
Jersey City, N.J., c. 1850
Daumont, Peter
Indianapolis, Ind., c. 1860
Davenport, James
Salem, Mass., c. 1780
Davenport, Joseph
Newton Upper Falls, Mass., c. 1800. Made tall case clocks.
Davenport, William
Philadelphia, Pa., c. 1800
Davidson, Barzillai
Norwich, Conn., c. 1770. Could also have been dealer.
Davidson, Barzillai
New Haven, Conn., c. 1825. Possibly son of Barzillai.
Davidson, Samuel
Maryland, c. 1775
Davies, B. F. and T.
Ithaca, N.Y., c. 1870
Davies, D.
Wellsburg, Va., 1830–1840
Davies, H. J.
New York, N.Y., c. 1855
Davies, Thomas
Utica, N.Y., c. 1820
Davies, Thomas
New York, N.Y., c. 1845. Was issued patent for lever movement used by Seth Thomas.
Davis, Ari
Boston, Mass., c. 1840. Made and repaired chronometers.
Davis, C. P.
Elizabethtown, N.J., n.d.
Davis, Caleb
Woodstock, Vt., c. 1815
Davis, D. P.
Roxbury, Mass., 1840–1850. With E. Howard in Howard and Davis.
Davis, Gabriel
Manheim, Lancaster Co., Pa., c. 1780
Davis, H. J.
New York, N.Y., c. 1860. Made illuminated alarm clock.
Davis, John
Fairfield, Conn., c. 1750. Church records indicate he was to keep clock in church in good repair.

Davis, John
New Holland, Pa., c. 1800. Made and painted dials for tall clocks.
Davis, Peter
Jaffrey, N.H., n.d.
Davis, Phineas
York, Pa., c. 1800. Lewis Miller's sketch books, owned by Historical Society of York County, contain a picture of Davis at work with this data: "In 1806 made a watch pocket clock which he sent to London." Davis was watch and clockmaker, silversmith, steamboat builder, and locomotive builder for the B&O., also a bell founder. His iron steamboat, *Codorus*, navigated on the Susquehanna River.
Davis, Richard
Philadelphia, Pa., c. 1830
Davis, Riley
New Bern, N.C., c. 1850
Davis, Robert
Concord, N.H., c. 1810
Davis, Robert, Jr.
Concord, N.H., c. 1824. Probably son of Robert.
Davis, Samuel
Pittsburgh, Pa., 1810–1820
Davis, Samuel
Boston, Mass., c. 1830
Davis, Thomas
New York, N.Y., c. 1840
Davis, W. M.
Morrisville, N.Y., c. 1825
Davis, William
Boston, Mass., 1683–1690
Davis & Babbitt
Providence, R.I., c. 1810
Davis and Barbour
Bristol, Conn., c. 1850. Made cases for E. Ingraham.
Davis Clock Co.
Columbus, Miss., c. 1880
Davis, Palmer and Comp.
Boston, Mass., c. 1840
Davis, Posley Comp.
Boston, Mass., n.d.
Davis, Toklas & Co.
San Francisco, Calif., c. 1880
Davison, C.
New York, N.Y., c. 1830
Dawes, Robert
Boston, Mass., c. 1842
Dawrey, Charles D.
Brooklyn, N.Y., c. 1850. Clock and dial painter.
Dawson, Jonas
Philadelphia, Pa., 1813–1824
Dawson, Thomas S.
Wilmington, Del., n.d.
Day, Benjamin
Euclid, Ohio, n.d.
Day, Israel
Baltimore, Md., c. 1802
Day, D. D. and R.
Westfield, Mass., n.d.
Day, D. N. & R.
Westfield, Mass., 1820–1840
Dayton, John D.
Brooklyn, N.Y., 1840-1850
Dean, George
Salem, Mass., c. 1800
Dean, William
Salem, Mass., c. 1800

Dean, William
Pleasant Valley, N.Y., c. 1820
Dean and Company
Salem, Mass., c. 1800
DeBenneville, N.
Philadelphia, Pa., 1820–1822
De Berard
Utica, N.Y., c. 1820
Debruhl, Michael Samuel
Charleston, S.C., 1795–1810. In partnership with Mary M. Dunsceth until 1804.
Deems, John
Baltimore, Md., c. 1842
DeForest & Co.
Salem Bridge, Conn., c. 1832. Made buttons as well as 8-day clocks.
DeGiy, Lewis
Boston, Mass., c. 1800
De Huff, A.
York, Pa., to c. 1850
Deibert, S. F.
Catawissa, Pa., n.d. Tall clocks known.
DeLachaux, Philip H.
Philadelphia, Pa., 1820–1822
Delaplaine, James
New York, N.Y., 1780–1800
De Long, Charles
Glens Falls, N.Y., c. 1890. Worked for Jones and Bardmore, M. Eliasoff & Co., Marsh and Hoffman, and McIntyre Watch Company.
Delong, Peter Angle: 1839–
De Longuemaire
Charleston, S.C., 1690–1700
Deloste, Francis
Baltimore, Md., c. 1817
DeLuxe Clock & Mfg. Co.
New York, N.Y., 1929
Delvin, Mark H.
Salem, Mass., c. 1864
Demilt, Benjamin
New York, N.Y., 1800–1820
Demilt, Samuel
New York, N.Y., c. 1840
Demilt, Thomas
New York, N.Y., 1800–1820; moved to Philadelphia, c. 1820
Demilt, Thomas and Benjamin
New York, N.Y., c. 1800. Listed in directory.
Deming, Phineas
Vienna, Ohio, c. 1830
Denham, John
Philadelphia, Pa., c. 1845
Dennett, Charles
Rochester, N.H., c. 1820
Derby, Charles
Salem, Mass., 1840–1850
Derby, John
New York, N.Y., c. 1810
De Reiemer & Mead
Ithaca, N.Y., 1830–1831
Derry Mfg. Co.
Derry, N.H., n.d.
De Saules & Co.
New York, N.Y., c. 1830
Deschamps, Francis
Philadelphia, Pa., 1846–1849
Deuble, G. M.
Philadelphia, Pa., c. 1820; Manahoy, Pa., and Canton, Ohio, c. 1830
Deuconner, G.
Philadelphia, Pa., c. 1810

Deull, James
Philadelphia, Pa., n.d.
Devacht, François
Gallipolis, Ohio, c. 1790
Devacht, Joseph
Gallipolis, Ohio, c. 1795
Develin, J. & M.
Philadelphia, Pa., c. 1848. Listed in directories.
Deverell, John
Boston, Mass., 1789–1803
Dewey, I.
Chelsea, Vt., n.d.
Dewitt, Garett
Sparta, Ga., c. 1840
De Wolf, Thomas
Westtown, Pa., 1810–1815. Cased wood movements.
Dexter, Dana
Roxbury, Mass., c. 1860
Dexter, H.
Stockbridge, N.Y., 1830–1840
Dexter, Joseph
Providence, R.I., c. 1820
Dexter, William
Stockbridge, N.Y., c. 1830. Possibly an assembler.
Dey, Alexander
Syracuse, N.Y., c. 1885. Patented time recorder made by Dey Time Register Co.
Dey Time Register Co.
Syracuse, N.Y., c. 1893
De Young, Michael
Baltimore, Md., c. 1832
Dickenson
Boston, Mass., c. 1800s. Tall case clock known.
Dickenson, Charles
Zanesville, Ohio, c. 1815
Dickenson, John
Philadelphia, Pa., 1822–1825
Dickenson, Richard
Mount Holly, N.J., 1760–1770
Dickenson, William
Philadelphia, Pa., 1843–1848
Dickerson, John
Morristown, N.J., 1770–1790. Adv. for apprentice, 1778. Migrated to Indiana.
Dickey, Thomas
Marietta, Lancaster Co., Pa., 1810–1820; Middletown, Pa., c. 1820; Harrisburg, Pa., c. 1821
Dickinson, John
Philadelphia, Pa., c. 1822
Dickson, White, & Co.
Philadelphia, Pa., c. 1837
Didier, Pierre
Gallipolis, Ohio, 1790–1800. Migrated to Saint Louis, Mo.
Diehl, Jacob
Reading, Berks Co., Pa., 1790–1820. Worked in shop of Daniel Rose during his absence in 1808.
Differential Clock Co.
Grand Rapids, Mich., c. 1910
Dikeman, A.
New York, N.Y., 1780–1800
Dikeman, Edward B.
Grand Rapids, Mich., 1837–1860
Dillon, J. F. M.
Adel, Iowa, c. 1860

Dillon, T. E.
New York, N.Y., c. 1860. Made chronometers.
Dillon and Tuttle
New York, N.Y., c. 1860
Dinsmore, James
Hopkinton, N.H., n.d. Tall case clock known.
Disturnell, William
New Haven, Conn., 1784–1786; Middletown, Conn., 1786–1790
Dittmeir, John
Rochester, N.Y., 1860–1870
Dix, Joseph
Philadelphia, Pa., c. 1770
Dixon, Isaac
Philadelphia, Pa., c. 1840
Doane, John
Scituate, Mass., c. 1790
Dobbs, Henry M.
New York, N.Y., 1795–1805
Dobson, John A.
Baltimore, Md., 1860–1870
Dodd, Abner
Newark, N.J., c. 1830
Dodge, Ezra
New London, Conn., 1787–1798; Providence, R.I., c. 1820. Apprenticed to Thomas Harland, carried general merchandise in his shop as well as clocks.
Dodge, George
Salem, Mass., c. 1837
Dodge, John
Catskill, N.Y., c. 1820
Dodge, Nehemiah
Providence, R.I., c. 1800. Worked with Seril Dodge for a time.
Dodge, Seril
Providence, R.I., c. 1788. Apprenticed to Thomas Harland.
Dodge, Garfield and Co.
Chillicothe, Ohio, c. 1840
Dodge and Whitaker
Providence, R.I., c. 1800
Dodge & Williams
Providence, R. I., 1799–1802
Dole, Daniel N.
Hallowell, Me., c. 1800
Dole, H. L., & Co.
Haverhill, Mass., 1865–1877
Doll, Joseph
Lancaster, Pa., 1800–1820; Harrisburg, Pa., after 1821
Dominick, Bernhardus
Philadelphia, Pa., c. 1775
Dominick, Frederick
Philadelphia, Pa., c. 1768
Dominy, Nathaniel IV
East Hampton and Sag Harbor, N.Y., 1764–1809
Dommett, John
Philadelphia, Pa., c. 1730
Don, Alexander (and William)
Albany, N.Y., c. 1810
Donaldson, George E.
Doylestown, Pa., 1850–1860
Doods, Joseph
n.p.; n.d.
Doogal & Russel
New York, N.Y., c. 1805
Doolittle, Enos
Hartford, Conn., 1790–1800. Apprenticed to his brother, Isaac. Made blanks

for other clockmakers and also cast bells.

Doolittle, Isaac
New Haven, Conn., 1742–1797. Made cast-brass blank parts for other makers besides clock and tower bells.

Doolittle, Isaac, Jr.
New Haven, Conn., 1780–1820. Made surveyors' instruments, buttons, scales, etc.

Doolittle, Lucius
New York, N.Y., c. 1850

Dorchester Clock & Bell Foundry
Dorchester, Mass., c. 1830. Made clocks, clock parts, and organs.

Dorey, Joseph L.
East Cahn Twp., Pa., c. 1825

Dorflinger, Joseph
Philadelphia, Pa., c. 1837

Doron, John
Vincentown, N.J., c. 1849

Dorsey, Philip
Baltimore, Md., c. 1800

Doty, George
Buffalo, N.Y., c. 1835

Doty, John F.
Albany, N.Y., c. 1813

Doughty, S. H.
New York, N.Y., c. 1850

Douglass, John
New Haven, Conn., 1800–1820

Douglass, Thomas
Niles, Mich., c. 1860

Doull, James
Charlestown, Mass., 1790–1820; Philadelphia after 1825

Douty, Hendrick
Philadelphia, Pa., c. 1774

Dover, Thomas
Dayton, Ohio, 1820–1830

Dow, David
Pittsfield, N.H., c. 1800

Dowdney, Burrows
Philadelphia, Pa., 1768–1771

Dowdney, Nathaniel
Philadelphia, Pa., n.d.

Dowig, George
Baltimore, Md., c. 1784

Dowle, Robert
New York, N.Y., c. 1790

Dowling, G. R. & B. Co.
Newark, N.J., c. 1832

Downes, Arthur
Charleston, S.C., c. 1760. In partnership with Joshua Lockwood, 1762–1765.

Downs, Anson
Bristol, Conn., c. 1830. Apprentice of Seth Thomas. Worked with Ephraim Downs and Luman Watson. Later at Plymouth, Conn. Moved to Waterville, where he made knives and buttons.

Downs, Ephraim
Bristol, Conn., c. 1820. Made shelf and tall clocks. Worked with Silas Hoadley, Eli Terry, Seth Thomas, and George Mitchell.

Dows and Fuller
New York, N.Y., c. 1840. Probably dealer.

Drawbaugh, Daniel
Eberly's Mills, Cumberland Co., Pa., c. 1875. Invented an electric clock, also

worked on the telephone, preceding Alexander Bell.

Drayer, William E.
Hamilton, Ohio, c. 1835

Dring, Thomas
West Chester, Chester Co., Pa., c. 1790

Dropsie, M. A.
Philadelphia, Pa., 1842–1849

Drown, Charles Leonard
Newburyport, Mass., c. 1849

Drown, John Boardman
Newburyport, Mass., c. 1850

Drown, Richard
Newburyport, Mass., c. 1795. Apprenticed to David Wood.

Drown and Barnaby
Dover, N.H., c. 1850

Droz, Charles A.
Philadelphia, Pa., c. 1810

Droz, Ferdinand Humbert
Pittsburgh, Pa., c. 1840; Cleveland, Ohio, 1850–1860

Droz, Hannah
Philadelphia, Pa., c. 1840. One of the few female clockmakers.

Droz, Humbert
Philadelphia, Pa., 1790–1810. Listed in directories.

Droz, John
Cincinnati, Ohio, c. 1825

Droz & Sons
Philadelphia, Pa., c. 1807

Dryer, C.
Louisville, Ky., c. 1840. Also made thermometers and other instruments.

Drysdale, William
Philadelphia, Pa., 1816–1850

Drysdale, William, Jr.
Philadelphia, Pa., 1842–1845

Duble, Charles
Zanesville, Ohio, c. 1815

DuBois, B. F.
Chester Co., Pa., n.d.

Dubois, Gabriel
New York, N.Y., c. 1810

DuBois, P. C.
Alameda, Calif., c. 1875. Made shelf and tall clocks with chimes.

Dubois & Folmar
New York, N.Y., c. 1810

Duchene, Andrew
Portsmouth, N.H., c. 1795

Ducommun, Henry
Philadelphia, Pa., c. 1830

Ducommun, Henry, Jr., & Co.
Philadelphia, Pa., c. 1840

Dudley, Benjamin
Newport, R.I., 1785–1825

Dudley, Thomas
Boston, Mass., c. 1800. Adv. for cabinetmakers, 1807.

Duff, George
Philadelphia, Pa., c. 1830

Duff, George C.
New Bern, N.C., c. 1845

Duffield, Edward
Philadelphia, Pa., 1741–1747; Lower Dublin, Pa., 1747–1801. Friend of Benjamin Franklin. Made tower clocks after moving to Lower Dublin. Few tall case clocks known.

Duffner, Vincent
Cincinnati, Ohio, 1830–1840

Dugan, Edgar E.
Fort Washington, Pa., c. 1905. Patent issued for "The Mouse" clock.

Duhme & Co.
Cincinnati, Ohio, 1850–1860

Dulty, John
Zanesville, Ohio, c. 1810

Dumesnil, Anthony
Boston, Mass., c. 1790

Dumesnil, Anthony
Lexington, Ky., c. 1820

Dumotette, J. B.
Philadelphia, Pa., c. 1820

Dunbar, Butler
Bristol, Conn., 1810–1830; Springville, Pa., 1830–1840. In partnership with Titus Merriman.

Dunbar, Edward B.
Bristol, Conn., c. 1865. Made clock springs.

Dunbar, Edward L.
Bristol, Conn., c. 1850. Son of Butler.

Dunbar, Jacobs & Warner
Bristol, Conn., c. 1849

Dunbar & Merriman
Bristol, Conn., c. 1810

Dunbar and Warner
Bristol, Conn., c. 1850

Duncan, Alex
Elgin, Ill., n.d. Made tall clocks.

Dungan & Klump
Philadelphia, Pa., c. 1910

Dunheim, Andrew
New York, N.Y., c. 1775

Dunlap, Archibald
New York, N.Y., c. 1800

Dunlap, John
Bedford, N.H., c. 1760. Cabinetmaker.

Dunn, Cary
New York, N.Y., 1776–1782; Morristown, N.J., 1782; Newark, N.J., 1782–1783. Doubtful whether he was clockmaker.

Dunn, Robert
New York, N.Y., c. 1840

Dunning, J. L.
Concord, Mass., c. 1815. Apprenticed to Lemuel Curtis, later became a partner; then moved to Burlington, Vt., with Curtis.

Dunning & Crissey
Rochester, N.Y., c. 1840

Dunnings
Wolcottville, Conn., n.d.

Dunseath, W. G.
Pittsburgh, Pa., n.d.

Dunyon, Augustine
Portsmouth, N.H., c. 1840

Dupuy, John
Philadelphia, Pa., 1765–1780. Probably moved to Reading, Pa.

Durand, Asher Brown
Boston, Mass., c. 1820. Later turned to engraving.

Durant, John H. G.
New Haven, Conn., n.d.

Duren, H.
New York, N.Y., 1820–1840

Durfee, Walter H.
Providence, R.I., c. 1870. Maker of tall clocks.

Durgin, Clark
Andover, N.H., c. 1840

Durgin, F.
Andover, N.H., n.d.

Durgin, Gersham
Andover, N.H., c. 1790

Durkin, John
Akron, Ohio, n.d.

Duryea, W.
New York, N.Y., c. 1855

Dusenberry, D. C.
Middletown, N.Y., 1790–1820

Dutch, Stephen
Boston, Mass., 1800–1810

Dutens, Charles
Philadelphia, Pa., c. 1755

Dutton, David
Mount Vernon, N.H., 1820–1830.
Made wood-movement shelf clocks.

Dutton, Hildreth
Lyndeborough, N.H., c. 1830. Brother
of Reed.

Dutton, Reed
Milford, N.H., c. 1840

Dutton, David and Sons
Mount Vernon, N.H., c. 1840

Dyar, George W.
Boston, Mass., c. 1825. In partnership
with John Sawin.

Dyar, Giles
Boston, Mass., c. 1675

Dyar, Harrison
New York, N.Y., c. 1825

Dyar, Warren
Lowell, Mass., c. 1831. Probably
dealer.

Dye, William
Fayetteville, N.C., c. 1805

Dyer, Joseph
Concord, Mass., c. 1815. Employed by
Curtis and Dunning. Later to Burling-
ton, Vt.

Dyer, Wadsworth and Comp.
Augusta, Ga., 1838–1843. Used Birge
and Mallory movements in triple-deck
clocks.

Dyer, W. and V.
Savannah, Ga., c. 1835

Dyffer, Daniel
Reading, Pa., c. 1820. Tall clocks.

Dyke, Albert
New York, N.Y., c. 1925

Dysart, James P.
Lancaster, Pa., c. 1850

Ealer, John
Northampton (now Allentown), Pa.,
c. 1800

Earp, Robert
Philadelphia, Pa., c. 1811

Easterley, John
New Holland, Pa., 1825–1840

Eastman, Abel B.
Belfast, Me., 1806–1821. Earliest clock-
maker in Belfast. Came in 1806 from
Concord, N.H.

Eastman, Cyrus
Amherst, N.H., c. 1815

Eastman, Edward
Sanbornton, N.H., c. 1805; later to
Cato Four Corners, N.Y., c. 1830

Eastman, Joseph
Boston and Chelsea, Mass. Apprenticed
to the Willards, c. 1820. Founded Eastman Clock Co., later Chelsea Clock Co.

Eastman, Robert
Belfast and Brunswick, Me., 1805–
1808

Eastman & Carey
Brunswick, Me., 1805–1810

Eastman Clock Co.
Chelsea, Mass., 1886–1888. Later be-
came Boston Clock Co., finally Chelsea
Clock Co.

Eaton, Elon
Grand Rapids, Mich., c. 1860

Eaton, Isaiah C.
Walpole, N.H., c. 1790. Also a silversmith.

Eaton, James
Boston, Mass., c. 1809

Eaton, John H.
Boston, Mass., c. 1820

Eaton, Samuel
Boston, Mass., 1825–1840

Eberman, Charles
Lancaster, Pa., c. 1820. Son of Joseph.

Eberman, Gottlieb
Lancaster, Pa., 1782–1801

Eberman, Jacob
Lancaster, Pa., 1773–1837

Eberman, John, Sr.
Lancaster, Pa., 1749–1835

Eberman, John, Jr.
Lancaster, Pa., 1776–1846

Eberman, Joseph
Lancaster, Pa., 1780–1884

Eby, Christian
Manheim, Pa., 1799–1837

Eby, George
Manheim, Pa., 1830–1860. Son of
Christian.

Eby, Jacob
Manheim, Pa., 1830–1860. Son of
Christian.

Eckel, Alexander Perry
Greensboro, N.C., 1821–1906. Adv.
1845.

Eckspewen, William
Pennsylvania, n.d.

Edgerly, Sylvester
Roxbury, Mass., 1820–1840. Willard
apprentice.

Edmands and Hamblett
Boston, Mass., c. 1867. Maker of electric clocks.

Edmund, William
Roxbury, Mass., 1820–1840

Edmund, William
Philadelphia, Pa., c. 1845

Edmunds, James
Charleston, S.C., c. 1745

Edmundson, Thomas
York County, Pa., 1790–1800. Apprentice of E. Kirk.

Edson, Jonah
Bridgewater, Mass., 1810–1830

Edwards, Abraham
Ashby, Mass., 1794–1840

Edwards, Calvin
Ashby, Mass., 1780–1830

Edwards, John
Ashby, Mass., 1810–1812

Edwards, Nathan
Acton, Mass., 1800–1810

Edwards, Samuel
Ashby, Mass., 1715–1783. Father of
Calvin.

Edwards, Samuel, Jr.
Ashby, Mass., 1800–1808; Gorham,
Me., 1808–1830

Edwards, A. & C. (partnership of Abraham and Calvin)
Ashby, Mass., c. 1790

Eells, Edward, Sr.
Stonington and Preston, Conn., c. 1773

Eells, Edward, Jr.
Middlebury, Vt., and Medina, N.Y.,
c. 1795

Effey, William
Davenport, Iowa, c. 1850

Egan, Robert
Williamsburg, Va., c. 1772

Ege, James
Fredericksburg, Va., c. 1830

Egerton, Matthew, Sr.
New Brunswick, N.J., 1760–1780.
Cabinetmaker.

Egerton, Matthew, Jr.
New Brunswick, N.J. Cabinetmaker,
1790–1820, for a number of clockmakers; worked with his father.

Egg, Edward
Columbia, S.C., c. 1860

Eggert, D.
New York, N.Y., c. 1826. Taught Simon Willard, Jr., the art of chronometer making.

Ehst, David K.
Boyertown, Berks Co., Pa., c. 1840

Electime Corp.
Brooklyn, N.Y., c. 1949

Electric Self Winding Clock Co.
Bristol, Conn., c. 1903

Eliasoff, M., & Co.
Albany, N.Y., c. 1888

Eliot, William
Baltimore, Md., c. 1799

Ellery, E.
Reported as working at Newburyport,
Mass., n.d.

Ellicott, Andrew
Solebury, Pa., c. 1780

Ellicott, Andrew, Sr.
Baltimore, Md., c. 1775

Ellicott, Andrew, Jr.
Buckingham, Bucks Co., Pa., n.d.
Father of Joseph.

Ellicott, Joseph
Buckingham, Bucks Co., Pa., c. 1750

Elliot, B. R.
Farmington, Me., c. 1850

Elliot, Hazen
Lowell, Mass., c. 1830

Elliot, J. R.
Minneapolis, Minn., c. 1880

Elliott, G. M.
Paterson, N.J., n.d.

Elliott, George
Wilmington, Del., c. 1855. Probably
only dealer and repairman.

Elliott, J.
Plymouth Meeting, Pa., c. 1770

Elliott, Luther
Amherst, N.H., 1840–1850

Elliott, Zebulon
New York, N.Y., c. 1810

Elliott & Burnham
Salisbury, N.C., from 1821. Zebulon Elliott and E. B. Burnham, clock and watchmakers.

Ellis, Arnold
Londonderry, N.H., n.d.

Ellis, Benjamin
Philadelphia, Pa., 1829–1833. Listed in directories.

Ellis, George
Philadelphia, Pa., c. 1850

Ellsworth, David
Windsor, Conn., 1742–1821. Probably apprenticed to either Seth or Benjamin Youngs.

Elmore, M. W.
Ottawa, Kan., c. 1860

Elson, Herman N.
Philadelphia, Pa., 1843–1848

Elson, Julius
Philadelphia, Pa., 1842–1844

Elvins, William
Fells Point, Md., 1780–1799; later to Baltimore, Md.

Elwyn, George
Bristol, Conn., n.d.

Ely, Hugh
New Hope, Bucks Co., Pa., c. 1800

Ely, John
Mifflinburg, Pa., 1800–1830

Emberson, George W.
Newport, Me., n.d.

Embree, Effingham
New York, N.Y., 1780–1790

Emerson, Dudley
Lyme, Conn., 1780–1790. Adv. c. 1788.

Emerson, T. P.
Lafayette, Ind., c. 1860

Emerson, William C.
Newport, Me., c. 1830

Emery, Jesse
Weare, N.H., c. 1800

Emery, Samuel
Salem, Mass., 1810–1855

Emmery, John
New York, N.Y., c. 1880

Emmett, Edward T.
Boston, Mass., c. 1765

Emmons, C. G.
Boston, Mass., c. 1844

Emmons, Erastus
Trenton, N.J., 1800–1820

Empire Calendar Clock Co.
Genoa, N.Y., n.d. Manufacturers of calendar clocks.

Empire Clock Co.
Bristol, Conn., c. 1854. An enterprise of Noble Jerome.

Endt (or Ent), John
New York, N.Y., c. 1794; Philadelphia, Pa., c. 1760. Son of Theodore.

Endt (or Ent), Theodore
Philadelphia, Pa., c. 1740

Engard, Samuel
Philadelphia, Pa., 1830–1840

England, James
Baltimore, Fells Point, Md., 1807–1819

Engle, Jacob
Carlisle, Pa., 1780–1800

Engle, Jacob
New Bedford and Millersburg, Ohio, c. 1880

Engle, Stephen D.
Hazelton, Luzerne Co., Pa., c. 1865. Also practiced dentistry.

Englehart, C. W. and Son
Philadelphia, Pa., c. 1880

Ensign, Charles
Troy, N.Y., c. 1842

Entwhistle, Edmund
Boston, Mass., c. 1740

Eoff, Garret
New York, N.Y., c. 1800

Eoff and Howell
New York, N.Y., c. 1805

Epps, W.
New Orleans, La., c. 1860

Erb, John
Conestoga Center, Pa., 1835–1860

Erickson, Laurence
Evanston, Ill., c. 1895

Ernst
Cooperstown, N.Y., 1810–1840

Erwin, Edward F.
Bethlehem, Pa., c. 1880

Erwin, Henry
Philadelphia, Pa., 1817–1842

Essex, Joseph
Boston, Mass., c. 1712. From Great Britain.

Esslinger, Charles
Buffalo, N.Y., 1840–1848

Est, John
New York, N.Y., 1750–1760. Probably dealer.

Estelle, Samuel
Germantown, Ohio, c. 1870

Esterlie, John
New Holland and Lebanon, Pa., c. 1812. Retired 1830.

Eubank, James
Glasgow, Ky., c. 1826

Eubank, Joseph
Glasgow, Ky., 1820–1841

Eubank and Jeffries
Glasgow, Ky., c. 1820

Eureka Manufacturing Co.
Bristol, Conn., 1830–1840; perhaps to 1868

Eureka Manufacturing Co.
Boston, Mass., 1850–1860. Adv. regulators, astronomical, marine, school, hotel, office, calendar, and house clocks; also clockwork-driven, self-stirring coffee roasters in 1860.

Eureka Shop, The
Bristol, Conn., c. 1835

Evans, Alfred
Kirkwood, N.Y., c. 1850

Evans, David
Philadelphia, Pa., 1770–1773; Baltimore, Md., 1773–1784. Nephew of David Rittenhouse.

Evans, E.
Cincinnati, Ohio, c. 1850

Evans, Elijah
Baltimore, Md., 1779–1780; Frederick, Md., after 1782

Evans, Henry
Newark, N.J., c. 1850

Evans, James
Chenango Point, N.Y., c. 1820

Evans, John
Charles County, Md., c. 1754

Evans, S.
Newport, Del., c. 1745

Evans, Septimus
Warwick, Pa., c. 1800

Evans, Stephen
Warwick, Pa., c. 1800

Evans, Thomas
New York, N.Y., c. 1760

Evans, William M.
Philadelphia, Pa., c. 1815

Evans, William M.
Cincinnati, Ohio, c. 1850.

Evans, David and Elijah
Baltimore, Md., c. 1789

Evans and Furness
Newport, Del., c. 1745

Evard, Charles C.
Philadelphia, Pa., c. 1837

Evens, Wm., Jr.
Kensington, N.H., c. 1770

Everman, Jacob
Lancaster, Pa., 1773 and later.

Eversole, H. E.
Logansport, Ind., c. 1860

Eves, William
Cincinnati, Ohio, c. 1830

Evits, R.
Kalamazoo, Mich., c. 1840

Eyre, Johan
Philadelphia, Pa., n.d.

Eyre, Matthias
Philadelphia, Pa., c. 1770

Faber, George
Sumneytown, Pa., c. 1770; Reading, Pa., 1772–1780

Faber, S.
New Bedford, Mass., 1810–1820

Fabian, H.
Chester and Lancaster, Pa., c. 1850

Fadeley, J. M.
Louisville, Ky., c. 1840

Faff, Augustus P.
Philadelphia, Pa., c. 1835

Fahrenbach, Pius
Boston, Mass., c. 1850

Fail, Philip
Lancaster Boro, Pa., c. 1830

Fainstern, J.
Boston, Mass., n.d.

Fairbanks, Joseph O.
Newburyport, Mass., c. 1860

Fairbanks and Co.
New Brunswick, N.J., c. 1830

Fairchild, G. W.
Bridgeport, Conn., c. 1860

Fairhaven Clock Co.
Fairhaven, Vt., c. 1890

Fairman, Gideon
Newburyport, Mass., c. 1775

Fales, G. S.
New Bedford, Mass., 1810–1820

Fales, James
New Bedford, Mass., 1810–1830

Fales, James, Jr.
New Bedford, Mass., c. 1830

Fales, James & Giles
New Bedford, Mass., c. 1840

Faller, Adam
Philadelphia, Pa., c. 1860

Faris, Charles
n.p.; c. 1796

Faris, Hyram
n.p.; c. 1790

Faris, William, Sr.
Philadelphia, Pa., c. 1749; Annapolis,

Md., c. 1757. Apprenticed to Peter Stretch. Father of William, Jr.

Faris, William, Jr.
Annapolis, Md., c. 1815

Farmer, John
Philadelphia, Pa., c. 1693. Documentary reference designates this clockmaker as establishing himself the 24th day, 8th month, 1693.

Farmer, M. G.
Salem, Mass., c. 1849

Farnham, Henry
Boston, Mass., c. 1780. Apprenticed to Thomas Harland.

Farnham, Rufus
Boston, Mass., c. 1780. Apprenticed to Thomas Harland.

Farnham, Samuel S.
Oxford, N.Y., c. 1840

Farnum, Henry and Rufus
Boston, Mass., c. 1780

Farr, Bela
Norwich, N.Y., c. 1830

Farr, John
Utica, N.Y., c. 1830

Farr, John C.
Philadelphia, Pa., c. 1825

Farr and Olmsted
Brandon, Vt., n.d.

Farr and Thompson
Philadelphia, Pa., c. 1822. Importers, not makers.

Fasbender, John H.
Charleston, S.C., c. 1800; Richmond, Va., c. 1820

Fasig, Conrad
Reading, Pa., 1790–1815

Fasoldt, Charles
New York and Albany, N. Y., c. 1850

Fasoldt, Dudley
Albany, N.Y., n.d.

Fasoldt, John G.
Albany, N.Y., c. 1865

Fasoldt, Max
Albany, N.Y., c. 1865

Fasoldt, Otto
Albany, N.Y., n.d.

Fasoldt Mfg. Co.
Albany, N.Y., c. 1880. Made regulators and tower clocks.

Fatman, Bros.
Philadelphia, Pa., c. 1843

Fatton, Frederick
Philadelphia, Pa., c. 1830

Fatton & Co.
Philadelphia, Pa., c. 1840

Faulkner, James
New York, N.Y., c. 1840

Faver, Christian
Lampeter, Pa., n.d.

Favre, John James
Philadelphia, Pa., c. 1797

Fay, Henry
Albany, N.Y., c. 1850

Fazier, William
Elizabeth Twp., Pa., c. 1850

Fearis, I.
Pittsburgh, Pa., c. 1800. Casemaker.

Feddersen, H. F.
Lancaster, Pa., c. 1850

Fehlinger, Samuel
Gettysburg, Pa., c. 1800

Fehrenbach, P.
Boston, Mass., c. 1860

Fehrer, George J.
Shawneetown, Ill., c. 1860

Felix, J.
Columbia, Lancaster Co., Pa., 1840–1850

Fellows, Abraham
Troy and Waterford, N.Y., 1810–1835

Fellows, Ignatius
Lowell, Mass., c. 1830

Fellows, James
Kensington, N.H., c. 1800

Fellows, James
Lowell, Mass., c. 1830

Fellows, Jeremiah, Jr.
Kensington, N.H., c. 1775

Fellows, I. W. and J. K.
Lowell, Mass., c. 1830

Fellows, Read & Olcott
New York, N.Y., 1820–1830. Probably dealers in watches and clocks.

Fellows, Storm & Cargill
New York, N.Y., c. 1832. Dealers.

Fellows, Wadsworth & Co.
New York, N.Y., c. 1840. Probably dealers only.

Felt, J. F.
Portland, Me., c. 1825

Felton, A. C.
Boston, Mass., c. 1860

Felton, J.
Philadelphia, Pa., 1820–1840

Fenlester, Alexander
Baltimore, Md., c. 1805

Fenn, Gibe
Brimfield, Ohio, c. 1850, Casemaker.

Fenn, William B.
Plymouth, Conn., c. 1820

Fenno, James
Lowell, Mass., 1830–1840

Fenton, Gamaliel
Walpole, N.H., c. 1795. Bell founder.

Fenton, Jr.
Philadelphia, Pa., 1828–1840

Ferguson, Elijah
New Bern, N.C., c. 1845

Ferguson, George
Philadelphia, Pa., 1820–1822

Ferris, Benjamin
Waterford, N.Y., c. 1810

Ferris, Benjamin C.
Philadelphia, Pa., c. 1810; Wilmington, Del., c. 1813

Ferris, Edward B.
Philadelphia, Pa., c. 1846

Ferris, W.
Philadelphia, Pa., c. 1810

Ferris, Ziba
Wilmington, Del., 1806–1850. Tall, shelf, and wall clocks. Brother of Benjamin.

Ferris, Ziba, Jr.
Wilmington, Del. Son of Ziba.

Ferris & McElwee
Philadelphia, Pa., c. 1810

Fertig, Benjamin
Philadelphia, Pa., c. 1810

Fertig, Jacob
Vincent, Chester Co., Pa., 1802–1823

Fertig, Jacob W.
Philadelphia, Pa., c. 1810

Fessler, John
Fredericktown, Md., c. 1800

Fessler, John, Jr.
Fredericktown, Md., c. 1820

Fessler and Son
Fredericktown, Md., c. 1810

Fest, Alfred
Philadelphia, Pa., c. 1840

Fest, Edward
Philadelphia, Pa., c. 1810

Fest and Brother
Philadelphia, Pa., c. 1850

Field, John
Poughkeepsie, N.Y., 1790–1820

Field, John H.
Batavia, N.Y., c. 1810

Field, Peter
New York, N.Y., c. 1800

Field, Peter, Jr.
New York, N.Y., c. 1830

Fiester, John
Lancaster, Pa., c. 1860. Maker of "Apostolic" clock. Finished and exhibited an "Apostolic" clock, 1878, upon which he had spent 11 years of labor.

Fiffe, H.
n.p.; c. 1810

Fifield, John
Kingston and Kensington, N.H., 1758–1759

Filber, John
York, Pa., 1790–1810; Lancaster, Pa., 1810–1820; York, after 1820

Finley, John
Charlestown, Md., c. 1754

Finney, John
Charlestown, Md., c. 1750

Fish, Isaac
Utica, N.Y., c. 1830

Fish, Isaac, Jr.
Utica, N.Y., c. 1850

Fisher, Charles F.
San Antonio, Tex., 1850–1860

Fisher, George
Lancaster, Pa., 1780–1800

Fisher, George
Troy, N.Y., c. 1835

Fisher, John
York Town (later known as York), Pa., c. 1759. Maker of an astronomical clock.

Fisher, Louis
New York, N.Y., c. 1800

Fisher, Thomas
York, Pa., 1775

Fisher, William
Charleston, Va., c. 1845

Fisher Electric Clock Co., Inc.
New York, N.Y., c. 1896

Fisk, Samuel
Boston, Mass., c. 1790. Cabinetmaker.

Fisk, William
Boston, Mass., c. 1790. Cabinetmaker. Brother of Samuel. Made cases for Simon Willard.

Fister, Amon
Philadelphia, Pa., c. 1794

Fitch, Eugene
New York, N.Y., c. 1890. Invented the "Plato" clock.

Fitch, John
Windsor, Conn., 1764–1769; Trenton, N.J., 1770–1776; Philadelphia, Pa., 1780. Clockmaker and inventor of steamboat.

Fitch, Jonas
Pepperell, Mass., 1770–1800

Fite, John
Baltimore, Md., 1800–1810
Fitts, George
Bangor, Me., 1830–1860
Fitz, William
Portsmouth, N.H., 1760–1780
Fix, George
Reading, Pa., c. 1805
Fix, Joseph
Reading, Pa., 1820–1840
Flach, George
Charleston, S.C., c. 1840
Flagg, Seth
Springfield, Mass., c. 1840
Flaig, E.
Danville, Ky., c. 1860
Fletcher, Charles
Philadelphia, Pa., c. 1817
Fletcher, George
Philadelphia, Pa., c. 1821
Fletcher, Thomas
Philadelphia, Pa., c. 1815
Fletcher, C. &. G.
Philadelphia, Pa., c. 1820
Fletcher, Charles & Thomas
Philadelphia, Pa., c. 1830. Importers of clocks and watches.
Fletcher, J. & S.
Philadelphia, Pa., n.d.
Flint, Daniel
Mount Holly, N.J., and Philadelphia, Pa., c. 1810
Flood, William
Philadelphia, Pa., c. 1837
Floto, William
Philadelphia, Pa., c. 1849
Flournay
Virginia, c. 1790
Flower, Henry
Philadelphia, Pa., c. 1750
Floyd, Thomas
Charleston, S.C., c. 1765. Adv. during this period.
Fole, Nathaniel
Northampton, Mass., 1819–1820
Folger, Peter
Nantucket, Mass., c. 1645. Daughter Abiah was mother of Benjamin Franklin. It is possible that he did not make clocks.
Folger, Walter, Jr.
Nantucket, Mass., 1787–1820. Cousin of B. Franklin. Made complicated astronomical tall clock. Also practiced medicine and operated factory for spinning cotton and wool.
Folkrod, William
Philadelphia, Pa., c. 1849
Follet, Marvill M.
Lowell, Mass., c. 1835
Follett, N. M.
Madrid, N.Y., c. 1840
Folmar, Andrew
New York, N.Y., c. 1810
Foote, Charles F.
Bristol, Conn., c. 1850. Purchased C. Boardman's factory.
Foote, William
Middletown and East Haddam, Conn., 1790–1820
Forbach, Joseph
New York, N.Y., c. 1850

Forbes, John
Philadelphia, 1760–1770s; Hartford, Conn., after 1771
Forbes, John
Hartford, Conn., c. 1770. From Philadelphia.
Forbes, Wells
Bristol, Conn., c. 1840
Forbes & Tucker
Concord, N.H., 1830–1840. Probably dealers.
Ford, George
Lancaster, Pa., 1810–1840. Also made surveyors' instruments.
Ford, George, Jr.
Lancaster, Pa., c. 1840
Ford, George H.
New Haven, Conn., c. 1850
Ford, Henry O.
Athol Depot, Mass., n.d.
Ford, Peter
Lancaster and York, Pa., c. 1780
Ford, Southerland
Charleston, S.C., c. 1741
Ford, William
Philadelphia, Pa., c. 1848
Forestville Clock Co.
Bristol, Conn., c. 1840
Forestville Clock Manufactory
Bristol, Conn., c. 1850
Forestville Hardware Co.
Bristol, Conn., 1852–1853. J. C. Brown was the president.
Forestville Hardware and Clock Company
Bristol, Conn., 1853–1855. Another of J. C. Brown's enterprises.
Forestville Manufacturing Co.
Bristol, Conn., 1835–1839. Factory built by J. C. Brown, J. Goodrich, L. Waters, C. Boardman, and W. Hills. Made 8-day movements. Used various labels in their clocks. Later became Forestville Clock Manufactory Co. and Forestville Hardware and Clock Co. Assets purchased by E. N. Welch. Later became Sessions Clock Co.
Forrer, Christian
Lampeter, Lancaster Co., Pa., c. 1760. From Switzerland, 1754.
Forrer, Daniel
Lampeter and Newberry, Pa., c. 1755. Brother of Christian.
Forsyth, Henry
Philadelphia, Pa., c. 1860
Fort Dearborn Watch and Clock Co.
Chicago, Ill., c. 1918
Foss, John
Somersworth, N.H., c. 1760
Foster, George
Boston, Mass., c. 1840
Foster, John C.
Portland, Me., c. 1830
Foster, Joseph H.
Bristol, Conn., n.d.
Foster, Nathaniel
Newburyport, Mass., c. 1818
Foster, Samuel
Amherst, N.H., c. 1800
Foster, Thomas
Newburyport, Mass., c. 1825. Brother of Nathaniel.
Foster, Thomas W.
Newburyport, Mass., c. 1850

Foster, Nathaniel and Thomas
Newburyport, Mass., c. 1820
Fournier, Stanislaus
New Orleans, La., 1830–1870. Made first public electric clock of record for Bank of Louisiana, 1849.
Fouston, John
New York, N.Y., c. 1805
Fowell, J. & N.
Boston, Mass., 1805–1809
Fowle, J. H.
Northampton, Mass., c. 1850
Fowle, John
Boston, Mass., c. 1805
Fowle, Nathan
Charleston, S.C., c. 1840
Fowle, Nathaniel
Boston, Mass., c. 1803
Fowler, John C.
Boston, Mass., c. 1842; Lynn, Mass., c. 1847; Groton, Mass., c. 1849
Fox, Arthur C.
Cherry Valley, N.Y., c. 1850
Fox, Asa
Buffalo, N.Y., c. 1810
Fox, Philetus
Boston, Mass., c. 1840
Foxcroft, James A.
Baltimore, Md., c. 1820
Foxcroft & Clark
Baltimore, Md., 1831–1839
Fragercrans, P.
Princeton, Ill., c. 1860
Francis, Basil
Baltimore, Md., 1760–1772; Albany, N.Y., 1772–1780
Francis, Field & Francis
Philadelphia, Pa., n.d. Toymakers; may have made only toy clocks.
Francis & Vuille
Baltimore, Md., c. 1760
Franciscus, George, Sr.
Baltimore, Md., c. 1776
Franck, Philip
New Berlin, Pa., 1800–1850
Francony, Jacob Hagey
n.p.; n.d.
Frank, L.
New York, N.Y., c. 1870
Frank and Lichtenauer
New York, N.Y., c. 1850
Frankfield, A. and Co.
New York, N.Y., c. 1860. Patented cuckoo clocks.
Franklin, Benjamin: 1706–1790
Philadelphia, Pa. Designed a 3-wheel clock.
Franklin & Marshall
Seneca Falls, N.Y., c. 1830. Cased Connecticut movements in cases designed by A. Munger of Auburn, N.Y.
Franks, J. and S.
Philadelphia, Pa., c. 1850
Franks, Jacob
Philadelphia, Pa., c. 1840. Listed in directories.
Franksen, B.
New York, N.Y., c. 1870
Frary, Obediah
Southampton, Mass., 1740–1770
Fraser, Alexander
Menallin Twp., Pa., c. 1840

Fraser, Jacob
New Ephrata (now Lincoln), Lancaster Co., Pa., 1830–1860

Fraser, William
Apprenticed to Samuel Parke, Philadelphia, Pa., 1814–1821; moved to New Holland, Lancaster Co., working for Esterlie and then, 1834, set up his own shop at New Ephrata, Pa.

Frazer, H. N.
Vienna, N.Y., c. 1830

Frazer, James
Logansport, Ind., c. 1830

Frazer, Samuel
Baltimore, Md., c. 1820

Frazer, Robert & Alexander
Philadelphia, Pa. before 1799; Paris, Ky., 1799. Robert to Lexington, Ky., 1799, listed in directory, 1818; Alexander after 1803.

Frazier, Samuel
Baltimore, Md., c. 1820

Frazier, William
Philadelphia, Pa., c. 1824

Free, Mathew
Elizabeth Twp., Pa., c. 1825

Freeman, Henry B.
West Chester, Pa., c. 1855

Freeman, William
Baltimore, Md., c. 1810

Freeman Brothers
Augusta, Ga., 1850–1860

French, Charles
Brattleboro and Rutland, Vt.; migrated to Ohio, c. 1825

French, David
New Ipswich, N.H., n.d.

French, James O.
Baltimore, Md., c. 1770

French, Lemuel
Boston, Mass., 1790–1820

Freytit, Peter
Pittsburgh, Pa., c. 1813

Frick Clock Co., Fred
Waynesboro, Pa., n.d. Maker of a complicated clock.

Friend, Engell
New York, N.Y., c. 1825

Friend, Frederick
Pittsburgh, Pa., c. 1813. Clock- and watchmaker in Diamond Alley.

Friend, George
New York, N.Y., c. 1820

Fries, John
Philadelphia, Pa., c. 1830

Fries, P.
Philadelphia, Pa., c. 1840

Fries, John and P.
Philadelphia, Pa., c. 1835

Frink, Urban
Brattleboro, Vt., 1870–1880

Frisbie, L. & J. & Co.
Chittenango, N.Y., c. 1830

Fritz, C.
Philadelphia, Pa., c. 1840

Frohn, Sebastian
Lancaster Boro, Pa., c. 1830

Fromanteel & Clark
Providence, R.I., c. 1710

Fromm, Sebastian
Hamilton, Ohio, c. 1825. Also casemaker.

Frost, Benjamin
Reading, Mass., c. 1840

Frost, Daniel
Reading, Pa., c. 1760. Made unique shelf clock, similar to hood portion of tall case clock. Carved ball-and-claw feet.

Frost, Jesse
Lynn, Mass., 1840–1850

Frost, Jonathan
Reading, Mass., c. 1820

Frost, N. A.
Hanover, N.H., c. 1880

Frost, Oliver
Providence, R.I., c. 1800

Frost, Merriman and Co.
Bristol, Conn., c. 1835; purchased Mitchell and Atkins firm.

Frost & Mumford
Providence, R.I., c. 1810

Frye, Jacob
Woodstock, Vt., n.d.

Frye, James
Haverhill, Mass., c. 1850

Frye & Shaw
New York, N.Y., c. 1830

Fryer, Peter
Albany, N.Y., 1824–1825; Norwich, N.Y., 1828–1840

Fuller, Artemas
Lowell, Mass., 1840–1850

Fuller, F. A.
Rutland, Vt., c. 1830

Fuller, Rufus
Francistown, N.H., n.d.

Fuller, Thomas Franklin
Bristol, Conn., c. 1845. Partner of John Birge, in Birge and Fuller.

Fuller and Ives
Bristol, Conn., c. 1835

Fuller and Kroeber
New York, N.Y., c. 1860

Fulton, James
Shelby County, Ky., c. 1830

Funk, Jacob
Lebanon, Pa., c. 1850

Furness, Samuel
New Castle, Md., c. 1760. Apprenticed to Benjamin Chandlee.

Furness, William
Newcastle County, Del., c. 1740. Father of Samuel.

Furnivall, James
Marblehead, Mass., 1770–1780

Fusselli, Peter
Bowling Green, Ky., c. 1850

Fyler, Orsamus R.
Vermont, c. 1815

Gaensle, Jacob
Philadelphia, Pa., c. 1755. Born in Germany; migrated to this country, 1743.

Gaillard, Peter
Reading, Pa., c. 1790. Adv. during this period. From France.

Gaines, John
Portsmouth, N.H., c. 1800

Gaines, Richard
Baltimore, Md., c. 1805

Gainey, W. B.
Pendleton, S.C., c. 1855

Galbraith, Patrick
Philadelphia, Pa., 1796–1811

Gale, Daniel
Bristol, Conn., c. 1850. Inventor of a calendar clock. Worked for Welch, Spring and Company.

Gale, James
Salem, Mass., c. 1815

Gale, Joseph
Fayetteville, N.C., c. 1795

Gale, Robert
n.p.; c. 1850

Galiay, John P.
Boston, Mass., c. 1825

Gallome, C.
Baltimore, Md., c. 1820

Galpin, Moses
Bethlehem, Conn., c. 1825. Not a maker, but a peddler. Purchased clocks from several makers.

Galt, James
Williamsburg, Va., c. 1765

Galt, Peter
Baltimore, Md., 1810–1812

Galt, Samuel
Williamsburg, Va., c. 1750

Galt, Stirling
Baltimore, Md., c. 1800

Galt, William
Washington, D.C., 1810–1840

Gannet, Aaron
Troy, N.Y., c. 1840

Gardiner, B.
New York, N.Y., 1830–1840. Probably dealer only.

Gardiner, John B.
Ansonia, Conn., c. 1855

Gardiner & McBride
Charlotte, N.C., c. 1810

Gardner, Barzillai
Charlotte, N.C., from 1807. It is believed he learned clockmaking at York, Pa.

Garlan, John R.
Greensboro, N.C., c. 1840

Garner, Edwin T.
Utica, N.Y., c. 1840

Garrett, Benjamin
Goshen, Chester Co., Pa., c. 1800

Garrett, Philip
Philadelphia, Pa., c. 1800

Garrett and Hartley
Philadelphia, Pa., c. 1825

Garrett, Philip & Sons
Philadelphia, Pa., c. 1825

Garrett, Thomas C. & Co.
Philadelphia, Pa., c. 1841. Jewelers, and dealers and importers of clocks.

Garrish, D. D.
Boston, Mass., c. 1854

Gartner, Jacob
York County, Pa., 1780–1800

Gate, Hiram
Connecticut or New Hampshire, c. 1842

Gates, Zacheus
Charlestown and Harvard, Mass., 1800–1820

Gaw, William
Philadelphia, Pa., 1810–1820

Gawne, W. A.
Oxford, Ohio, c. 1850

Gay, Levi
  Nashua, N.H., c. 1860
Gayhart, S.
  Camden, N.J., c. 1840
Gaylord, C. E.
  Chicago, Ill., c. 1850
Gaylord, Homer
  Norfolk, Conn., c. 1800; Homer, N.Y., c. 1810
Gebhard, R. L.
  n.p.; c. 1850. Maker of astronomical clocks.
Geddes, Charles
  Boston, Mass., c. 1770; New York, N.Y., c. 1776
Geddy, James
  Williamburg, Md., c. 1770
Geer, Elihu
  Hartford, Conn., 1830–1885. Printer who printed clock labels in his shop.
Gegye, Rene
  Charleston, S.C., 1740–1760
Gehring, John G.
  Baltimore, Md., c. 1825
Geiger, Jacob
  Northampton (now Allentown), Pa., 1787–1790; Maryland after 1793
Geiger, Joseph
  Whitehall, Pa., c. 1750
Geissler, C. A.
  New York, N.Y., c. 1895
Gelston, George S.
  New York, N.Y., c. 1830. Also imported clocks.
Gelston, Hugh
  Baltimore, Md., c. 1832
Gemmel, Matthew
  New York, N.Y., c. 1805
Gemmill, John
  Carlisle, Lancaster, and York, Pa., c. 1755
General Electric Co.
  Bridgeport, Conn., and Schenectady, N.Y., c. 1920. Electric clocks.
General Time Corporation
  New York, N.Y., Successor to General Time Instruments Corp., 1949.
General Time Instruments Corp.
  New York, N.Y. Merged with Seth Thomas and others to form General Time Instruments Corp., 1930–1949. Merger of Seth Thomas Clock Co., Western Clock Co., and others.
Gensel, John
  Philadelphia, Pa., n.d. There is extant a one-hand wall clock with brass dial that was made by Gensel in Germantown.
George, William
  Philadelphia, Pa., c. 1720. Apprenticed to John Cowper, 1716.
George, William L.
  Coal Creek, Tenn., c. 1845
Gerbie, Charles
  Atlanta, Ga., c. 1820
Gerding & Siemon
  New York, N.Y., c. 1830. Importers of French clocks.
Gere, Isaac
  Northampton, Mass., c. 1790. Made musical clocks as well as others.
Gerrish, Oliver
  Portland, Me., c. 1830

Gerrish, William
  Dover, N.H., c. 1830
Gerrish and Pearson
  Portland, Me., c. 1850
Gerry, James H.
  Newark, N.J., c. 1880. Patented one arbor for winding both time and strike.
Gerwich, H.
  Hartford, Conn., n.d.
Gery, Herman
  Philadelphia, Pa., c. 1800
Getz, Peter
  Lancaster, Pa., 1790–1820. Also a silversmith.
Gibble, Lewis
  Rapho, Warwick (Manheim), Pa., 1832–1850
Gibbons, Thomas
  Boston, Mass., c. 1735. Cabinetmaker.
Gibbons, Thomas
  Philadelphia, Pa., c. 1750
Gibbons, William
  Philadelphia, Pa., n.d.
Gibbs, Benjamin
  Newburyport, Mass., 1810–1820
Gibbs, James
  Philadelphia, Pa., c. 1845
Gifford, S. K.
  Camden, S.C., c. 1830
Gifft, Peter
  Kutztown, Pa., 1800–1820
Gilbert, J. F.
  Rochester, N.Y., c. 1830
Gilbert, Jesse
  Brooklyn, N.Y., c. 1843
Gilbert, T.
  Atlanta, Ga., c. 1865
Gilbert, William L.
  Winsted, Conn., c. 1850. Worked with Lucius Clarke and Ezra Baldwin.
Gilbert, William Lewis
  Farmington, Bristol, and Winsted, Conn., 1828–1871. Partner in many companies: Marsh and Gilbert, c. 1830; Birge, Gilbert and Co., c. 1835; Jeromes, Gilbert, Grant and Co.; Clarke, Gilbert and Co., c. 1850; Wm. L. Gilbert Co., c. 1866; Gilbert Manufacturing Co., c. 1871; and, finally, William L. Gilbert Clock Co. Prolific maker of shelf clocks.
Gilbert and Hubbard
  Meriden, Conn., c. 1860
Gilbert, Jordan & Smith
  New York, N.Y., c. 1830. Probably dealer only.
Gilbert Manufacturing Co.
  Winsted, Conn., 1866–1871
Gilbert, Marsh and Co.
  Winsted, Conn., c. 1830
Gilbert, Richards & Co.
  Chester, Conn., c. 1830
Giles, Joseph
  Concord, N.H., c. 1795. Worked in the L. & A. Hutchins Shop.
Giles, Joseph
  Trenton, N.J., 1800–1820
Giles, Wales and Co.
  New York, N.Y., n.d.
Gill, Caleb
  Hingham, Mass., c. 1785
Gill, E.
  Philadelphia, Pa., c. 1800. Bell founder.

Gill, Isaac
  Charleston, S.C., c. 1810
Gill, Leavitt
  Hingham, Mass., c. 1790
Gillespie, William
  New London, Pa., n.d.
Gilliam, Edward
  Pittsburgh, Pa., c. 1830
Gillman
  Hallowell (probably Me.), n.d.
Gilman, B. C.
  Exeter, N.H., 1790–1830
Gilman, John
  Kensington, N.H., n.d.
Gilman, John H.
  Portsmouth, N.H., n.d.
Gilman, Thomas
  Either Massachusetts or New Hampshire, n.d.
Gilmartin, John
  Augusta, Ga., c. 1820
Gilmore, William
  Pittsburgh, Pa., c. 1830
Gilmur, George
  Philadelphia, Pa., c. 1800
Girard, A.
  Mobile, Ala., c. 1849. Inventor.
Gird, W. F.
  Alexandria, Va., c. 1800
Gladman & Williams
  New York, N.Y., c. 1770
Gleason, F. A.
  Rome, N.Y., c. 1845
Gligeman
  Reading, Pa., c. 1784
Globe Clock Co.
  Milldale, Conn., c. 1880. Makers of the globe clock, Pat. 1883.
Glore, S.
  New Hampshire, c. 1830
Glover, Edwin
  Fayetteville, N.C., c. 1843
Glover, Henry
  New York and Brooklyn, N.Y., c. 1840
Glover, William
  Boston, Mass., c. 1823
Gnech (Gnecht; Knecht), Charles D.
  Charleston, S.C., c. 1820
Gobel, Henry
  New York, N.Y., c. 1850
Gobrecht, David
  Hanover, Pa., 1795–1829
Gobrecht, Eli
  Pennsylvania, c. 1800
Gobrecht, George S.
  Boston, Mass., c. 1815
Gobrecht, John
  Newport, R.I., c. 1723. Cabinetmaker, worked with J. Townsend.
Goddard, Benjamin
  Worcester, Mass., c. 1850
Goddard, George S.
  Boston, Mass., c. 1823
Goddard, John
  Newport, R.I., 1789–1843. Cabinetmaker.
Goddard, Nicholas
  Northampton, Mass., c. 1795; Rutland, Vt., c. 1797
Goddard, Stephen
  Newport, R.I., 1804. Cabinetmaker.
Goddard, D. and Co.
  Worcester, Mass., c. 1850

Godfrey, Thomas
Philadelphia, Pa., c. 1730
Godfrey, William
Philadelphia, Pa., c. 1730
Godshalk, Jacob
Towamencin Twp., Montgomery Co., and Philadelphia, Pa., c. 1770. A famous apprentice was Griffith Owen.
Godsoe, B. F.
New York, N.Y., c. 1850
Goewey, P. P.
Albany, N.Y., c. 1855
Goff, Charles
n.p.; n.d.
Golder, John
New York, N.Y., c. 1810
Goldsbury
Saint Albans and Granville, Ohio, c. 1825
Goldsmith & Co.
Salem, Mass., 1850–1860. Firm composed of William H. Chase, Caleb Newcomb, Nathaniel Goldsmith, and James Fairless.
Goldstone, B.
Philadelphia, Pa., c. 1830
Golefiel, S.
Lancaster, Pa., c. 1850
Goodell, David
Pomfret, Conn., c. 1790
Goodfellow, William
Philadelphia, Pa., c. 1790
Goodfellow, William
Philadelphia, Pa., 1810s–1820
Goodfellow & Sons
Philadelphia, Pa., c. 1790
Goodfellow, William, & Son
Philadelphia, Pa., 1796–1799
Goodhart, Jacob
Lebanon, Lebanon Co., Pa., c. 1815
Goodhue, D. T.
Providence, R.I., c. 1820
Goodhue, Richard S.
Portland and Augusta, Me., c. 1830
Gooding, Alanson
New Bedford, Mass., c. 1810
Gooding, Henry
Boston, Mass., c. 1810
Gooding, John
Plymouth, Mass., c. 1805
Gooding, Joseph
Dighton and Fall River, Mass., c. 1800
Gooding, Josephus
Bristol, Conn., c. 1820
Gooding, Josiah
Dighton, Mass., Bristol, R.I., and Boston, Mass., c. 1820
Goodman, John
Cleveland, Ohio, c. 1850
Goodman, Thomas
Charleston, S.C., 1730–1750
Goodnow, Silas B.
Fitchburg, Mass., c. 1835
Goodrich, Chauncey
Bristol and Forestville, Conn., prior to 1830; then Ingraham & Goodrich, 1833; Smith & Goodrich, Brown & Goodrich, 1845–1847
Goodrich, Jared
Bristol, Conn., c. 1835. Partner in Forestville Manufacturing Co. and Hills, Goodrich & Co.

Goodspeed, Lot
Middletown, Conn., c. 1820. Cased movements. Not a maker.
Goodwin, E. O.
Bristol, Conn., c. 1850. Casemaker. Purchased movements from other makers.
Goodwin, Henry
Boston, Mass., c. 1820
Goodwin, Horace, Jr.
Hartford, Conn., c. 1830. Probably not a maker.
Goodwin, James
Baltimore, Md., c. 1805
Goodwin, Samuel
Baltimore, Md., c. 1805
Goodwin, Samuel
Philadelphia, Pa., c. 1820
Goodwin, V. C.
Unionville, Conn., c. 1830. Probably cased movements only. Not a maker.
Goodwin, Wallace
Attleboro, Mass., c. 1850
Goodwin, William
Hartford, Conn., n.d.
Goodwin and Dodd
Hartford, Conn., c. 1815
Goodwin and Frisbie
Unionville, Conn., c. 1830
Gorden, Smyley
Lowell, Mass., c. 1832. Casemaker.
Gordon, Albertus
Laconia, N.H., c. 1885
Gordon, George
Philadelphia, Pa., c. 1845
Gordon, George I.
New York, N.Y., c. 1850
Gordon, Thomas
Boston, Mass., c. 1750
Gorgas, Benjamin
Ephrata, Pa., c. 1790
Gorgas, Jacob
Ephrata, Pa., c. 1765
Gorgas, John
Germantown, Pa., c. 1720. Father of Benjamin and Jacob.
Gorgas, Joseph
Ephrata, Pa., c. 1791
Gorgas, Solomon
Ephrata, Pa., c. 1785
Gorgas, William
Greensboro, Pa., c. 1850
Gorham, Charles L.
Barre, Mass., n.d.
Gorham, Brown and Co.
Providence, R.I., n.d.
Goron, Thomas
Boston, Mass., c. 1750
Gosler, George A.
York, Pa., c. 1800
Gostelowe, Jonathan
Philadelphia, Pa., c. 1770. Cabinetmaker.
Gotshalk, Henry
New Britain, Pa., c. 1760
Gottier, Francis
Charleston, S.C., c. 1750
Gould, Abijah
Nashua, N.H., 1800–1820; Rochester, N.Y., c. 1830
Gould, James
Baltimore, Md., c. 1840

Govett, George
Norristown, Pa., 1810–1830
Govett, George
Norristown, Montgomery Co., and later Philadelphia, Pa., 1840–1850
Gowan, Peter D.
Charleston, S.C., c. 1820
Graff, Jacob
Lancaster, Pa., c. 1775
Graff, John
Lebanon Twp., Pa., 1770–1781
Graff, Joseph
Allentown, Lehigh Co., Pa., c. 1795. Moved to Maryland.
Graffenberg, Thomas
n.p.; n.d.
Graham, Daniel
New York, N.Y., c. 1805
Graham, Mitchell
Philadelphia, Pa., c. 1835
Graham, William
Philadelphia, Pa., c. 1733
Graham & Co.
n.p.; n.d.
Grant, Alfred
New Haven, Conn., 1840–1850
Grant, Israel
Saint Louis, Mo., c. 1810
Grant, James
Hartford, Conn., c. 1790, adv. 1794; Wethersfield, Conn., c. 1796
Grant, William
Boston, Mass., c. 1815
Grant, Zelotes
Bristol, Conn., c. 1840. Partner with the Jeromes in Jeromes and Grant.
Grant and Loring
Boston, Mass., n.d.
Grant and Matthews
Bristol, Conn., c. 1840
Grau Electric Clock Co.
New York, N.Y., c. 1895
Graves, Alfred
Willow Grove, Montgomery Co., Pa., c. 1845
Gray, James
New York, N.Y., c. 1840
Gray and Alder
New York, N.Y., c. 1865
Gray & Bail
Boston, Mass., c. 1860
Gray Electric Clock Co.
New York, N.Y., c. 1895
Green, J.
Albany, N.Y., c. 1795
Green, John
Boston, Mass., c. 1795
Green, John
Philadelphia, Pa., c. 1795
Green, John
Carlisle, Pa., c. 1805
Green, Samuel
Boston, Mass., c. 1820
Green, Samuel, Jr.
Boston, Mass., c. 1825
Green, William
n.p.; n.d.
Greenawalt, William
Halifax, N.C., c. 1825
Greenleaf, David
Hartford, Conn., c. 1795

Greenleaf, Stephen
Boston, Mass., c. 1740. Maker of sundials.

Greenough, Norman C.
Newburyport, Mass., c. 1825

Greenwich Clock & Instrument Co.
New York, N.Y., c. 1888

Greer, John
Carlisle, Pa., c. 1770

Gregg, Jacob
Alexandria, Va., c. 1810

Gregg and Pomeroy
Hamilton, Ohio, c. 1830

Greiner, Charles
Charleston, S.C., c. 1780

Greishaber, E.
Louisville, Ky., c. 1840. Had shop at corner of 3rd and Market streets.

Gridley, F. R.
Attica, Ind., n.d.

Gridley, Martin
Logansport, Ind., 1830–1840

Gridley, Timothy
Sanbornton, N.H., c. 1810

Gridley, L. P. & C. E.
Logansport, Ind., 1860–1870

Griffen, Bryen
Philadelphia, Pa., c. 1800. Clockmaking is doubtful. Made scientific instruments.

Griffen, Peter
New York, N.Y., c. 1810

Griffin, Henry
New York, N.Y., c. 1795; Brooklyn, N.Y., c. 1810

Griffin & Hoyt
New York, N.Y., 1820–1830

Griffith, Edward
Litchfield, Conn., c. 1790; Charleston, S.C., c. 1794; Savannah, Ga., after 1796

Griffith, Greenbury
Alexandria, Va., c. 1811

Griffith, Humphrey
Huntington, Pa., c. 1818; Lebanon, Ohio, c. 1819; Indianapolis, Ind., c. 1825

Griffith, L.
Philadelphia, Pa., c. 1840

Griffith, Nathaniel
Portsmouth, N.H., c. 1770

Griffith, Samuel
Philadelphia, Pa., c. 1845

Griffith and Gaither
Alexandria, Va., c. 1809

Griffiths, James
Glens Falls, N.Y., c. 1830

Griffiths, John
Greenville, S.C., c. 1850

Griger, Jacob
Pennsylvania, n.d.

Griggs, Ebenezer
Bristol, Conn., c. 1810

Griggs, Solomon
Bristol, Conn., c. 1810

Grilley, Silas
Waterbury, Conn., c. 1808, with Abel, Porter and Co.

Grim, George
Orwigsburg, Berks Co., Pa., c. 1820

Griswold, Charles
New Haven, Conn., 1840–1850

Griswold, Chauncey
Troy, N.Y., c. 1840

Griswold, Daniel W.
East Hartford, Conn., 1789–1840

Griswold, H. D.
Framingham, Mass., n.d.

Griswold, Joab
Buffalo, N.Y., c. 1830

Griswold, A. B. & Co.
New Orleans, La., 1850–1860

Griswold, J. and W. W.
Fitchburg, Mass., c. 1830

Groff, Amos
Rawlinsville, Lancaster Co., Pa., c. 1850

Gropengiesser, Louis C.
Philadelphia, Pa., c. 1870. Brother of John. Also worked with him.

Groppengiesser, J. L.
Philadelphia, Pa., c. 1840. Chronometer and clockmaker.

Grosch, Samuel
Marietta, Pa., c. 1820. Clockmaker and lumber dealer.

Grosclaude, F.
Savannah, Ga., c. 1850

Grosh, Peter Lehn
Lancaster, Pa., c. 1825. Artist, painted clock dials.

Grotz, Isaac
Bethlehem and Easton, Pa., 1810–1830

Grout, William
Philadelphia, Pa., c. 1815

Grove, Christian
Heidelberg, York Co., Pa., c. 1800

Grove, Jacob
Lebanon, Pa., 1759–1782

Grove, William
Hanover, Pa., 1830–1870

Grubb, William, Jr.
Boston, Mass., c. 1815

Gruber, George
Berryville, Va., c. 1840

Gruby, Edward L.
Portland, Me., c. 1830

Grueby, George A.
Boston, Mass., c. 1860. Calendar clocks.

Gruen, D. & Sons
Cincinnati, Ohio, 1890–1898

Gruez, John
New York, N.Y., c. 1820. Cabinetmaker.

Grumbine, Daniel
East Berlin and Hanover, Pa., 1820–1870

Guild, Benjamin
New Jersey, n.d.

Guild, Isaac
Francestown, N.H., c. 1820

Guild, Jeremiah
Cincinnati, Ohio, c. 1830

Guild, John
Philadelphia, Pa., c. 1818

Guile, John
Philadelphia, Pa., 1810–1820

Guimartin, John
Augusta, Ga., c. 1820

Guimartin, T. J.
Atlanta, Ga., c. 1870

Guinard, F. E.
Baltimore, Md., c. 1817

Gulick, Nathan
Easton, Pa., c. 1790

Gulick, Samuel
Northampton, Pa., 1756–1825. Father of Nathan.

Gunkle (Kunkle), John
Cocalico, Lancaster, Pa., 1830–1840

Gurney, L. F.
Bridgeport, Conn., c. 1870

Guth, John
Whitepaint Twp., Pa., c. 1800

Guyer, Benjamin
Philadelphia, Pa., c. 1845

Haas, Gottlieb
Red Hook, Dutchess Co., N.Y., c. 1830

Haas, James A.
Philadelphia, Pa., c. 1845

Haas, N.
Philadelphia, Pa., c. 1845

Haas & Co.
New York, N.Y., 1820–1830. Maker of musical clocks.

Haas & Goetz
New York, N.Y., 1820–1830

Hacker, Michael
Tewksbury, N.J., and Philadelphia, Pa., c. 1755

Hadder, William
Philadelphia, Pa., c. 1837

Hadley Bros. & Estell
Chicago, Ill., c. 1860

Haettich, Andrew
Cleveland, Ohio, c. 1850

Hagey, George
Trappe, Pa., and Sterling, Ohio, c. 1840

Hagey, Jacob
Salford Twp., Pa., c. 1800. Son of Samuel.

Hagey, John
Philadelphia, Pa., c. 1830

Hagey, Jonas
Springtown, Pa., c. 1830

Hagey, M.
Germantown, Pa., 1820–1840

Hagey, Samuel
Franconia and Germantown, Pa., c. 1820

Hague, B.
New York, N.Y., c. 1850

Hahl Mfg. Co., The
Baltimore, Md., c. 1875. Maker of Wenzell Air Clock.

Hahn, C. G.
Philadelphia, Pa., c. 1790

Hahn, Henry
Reading, Pa., c. 1790

Hahn, Jacob
Reading, Pa., c. 1790

Haigh, T. Jefferson
Baltimore, Md., 1829–1831

Haight, Nelson
Newburgh, N.Y., n.d.

Hale, David R.
Lowell, Mass., n.d.

Hale, Joshua
Lowell, Mass., c. 1840

Hale, Nathan
Windsor, Vt., c. 1800

Hale, William C.
Salem, Mass., c. 1850

Hall, A. B.
Cleveland, Ohio, c. 1825

Hall, Amasa W.
Atlanta, Ga., c. 1860

Hall, Asa
Boston, Mass., c. 1805

Hall, Asaph
Goshen and Hart Hollow, Conn.,
c. 1805

Hall, Charles
Lancaster, Pa., c. 1770

Hall, Christian
Lititz, Lancaster Co., Pa., c. 1810

Hall, D. G.
Lewiston, Me., c. 1850

Hall, David
Philadelphia, Pa., and Burlington, N.J.,
c. 1775

Hall, Henry William
Lititz, Lancaster Co., Pa., c. 1835. Son
of Christian. Continued father's business.

Hall, Ivory
Concord, N.H., c. 1830. Besides making clocks, he operated a jewelry store
in Concord.

Hall, John
Geneva, N.Y., c. 1810

Hall, John
Philadelphia, Pa., c. 1810. Listed in
directories.

Hall, John
West Chester, Chester Co., Pa., c. 1820

Hall, John H.
New Haven, Conn., c. 1785

Hall, Peter
Philadelphia, Pa., c. 1820

Hall, Samuel
Harrisburg, Pa., n.d.

Hall, William
Warwick, Pa., 1832–1835

Hall and Bliss
Albany, N.Y., c. 1815

Hall, Seymour & Co.
Unionville, Conn., c. 1820

Hall and Stillman
Flemington, N.J., c. 1770

Hall & Wade
Newfield, Conn., 1793–1797

Halle, A.
Louisville, Ky., c. 1840

Haller, Jacob
Aaronsburg, Center Co., Pa., c. 1810

Halliday, E. H.
Camden, N.J., 1790–1820

Halliday, Hiram
Albany, N.Y., 1830–1840

Halliwell, George
New York, N.Y., c. 1805

Hallowell, Robert
Baltimore, Md., c. 1830

Ham, Daniel
Portsmouth, N.H., c. 1805

Ham, Francis
Portsmouth, N.H., c. 1840

Ham, George
Portsmouth, N.H., c. 1810

Ham, Henry
Portsmouth, N.H., n.d.

Ham, James
New York, N.Y., c. 1755. Maker of
mathematical instruments.

Ham, Supply
Portsmouth, N.H., c. 1820

Hamilton, Daniel S.
Elmira, N.Y., c. 1850

Hamilton, James
Philadelphia, Pa., c. 1850

Hamilton, R. J.
Philadelphia, Pa., c. 1835

Hamilton, S. P.
Savannah, Ga., c. 1860

Hamilton, Samuel
Philadelphia, Pa., c. 1835

Hamilton and Adams
Elmira, N.Y., c. 1835

Hamilton-Sangamo Corp.
Springfield, Ill., c. 1928. Maker of electric clocks.

Hamlen, Nathaniel
Augusta, Me., c. 1800

Hamlin, William
Providence, R.I., c. 1790

Hamman, Peter
Philadelphia, Pa., c. 1815

Hammerer, Jacob
n.p.; n.d.

Hammond, Samuel
New York, N.Y., 1840–1860

Hammond Clock Co.
Chicago, Ill., c. 1935

Hampson, Robert
New York, N.Y., n.d.

Hampton, James B.
Salisbury, N.C., c. 1820

Hampton, Samuel
Chelsea, Mass., c. 1840

Hampton and Palmer
Salisbury, N.C., c. 1830

Hamson, Clark
Waterbury, Conn., c. 1812

Handel, Bernard
Carlisle, Pa., c. 1800

Hanebarger, Peter
Ralpho, Pa., c. 1807

Haneye, Nathaniel
Bridgewater, Mass., n.d.

Hanks, Benjamin
Litchfield, Windham, and Mansfield,
Conn., c. 1800. Also bell founder.

Hanna, Hugh
Wabash, Ind., c. 1834. Probably dealer
only.

Hannum, John
Northampton, Mass., c. 1840

Hansell, James
Philadelphia, Pa., 1810–1840

Hansen Mfg. Co.
Princeton, Ind., c. 1936

Harden, James
Philadelphia, Pa., c. 1810. Made clock
dials.

Harder, W. A.
New York, N.Y., c. 1840

Harding, Newell
Haverhill and Boston, Mass., c. 1840

Hardman, J.
Lebanon, Ohio, c. 1820

Hardy, William
Charleston, S.C., c. 1770

Harlacher, Benjamin
Washington Twp., Pa., c. 1810

Harland, Thomas
Norwich, Conn., c. 1780. D. Burnap,
Seril and Ezra Dodge, Jabez Baldwin,

and others were apprenticed to him.
Father of Thomas, Jr.

Harland, Thomas, Jr.
Norwich, Conn., c. 1800

Harmson, Henry
Newport, R.I., c. 1720

Harper, Benjamin
Philadelphia, Pa., c. 1843

Harper, John M.
Philadelphia, Pa., c. 1841

Harrington, Charles
Brattleboro, Vt., c. 1830

Harrington, Henry
Salem, Mass., c. 1855

Harrington, Samuel
Amherst, Mass., 1842–1845

Harrington, William
Philadelphia, Pa., c. 1849

Harris, John
Charleston, S.C., c. 1729

Harris & Co.
Philadelphia, Pa., c. 1830

Harris & Harrington
New York, N.Y., c. 1880

Harris & Stanwood
Boston, Mass., c. 1842

Harris and Wilcox
Troy, N.Y., c. 1840. Could be dealers
only.

Harrison, James
Waterbury, Conn., 1790–1830

Harrison, John
Philadelphia, Pa., n.d.

Harrison, John M.
Philadelphia, Pa., n.d.

Harrison, Lemuel
Waterbury, Conn., c. 1800

Harrison, Susannah
New York, N.Y., c. 1850

Harrison, Wooster
Trumbull, Conn., c. 1795. Brother of
James and Lemuel.

Hart, Alpha
Goshen, Conn., c. 1820. Brother of
Henry.

Hart, Eliphaz
Norwich, Conn., c. 1810

Hart, G.
Bridgeport, Pa., c. 1850

Hart, Henry
Goshen, Conn., c. 1820

Hart, Judah
Norwich, Conn., 1810–1820

Hart, M.
Pittsburgh, Pa., c. 1820

Hart, Orrin
Bristol, Conn., 1824–1833

Hart and Brewer
Middletown, Conn., c. 1800

Hart and Sons
Goshen, Conn., c. 1830

Hart and Truesdale
Hartford, Ohio, n.d.

Hart and Way
Brookfield, Conn., c. 1800

Hart & Wilcox
Norwich, Conn., c. 1805

Harth, H. C.
New York, N.Y., c. 1850

Hartley, Jeremiah
Philadelphia, Pa., c. 1835

Hartley, John
York, Pa., c. 1810

Hartman, A.
New York, N.Y., c. 1840
Hartman, Emil
New York, N.Y., c. 1840
Hartman, Emil
San Francisco, Calif., 1875–1876
Hartzler, Joseph
Bear Town, Pa., c. 1850. Also a mill-
wright.
Harvard Clock Co.
Boston, Mass., c. 1880. Became Boston
Clock Co., then Chelsea Clock Co.
Harwood, George
Rochester, N.Y., c. 1830. Probably
dealer only.
Harwood Bros.
Boston, Mass., c. 1865
Hascy, Alexander R.
Albany, N.Y., c. 1830
Hascy, Samuel
Albany, N.Y., c. 1820. Father of Alex-
ander.
Haseltine and Wentworth
Lowell, Mass., c. 1830
Hasey, S.
Rensselaerville, N.Y., c. 1850
Hasham, Stephen
Charlestown, N.H., 1780s through first
quarter of 19th century. Originally
from Boston.
Hasie, Mark
New York, N.Y., c. 1855
Haskell, Moody
Burlington, Vt., c. 1820
Hass, James
Philadelphia, Pa., c. 1860
Hasting, B. B.
Cleveland, Ohio, c. 1837
Hastings, David B.
Boston, Mass., c. 1840. Probably dealer
only.
Hastings, T. D.
Boston, Mass., c. 1854
Hatch, George D.
Attleboro, Mass., 1810–1850
Hatch, John B.
Attleboro, Mass., c. 1870
Hatch, Jonathan
Westtown, Pa., c. 1810
Hatton, Thomas
Connecticut, n.d.
Haughton, S.
New Haven, Conn., c. 1810. Very likely
a casemaker.
Haughwout, E. V., & Co.
New York, N.Y., c. 1850
Haupt, H.
Cairo, Ill., c. 1860
Hausburg, E. O.
New York, N.Y., c. 1895
Haushall, John
Philadelphia, Pa., 1816–1817
Hawchurst, Nathaniel
New York, N.Y., c. 1785
Hawchurst and DeMilt
New York, N.Y., c. 1790
Hawes, J. H.
Ithaca, N.Y., c. 1850. Patented calen-
dar clock.
Hawley, F.
Panora, Iowa, c. 1860
Hay, Samuel
Lancaster Boro, Pa., c. 1789

Hayden, David
Waterbury, Conn., c. 1805
Hayden, Samuel
Boston, Mass., c. 1795
Hayden, Stephen
Butler, Ohio, c. 1805
Hayden and Freeman
New York, N.Y., c. 1785
Hayden, S. and Son
Boston, Mass., 1790s–1800
Haydock, C. G.
Philadelphia, Pa., 1785–1798
Hayes, Peter
Poughkeepsie, N.Y., c. 1825. Could be
dealer.
Hayes & Thomas
Philadelphia, Pa., c. 1860
Haynes, Lafayette
Troy, N.Y., c. 1835
Hays, Michael
New York, N.Y., c. 1765
Hazelton, E. L.
Springfield, Vt., n.d.
Hazen, N. S.
Cincinnati, Ohio, 1830–1840
Headman, William
Philadelphia, Pa., 1830–1840
Heagy, Jacob: See Hagey
Healy, Charles
Syracuse, N.Y., 1840–1850
Healy, John W.
Worcester, Mass., c. 1850
Heath, Reuben
Scottsville, N.Y., 1790–1810
Heath, Stevens
Chillicothe, Ohio, c. 1810
Heath, Willard B.
Bangor, Me., 1830–1870
Hedderley, Charles
Philadelphia, Pa., c. 1790. Maker of
clock parts, brass founder, clocksmith,
and machinist.
Hedges, George
Waterford, N.Y., 1820–1830; Buffalo,
N.Y., c. 1830
Heebner, David S.
Worcester Twp., Montgomery Co., Pa.,
c. 1830
Heffards, S. M.
Middleboro, Mass., n.d.
Heffley, Annanias
Berlin, Somerset Co., Pa., c. 1840
Heffley, Daniel
Berlin, Somerset Co., Pa., c. 1840
Heffords, M.
Middleboro, Mass., n.d.
Hege, Jacob: See Hagey
Hege, Samuel: See Hagey
Heilburn, Michael
Baltimore, Md., c. 1840
Heilig, Albert Elijah
Germantown, Pa., c. 1860
Heilig, Frederick
Philadelphia, Pa., n.d.
Heilig, Herman
Germantown, Pa., c. 1850
Heilig, Jacob
Lancaster and Philadelphia, Pa., 1770–
1820
Heilig, John
Germantown, Pa., c. 1820
Heineman, George
Philadelphia, Pa., 1847–1849

Heineman, L. C.
Philadelphia, Pa., c. 1849
Heinitsch, Charles
Lancaster, Pa., c. 1780
Heinrich, H. H.
New York, N.Y., n.d.
Heintzelman, Hieronymus
Lampeter Sq., Pa., c. 1750
Heintzelman, John Conrad
Manheim, Pa., c. 1785
Heintzelman, Peter
Manheim, Pa., c. 1800
Heiny, Clements
New York, N.Y., c. 1840
Heisley, Frederick
Frederick, Md., c. 1780; Lancaster,
Pa., c. 1793; Harrisburg, Pa., c. 1801;
Pittsburgh, Pa., c. 1820
Heisley, George J.
Frederick, Md., and Harrisburg, Pa.,
c. 1820
Heiss, James P.
Philadelphia, Pa., c. 1850
Helm, Christian
Philadelphia, Pa., c. 1800
Hemingway, A.
Chicago, Ill., c. 1856. Possibly dealer
only.
Hemley, Nathaniel
Kensington, N.H., c. 1760. Also black-
smith.
Hemphill, Thomas J.
Philadelphia, Pa., 1836–1841
Hempson, Robert
New York, N.Y., 1820–1830
Hempsted, Daniel Booth: 1784–1852
New London, Conn., c. 1810. Cabinet-
maker.
Hendel, Bernard
Carlisle, Pa., c. 1785
Hendel, Jacob
Carlisle, Pa., c. 1800
Henderson, Adam
Poughkeepsie, N.Y., c. 1830
Henderson, William
New Castle, Del., c. 1770
Henderson & Lossing
Poughkeepsie, N.Y., 1830–1840
Hendrick, Ebenezer
Bristol, Conn., c. 1850
Hendrick, Barnes & Co.
Forestville, Conn., c. 1845
Hendrick and Churchill
Bristol, Conn., c. 1847
Hendrick and Hubbel
Bristol, Conn., c. 1848
Hendrick, Hubbel and Beach
Bristol, Conn., c. 1854
Hendricks, Uriah
New York, N.Y., c. 1760
Hendrie, William A.
Chicago, Ill., 1880–1882
Hendrix, Uriah W.
New York, N.Y., 1756 and after. Could
also be Uriah Hendricks.
Heneberger, Peter
Harrisburg, Pa., c. 1800
Henry, James
Maysville, Ky., c. 1820
Hense, J. E.
Central City, Colo., c. 1870
Hense, Gottesleben and Jones
New York, N.Y., c. 1860

Heppleman, John
Manheim, Pa., c. 1800
Hepton, Frederick
Philadelphia, Pa., c. 1785
Hequembourg, C.
New Haven, Conn., 1810–1830. Could be dealer only.
Herancourt & Dresbache
Columbus, Ohio, c. 1830
Herdsal, Joseph
Florida, N.Y., n.d.
Herman, George
Newport, R.I., c. 1870. Patented a swinging clock.
Herman, John
Lancaster, Pa., n.d.
Heron, Erskine
Charleston, S.C., 1780–1790
Heron, Isaac
Bound Brook, N.J., c. 1765
Heron, James
Newtown, Pa., 1760–1780
Herr, William, Jr.
Providence, R.I., c. 1848
Herrican, William
Philadelphia, Pa., c. 1850
Hersheide Clock Co.
Cincinnati, Ohio, c. 1904; Starkville, Miss., 1960
Hertz, Jacob
Lancaster, Pa., c. 1810
Hervey, C. P.
New York, N.Y., c. 1810
Herwick, Jacob
Carlisle, Pa., c. 1780
Hetzel, John M.
New Town (Newton), N.J., c. 1795
Heurton, William, Jr.
New York, N.Y., c. 1729
Hewitt, E. A.
North Bridgewater, Mass., c. 1860
Heydorn, C.
Hartford, Conn., c. 1808
Heydorn and Imlay
Hartford, Conn., c. 1808. Purchased the business of Isaac Doolittle.
Hibbard, Caleb: 1781–1835
Willistown, Chester Co., Pa., c. 1800; to Ohio, 1818
Hibben, Andrew
Charleston, S.C., 1760–1770
Hickcox, Samuel R.
Humphreysville, Conn., c. 1830
Hicks, Willet
New York, N.Y., c. 1790
Higby, S. S.
New Hartford Center, Conn., c. 1800
Hight, Christian
Philadelphia, Pa., 1819–1822
Hilburn, John Jacob
Bowling Green, Ky., c. 1840
Hildeburn, Samuel
Philadelphia, Pa., c. 1810
Hildeburn & Watson
Philadelphia, Pa., c. 1830
Hildeburn & Woodworth
Philadelphia, Pa., 1810–1819
Hildreth, Jonas
Salisbury, Vt., c. 1805
Hile, J. W.
Kansas City and Topeka, Kans., c. 1860
Hileinger, Joshua
Pennsylvania, n.d.

Hill, A.
Steubenville, Ohio., n.d.
Hill, Arundel
Richmond Twp., Berks Co., Pa., c. 1810. Son of Benjamin Hill.
Hill, Benjamin
Richmond Twp., Berks Co., Pa., c. 1760
Hill, Charles
Zanesville, Ohio, c. 1815
Hill, Charles
Steubenville, Ohio, c. 1820
Hill, D.
Reading, Pa., 1820–1840
Hill, E. J.
Albion, N.Y., 1850–1860
Hill, Henry
New York, N.Y., 1740–1760
Hill, J. W.
Kansas, c. 1870
Hill, Joachim
Flemington, N.J., c. 1800
Hill, John B.
Beverly, Mass., 1850–1860
Hill, Noble S.
Bennington, Vt., c. 1790
Hill, Peter
Burlington, N.J., c. 1795. One of the few black clockmakers.
Hill, Samuel
Harrisburg, Pa., c. 1780
Hill, William
Boston, Mass., c. 1805
Hill, William
New York, N.Y., c. 1810
Hill, William J.
Bristol, Conn., c. 1850
Hill & Ross
Zanesville, Ohio, c. 1830
Hillard, Christopher
Hagerstown, Md., c. 1825
Hillard, George
Fayetteville, N.C., c. 1823
Hillard, James
Charleston, S.C., c. 1730
Hillard, William
Fayetteville, N.C., c. 1801
Hilldrop, Thomas
Hartford, Conn., c. 1773
Hiller, Joseph
Boston and Salem, Mass., c. 1770
Hillerd, Christopher
Hagerstown, Md., 1800–1840
Hillier, Thomas A.
Pittsburgh, Pa., 1840–1850. Probably dealer.
Hillman, F.
New York, N.Y., c. 1850
Hills, Amariah
New York, N.Y., c. 1845
Hills, Charles C.
Haverhill, Mass., n.d.
Hills, D. B.
Plainville, Conn., 1870–1880
Hills, Dwight B.
Bristol, Conn., c. 1895
Hills, George
Plainville, Conn., c. 1850
Hills, William
Farmington, Conn., c. 1830. Partner in Forestville Manufacturing Co., J.C. Brown and Hills, Goodrich and Co.

Hills, Brown and Co.
Bristol, Conn., c. 1840
Hills, George and Son
Plainville, Conn., c. 1870
Hills, Goodrich and Co.
Plainville, Conn., c. 1841
Hillworth, Frederick
Philadelphia, Pa., c. 1845
Hillyartiner, Philip
Philadelphia, Pa., c. 1840
Himele, James
New York, N.Y., c. 1786
Himely, John James
Philadelphia, Pa., c. 1786; Charleston, S.C., c. 1796
Hinkle, John P.
Philadelphia, Pa., c. 1824
Hinman, Alonzo
New Haven, Conn., 1840–1850
Hinsdale, Epaphras
Newark, N.J., c. 1795. Also made jewelry.
Hinshon, J. P.
Terre Haute, Ind., c. 1850
Hinton, George
Paterson, N.J., c. 1825
Hirsh, A., H. & L.
Lancaster, Pa., c. 1850. Probably jewelers only.
Hitchcock, H.
Lodi, N.Y., c. 1800
Hitchcock, R.
n.p.; c. 1870
Hoadley, Ammi: 1762–1834
Bethany and Plymouth, Conn. Operated a gristmill. Father of Silas.
Hoadley, Luther
Winsted, Conn., c. 1807. Worked with Riley Whiting.
Hoadley, Samuel
Winsted, Conn., c. 1807. Worked with Luther and Riley Whiting.
Hoadley, Silas: 1780–1870
Plymouth, Conn. Made various types of shelf and tall clocks with wood movements. Worked with Seth Thomas and Eli Terry. Made a few clocks with brass movements.
Hoadley, Samuel and Co.
Winchester, Conn., c. 1805
Hobart, Aaron
Boston, Mass., c. 1770. Was brass founder, making clock parts.
Hobbs, James
Baltimore, Md., 1790–1800
Hobbs, Nathan
Boston, Mass., c. 1840
Hockers, G.
Ephrata, Lancaster Co., Pa., c. 1760
Hockley, Thomas
Philadelphia, Pa., c. 1800
Hodges, Edwin
Torrington Hollow, Conn., c. 1850. Son of Erastus.
Hodges, Erastus
Torrington, Conn., c. 1830. Made pillar-and-scroll clocks with Torrington or "East and West" movements.
Hodges & North
Wolcottville (now Torrington), Conn., c. 1830
Hodgson, William
Philadelphia, Pa., c. 1785

Hoelsche, Killian
Mount Joy, Lancaster Co., Pa., c. 1850
Hofer, Charles
Macon, Miss., c. 1850
Hoff, George
Lancaster, Pa., 1760–1816. Father of George, Jr.
Hoff, George, Jr.
Lancaster, Pa., c. 1790 to 1830 or 1840
Hoff, George F.
Lancaster Boro, Pa., 1770–1822
Hoff, Jacob
Lancaster Boro, Pa., 1807–1817
Hoff, John
Lancaster Boro, Pa., 1799–1809
Hoff, Mrs. John
Lancaster, Pa., c. 1810. Carried on her husband's business after his death.
Hoff & Heisely
Lancaster, Pa., 1796–1800
Hoffard, Samuel
Berlin, Somerset Co., Pa., c. 1825
Hoffman, C. M.
Lebanon, N.H., 1850–1860
Hoffman, C. W.
Greensburg, Pa., 1850–1870
Hoffner, Henry
Philadelphia, Pa., c. 1790
Hoguet, Augustus
Philadelphia, Pa., 1814–1833
Hoke, George
Hanover, Pa., 1810–1820
Holbrook, George, Major
Wrentham, Brookfield, Medway, Mass., c. 1800. Bell founder.
Holbrook, H.
Medway, Mass., c. 1830
Holden, Eli
Philadelphia, Pa., c. 1840
Holden, Henry
New Haven, Conn., c. 1840
Holden, J.
Boston, Mass., c. 1830
Holden, Joseph
Dayton, Ohio, c. 1830
Holdredge, A. A.
Glens Falls, N.Y., c. 1840
Hollenbach, David
Reading, Pa., c. 1826. Worked for Daniel Oyster.
Holler, Henry
Center County, Pa., c. 1815
Hollinger, A.
Philadelphia, Pa., c. 1835
Hollinshead, George
Woodstown, N.J., c. 1760
Hollinshead, Hugh
Mount Holly and Moorestown, N.J., c. 1760
Hollinshead, Jacob
Salem, N.J., c. 1770
Hollinshead, Job
Newtown, Bucks Co., Pa. Adv. as clock- and watchmaker, 1821.
Hollinshead, John
Burlington, N.J., 1770–1780
Hollinshead, Joseph
Burlington, N.J., c. 1740
Hollinshead, Joseph, Jr.
Burlington, N.J., c. 1770
Hollinshead, Morgan
Philadelphia, Pa., c. 1775
Hollis, Joseph
West Chester, Pa., c. 1820

Hollister, J. H.
Greenfield, Mass., 1850–1860
Holloway, Robert
Baltimore, Md., c. 1820
Holman, D.
Baltimore, Md., 1800–1820. Produced excellent banjo clocks.
Holman, Salam
Hartford, Conn., c. 1810
Holmes, Aaron
Boston, Mass., c. 1842
Holmes, A. B.
Newark, N.J., n.d.
Holmes, J.
Philadelphia, Pa., c. 1842
Holmes, Weaver
Newport, R.I., n.d. Cabinetmaker.
Holmgreen, Charles
Hamilton, N.Y., 1850–1860
Holt, David
Harpers Ferry, W.Va., c. 1830
Holton, Harry
Wells River, Vt., c. 1860
Holway, Philip
Falmouth, Mass., c. 1800
Homan, Samuel
Marblehead, Mass., n.d.
Homer, William
Moreland, Pa., c. 1840
Hood, Francis
New York, N.Y., c. 1810
Hood, Jacob
Philadelphia, Pa., c. 1820. Jeweler, probably not a maker.
Hood, John
Philadelphia, Pa., n.d.
Hook, Michael
Lancaster, Pa., c. 1708
Hooker & Goodenough
Bristol, Conn., c. 1840
Hooker & Morgan
Pine Plains, N.Y., 1810–1820
Hooley, Richard
Flemington, N.J., 1810–1830. From England.
Hoops, Adam
Somerset, Pa., c. 1800
Hoover, John
Emmitsburg, Md., c. 1754
Hope, F. M.
Sag Harbor, N.Y., 1870
Hopkins, Asa
Litchfield, Conn., 1810–1820
Hopkins, Henry P.
Philadelphia, Pa., c. 1830
Hopkins, Joseph
Waterbury, Conn., c. 1750
Hopkins, Orange
Litchfield, Campville, and Terryville, Conn., c. 1820
Hopkins, Robert
Philadelphia, Pa., c. 1820
Hopkins, William
Geneva, N.Y., c. 1840
Hopkins & Alfred
Harwinton, Conn., 1820–1825; Hartford, Conn., 1825–1845
Hopkins & Lewis
Litchfield, Conn., c. 1820
Hopper, B. C.
Philadelphia, Pa., c. 1840
Hopper, Benjamin
Philadelphia, Pa., c. 1850

Hopper, John
Philadelphia, Pa., c. 1835
Hopper, Joseph
Philadelphia, Pa., 1810–1820
Hopper, S.
Philadelphia, Pa., 1840–1850
Hoquet, Augustus
Philadelphia, Pa., c. 1820
Horah, James
Salisbury, N.C., c. 1840
Horn, E. B.
Boston, Mass., c. 1840
Horn, Eliphalet
Lowell, Mass., c. 1832
Horne, James A.
Dover, N.H., c. 1850
Horst, David
Sporting Hill, Lancaster Co., Pa., 1850–1860
Horton, Alfred
New Haven, Conn., 1840–1850
Horton, Henry B.
Akron, Ohio, c. 1845. Inventor of Horton Calendar used by Ithaca Calendar Clock Co.
Horton and Burgi
New York, N.Y., c. 1775
Horton & Peck
Litchfield, Conn., c. 1800
Horwood, Charles
Bristol, Conn., 1750–1780
Hosmer, M.
Hartford, Conn., 18th century
Hostetter, Jacob
Hanover, York Co., Pa., c. 1800
Hostetter, Jacob, Jr.
Hanover, Pa., 1806–1818; later, New Lisbon, Ohio, to the 1830s
Hostetter, S.
Hanover, Pa., c. 1820
Hotchkiss, A. E.
Cheshire, Conn., c. 1880. Founder of Cheshire Clock Co.
Hotchkiss, Alva
Poughkeepsie, N.Y., 1820–1830; later, New York, N.Y., 1830–1840
Hotchkiss, Andrew S.
Brooklyn, N.Y., c. 1860
Hotchkiss, Elisha
Burlington, Conn., c. 1815
Hotchkiss, Hezekiah
New Haven, Conn., c. 1748
Hotchkiss, John
Rochester, N.Y., c. 1840
Hotchkiss, William
Maryland, c. 1775
Hotchkiss, A. S. and Co.
New York, N.Y., c. 1870
Hotchkiss & Benedict
Auburn, N.Y., c. 1820
Hotchkiss & Field
Burlington, Conn., c. 1820
Hotchkiss & Pierpont
Plymouth, Conn., c. 1811
Hotchkiss, Robert & Henry
Plymouth, Conn., c. 1840
Hotchkiss, Spencer & Co.
Salem Bridge, Conn., c. 1830
Hough, J. G.
Bridgeport, Conn., c. 1810
Hough, John
Newport, Ind., c. 1820. Also cabinetmaker.

Hough, Joseph G.
  Hamilton and Lebanon, Ohio, c. 1805
Houguet, Augustus
  Philadelphia, Pa., 1819–1825
House, G. V.
  New York, N.Y., c. 1830
House, George
  Hanover, Pa., 1790–1830
House & Robinson
  Bristol, Conn., c. 1850
Houston, James
  Lancaster Boro, Pa., 1809
Houston, William
  Philadelphia, Pa., c. 1800
Hovey, Cyrus
  Lowell, Mass., c. 1860
Hovey, J. R.
  Norwich, Conn., c. 1815
Hovey, S. and Co.
  Manchester, N.H., n.d.
Howard, Albert
  Boston, Mass., c. 1878
Howard, Edward
  Boston, Mass., c. 1840. Maker of ex-
  cellent watches and clocks. In business
  with Howard and Davis, 1842–1857,
  and Howard, Davis and Dennison,
  Roxbury, Mass., c. 1850. Howard and
  Davis produced first scales used by
  U.S. Post Office Dept.
Howard, E.
  New York, N.Y., n.d.
Howard, J.
  Boston, Mass., c. 1870
Howard, Thomas
  Philadelphia, Pa., 1770–1780
Howard, William
  Boston, Mass., c. 1815
Howard, A. and Co.
  Boston, Mass., c. 1878
Howard Clock Co.
  Roxbury, Mass., c. 1903
Howard Clock Products Co.
  Waltham, Mass., c. 1934
Howard Clock and Watch Co.
  Boston, Mass., c. 1861
Howard and Davis
  Boston, Mass., c. 1842
Howard, Davis and Dennison
  Roxbury, Mass., c. 1850
Howard, E. & Co.
  Boston, Mass., c. 1857
Howard, E. Watch and Clock Co.
  Boston, Mass., c. 1861
Howard Watch & Clock Co.
  Boston, Mass., c. 1867
Howcott, Nathaniel
  Edenton, N.C., c. 1830
Howe, Jubal
  Boston, Mass., c. 1830
Howell, Nathan
  New Haven, Conn., 1762–1784
Howell, Silas W.
  New Brunswick, N.J., c. 1790
Howell & Hall
  Albany, N.Y., c. 1800
Hoyt, Freeman
  Sumter, S.C., 1830–1860
Hoyt, George A.
  Albany, N.Y., c. 1830
Hoyt, George B.
  Albany, N.Y., c. 1845

Hoyt, Henry
  New York, N.Y., c. 1810; Albany, N.Y.,
  1820–1830
Hoyt, James
  Troy, N.Y., c. 1830
Hoyt, Seymour
  Brooklyn, N.Y., c. 1840
Hoyt, Badger and Dillon
  New York, N.Y., n.d.
Hoyt, George A. and Co.
  Albany, N.Y., c. 1840
Hoyt, S. & Co.
  New York, N.Y., c. 1830
Hubbard, C.
  Boston, Mass., n.d.
Hubbard, C. K.
  Hartford, Conn., c. 1860
Hubbard, Daniel
  Medfield, Mass., c. 1820
Hubbard Brothers
  New York, N.Y., c. 1860
Hubbard, Gilbert and Co.
  Bristol, Conn., c. 1850
Hubbard & Hitchcock
  Buckland, Mass., 1800–1820
Hubbell, La Porte
  Bristol, Conn., 1849–1880
Hubbell & Beach
  Bristol, Conn., 1859–1863
Hubbell & Boardman
  New Haven, Conn., c. 1860
Hubbell, L. and Son
  Bristol, Conn., c. 1870
Huber, Christian
  Cocalico Twp., Lancaster Co., Pa.,
  c. 1760
Huckel, Samuel
  Philadelphia, Pa., c. 1820
Hudson, Edward
  Mount Holly, N.J., c. 1810
Hudson, J. C.
  San Francisco, Calif., c. 1860
Hudson, Joseph
  Albany, N.Y., c. 1850. Probably dealer
  only.
Hudson, William
  Mount Holly, N.J., c. 1810
Hugenin, Charles Frederick
  Philadelphia, Pa., c. 1790
Hughes, Christopher
  Baltimore, Md., 1859–1873
Hughes, Edmund
  Hampton and Middletown, Conn., n.d.
Hughs, John
  Taneytown, Md., c. 1810. Maker of
  tower clocks.
Huguenail, Charles T.
  Philadelphia, Pa., c. 1799
Huguenin, J. C.
  San Francisco, Calif., 1860–1870
Hugus, Jacob
  Greensburg, Pa., 1800–1820
Hugus, Michael
  Berlin, Somerset Co., Pa., 1794–1825
Hulburt, Horace
  New Haven, Conn., c. 1850
Humbert, Charles
  New York, N.Y., c. 1810
Humbert & Droz
  Philadelphia, Pa., c. 1790
Hummely & Thomas
  Piqua, Ohio, c. 1825
Humpary, W. and D. S.
  Parma, Ohio, c. 1830

Humphrey, David
  Lexington, Ky., 1780–1790
Humphrey, Joshua
  Charlestown and East Whiteland,
  Chester Co., Pa., c. 1770
Humphrey, Norman
  New York, N.Y., c. 1840. Casemaker
  and probably dealer.
Hunchburger, Isaac
  West Earl, Pa., 1849–1850
Hunt, E.
  New York, N.Y., c. 1780
Hunt, Hiram
  Bangor and Robbinston, Me., c. 1835
Hunt, John
  Plainville and Farmington, Conn.,
  1830–1840
Hunt and Clark
  Vermont, c. 1795. Later alone.
Hunt and Colgrove
  Farmington, Conn., c. 1840
Huntington, Gurdon
  Windham, Conn., 1784–1789; Walpole,
  N.H., 1790–1804
Huntington, M.P. and Co.
  Milton, N.C., c. 1820. Dealers in
  clocks.
Huntington & Platto
  Ithaca, N.Y., 1854; Plymouth Hollow,
  Conn., 1855–1868; Ithaca after 1868.
  Later, Ithaca Calendar Clock Co.
Huntzecker, Jacob
  East Donegal, Marietta, Pa., 1842–
  1850
Huply, Frederick
  Lancaster Boro, Pa., c. 1797
Hurdus, Adam
  Cincinnati, Ohio, c. 1820. Worked with
  Luman Watson.
Hurdus, Allen
  Cincinnati, Ohio, c. 1810
Hurlbut, Horace
  New Haven, Conn., c. 1850
Hurst, David
  Sporting Hill, Lancaster Co., Pa.,
  c. 1850
Hurtin, Christian
  Goshen, N.Y., c. 1790
Hurtin, Joshua
  Bound Brook, N.J., 1760. Brother of
  William.
Hurtin, William
  Bound Brook, N.J., c. 1775
Hurtin & Burgi
  Bound Brook, N.J., c. 1775
Huston, James
  Trenton, N.J., c. 1760; Philadelphia,
  Pa., c. 1770
Huston, Joseph
  Albany, N.Y., c. 1850
Huston, William
  Philadelphia, Pa., 1770–1800
Hutchins, Abel
  Concord, N.H., 1788–1819. Apprentice
  of Simon Willard. Worked with his
  brother Levi, and signed their clocks
  Levi and Abel Hutchins.
Hutchins, Levi
  Concord, N.H., 1786–1819. Apprentice
  of Simon Willard.
Hutchins, Nicholas
  Baltimore, Md., c. 1810
Hutchinson, Samuel
  Philadelphia, Pa., c. 1830

Hutchinson, Thomas
Philadelphia, Pa., c. 1820
Hutinson, William
Philadelphia, Pa., c. 1805
Huver, I.
Pennsylvania, n.d.
Hyde, J. O.
New York, N.Y., c. 1850
Hyde, John E.
New York, N.Y., c. 1880
Hyland, William C.
New York, N.Y., c. 1845
Hyman, Henry
Lexington, Ky., 1800–1810
Hyman, Samuel
Philadelphia, Pa., c. 1790; Baltimore, Md., c. 1800
Hyver, G. A.
New Orleans, La., c. 1850

Ihrie, Edward
Easton, Pa., 1790–1810
Imay, K. K.
n.p.; n.d.
Imbery, J. and A.
New York, N.Y., c. 1820
Imhauser Time Clock Co.
New York, N.Y., c. 1870. Received Pat., 1873, for watchman's time detector.
Imhoff, Jacob
New York, N.Y., c. 1840
Imlay
New Haven and Hartford, Conn., 1801–1807
Imperial Clock Co.
Hyland, Ill., c. 1936
Inch, John
Annapolis, Md., c. 1740. Adv. 1745 to 1749.
Ingraham, Elias
Bristol and Ansonia, Conn., 1827–1885. Started as cabinetmaker and joiner. One of the outstanding case designers of the period; designed the sharp gothic or steeple clock. Involved in many companies, such as Ingraham & Bartholomew, Ingraham & Goodrich, Ray and Ingraham, Brewster & Ingraham, E. and A. Ingraham, Ingraham and Company, The Ingraham and Company and The E. Ingraham Company.
Ingraham, Henry
Philadelphia, Pa., c. 1830
Ingraham, Reuben
Preston and Plainfield, Conn., c. 1770. Apprenticed to John Avery.
Ingraham and Andrew
Bristol, Conn., 1852–1855. Moved to Ansonia, Conn., after a disastrous fire.
Ingraham and Bartholomew
Bristol, Conn., 1831–1832
Ingraham, Elias and Company
Bristol, Conn., probably c. 1857
Ingraham Company, The E.
Bristol, Conn., c. 1884. Company was one of largest and foremost clock manufacturing companies in the world.
Ingraham and Company, The
Bristol, Conn., 1880–1884. Elias Ingraham, President.
Ingraham, E. and A.
Bristol, Conn., 1852–1855

Ingraham and Goodrich
Bristol, Conn., 1832–1833
Ingraham and Steadman
New York, N.Y., and Conn., c. 1850
Ingram, Alex
Greenwich, N.Y., c. 1870
Inskeep, Joseph
Philadelphia, Pa., 1790–1800
International Time Recorders
New York, N.Y., c. 1936
Irish, Charles
New York, N.Y., c. 1810
Ithaca Calendar Clock Co.
Ithaca, N.Y., 1868–1919. Made clocks under Hawes, Atkins, and Horton patents.
Itnyer, John
Hagerstown, Md., 1750–1770
Ives, Amasa, Sr.
Bristol, Conn., 1770–1790. Father of the famous Ives brothers.
Ives, Chauncey
Bristol, Conn., 1811–1838
Ives, Enos
New York, N.Y., c. 1845
Ives, George
Lebanon, Pa., n.d.
Ives, Ira
Bristol, Conn., 1810–1820. Brother of Chauncey.
Ives, James S.
Bristol, Conn., c. 1835. Received Pat. for clock springs.
Ives, Joseph
Bristol, Conn., and Brooklyn, N.Y., 1811–1825. Made wood movements, both 30-hour and 8-day. Invented the wagon spring in New York c. 1825. Experimented with pillar-and-scroll clock. Invented the tin plate movement c. 1859; also invented the "roller pinions." Worked with many other companies and men, including Amasa Ives & Company, Thomas Barnes, Jr., Merriman, Birge & Co., Levi Lewis, etc. Also worked in Farmington and Plainville, Conn. One of the great names in the clock industry.
Ives, Joseph S.
Bristol, Conn., c. 1830. Worked with his father Joseph. Had many patents on clock parts.
Ives, Lawson
Bristol, Conn., 1820–1830
Ives, Philo
Bristol, Conn., c. 1800
Ives, Porteus R.
Bristol, Conn., c. 1840. Son of Joseph Ives.
Ives, Rollin
Bristol, Conn., c. 1855. Grandson of Joseph Ives and son of Porteus.
Ives, Shaylor
Bristol, Conn., c. 1840. Worked with Elisha C. Brewster.
Ives, Amasa, Jr., & Co.
Bristol, Conn., 1811–1812. Same firm as Amasa and Chauncey Ives.
Ives, Blakeslee & Co.
Bridgeport, Conn., 1870–1880. Made mechanical motion novelty clocks.
Ives and Brewster
Bristol, Conn., c. 1840

Ives Brothers
Bristol, Conn., various dates between 1808–1862. Birth and death dates as follows: Ira, 1775–1848; Amasa, 1777–1817; Philo, 1780–1822; Joseph, 1782–1862; Shaylor, 1785–1840; Chauncey, 1787–1857.
Ives, Chauncey & Lawson
Bristol, Conn., 1830–1838. Movements for cases made by Elias Ingraham.
Ives, Lawson and Company
Bristol, Conn., c. 1840
Ives & Lewis
Bristol, Conn., 1819–1823

Jaccard, E.
Saint Louis, Mo., c. 1824
Jacks, James
Charleston, S.C., 1780–1790 and 1800–1820; Philadelphia, Pa., 1797–1799
Jacks & Gibson
Charleston, S.C., 1780–1790
Jackson, Alfred
Norwalk, Conn., n.d.
Jackson, Charles
Schenectady, N.Y., c. 1815
Jackson, George
Unionville, East Marlborough Twp., Chester Co., Pa., c. 1800
Jackson, Isaac
London Grove and New Garden, Chester Co., Pa., c. 1760
Jackson, John
East Marlborough Twp., Chester Co., Pa., c. 1775
Jackson, John
Boston, Mass., c. 1790
Jackson, Joseph H.
Philadelphia, Pa., c. 1802
Jackson, Richard
East Springfield, Jefferson Co., Ohio, c. 1801
Jackson, Thomas
Kittery, Me.; Portsmouth, N.H.; Boston, Mass.; and Preston, Conn., c. 1775
Jacob, Charles
Annapolis, Md., c. 1773; Baltimore, Md., c. 1778
Jacobs, J.M. and Co.
Brooklyn, N.Y., n.d.
Jacot, A.
Baltimore, Md., c. 1840
Jacques, Charles
New York, N.Y., c. 1880. Agent for V. Blanpain, Paris.
James, Edward
Philadelphia, Pa., c. 1780. Case- and cabinetmaker.
James, Henry B.
n.p.; c. 1860
James, J. J.
Augusta, Ga., c. 1820
James, Joshua
Boston, Mass., c. 1823
James, William
Portsmouth, R.I., c. 1717
Jameson, Jacob
Columbia, Lancaster Co., Pa., c. 1820. Later moved to Dayton, Ohio.
Jamin, Jean Baptiste
Baltimore, Md., 1790–1800
Jarrett, Sebastian
Germantown, Pa., 1760–1780
Jarves, John J.
Boston, Mass., c. 1790. Also cabinetmaker.

Jeanes, Thomas
Philadelphia, Pa., c. 1830
Jefferis, Curtis
West Chester, Chester Co., Pa., c. 1816.
Left for Kentucky and worked there
c. 1822. Also silversmith.
Jefferson, Thomas
Monticello, Va. Designed clock for
his home, Monticello.
Jeffreys, Samuel
Philadelphia, 1760–1770
Jeffreys, Samuel Fuller
Philadelphia, Pa., c. 1760
Jeffries, George, Rev.
Franklintown, Ohio, c. 1814
Jencks, John E.
Providence, R.I., c. 1800
Jengens, R.
Sag Harbor, N.Y., n.d.
Jenkins, Harman
Albany, N.Y., c. 1817
Jenkins, Ira
Albany, N.Y., c. 1813
Jenkins, Osmore
New Bedford, Mass., c. 1840
Jenkins, W.
Richmond, Ind., 1800–1820
Jenkins, I. and H.
Albany, N.Y., c. 1815
Jenne & Andersons
Big Rapids, Mich., c. 1860
Jennerer, Charles E.
Saint Louis, Mo., c. 1810
Jennings Bros. Mfg. Co.
Bridgeport, Conn., n.d.
Jennis, F. S.
Barnstead Parade, N.H., c. 1880
Jensen, Fred, & Son
New York, N.Y., c. 1900
Jepson, William
Boston, Mass., c. 1825
Jerome, Andrew
New Haven, Conn., 1840–1850
Jerome, Charles
New Haven, Conn., 1840–1850
Jerome, Chauncey
Plymouth, Conn., 1816–1822; Bristol,
Conn., 1822–1845; New Haven, Conn.,
1845–1855. One of the more important
clockmakers. In various companies:
Jerome and Company, 1833–1837; C.
& N. Jerome, 1834–1839; Jerome &
Company, c. 1850; Jerome & Grant,
1842–1843; Jerome, Darrow and Com-
pany, c. 1825; Jerome & Jewell, 1847–
1849; Jerome Mfg. Co., 1845–1855;
Jerome & Noble, 1835–1837, etc.
Brother of Noble.
Jerome, Noble
Bristol, Conn., c. 1824. Worked with
brother Chauncey. Invented 30-hour
weight-driven movement made of strip-
rolled brass.
Jerome and Barnes
Bristol, Conn., 1833–1837
Jerome, C. & N.
Bristol, Conn., 1834–1839. Succeeded
Jeromes and Darrow.
Jerome & Company
New Haven, Conn., c. 1850
Jerome and Company
Philadelphia, Pa., c. 1850. Dealers only.
Jerome and Darrow
Bristol, Conn., c. 1825

Jerome and Grant
Bristol, Conn., 1842–1843
Jerome, Jewell & Company
Bristol, Conn., 1847–1849
Jerome Manufacturing Company
Boston, Mass., c. 1852
Jerome Manufacturing Co.
New Haven, Conn., 1845–1855
Jerome and Noble
Richmond, Va., and Hamburg, S.C.,
1835–1837. Assembly plant only for
clock parts from Bristol.
Jerome, S. B. & Co.
New Haven, Conn., 1856–1858
Jerome, Thompson and Company
Bristol, Conn., n.d.
Jeromes and Company
Bristol, Conn., n.d.
Jeromes and Darrow
Bristol, Conn., 1824–1833. Chauncey
and Noble were in this firm. Noble
made movements; Chauncey, the cases;
Darrow painted the tablets.
Jeromes, Gilbert, Grant and Co.
Bristol, Conn., 1839–1840. Both broth-
ers, Chauncey and Noble, were in this
firm.
Jessop, Jonathan
Yorktown, York Co., Pa., c. 1800.
Brother of Joseph.
Jessop, Joseph Updegraff
Philadelphia, Pa., c. 1820. Brother of
Jonathan.
Jewell, Jessop & Co.
Bristol, Conn., c. 1845
Jewell, Matthews and Company
Bristol, Conn., 1847
Jewell and Warner
Bristol, Conn., c. 1845
Jewett, Amos
Canaan, N.Y., c. 1790; New Lebanon
Community to c. 1830. Made and num-
bered tall case clocks.
Jewett, Augustine
Newburyport, Mass., c. 1855
Job, John
Philadelphia, Pa., c. 1815
Jocelyn, Albert H.
New Haven, Conn., c. 1840. Son of
Nathaniel and grandson of Simeon.
Jocelyn, Nathaniel
New Haven, Conn., c. 1800. Father of
Albert.
Jocelyn, Simeon
New Haven, Conn., 1770–1800. Prob-
ably apprenticed to Isaac Doolittle.
Patented silent timepiece with fewer
wheels. Also a mathematician. Father
of Nathaniel.
Johns, Daniel
Charlestown, Ohio, c. 1835
Johnson, Addison
Wolcottville, Conn., c. 1820
Johnson, Andrew
Boston, Mass., c. 1840
Johnson, Caleb
Boston, Mass., c. 1800
Johnson, Charles F.
Owego, N.Y., c. 1835
Johnson, Chauncey
Albany, N.Y., c. 1820. Maker of mu-
sical clocks.
Johnson, Daniel B.
Utica, N.Y., c. 1835

Johnson, David
Limerick Twp., Pa., c. 1850
Johnson, Edward
n.p.; c. 1774
Johnson, Eli
Boston, Mass., c. 1820
Johnson, Elisha
Greensboro, N.C., c. 1840
Johnson, F.
Belmont, N.H., c. 1880
Johnson, Israel
Easton, Md., c. 1790
Johnson, J. J.
New York, N.Y., c. 1850
Johnson, Jabez
Charleston, S.C., 1780–1790
Johnson, John
Charleston, S.C., c. 1765
Johnson, M. B.
Watertown, N.Y., c. 1835
Johnson, Michael
Yellow Creek, Ohio, c. 1820
Johnson, Miles
Wallingford, Conn., n.d.
Johnson, Nels
Manistee, Mich., n.d.
Johnson, P.
Sheward, Del., n.d.
Johnson, Robert
Philadelphia, Pa., c. 1830
Johnson, Samuel
Hagerstown, Md., n.d.
Johnson, Simon
Sanbornton, N.H., 1830–1860
Johnson, William
New York, N.Y., 1830–1840
Johnson Brothers
Sanbornton, N.H., c. 1830
Johnson and Crowley
Philadelphia, Pa., c. 1825
Johnson and Lewis
Philadelphia, Pa., c. 1835
Johnson, R.S. and R.D.
Sanbornton, N.H., c. 1840
Johnson, W.N. and Co.
New York, N.Y., n.d.
Johnston, Arthur
Hagerstown, Md., 1785–1825
Johnston, John
Boston, Mass., c. 1810. Dial and tablet
painter.
Johnston, Robert
Cincinnati, Ohio, c. 1850
Johnston, A. & W.
Hagerstown, Md., 1785–1815
Johnston and Davis
Pittsburgh, Pa., c. 1800
Johnston & Fisher
Frederick, Md., c. 1845
Johnston and Foss
Pittsburgh, Pa., c. 1800
Johnston & Melhorn
Boonesboro and Hagerstown, Md.,
1785–1818
Johnston, J.H. & Co.
New York, N.Y., 1800–1820
Jonas, Joseph
Philadelphia, Pa., c. 1815
Jonas, Joseph
Cincinnati, Ohio, 1810–1820
Jonckheere, Francis
Baltimore, Md., c. 1817
Jones, Abner
Weare, N.H., c. 1780

Jones, Albert
Greenfield, Mass., n.d.
Jones, Daniel
Steubenville, Ohio, c. 1808
Jones, Edward K.
Bristol, Conn., c. 1820
Jones, Ezekiel
Boston, Mass., c. 1815. Worked with
Daniel Monroe, Jr., 1807–1809.
Jones, George, Jr.
Wilmington, Del., c. 1814
Jones, George A.
Zanesville, Ohio, c. 1830
Jones, George A.
Bristol, Conn., c. 1870
Jones, Griffith
Baltimore, Md., c. 1820
Jones, Harlow
Canandaigua, N.Y., c. 1810
Jones, Henry B.
Easton, Md., c. 1820
Jones, J. B.
Boston, Mass., c. 1820. Probably dealer.
Jones, Jacob
Pittsfield, N.H., c. 1800
Jones, Jacob
Baltimore, Md., c. 1815
Jones, John
Philadelphia, Pa., c. 1775
Jones, Noel
Hudson, N.Y., c. 1800
Jones, Richard
Baltimore, Md., c. 1815
Jones, Richard
Baltimore, Md., c. 1835
Jones, Roland
Utica, N.Y., c. 1835
Jones, Samuel
Philadelphia, Pa., c. 1800
Jones, Samuel G.
Baltimore, Md., c. 1810
Jones, William
New York, N.Y., c. 1845
Jones, William H.
Charleston, S.C., c. 1835
Jones & Aspinwall
Boston, Mass., c. 1809
Jones, Ball & Poor
Boston, Mass., c. 1840
Jones & Frisbie
New Hartford, Conn., c. 1830
Jones, George A. and Company
Bristol, Conn., and New York, N.Y.,
c. 1870
Jones, Low and Ball
Boston, Mass., c. 1835
Jones & Olney
Newark, Wayne Co., N.Y., c. 1830.
Probably dealer only.
Jones and Pardmore
Troy, N.Y., c. 1885
Jones, Shreve, Brown & Company
Boston, Mass., c. 1850
Jones & Wood
Syracuse, N.Y., c. 1845
Jordan, R.
Richmond, Va., c. 1820
Joseph, Isaac
Boston, Mass., c. 1820
Joseph, J. G.
Cincinnati, Ohio, 1820–1840
Joslin, Gilman
Boston, Mass., c. 1850. Made globes
for Timby Clock.

Joslin, James
New Haven, Conn., c. 1800
Joyce, Robert
New York, N.Y., c. 1795
Joyce, Thomas
Philadelphia, Pa., c. 1820
Judd, Henry
Torrington, Conn., n.d.
Judd, Henry G.
New York, N.Y., c. 1840
Just, William F.
New Britain, Conn., c. 1890
Justice, Joseph
Philadelphia, Pa., c. 1840
Juvet, Louis P.
Glens Falls, N.Y., 1879–1886. In part-
nership with James Arkell, manufac-
tured the time globes.

Kabel, Joseph
New York, N.Y., c. 1850
Kadmus, J.
Dubuque, Iowa, n.d.
Kalish, B. S.
Bangor, Me., c. 1870
Kallman, Charles
Newburgh, N.Y., c. 1865
Kapp, Phillip
Warwick, Pa., 1840–1850
Karn, A. L.
Philadelphia, Pa., c. 1805
Karner, C.
Philadelphia, Pa., c. 1809
Kayton, B.
Fredericksburg, Va., c. 1845
Kearn, Felix
New Haven, Conn., c. 1840
Kearney, Hugh
Wolcottville, Conn., c. 1825. Shelf
clocks.
Kedzie, J.
Rochester, N.Y., c. 1840
Kee, John M.
Chester, S.C., c. 1860
Keel, John
Philadelphia, Pa., c. 1835
Keeler, Joseph
Norwalk, Conn., c. 1870
Kehew, William Henry
Salem, Mass., c. 1855
Keim, John
Reading, Pa., c. 1777
Kelley, Allen
New Bedford, Hingham, Hanover,
Sandwich, Provincetown, and Nan-
tucket, Mass., 1805–1838. Actual dates
in each location unknown.
Kelley, Benjamin
Atlanta, Ga., c. 1870
Kelley, David
Philadelphia, Pa., c. 1810
Kelley, Zeno
New Bedford, Mass., c. 1840. Adv. as
clockmaker.
Kellogg, Daniel
Hebron, Conn., c. 1787. Apprenticed to
Daniel Burnap. Later at Colchester,
Conn., c. 1811 and Hartford, Conn.,
c. 1833.
Kelly, Ezra
New Bedford, Mass., 1823–1845
Kelly, Hezekiah
Norwich, Conn., c. 1790

Kelly, John
New Bedford, Mass., c. 1835
Kelly, Michael
New York, N.Y., c. 1850
Kelly, O. H.
New York, N.Y., c. 1850
Kelly, Ezra and Son
New Bedford, Mass., c. 1840
Kelvey, Thomas
West Union, Ohio, n.d. Probably
cabinetmaker.
Kemble, William
New York, N.Y., c. 1780
Kemlo, Francis
Chelsea, Mass., c. 1847
Kendall, Caleb
South Woodstock, Vt., c. 1811
Kendall, D. C.
Boston, Mass., c. 1842
Kennard, John
Newfields, N.H., c. 1825
Kennedy, Elisha
Easton, Pa., c. 1785
Kennedy, Patrick
Philadelphia, Pa., c. 1800
Kennedy, S. A.
New York, N.Y., c. 1860. Inventor of
an electric clock. Associated with
Samuel F. B. Morse.
Kenney, Asa
West Millbury, Mass., c. 1800
Kent, Luke
Cincinnati, Ohio, 1810–1840
Kent, Thomas
Cincinnati, Ohio, 1820–1840. Son of
Luke.
Kepplinger, John
Baltimore, Md., c. 1800. Son of Samuel.
Kepplinger, Samuel
Gettysburg, Pa., c. 1785; Baltimore,
Md., after 1800
Kepplinger, William
Baltimore, Md., c. 1820
Kern, Herman
Mount Joy, Lancaster Co., Pa., c. 1850
Kerner, Louis
Muskingum County, Ohio, c. 1850
Kerner, Nicholas
Marietta, Lancaster Co., Pa., c. 1850
Kerner & Paff
New York, N.Y., c. 1790. Importers of
clocks.
Kerr, William, Jr.
Providence, R.I., c. 1850. Manufac-
turer.
Kerrison, Robert M.
Philadelphia, Pa., c. 1842
Kersey, Robert
Easton, Md., c. 1790
Kesselmeir, Frederick
Wooster, Ohio, c. 1840
Kessler, John, Jr.
Philadelphia, Pa., c. 1805
Ketcham & Hitchcock
New York, N.Y., c. 1818
Kew, George
Philadelphia, Pa., c. 1840
Keyes, Rufus
Lowell, Mass., c. 1830
Keyser, Joseph
Philadelphia, Pa., c. 1825
Keyworth, Robert
Washington, D.C., c. 1822

Keyworth, T.
York, Pa., c. 1850

Kilborn, Henry
New Haven, Conn., c. 1840

Kilbourne, Lemuel J.
Pennsylvania, c. 1805

Kilburn, Hiram
Lowell, Mass., c. 1835

Killam, George
Pawtucket, R.I., 1899–1930. Made banjo movements cased and sold by Tilden-Thurber, Providence, R.I.

Killam, Guy
Pawtucket, R.I., c. 1939

Killam and Co.
Pawtucket, R.I., c. 1939

Kimball, Jacob
Montpelier, Vt., c. 1810

Kimball, James
Montpelier, Vt., c. 1800

Kimball, John, Jr.
Boston, Mass., c. 1820

Kimball, N.
Boston, Mass., c. 1810

Kimball and Gould
Haverhill, Mass., c. 1865

Kimberly, R.
Ansonia, Conn., n.d. Made ogee brass movements.

Kincaird, Thomas
Christiana Bridge, Del., c. 1775

King, Abraham
Lancaster Boro, Pa., c. 1759

King, Henry: See Roi, Henry

King, Henry N.
New York, N.Y., c. 1810

King, John
Portsmouth, N.H., c. 1795

King, Ormand
Paterson, N.J., c. 1825

King, Samuel
Newport, R.I., 1748–1820. Also painter and maker of instruments.

King, Thomas
Baltimore, Md., c. 1820

King, W. B.
Boston, Mass., n.d.

Kinkaid, George
Cincinnati, Ohio, c. 1830

Kinkead, Alexander
Christiana Bridge, Del., c. 1785

Kinkead, James
Philadelphia, Pa., c. 1760

Kinkead, Joseph
Christiana Bridge, Del., c. 1790

Kinkead, Joseph and Alexander
Christiana, Del., c. 1790

Kinnan, John
Philadelphia, Pa., n.d.

Kippen, George
Bridgeport, Conn., c. 1822

Kirby, John B.
New Haven, Conn., c. 1855

Kirby, Samuel H.
New Haven, Conn., c. 1885

Kirchoff, J. H.
Philadelphia, Pa., c. 1800

Kirckhaff, E. H.
Philadelphia, Pa., c. 1800

Kirk, Aquilla
York, Pa., c. 1790; Baltimore, Md., after 1800. Son of Elisha.

Kirk, Charles
Bristol, Conn., c. 1828; Wolcott, Conn.,

c. 1837; New Haven, Conn., c. 1847. Made marine movements.

Kirk, Elisha
York, Pa., c. 1780. Made both 30-hour and 8-day movements. Also pewterer.

Kirk, John
Bristol, Conn., c. 1831

Kirk, Timothy
York, Pa., c. 1780. Also cabinetmaker.

Kirke & Todd
Wolcott, Conn., c. 1840. Brass movement clocks with cast-iron plates and musical attachments.

Kirkland, Samuel W.
Northampton, Mass., c. 1835

Kirkpatrick, Thomas
New York, N.Y., c. 1845

Kirkwood, Alexander
Charleston, S.C., c. 1768

Kirkwood, John
Charleston, S.C., c. 1761; Wilmington, N.C., 1770–1780

Kirtland Brothers
New York, N.Y., c. 1895

Kissam & Keeler
New York, N.Y., c. 1840

Kitts, John
Louisville, Ky., c. 1835

Kleckner, Solomon
Mifflinburg, Pa., 1818–1860

Klein, John
Philadelphia, Pa., c. 1835

Kleiser, Jacob
Philadelphia, Pa., c. 1820

Kline, B.
Philadelphia, Pa., c. 1840

Kline, John
Amity and Lancaster, Pa., c. 1800; Philadelphia, Pa., c. 1812; Reading, Pa., c. 1820

Kline & Co.
New York, N.Y., c. 1860

Kling, Jacob
Reading, Pa., 1790s–1800; York, Pa., 1810–1820

Klingle, Joseph
Philadelphia, Pa., c. 1820

Klingman, Daniel
York, Pa., 1800–1830

Klingman, Jacob
Reading, Pa., c. 1775

Klingman, Jesse
Boston, Mass., c. 1820

Klingman, William
Annapolis, Md., c. 1760

Kneedler, Jacob
Horsham, Pa., c. 1790

Kneeland, Samuel
Hartford, Conn., c. 1785

Kneeland and Adams
Hartford, Conn., c. 1792. May have been casemakers only.

Knight, Benjamin
Statesville, R.I., c. 1840

Knight, Elijah
Hancock, N.H., c. 1830. Also worked in Goffstown, Concord, and Nashua, N.H.; Charlestown and Boston, Mass.

Knight, Levi
Salem, Ind., c. 1845. Made wood movements.

Knower, Daniel
Roxbury, Mass., c. 1800

Knowles, John
Philadelphia, Pa., 1780

Knowles, Robert
Bangor, Me., c. 1830

Knox, William
Dover, N.H., c. 1840

Koch, Jacob
York, Pa., c. 1800. May have been casemaker only.

Koch, Richard
York, Pa., c. 1805

Kocksperger, Henry
Philadelphia, Pa., c. 1835

Koecker, L. B.
Philadelphia, Pa., c. 1890

Kohl, Nicholas
Willow Grove, Pa., c. 1830

Kolb, Martin
Columbia, Lancaster Co., Pa., 1840–1850

Koplin, T.
Norristown, Pa., c. 1850

Koplin, Washington
Norristown, Pa., c. 1850

Korfhage, Charles
Brooklyn, N.Y., c. 1875

Kraemer, F.
New York, N.Y., c. 1840

Kraft, Jacob
Shepherdstown, W.Va., c. 1790

Krahe, William
San Francisco, Calif., c. 1860. Worked with Wenzell on air clock.

Kramer, M. & Co.
Boston, Mass., c. 1840. Importers and dealers.

Krause, John Samuel
Bethlehem, Pa., c. 1800

Krauss, John
Allentown, Pa., c. 1830

Krauss, Samuel
Upper Hanover Twp., Montgomery Co., Pa., c. 1840. Also miller and farmer. Family originally built organs.

Kretman, Ernest
Philadelphia, Pa., c. 1880

Kreuzer, Fidel
Pennsylvania, n.d.

Kringe, Jacob
New Market, Va., c. 1790

Kroeber, F.
New York, N.Y., c. 1870

Kroeber Clock Co.
New York, N.Y., c. 1880. Used Seth Thomas movements.

Kroeber, Frederic J., Clock Co.
New York, N.Y., c. 1887

Kronenberge, F.
New York, N.Y., n.d.

Krouse, John J.
Northampton (now Allentown), Pa., c. 1830

Krouse, John S.
Bethlehem, Pa., n.d.

Krout, Jacob
Plumstead, Pa., c. 1830

Krueger, Adolph
Camden, N.J., c. 1850

Kruger, L.
Cleveland, Ohio, c. 1850

Kulp, Jacob
Franconia Sq., Montgomery Co., Pa., 1840–1850

Kulp, William
  Lower Salford, Pa., c. 1800
Kumbel, William
  New York, N.Y., c. 1770
Kuner, Maximilian
  Vicksburg, Miss., c. 1850
Kunkle, John
  Ephrata, Pa., c. 1830
Kunsman, Henry
  Raleigh, N.C. Adv. c. 1820.
Kuntz, M. S.
  South Whitehall Twp., state unknown,
  c. 1820

Labbart, John
  New York, N.Y., c. 1805
Labhart, W. L.
  New York, N.Y., c. 1810
Lacey, John
  Philadelphia, Pa., c. 1820
Lachow, John
  Baltimore, Md., c. 1830
Lackey, Henry
  Philadelphia, Pa., 1808–1811
Lacour, Henry
  Mobile, Ala., c. 1860
Ladd & Bigelow
  New York, N.Y., n.d.
Ladomus, Charles Alexander
  Chester, Pa., 1825–1854
Ladomus, Jacob
  Philadelphia, Pa., c. 1843
Ladomus, Joseph
  Chester, Pa., c. 1850
Ladomus, Louis
  Philadelphia, Pa., c. 1846
LaDue, S. P.
  Rockford, Iowa, c. 1850. Pat. 1859 for
  a calendar clock.
Lafever & Beary
  New York, N.Y., c. 1855
LaFoy, Theodore
  Newark, N.J., c. 1850
Lakeman, Ebenezer Knowlton
  Salem, Mass., c. 1820
Lamb, Anthony
  New York, N.Y., 1740–1750. Made
  mathematical and surveying instru-
  ments.
Lamb, Cyrus
  Oxford, Mass., c. 1830
Lambert, L. C.
  New York, N.Y., c. 1870
Lambertoz, D.
  Wilmington, N.C., c. 1795
Lamoyne, Augustus
  Philadelphia, Pa., c. 1815
Lampe, John
  Annapolis, Md., 1770–1780; Baltimore
  after 1780
Lamson, Charles
  Salem, Mass., c. 1850. Worked with
  James Balch.
Lamvine, Augustus
  Philadelphia, Pa., 1811–1816
Landah, John
  Pennsylvania, c. 1792
Lander, T. D.
  Newburgh, N.Y., n.d.
Landis, C. E.
  Newburgh, N.Y., n.d.
Landis, Isaac
  Coatesville, Pa., c. 1845

Landis, Isaac C.
  Coatesville, Pa., 1898–1914
Landry, Alexander
  Philadelphia, Pa., c. 1790
Lane, Aaron
  Elizabethtown, N.J., 1785–1800; also
  worked in Bound Brook, N.J., c. 1780
Lane, Frederick A.
  New Haven, Conn., c. 1880
Lane, H.
  Bristol, state and date unknown
Lane, J.
  Southington, Conn., probably 1830s
Lane, James
  Philadelphia, Pa., c. 1810
Lane, Lyman, J.
  New Haven, Conn., 1840–1850
Lane, Mark
  Southington, Conn., c. 1830; Elizabeth-
  town, N.J., after 1835
Lane, N.
  New York, N. Y., c. 1845
Langdon, Edward
  Bristol, Conn., c. 1850
Langdon, George
  Bristol, Conn., c. 1835
Langdon & Jones
  Bristol, Conn., 1845-1855
Langdon & Root
  Bristol, Conn., 1851–1854
Lange & Wyleys
  Charleston, S.C., c. 1780
Langmack, H.
  Davenport, Iowa, c. 1850
Langworthy, William Andrews
  Saratoga Springs, N.Y., c. 1820
Lanny, David F.
  Boston, Mass., c. 1789; moved to New
  York c. 1793
Lansing, Jacob H.
  Rochester, N.Y., c. 1845
LaPierre, Bennet
  Baltimore, Md., c. 1800
LaPlace, Charles
  Wilmington, N.C., c. 1790; moved to
  Philadelphia at a later date
Lapp and Fleirghein
  Chicago, Ill., c. 1880. Probably dealers.
Laquain, Francis
  Philadelphia, Pa., c. 1794
Large, "Squire"
  Putnam, Ohio, c. 1810. Cabinetmaker.
Largen, Robert
  Philadelphia, Pa., c. 1860
Larkin, Joseph
  Boston, Mass., c. 1840
Laroy, Abrum
  Lancaster Boro, Pa., c. 1757
Latham
  Marple, Delaware Co., Pa., n.d. One
  clock known.
Latham, James
  Albany, N.Y., c. 1790
Latham & Clark
  Charleston, S.C., c. 1790
Latimer, J.
  Philadelphia, Pa., 1810–1820
Latimer, J. E.
  Saybrook, Conn., n.d.
Latournau (also LeTournay), John B.
  Baltimore, Md., 1820–1850
Latshar, John
  York, Pa., c. 1780

Latta, A.
  Philadelphia, Pa., c. 1835
Laughlin, A. S.
  Barnett, Vt., c. 1860
Launay, David
  New York, N.Y., c. 1800
Laundry, A.
  Philadelphia, Pa., n.d.
Law, William
  Philadelphia, Pa., c. 1840
Lawing, Samuel
  Charlotte, N.C., c. 1840. In Lawing &
  Brewer, 1842–1843; later alone.
Lawrence, George
  Lowell, Mass., c. 1830
Lawrence, John
  Philadelphia, Pa., c. 1790
Lawrence, Silas H.
  New York, N.Y., c. 1840
Lawrence, William
  Sing Sing Landing, Mount Pleasant,
  N.Y., c. 1850
Lawse, John
  Amwell, N.J., 1780–1810
Lawson, William H.
  Waterbury, Conn., n.d.
Lawyer, Loring
  Newark, N.Y., c. 1835. Possibly dealer
  only.
Lay, Asa, Jr.
  Hartford, Conn., c. 1784
Leach, Caleb
  Plymouth, Mass., 1770–1790
Leach, Charles
  Utica, N.Y., c. 1840
Leach & Bradley
  Utica, N.Y., c. 1832
Leacock, Joseph
  Philadelphia, Pa., n.d.
Leavenworth, Mark
  Waterbury, Conn., 1810–1830. Also
  worked as gunsmith. Later, after de-
  mise of wood movements, concentrated
  on buttons.
Leavenworth, William
  Waterbury, Conn., c. 1802; Albany,
  N.Y., c. 1817
Leavenworth and Company
  Waterbury, Conn., c. 1830
Leavenworth, Mark and Son
  Waterbury, Conn., n.d.
Leavenworth & Son
  Albany, N.Y., c. 1815
Leavenworth, William and Son
  Waterbury, Conn., c. 1807
Leavit, M. F.
  Kalamazoo, Mich., c. 1860
Leavitt, Dr. Josiah
  Hingham, Mass., c. 1775. Built organs
  at a later date.
Lee, Stephen
  Charleston, S.C., c. 1780
Lee, William
  Charleston, S.C., c. 1760
Lee and Goddard
  Rutland, Vt., c. 1820
Leeds, Gideon
  Philadelphia, Pa., 1841–1842
Leeds, Howard G.
  Philadelphia, Pa., c. 1840
Lefferts, Charles
  Philadelphia, Pa., c. 1820

Lefferts, Charles
Ovid, N.Y., c. 1825
Lefferts & Hall
Philadelphia, Pa., c. 1820
LeGoux, J. F.
Charleston, S.C., 1780–1790
Legros, John F.
Baltimore, Md., c. 1790
LeHuray, Nicholas
Philadelphia, Pa., c. 1810
LeHuray, Nicholas
Ogletown, Del., c. 1835. Son of Nicholas.
LeHuray, Nicholas, Jr.
Philadelphia, Pa., c. 1810
Leibert, Henry
Norristown, Pa., c. 1850
Leigh, David
Pottstown, Pa., c. 1840
Leigh, W.
Newtown, Pa., n.d.
Leinbach, Elias
Reamstown, Lancaster Co., Pa., c. 1790
Leinbach, John
Reamstown, Lancaster Co., Pa., c. 1790. Made, for the most part, 30-hour clocks.
Leinbay, Elias
Earl, Pa., 1805–1817
Leinhardt, Christian
Carlyle, Pa., c. 1782
Lemist, William King
Dorchester, Mass., c. 1812. Apprentice of Simon Willard c. 1806 or 1808.
Lemist, Wm., & Tappan, W. B.
Philadelphia, Pa., c. 1820
Lemmerman, Leonard
Earl, Pa., c. 1806
Lemoine, A.
Philadelphia, Pa., 1810–1817
Lemon, J. J.
Louisville, Ky., c. 1840
Lenhardt, Godfrey
York, Pa., c. 1790
Lenhart, Christian
Carlisle, Pa., c. 1780
Lennet (also Lehnert), Francis
Warwick, Pa., 1833–1846
Lentz, George K.
Philadelphia, Pa., c. 1825
Leonard, Charles
Newburyport, Mass., c. 1850
Leonard, Jacob
Fredericksburg, Va., c. 1825
Leoni & Co.
New York, N.Y., c. 1840
Leppleman, Edward
Buffalo, N.Y., 1836–1839
Lerow, Lewis
Boston, Mass., 1813–1825
Leroy, Abraham
Lancaster, Pa., c. 1757. Daughter in charge of business after he returned to Switzerland.
Leschey, Thomas
Middletown, Pa., c. 1800
Leschot, Louis A.
Virginia, c. 1810. Constructed the clock for Monticello for Thomas Jefferson. Also mathematician.
Lescoit, Lambert
Providence, R.I., 1760–1780; and Hartford, Conn., c. 1770

Leslie, Robert
Philadelphia, Pa., 1791–1803. Made several improvements on clocks and watch movements.
Leslie, William J.
Trenton, N.J., 1799–1830; also Philadelphia, Pa.
Leslie & Parry
Philadelphia, Pa., c. 1800
Leslie & Price
Philadelphia, Pa., 1793–1799
Leslie, Robert and Co.
Baltimore, Md., c. 1795
Leslie & Williams
New Brunswick, N.J., 1780–1790; Trenton, N.J., 1799–1805
Lesquereux, L. & Son
Columbus, Ohio, 1840–1850
Lester, J. U.
Oswego, N.Y., c. 1840
Lester, Robert
Philadelphia, Pa., c. 1790
LeTellier
Philadelphia, Pa., c. 1770
Leuba, Henry
Lexington, Ky., c. 1818
Levely, George
Philadelphia, Pa., 1770–1774; Baltimore, Md., c. 1780
Levi, Garretson
Philadelphia, Pa., c. 1840
Levi, Isaac
Philadelphia, Pa., c. 1790
Levi, Michael
Philadelphia, Pa., c. 1750; Baltimore, Md., 1802–1816
Levi and Isaac
Baltimore, Md., c. 1780
Levin & Ferguson
Alexandria, La., 1850–1860
Levy, Abraham
New York, N.Y., c. 1910. Founder of United Clock Co.
Levy, Henry
Philadelphia, Pa., c. 1840
Levy, Michael
Philadelphia, Pa., c. 1800
Levy, M. & Co.
Philadelphia, Pa., c. 1815
Lewis, Benjamin
Bristol, Conn., 1864–1870
Lewis, Charles
St. Albans, Ohio, c. 1820
Lewis, Curtis
Reading, Pa., 1790–1820
Lewis, Erastus
New Britain (later Waterbury), Conn., c. 1800
Lewis, Frederic H.
Rochester, N.H., c. 1850
Lewis, G. H.
New York, N.Y., n.d.
Lewis, George
Canonsburg, Pa., c. 1830. Also cabinetmaker.
Lewis, Isaac
Newark, N.J., c. 1782
Lewis, Jackson
San Jose, Calif., c. 1860
Lewis, John
Philadelphia, Pa., c. 1840

Lewis, Levi
Bristol, Conn., c. 1810. In partnership with Joseph Ives.
Lewis, R. W.
n.p.; n.d.
Lewis, Sheldon
Bristol, Conn., c. 1830. With Birge and Mallory.
Lewis, Tunis
New York, N.Y., c. 1820
Lewis, Benjamin and Son
Bristol, Conn., c. 1870
Lewis and Catlin
Litchfield, Conn., n.d.
Lewis & Co.
Bristol, Conn., c. 1875
Lewis & Ives
Bristol, Conn., c. 1825
Lidell, Thomas
Frederick, Ind., c. 1860
Liebert, Henry
Norristown, Pa., c. 1849
Lilienthal, J.
New Orleans, La., c. 1850
Limeburner, John
Philadelphia, Pa., c. 1790
Lincoln and Reed
Boston, Mass., c. 1840
Lind, John
Philadelphia, Pa., 1791–1799
Linder, Charles
Geneva, N.Y., c. 1810
Lindsay, Morton
Rising Sun, Pa., n.d.
Lindsay, Thomas
Frankford, Pa., c. 1810
Lindsay, W. K.
Pittsburgh, Pa., c. 1825
Lindsay, W.K. and Co.
Pittsburgh, Pa., c. 1830
Lindsey, Thomas
n.p.; c. 1800
Lindsey, W. R.
Davenport, Iowa, c. 1850
Lindsley, William
Portsmouth, Ohio, c. 1825
Lindsly, Timothy
Reading, Pa., c. 1815
Linebach, Elias
Brecknock, Pa., 1846–1850
Linebaugh, H. W.
Keokuk, Iowa, c. 1860
Linerd, John
Philadelphia, Pa., c. 1816
Lingo, J. W.
Philadelphia, Pa., n.d.
Linnel, Knowles
St. Albans, Ohio, c. 1825
Lisney, Wm.
New York, N.Y., c. 1840
Lister, Thomas
Halifax, Nova Scotia, c. 1760
Litchfield Manufacturing Co.
Litchfield, Conn., 1850–1860. Made both spring- and weight-driven movements, papier-mâché and mother-of-pearl inlay cases.
Little, Archibald
Reading, Pa., c. 1815
Little, Peter
Baltimore, Md., 1790–1820
Little and Elmer
Bridgeton, N.J., c. 1830

Littlejohn, James
Charleston, S.C., c. 1760
Lloyd, Thomas R.
West Chester, Pa., n.d.
Lloyd, William
Springfield, Mass., c. 1802. Probably cabinetmaker. "Sideboards and clock cases."
Locke, John
Cincinnati, and Newark, Ohio, c. 1835. Professor of chemistry at Ohio Medical College and scientist.
Lockwood, Alfred (later Lockwood & Scribner)
New York, N.Y., c. 1830
Lockwood, Fred
New York, N.Y., c. 1830
Lockwood, Joshua
Charleston, S.C., 1756–1781
Lockwood, William
Charlestown, Mass., n.d.
Lockwood and Palmquist
New York, N.Y., n.d.
Lockwood & Scribner
New York, N.Y., c. 1840
Loew, John J.
Philadelphia, Pa., 1846–1848
Logan, A. Sidney
Goshenville, Pa., c. 1875
Logan, Adam
New York, N.Y., c. 1805
Logan, Robert
Saint Louis, Mo., c. 1819
Loheide Manufacturing Co.
Saint Louis, Mo., c. 1880. Maker of coin clocks.
Lomas, John
Chambersburg, Pa., n.d.
Lombard, Daniel, Jr.
Boston, Mass., c. 1825
Lombard, Nathaniel
Boston, Mass., c. 1825
Lomes, William
New York, N.Y., c. 1840
Londrefmith, Alex
Strasburg, Pa., 1796–1826
Long, George
Hanover, Pa., c. 1800
Long, John
Hanover, Pa., c. 1800
Long, Samuel
Philadelphia, Pa., c. 1840
Long and Price
Cincinnati, Ohio, c. 1805
Longin, R.
n.p.; c. 1865
Longmire, W. B.
Knox County, Tenn., c. 1795
Loomis, Henry K.
Bristol, Conn., c. 1825
Loomis, William
Wethersfield and Middletown, Conn., c. 1820. Made wood movements.
Lord, James
Woodbury, N.J., c. 1820
Lord and Gale
Fayetteville, N.C., c. 1790
Lord & Goddard
Rutland, Vt., 1790–1830
Loring, Henry W.
Boston, Mass., c. 1810
Loring, Joseph
Sterling, Mass., c. 1790. Account books still in existence.

Lorton, William
New York, N.Y., c. 1810
Loss, Augustus
Pittsburgh, Pa., c. 1830
Loss, P.
Germantown, Pa., c. 1850
Loucheim, P.
New York, N.Y., n.d.
Love, John
Baltimore, Md., c. 1802
Lovell, A. E.
Philadelphia, Pa., c. 1840
Lovell, George
Philadelphia, Pa., c. 1860
Lovell and Co.
Philadelphia, Pa., c. 1885
Lovell Mfg. Co.
Erie, Pa., c. 1880. Besides clocks, also made washers and wringers.
Lovell & Smith
Philadelphia, Pa., c. 1840
Lovern and Ritz
Boston, Mass., n.d.
Lovett, James
Mendon, Mass., c. 1750
Lovett, William
Boston, Mass., n.d. Tablet painter.
Lovis, Joseph
Hingham, Mass., c. 1770
Lowe, Thomas
Philadelphia, Pa., c. 1780
Lowery, Alfred
Bristol, Conn., n.d.
Lowery, David and Alfred
Bristol, Conn., n.d.
Lownes, David
Philadelphia, Pa., c. 1785
Lownes, Hyatt
Hagerstown, Md., c. 1790
Lowrey, David
Newington, Conn., c. 1760. Apprenticed to Ebenezer Balch.
Lows, Ball & Co.
Boston, Mass., c. 1842
Lucke, John P.
Philadelphia, Pa., c. 1845
Lucy, D. E.
Houlton, Me., c. 1850
Luden, Jacob
Reading, Pa., c. 1850
Ludwig, John
Philadelphia, Pa., c. 1791
Lufkin, Asa
Bucksport, Me., n.d.
Lufkin & Johnson
Boston, Mass., c. 1800
Lukens, Isaiah
Philadelphia, Pa., c. 1810. Son of Seneca. Made tower clocks for Hatboro Academy and State House. V-P of Franklin Institute. Horologist, town clockmaker, and machinist.
Lukens, J.
Philadelphia, Pa., c. 1830
Lukens, Seneca
Horsham Meeting, Montgomery Co., Pa., c. 1770. Father of Isaiah.
Lupp, Charles
New Brunswick, N.J., c. 1810. Brother of Lawrence and William.
Lupp, Harvey
New Brunswick, N.J., c. 1810

Lupp, Henry
New Brunswick, N.J., c. 1810. Son of Peter.
Lupp, John
New Brunswick, N.J., c. 1780. Father of Charles, Lawrence, and William.
Lupp, John H.
New Brunswick, N.J., c. 1830. Son of William.
Lupp, Lawrence
New Brunswick, N.J., c. 1805. Brother of Charles and William.
Lupp, Peter
New Brunswick, N.J., c. 1760. Father of Henry.
Lupp, Samuel V.
New Brunswick, N.J., c. 1809. Son of Henry.
Lupp, William
New Brunswick, N.J., c. 1790. Father of John H.
Luscomb, Samuel
Salem, Mass., c. 1770. Made tower clock for East Meeting House.
Lusk, U. S.
Fremont, Ohio, c. 1910
Lusk, William
Columbus, Ohio, c. 1840
Lux, Paul
Waterbury, Conn., c. 1914. Established Lux Clock Manufacturing Co., 1917.
Lyman, C. A.
Palmer, Mass., c. 1880
Lyman, G. E.
Providence, R.I., c. 1840
Lyman, Roland
Lowell, Mass., c. 1832
Lyman, Thomas
Windsor, Conn., c. 1790; Marietta, Ohio, 1792. Apprenticed to Daniel Burnap.
Lynch, Abraham
Baltimore, Md., c. 1790
Lynch, John
Baltimore, Md., c. 1800
Lyndall, William
Philadelphia, Pa., c. 1840
Lynn, Adam
Alexandria, Va., c. 1795
Lyon, George
Wilmington, N.C., c. 1820
Lyons, John, Jr.
New Haven, Conn., c. 1840

Maag, Henry
Philadelphia, Pa., n.d.
Maas (Manns), Frederick
Pennsylvania, n.d.
MacAllister, A. L.
n.p.; c. 1820
MacFarlane, John
Boston, Mass., c. 1800
MacFarlane, William
Philadelphia, Pa., c. 1805
Machen, Thomas W.
New Bern, N.C., c. 1810
Mackay, Crafts
Boston, Mass., c. 1785. May also have worked in Philadelphia, Pa.
Macomb Co., The
Macomb, Ill., c. 1885. Maker of calendar clocks.

Magann, Patrick
  Charleston, S.C., c. 1790
Magnin, David
  New York, N.Y., c. 1810
Magnin, John
  New York, N.Y., c. 1840. Probably importer and assembler of clocks and watches.
Maholland, Robert
  Philadelphia, Pa., c. 1850
Maire, Charles
  Louisville, Ky., c. 1840
Maker, Matthew
  Charleston, S.C., c. 1770
Mallory, George
  New York, N.Y., c. 1840. Probably dealer.
Mallory, Ransom
  Bristol, Conn., 1800–1850. Probably cabinetmaker.
Mallory and Merriman
  Bristol, Conn., c. 1830
Malls, Philip
  Washington, D.C., c. 1800
Manchester, Cyril B.
  Pawtucket, R.I., c. 1865
Manchester, G. D.
  Plainfield, Conn., c. 1850
Manhattan Clock Co.
  New York, N.Y., c. 1895
Mann, William
  Baltimore, Md., c. 1860
Manning, Richard
  Ipswich, Mass., c. 1798
Manning Bowman Co.
  Meriden, Conn., c. 1905. Maker of electric clocks.
Manross, Elijah
  Bristol, Conn., c. 1860
Manross, Elijah, Jr.
  Bristol, Conn., c. 1870
Manross, Elisha
  Bristol, Conn., c. 1820. Father of Elijah. Made clocks for other makers. Partner in several other clock businesses.
Manross Brothers
  Bristol, Conn., 1856–1861
Manross, E. & C.H.
  Bristol, Conn., 1854–1856
Manross & Norton
  Bristol, Conn., 1838–1840
Manross, Prichard & Co.
  Bristol, Conn., 1841–1842
Mans, John
  Columbia, Pa., c. 1810
Mansfield, Samuel A.
  Philadelphia, Pa., c. 1845
Manuel, Jules
  Philadelphia, Pa., c. 1845
Marache, Solomon
  New York, N. Y., c. 1750
Marand, Joseph
  Baltimore, Md., c. 1800
Maranville, Galusha
  Winsted, Conn., c. 1855. Patented The Maranville Calendar.
Marble, Simeon
  New Haven, Conn., c. 1815
Marchist, Joseph
  Utica, N.Y., c. 1845
Marie, M.
  Charleston, S.C., c. 1795

Marien, John
  New York, N.Y., c. 1840
Marine Clock Co.
  New Haven, Conn., c. 1845. Made 30-hour and 8-day clocks.
Markham & Case
  Columbia, S.C., c. 1845
Marks, Isaac
  Philadelphia, Pa., c. 1795
Marlow & Co.
  York, Pa., c. 1920
Marquand, Frederic
  New York, N.Y., c. 1825
Marquand, Isaac
  Fairfield, Conn., c. 1755; moved to New York c. 1801
Marquand, Isaac
  Edentown, N.C., c. 1790; New York, N.Y., c. 1803
Marquand and Brothers
  New York, N.Y., c. 1820
Marrian, John H.
  New York, N.Y., c. 1845
Marris, John
  Middletown and Hartford, Conn., n.d.
Marsh, B. B.
  Paris, Ky., 1810–1840
Marsh, George C.
  Winchester, Winsted, and Bristol, Conn., c. 1828; also Farmington and Wolcottville, Conn. Made both brass and wood and 30-hour and 8-day movements. Partner in various enterprises.
Marsh, T. K.
  Paris, Ky., c. 1804
Marsh, B.B. and T.K.
  Paris, Ky., c. 1804
Marsh, George and Co.
  Farmington, Conn., c. 1830
Marsh, Gilbert & Co.
  Bristol, Conn., c. 1830
Marsh and Hoffman
  Albany, N.Y., c. 1890
Marsh, Williams & Co.
  Dayton, Ohio, c. 1830. Probably first clock factory beyond Allegheny Mountains.
Marsh, Williams & Hayden and Company
  Dayton, Ohio, 1833–1840
Marshall, George
  Bristol, Conn., n.d.
Marshall & Adams
  Seneca Falls, N.Y., c. 1820
Marshall and Card
  Cazenovia, N.Y., c. 1860
Marshall & White
  Petersburg, Va., c. 1820
Martin, Alex
  New York, N.Y., n.d.
Martin, George
  Lancaster, Pa. Also made rope.
Martin, George A.
  Bethel, Me., 1850–1860
Martin, John
  New York, N.Y., c. 1830
Martin, John J.
  Philadelphia, Pa., c. 1845
Martin, Patrick
  Philadelphia, Pa., c. 1820
Martin, Peter
  New York, N.Y., c. 1810
Martin, Samuel
  New York, N.Y., 1800–1810

Martin, Thomas
  Baltimore, Md., c. 1860
Martin, Valentine
  Boston, Mass., c. 1840
Martin & Mullan
  Baltimore, Md., c. 1760. Thomas Martin and Robert Mullan.
Mascher, John F.
  Philadelphia, Pa., c. 1845
Masham, Samuel
  Wiltshire, Md., c. 1774
Masi, George
  Waseca, Minn., c. 1870. Made wagon-wall clocks.
Masi, Seraphim
  Washington, D.C., c. 1830. Probably dealer only.
Masi and Company
  Washington, D.C., c. 1830
Mason, George
  Waseca, Minn., 1860–1870. Also casemaker.
Mason, H. G.
  Boston, Mass., c. 1840
Mason, Morris
  Franconia Twp., Pa., c. 1800
Mason, P.
  Somerville, N.J., c. 1815
Mason, Timothy B.
  Boston, Mass., c. 1825
Mason, William R.
  Mount Holly, N.J., c. 1835
Massey, Charles R.
  Philadelphia, Pa., c. 1835
Massey, John
  Charleston, S.C., c. 1730
Massey, Joseph
  Charleston, S.C., c. 1720
Massot, Horace
  Charleston, S.C., c. 1780
Masters, John
  Boston, Mass., and Bath, Me., 1820–1840. Father of William.
Masters, William
  Bath, Me., 1820–1850
Mather, Eli
  West Bradford Twp., Pa., c. 1825. Probably dealer.
Mathews, David and Edwin
  Bristol, Conn., c. 1830
Mathews, Jewell and Co.
  Bristol, Conn., c. 1850
Mathewson and Harris
  New Hartford Centre, Conn., c. 1830
Mathey, Lewis
  Philadelphia, Pa., c. 1795
Mathias, J.
  Gettysburg, Pa., c. 1830
Mathieu, Gaston
  New York, N.Y., c. 1840
Matlack, White C.
  New York, N.Y., 1769–1775
Matlack, William
  Philadelphia, Pa., c. 1780
Matlack, White & William
  Philadelphia, Pa., c. 1780
Matthews, Thomas
  Charleston, W.Va., c. 1810
Matthews & Pennoyer
  Bristol, Conn., c. 1830
Matthewson, J.
  Providence, R.I., c. 1845
Maurepas, M.
  Bristol, Conn., c. 1850

Maus, Frederick
Philadelphia, Pa., 1785–1793
Maus, Jacob
Trenton, N.J., 1780s and Philadelphia, Pa.
Maus, John J.
Columbia, Lancaster Co., Pa., c. 1812
Maus, Philip
Lebanon, Pa., c. 1800
Maus, Samuel
Pottstown, Pa., c. 1790
Maus, William
Hilltown, Bucks Co., Pa., c. 1810
Mauser Mfg. Co.
New York, N.Y., n.d.
Mautz, John
Philadelphia, Pa., c. 1840
Mawdsley, John
Philadelphia, Pa., c. 1845
Maxant, E. M. L.
n.p.; c. 1870
Maxwell, A.
Philadelphia, Pa., c. 1800
Maxwell, James
Boston, Mass., c. 1730
May, Samuel
Philadelphia, Pa., c. 1760
May and Payson
Baltimore, Md., c. 1785
Mayer, Elias
Philadelphia, Pa., c. 1830. Probably dealer.
Maynard, George
New York, N.Y., c. 1705
McBride and Garner
Charlotte, N.C., c. 1805
McCabe, John
Baltimore, Md., c. 1770
McCabe, William
Richmond, Va., 1790–1820
McCarter, John
New York, N.Y., c. 1850
McCarthey, Thomas
Philadelphia, Pa., c. 1805. Cabinet-maker. Worked for David Rittenhouse.
McClary, Samuel
Wilmington, Del., 1803–1815. Partner of Jacob Alrichs.
McClary, Samuel, Jr.
Wilmington, Del., 1810–1850. Son of Samuel.
McClary, Thomas
Wilmington, Del., 1810–1850. Brother of Samuel, Jr.
McClintock, O. B.
Minneapolis, Minn., c. 1940. Maker of electric clocks.
M'Closkey, F.
Philadelphia, Pa., c. 1850
McCluer, Heman
Hamburg, N.Y., c. 1830
M'Clure, David
Boston, Mass., c. 1810
McClure, John
Boston, Mass., c. 1823
M'Collins, Thomas
Philadelphia, Pa., c. 1820
McConnell, J. C.
Waynesburg, Pa., 1830–1840
McCormack, Henry
Philadelphia, Pa., c. 1830
McCormick, Robert
Philadelphia, Pa., n.d.

M'Coy, George W.
Philadelphia, Pa., c. 1835
M'Cully, William
Philadelphia, Pa., c. 1840
McDaniel, William H.
Philadelphia, Pa., c. 1820
McDonald, Charles
Lexington, Ky., c. 1815
McDowell, F.
Philadelphia, Pa., 1790–1800
McDowell, James
Philadelphia, Pa., c. 1790
McDowell, James, Jr.
Philadelphia, Pa., c. 1805
McDowell, John
Philadelphia, Pa., c. 1810
M'Dowell, William Hanse
Philadelphia, Pa., c. 1815
McElwain, David
Rochester, N.Y., c. 1840
McElwain, George
Rochester, N.Y., c. 1840
McElwee, James
Philadelphia, Pa., c. 1813
M'Fadden, J. B.
Pittsburgh, Pa., c. 1830
M'Fadden, John B. & Co.
Pittsburgh, Pa., 1840–1850
McGann, Patrick
Charleston, S.C., c. 1780
McGibbon, James
Boston, Mass., c. 1810. Artist who also painted clock glasses.
McGraw, Donald
Annapolis, Md., c. 1765
McGregor, J.
San Francisco, Calif., c. 1850. Also made chronometers.
McGrew, Alexander
Cincinnati, Ohio, c. 1810
McGrew, Wilson
Cincinnati, Ohio, c. 1820
M'Harg, Alexander
Albany, N.Y., c. 1810
M'Harg and Selkirk
Albany, N.Y., c. 1815
McHugh, James
Lowell, Mass., c. 1860
McIlhenny, Joseph E.
Philadelphia, Pa., c. 1810
McIlhenny & West
Philadelphia, Pa., c. 1810
McIvor, Colin
Alexandria, Va., c. 1780
McIvor, Murdo
Rochester, N.Y., c. 1840
McKay, H.
Haverhill, Mass., c. 1905
McKay, Spear and Brown
Boston, Mass., c. 1854. Successors to McKay, William P. & Co.
McKay, William P. & Co.
Boston, Mass., c. 1840
M'Kee, John
Chester, S.C., c. 1815
M'Keen, Henry
Philadelphia, Pa., c. 1830
M'Kinley, Edward
Philadelphia, Pa., c. 1825
McKinney, Robert
Wilmington, Del., c. 1840
McLean, Homer
Williamsburg, Ohio, c. 1870

M'Manus, John
Philadelphia, Pa., c. 1840
McMarble, A.
Wilmington, Ohio, c. 1880. Cabinet-maker.
M'Masters, Hugh A.
Philadelphia, Pa., c. 1835
McMillian, J. W.
Greenville, Ala., c. 1860
M'Mullen, Edward
Philadelphia, Pa., c. 1845
McMyers, John
Baltimore, Md., c. 1795
McNeil, E.
Binghamton, N.Y., c. 1810
M'Niesh, John
New York, N.Y., c. 1810
McParlin, William
Annapolis, Md., c. 1800
M'Pherson, Robert
Philadelphia, Pa., c. 1835
M'Pherson, Sweeney Eugene
Boston, Mass., c. 1825
McQuillan, B.
New York, N.Y., c. 1850
M'Stocker, Francis
Philadelphia, Pa., c. 1830
Meacham, W. J.
Holyoke, Mass., c. 1850
Mead, Benjamin
Castine, Me., c. 1800
Mead & Addy
Boston, Mass., c. 1850. Made Tower clocks.
Mead, Adriance & Co.
Ithaca, N.Y., c. 1830. Probably dealers. only.
Meagear, Thomas J.
Wilmington, Del., and Philadelphia Pa., c. 1830
Mears, Charles
Philadelphia, Pa., c. 1825
Mears, William
Reading, Pa., c. 1785
Mechlin, Jacob
Alsace Twp., Berks Co., Pa., c. 1750
Mecke, John
Philadelphia, Pa., c. 1849
Mecom, John
New York, N.Y., c. 1765. Dealer.
Medinger, Thomas G.
New York, N.Y., n.d.
Medley, A. F.
Louisville, Ky., c. 1835
Meek, Benjamin
Frankfort, Ky., c. 1830
Meek, J.F. & Son
Louisville, Ky., c. 1860
Meeks, Edward, Jr.
New York, N.Y., c. 1796
Meer Bros.
Frankfort, Ky., c. 1835
Megary, Alexander
New York, N.Y., c. 1830
Megear, Thomas J.
Philadelphia, Pa., c. 1790
Megonegal, W. H.
Philadelphia, Pa., c. 1840
Meier, Felix
New York, N.Y., c. 1880
Meily, Emanuel
Lebanon, Pa., c. 1810

Melcher
Plymouth Hollow, Conn., c. 1790

Melholm, Michael
Boonesboro, Ind., c. 1830

Melly Brothers
New York, N.Y., c. 1830. Probably dealers.

Melville, Henry
Wilmington, N.C., c. 1798

Mendenhall, Thomas
Lancaster, Pa., c. 1775; later to Philadelphia

Mends, Benjamin
Philadelphia, Pa., c. 1795

Mends, James
Philadelphia, Pa., c. 1790

Menzies, James
Philadelphia, Pa., c. 1800

Menzies, John
Philadelphia, Pa., c. 1810

Menzies, John, Jr.
Philadelphia, Pa., c. 1830

Menzies, Thomas
Philadelphia, Pa., c. 1805

Merchant, William
Philadelphia, Pa., n.d.

Meredith, Joseph P.
Baltimore, Md., c. 1824

Meriden Clock Co.
Meriden, Conn., n.d.

Merimee, William
Brownsville, Fayette Co., Pa., c. 1795. From Kentucky

Mermad, Jaccard
Saint Louis, Mo., c. 1880

Merrell, A.
Vienna, Ohio, c. 1828

Merriam, Silas
New Haven, Conn., c. 1800

Merrie, John P.
Utica, N.Y., c. 1833

Merriman, Marcus
New Haven, Conn., c. 1805

Merriman, Reuben
Cheshire and Litchfield, Conn., c. 1840

Merriman, Samuel
New Haven, Conn., c. 1805. Son of Silas.

Merriman, Silas
New Haven, Conn., c. 1770

Merriman, Titus
Bristol, Conn., c. 1805. Worked in Merriman & Dunbar and Merriman, Birge companies.

Merriman, Birge & Co.
Bristol, Conn., 1820–1830. Made clocks invented by Joseph Ives.

Merriman, Bradley and Company
New Haven, Conn., c. 1815

Merriman & Bradley
New Haven, Conn., 1810–1820

Merriman & Dunbar
Bristol, Conn., c. 1805

Merriman and Ives
Bristol, Conn., c. 1818

Merriman, R. and Co.
Bristol, Conn., c. 1820

Merry, F.
Philadelphia, Pa., c. 1795

Mestier, B.
Philadelphia, Pa., c. 1815

Metcalf, F.
Hopkinton, Mass., c. 1825

Metcalf, Luther
Medway, Mass., c. 1800. Casemaker.

Metten, Laurens
Saint Louis, Mo., c. 1850

Mevrey, F.
Philadelphia, Pa., c. 1795

Meyer, Albert
Cincinnati, Ohio, c. 1850

Meyer, David
Myerstown, Lebanon Co., Pa., n.d.

Meyer, Felix
New York, N.Y., c. 1800. Maker of complicated clock that indicated local time as well as time in many parts of the world. Day, month, signs of zodiac, moon phase, etc. Made over a period of about 10 years.

Meyer, J. A.
New York, N.Y., c. 1832. Importer of clocks. To Canton, Ohio, c. 1850.

Meyers, John
Fredericktown, Md., c. 1800

Michael, Lewis
York, Pa., c. 1785

Middle, James
Paterson, N.J., c. 1820

Middleton, Aaron
Burlington, N.J., c. 1735

Miety, Emanuel
Lebanon, Pa., n.d.

Miksch, John M.
Bethlehem, Pa., c. 1825

Miles, E., Jr.
Sag Harbor, L.I., N.Y., c. 1860

Miley, Emanuel
Lebanon, Pa., n.d.

Milk, Thomas
Maryland, c. 1775

Millar, Thomas
Philadelphia, Pa., c. 1820. Dealer only.

Millard, Squire
Warwick, R.I., c. 1775

Miller, Aaron
Elizabethtown, N.J., c. 1740. Father in law of Isaac Brokaw.

Miller, Abraham
Easton, Pa., c. 1810

Miller, Alexander
Uniontown, Ohio, n.d.

Miller, Benjamin
Germantown, Pa., n.d.

Miller, Cornelius
New Jersey, c. 1790

Miller, Edward
Providence, R.I., c. 1820

Miller, George
Lancaster Boro, Pa., c. 1800

Miller, George H.
Philadelphia, Pa., c. 1828

Miller, Harry, Rev.
Lebanon, Pa., c. 1900

Miller, Henry
East Hanover, Pa., c. 1820

Miller, Henry A.
Southington, Conn., c. 1830

Miller, J. B.
Portland, Ore., c. 1860

Miller, John
Germantown, Pa., c. 1730

Miller, John J.
Germantown and Philadelphia, Pa., n.d.

Miller, Kennedy
Elizabethtown, N.J., c. 1830

Miller, Pardon
Providence and Newport, R.I., c. 1820

Miller, Peter
Lynn Twp. and Ephrata, Pa., c. 1800

Miller, Philip
New York, N.Y., c. 1763

Miller, Richard
n.p.; n.d.

Miller, S. W.
Philadelphia, Pa., c. 1840

Miller, Thomas
Philadelphia, Pa., c. 1825

Miller, William S.
Philadelphia, Pa., c. 1840

Miller Clock Company
Zeeland, Mich., c. 1930

Miller, W.H.C. and Co.
Chicago, Ill., c. 1860

Miller and Williams
Cincinnati, Ohio, c. 1830

Millington, Isaac
Lancaster County, Pa., c. 1850

Mills, Alexander
Brooklyn, N.Y., c. 1850

Mills, Joseph
Philadelphia, Pa., c. 1720

Mills, William
New York, N.Y., c. 1840

Mills & Chase
New York, N.Y., c. 1850

Mills, J.R. and Company
New York, N.Y., c. 1850. Made the Aaron Crane month clock.

Millum, Moses
Baltimore, Md., c. 1820

Milne, Robert
New York, N.Y., c. 1800; Philadelphia, Pa., c. 1817

Mily, Samuel
Lebanon, Pa., 1769–1783

Minchin & Willis
Boston, Mass., n.d.

Mindel, Gustavus
Philadelphia, Pa., c. 1850

Minor, E. C.
Jonesville, Mich., c. 1860

Minor, Richardson
Stratford, Conn., c. 1760

Minot, J.
Boston, Mass., c. 1800. Dial painter.

Mitchell, George
Bristol, Conn., c. 1825

Mitchell, Henry
New York, N.Y., c. 1785

Mitchell, Jesse C.
Buffalo, N.Y., c. 1830

Mitchell, Phineas
Boston, Mass., c. 1820

Mitchell, Professor
Cincinnati, Ohio, c. 1850. Maker of astronomical electric clocks.

Mitchell, William, Jr.
Richmond, Va., c. 1820

Mitchell & Atkins
Bristol, Conn., c. 1830

Mitchell and Bailey
New York, N.Y., c. 1854

Mitchell & Hinman
Bristol, Conn., c. 1830

Mitchell & Mott
New York, N.Y., c. 1795
Mitchell, Vance and Co.
New York, N.Y., c. 1860
Mitchell and Whitney
Boston, Mass., c. 1815
Mitchelson, David
Boston, Mass., c. 1774
Mix, Elisha
New Haven, Conn., c. 1840
Mix Bros.
Ithaca, N.Y., c. 1854
Mockford, Richard
Medina, N.Y., c. 1860
Moellinger, Henry
Philadelphia, Pa., c. 1795
Mohler, Jacob
Baltimore, Md., c. 1760
Moir, William
New York, N.Y., c. 1875. Dealer and
importer.
Moll, John
Wilmington, Del., c. 1675
Molloy, George
Lowell, Mass., c. 1840
Monarch Calendar Clock Company
Knoxville, Tenn., c. 1870
Mongin, David
Charleston, S.C., c. 1740
Monitor Clock Works
Medina, N.Y., c. 1910
Monnier, Daniel
Philadelphia, Pa., c. 1825
Monroe, Charles
Bangor, Me., c. 1835
Monroe, John
Barnstable, Mass., n.d.
Monroe & Co., E. & C.H.
Bristol, Conn., c. 1850
Montanden, Albert
Lancaster, Pa.; Baltimore, Md.; and
Clarksburg, Va; dates in each location
unknown, c. 1815
Montanden, Hannah
Lancaster, Pa., c. 1800. Continued
business after death of husband, Henry.
Montanden, Henry Lewis
Lancaster, Pa., c. 1778
Montanden (Hannah) & Roberts (Oliver)
Lancaster, Pa., c. 1800
Montcastle, William R.
Warrenton, N.C., c. 1845
Montgomery, Andrew
Baltimore, Md., c. 1820
Montgomery, Robert
New York, N.Y., c. 1780
Montieth, Benjamin
Philadelphia, Pa., c. 1815
Montieth, Charles
Philadelphia, Pa., c. 1840
Montieth and Company
Philadelphia, Pa., c. 1845
Montieth and Shippen
Philadelphia, Pa., c. 1820
Mooar, Lot
Nashua, N.H., c. 1830
Moon, Robert
Philadelphia, Pa., c. 1768. Casemaker
only.
Moonlinger, Henry
Philadelphia, Pa., c. 1795
Moore, Frederick
New Haven, Conn., c. 1840

Moore, George H.
Lynn, Mass., c. 1850
Moore, Nelson A.
Newark, N.J., c. 1850
Moore, R.
Nashua, N.H., c. 1860
Moore, Robert
Philadelphia, Pa., c. 1795
Morgan, Elijah
Poughkeepsie, N.Y., c. 1832. Dealer in
clocks.
Morgan, Gideon
Pittsburgh, Pa., c. 1810. Member of
Morgan & Hart.
Morgan, Luther S.
Salem, Mass., c. 1840
Morgan, Theodore
Salem, Mass., c. 1837
Morgan, Thomas
Philadelphia, Pa., c. 1770; Baltimore,
Md., 1772; back to Philadelphia
c. 1779
Morgan, William S.
Poughkeepsie, N.Y., c. 1820. Son of
Elijah.
Morgan & Hart
Pittsburgh, Pa., c. 1810
Morgan, Walker & Smith
New York, N.Y., c. 1830. Probably
dealers in glasses for clocks.
Morgue, Peter
Charleston, S.C., c. 1720
Morin, Augustus
Philadelphia, Pa., c. 1830
Morley, William
Burlington, N.J., c. 1725. Apprenticed
to Isaac Pearson.
Morrell, John
Baltimore, Md., c. 1820
Morrell & Mitchell
New York, N.Y., c. 1815
Morrill, Benjamin
Boscawen, N.H., c. 1810. Prolific maker
of New Hampshire mirror clocks; also
made dwarf tall case clocks and Massa-
chusetts shelf clocks.
Morrill, H. C.
Baltimore, Md., c. 1835
Morrill, Harrison O.
New Hampshire, c. 1825. New Hamp-
shire mirror clock known.
Morrill, John
Baltimore, Md., c. 1820
Morris, Abel
Reading, Pa., c. 1770
Morris, Benjamin
Hilltown, Bucks Co., Pa., c. 1760
Morris, Elijah
Canton, Mass., c. 1820
Morris, Enos
Hilltown, Bucks Co., Pa., c. 1780. Son
of Benjamin. Also a lawyer.
Morris, John
Grafton, Mass., c. 1760. Simon Willard
apprenticed to him. Name, along with
Willard's, stamped on a pendulum.
Morris, Myles
Plymouth, Conn., c. 1840
Morris, Robert
New Britain, Pa., n.d.
Morris, Sheldon
Litchfield, Conn., n.d.

Morris, William
Grafton, Mass., c. 1765
Morris, William
Bridgeton, N.J., c. 1816; Camden, N.J.,
c. 1831; Philadelphia, Pa., 1860
Morris, William
Utica, N.Y., c. 1830
Morris, Wollaston
Maryland, c. 1775
Morris & Cornell
Waterloo, Iowa, c. 1860
Morris & Willard
Grafton, Mass., c. 1769
Morse, Andrew, Jr.
Bloomfield, Me., c. 1830
Morse, Joseph
Walpole, Mass., n.d.
Morse, Moses L.
Keene, N.H., and Cambridge, Mass.,
c. 1804
Morse, Moses L.
Boston, Mass., c. 1810
Morse, R. C.
Baltimore, Md., c. 1840
Morse & Blakeslee
Plymouth, Conn., 1845
Morse & Co.
Plymouth Hollow, Conn., c. 1840
Morse, H. and D.
Canton, Mass., c. 1820
Morse and Mosley
Albany, N.Y., c. 1820
Mort, Jordan
New York, N.Y., c. 1805
Mort and Mitchell
New York, N.Y., c. 1826
Morton, E. Daniel & Co.
Bristol, Conn., c. 1850
Mosely, R. E.
Newburyport, Mass., c. 1840
Moses, Thomas
Sennett, N.Y., n.d.
Moses, Thomas
Wolcottville, Conn., c. 1830
Mosher, S.
Hamilton, N.Y., c. 1830
Moss
Rochdale, state unknown, c. 1818
Mott, James
New York, N.Y., c. 1820
Mott Brothers
New York, N.Y., c. 1800
Mott & Morrel
New York, N.Y., c. 1800
Mott and Mourne
New York, N.Y., c. 1800. May have
been assemblers only.
Moulton, E. G.
Saco, Me., c. 1810; and Rochester,
N.H.
Moulton, Edward S.
Rochester, N.H., c. 1810
Moulton, Francis
Lowell, Mass., c. 1830
Moulton, Joseph
Newbury (now Newburyport), Mass.,
c. 1755
Moulton, Thomas
Rochester, N.H., c. 1800
Moulton, Thomas M.
Dunbarton, N.H., c. 1800
Moulton and Carr
Lowell, Mass., c. 1830

Mountain, Samuel P.
  Philadelphia, Pa., c. 1840
Mountford, John
  Philadelphia, Pa., c. 1815
Mountjoy, John
  New York, N.Y., c. 1810
Mountjoy, William
  New York, N.Y., c. 1805
Moutoux, Carl
  Brooklyn, N.Y., c. 1850
Mowroue, Francis
  New York, N.Y., c. 1815
Mowroue, Peter
  Charleston, S.C., c. 1735
Moyer, Jacob
  Montgomery County, Pa., n.d.
Moyer, Joseph
  Skippackville, Pa., n.d.
Moyer, Solomon
  Allentown, Pa., c. 1880. Pat. received
  for a universal clock.
Moyston, John Hugan
  Schenectady, N.Y., c. 1795
Mueller, Frederic
  Savannah, Ga., c. 1735
Muhlenberg, George
  Morgantown, Pa., c. 1900
Mulford, E.
  Princeton, N.J., c. 1830
Muller, Nicholas
  New York, N.Y., c. 1875. Made cast-
  iron cases.
Muller's Sons
  New York, N.Y., c. 1880. Made bronze
  and cast-iron clocks.
Mulliken, Benjamin
  Bradford, Mass., c. 1740
Mulliken, John
  Bradford, Mass., c. 1690
Mulliken, Jonathan
  Newburyport, Mass., c. 1775
Mulliken, Jonathan
  Bradford, Mass., c. 1805
Mulliken, Joseph
  Concord, Mass., c. 1775
Mulliken, Joseph
  Newburyport, Mass., c. 1790
Mulliken, Joseph
  Salem, Mass., c. 1790
Mulliken, Nathaniel
  Newburyport, Mass., c. 1775; later to
  Hollowell, Me. Son of Jonathan.
Mulliken, Nathaniel, Jr.
  Lexington, Mass., c. 1777. Son of Na-
  thaniel, Sr.
Mulliken, Nathaniel, Sr.
  Lexington, Mass., c. 1765. Brother of
  Samuel, father of Nathaniel, Jr., and
  Joseph. Excellent maker of tall clocks.
Mulliken, Robert
  Boston, Mass., 1683; later to Bradford,
  Mass.
Mulliken, Samuel
  Haverhill, Mass., n.d.
Mulliken, Samuel
  Newburyport, Mass.; later to Hollowell,
  Me., c. 1780
Mulliken, Samuel, Sr.
  Newbury (now Newburyport), Mass.,
  c. 1740
Mulliken, Samuel, Jr.
  Newburyport, Salem, and Lynn, Mass.,
  c. 1780

Multer, Peter A.
  New York, N.Y., c. 1850
Mumford
  Providence, R.I., c. 1810
Munchin, M.
  n.p.; c. 1870
Munger, Asa
  Auburn, N.Y., c. 1820. Maker of hol-
  low-column clocks. Used eagle pendu-
  lums.
Munger, Austin E.
  Syracuse, N.Y., c. 1839 with A. Mun-
  ger and Son. Later with Pliney Dickin-
  son.
Munger, Sylvester
  Clinton, Onondaga, Elmira, and Ithaca,
  N.Y., c. 1820. Brother of Asa. In
  several companies.
Munger, A. and Son
  Auburn, N.Y., c. 1839
Munger & Benedict
  Auburn, N.Y., c. 1826
Munger & Pratt
  Ithaca, N.Y., c. 1826
Munk, D.
  New York, N.Y., n.d.
Munro and Company
  Charleston, S.C., c. 1795
Munroe, Daniel
  Concord, Mass., 1800–1850. Appren-
  ticed to Simon Willard. Brother of
  Nathaniel. Later to Boston, working
  with E. Jones.
Munroe, Deacon N.
  Boston, Mass., c. 1775. Cabinetmaker.
Munroe, Nathaniel
  Concord, Mass., c. 1800. Apprenticed
  to Abel Hutchins. Worked with his
  brother Daniel c. 1800. With Samuel
  Whiting c. 1808.
Munroe, William
  Concord, Mass., c. 1800. Cabinet-
  maker, made some clocks.
Munroe, Daniel and Nathaniel
  Concord, Mass., c. 1800
Munroe and Jones
  Boston, Mass., c. 1807
Munroe and Whiting
  Concord, Mass., c. 1809
Munsell, William
  n.p.; n.d.
Munyan, A. H.
  Northampton, Mass., c. 1845
Munyan Brothers
  Pittsfield, Mass., c. 1850
Murdock, John
  Woodbury, N.J., c. 1775. Possibly
  dealer only.
Murdock & Co., J.
  Utica, N.Y., c. 1820
Murdock & Mellish
  Woodstock, Vt., n.d.
Murphy, James
  Boston, Mass., c. 1800
Murphy, John
  Allentown, Lehigh Co., Pa., c. 1775
Murphy, John
  Charlestown, Pa., c. 1790
Murphy, Robert
  Philadelphia, Pa., c. 1848
Murphy, Thomas
  Allentown, Lehigh Co., Pa., c. 1835

Murray, Robert
  Trenton, N.J., c. 1800
Murray & Son
  Fredericksburg, Va., c. 1880
Musgrave & Kelly
  Buffalo, N.Y., c. 1810
Myer, George
  New York, N.Y., c. 1840
Myers, Frederick
  Maryland, c. 1790
Myers, Moses
  Poughkeepsie, N.Y., c. 1840
Myers and Company
  New York, N.Y., c. 1889. Successors to
  Prentiss Calendar and Time Co.
Mygatt, Comfort S.
  Danbury, Conn., c. 1783
Myle, Samuel
  Lebanon, Pa., c. 1800

Narney, Joseph
  Charleston, S.C., c. 1750
Nash, Thomas
  New Haven, Conn., c. 1640. Also gun-
  smith.
Nation, Sylvan
  New Lisbon, Ind., c. 1860
National Clock Company
  Brooklyn, N.Y., c. 1875
National Self Winding Clock Co.
  Bristol, Conn., c. 1905
Neal, Daniel
  Philadelphia, Pa., c. 1820
Neal, Elisha
  New Hartford, Conn., c. 1820
Neal, J. and Co.
  Philadelphia, Pa., n.d.
Negrin, Paul
  Charlottesville, Va., c. 1820
Negus, T.S. and J.D.
  New York, N.Y., c. 1845
Neil, Elisha
  New Hartford, Conn., c. 1820. As-
  sembled movements in cases.
Neilson
  Annapolis, Md., c. 1734
Neilson, George
  Boston, Mass., c. 1830
Neisser, Augustin
  Georgia, c. 1736; Philadelphia, Pa.,
  c. 1739; Germantown, Pa., c. 1770
Nelson, Alexander
  West Chester, Pa., c. 1820
Nelson, John A.
  Boston, Mass., to 1830s
Nelson, R. J.
  Davenport, Iowa, c. 1850
Nelson, Thomas
  Philadelphia, Pa., c. 1800
Nemert, Gottlieb Christian
  Reading, Pa., c. 1830. Also jeweler and
  silversmith.
Nerle, John L.
  Catawissa, Pa., n.d.
Nettleton, W. K.
  Rochester, N.Y., c. 1830
Nettleton, Wilford H.
  Bristol, Conn., c. 1860. Made clock
  parts.
Nettleton, Heath & Co.
  Scottsville, N.Y., c. 1800
Newall, James J.
  Utica, N.Y., c. 1830

Newall, Theodore
Poultney, Vt., c. 1815
Newall, Thomas
Sheffield, Mass., c. 1805
Newberry, James
Annapolis, Md., c. 1750
Newberry, James, Jr.
Philadelphia, Pa., c. 1810
Newberry, J. & R.
Philadelphia, Pa., c. 1815
Newberry, Thomas
Boston, Mass., c. 1810
Newcomb, Henry
Lowell, Mass., c. 1835
Newell, A.
Boston, Mass., c. 1780
Newell, E. E.
Bristol, Conn., c. 1890
Newell, Lott
Bristol, Conn., c. 1818. Was partner in
J. Ives and Co.
Newell, Norman
Rochester, N.Y., c. 1840
Newell, Sextus
Bristol, Conn., c. 1809
Newell, Thomas
Sheffield, Mass., c. 1810
New England Clock Co.
Bristol, Conn., c. 1851. Probably deal-
ers only.
Newhall, Frederick A.
Salem, Mass., c. 1850
Newhall, William
Boston, Mass., c. 1850
Newhart
Lebanon, Pa., c. 1840
New Hartford Mfg. Co.
New Hartford, Conn., c. 1850
New Haven Clock Co.
New Haven, Conn., c. 1850. Made
movements for Jerome; Hiram Camp
was president. Made shelf and ogee
clocks.
Newhouse, Adam
Paterson, N.J., c. 1820
Newlin, Edward G.
Philadelphia, Pa., c. 1848
Newman, John
Boston, Mass., c. 1760
Newman Clock Co.
Chicago, Ill., c. 1878
Newth, William
Schenectady, N.Y., c. 1835
Newton, Isaac
Salem, Mass., c. 1795
Newton, J. L.
Trenton, N.J., c. 1800
Newton, William
New York, N.Y., c. 1840. Casemaker.
Neyser, Augustine
Philadelphia, Pa., c. 1750
Neyser, William
Germantown, Pa., c. 1790
Nicaise, Gabriel
Nauvoo, Ill., c. 1848
Nichol, John L.
Belvedere, N.J., c. 1790
Nicholas, William C.
Winchendon, Mass., c. 1840
Nicholet, Joseph A.
Philadelphia, Pa., c. 1795
Nicholet, Julian
Baltimore, Md., c. 1820; Pittsburgh,
Pa., c. 1830

Nichols, C. R.
Fulton, N.Y., c. 1860
Nichols, George
New York, N.Y., c. 1728
Nichols, Walter
Newport, R.I., c. 1850
Nicolai, George
Belleville, Ill., c. 1850
Nicolet, Joseph Marci
Philadelphia, Pa., c. 1795
Niebergall, Frederick
Rondout, N.Y., c. 1850
Nieilly, Emanuel
Lebanon, Pa., c. 1840
Ninde, J.
Baltimore, Md., c. 1790
Nixon, John
New York, N.Y., c. 1770. Musical
clocks.
Noble, Philander
Pittsfield, Mass., c. 1830
Noel, Theodore
Frankfort, Ky., c. 1830
Nolen, Spencer
Boston, Mass., c. 1813; to Philadelphia,
Pa., c. 1819. Brother-in-law of Aaron
Willard, Jr. Dial painter; in partner-
ship with Aaron Willard, Jr., as dial
and sign painters.
Nolen & Curtis
Boston, Mass., and Philadelphia, Pa.,
c. 1805
Norman, James S.
Lincolnton, N.C., c. 1840
Norris, Benjamin
New Britain, Pa., n.d.
Norris, Patrick
Philadelphia, Pa., c. 1840
Norris, William
n.p.; c. 1810
North, Ethel
Wolcottville, Conn., c. 1820. Brother of
Norris. Made Torrington-type move-
ments for shelf clocks.
North, Norris
Wolcottville, Conn., c. 1820. Made
pillar-and-scroll and other types of shelf
clocks with wood movements.
North, Phineas
Torrington, Conn., 1790–1800
Northey, Elijah
Philadelphia, Pa., c. 1840
Northey, R. F.
New Haven, Conn., c. 1820
Northrop & Smith
Goshen, Conn., c. 1820
Norton, Elijah
Utica, N.Y., c. 1820
Norton, John
York County, Pa., c. 1790
Norton, Nathaniel
New Haven, Conn., c. 1840
Norton, Samuel
Hingham, Mass., c. 1780
Norton, T. B.
Pennsylvania, n.d.
Norton, Thomas
Rising Sun and Germantown, Md.,
c. 1800
Norton, Thomas and Samuel
Philadelphia, Pa., c. 1820
Nowland, Thomas
Philadelphia, Pa., c. 1800

Nowlens Manufacturing Co.
Boston, Mass., n.d.
Nowlin, L.
Chicago, Ill., c. 1840
Noxon, Martin
Edenton, N.C., c. 1800
Noyes, L. W.
Boston, Mass., c. 1840
Noyes, Leonard W.
Nashua, N.H., c. 1830
Noyes, William
Boston area, Mass., c. 1870
Nusz, Frederick
Frederick, Md., c. 1815
Nutter, Enoch H.
Dover, N.H., c. 1820
Nutter, John D.
Mount Vernon, N.H., c. 1820
Nutz, L. N.
Cincinnati, Ohio, c. 1830
Nye, William F.
New Bedford, Mass., c. 1860. Probably
not a clockmaker.

Oabike, Charles
Bristol, Conn., c. 1840
Oakes, Frederick
Hartford, Conn., c. 1828
Oakes, Henry
Hartford, Conn., c. 1839. Possibly only
a watch dealer.
Oakes, Tila
Ashby, Mass., c. 1800. Dial painter.
Oakes, Henry & Co.
Hartford, Conn., c. 1830
Oakland Clock Works
Sag Harbor, L.I., N.Y., c. 1860
Ober, Henry
Elizabethtown, Lancaster Co., Pa.,
c. 1820
O'Brien, James
Philadelphia, Pa., c. 1850
O'Brien, John
Philadelphia, Pa., c. 1840
Ochs, G.
New York, N.Y., c. 1870
O'Claire, Narcis
Albany, N.Y., c. 1815
O'Connell, Maurice
Boston, Mass., c. 1840
O'Daniel, Perry
Philadelphia, Pa., c. 1850
O'Daniel, Thomas
West Chester, Pa., c. 1820
Ogle, William
Philadelphia, Pa., c. 1825
O'Hara, Charles
Philadelphia, Pa., c. 1895
Olewine, Abraham
Pikeland, Pa., c. 1830
Olewine, Henry
Pikeland, Pa., c. 1810
Oliver, D.
Plainfield, N.J., c. 1825
Oliver, Griffith
Philadelphia, Pa., c. 1785
Oliver, John
New York, N.Y., c. 1850. Lived in
Brooklyn, N.Y.
Oliver, John S.
Reading, Pa., c. 1830
Oliver, Welden
Bristol, Conn., c. 1820

Olmstead, Gideon
Charlotte, N.C., c. 1830
Olmstead, Nathaniel
New Haven, Conn., c. 1825
Olmstead, Norman
Brooklyn, N.Y., c. 1829
Olmstead and Barnes
Brooklyn, N.Y., 1820–1840
Olmstead, Nathaniel, & Son
New Haven, Conn., c. 1825
O'Neil, Charles
New Haven, Conn., c. 1823
O'Neil, H.
Philadelphia, Pa., c. 1860
Oosterhoudt, Peter E.
Kingston, N.Y., c. 1790
Oosterhout, Dirk
Yonkers, N.Y., c. 1850
Orberts, E. and Co.
Bristol, Conn., n.d.
Ormsby, Henry
Philadelphia, Pa., c. 1835
Ormsby, James
Baltimore, Md., c. 1771
Orne, R. S.
Boston, Mass., c. 1840
Ornstead & Barns
Brooklyn, N.Y., c. 1850
Orr, Thomas
Philadelphia, Pa., c. 1810; Louisville, Ky., c. 1825
Orton, Robert
Rochester, N.Y., c. 1845
Orton, W. R.
Watertown, N.Y., c. 1850
Orton, Preston & Co.
Farmington, Conn., c. 1820
Osborn, Sheldon
Harwinton, Conn., c. 1830
Osborne, John
Lynn, Mass., c. 1800
Osgood, John
Andover, Mass., c. 1790, Haverhill, N.H., c. 1795
Osgood, John, Jr.
Boston, Mass., c. 1820
Osgood, Orlando
Haverhill, Mass., c. 1845
Otis, F. S.
New York, N.Y., c. 1860
Otis, Frederick S.
Bristol, Conn., 1853–1854
Ottick, M.
Baltimore, Md., c. 1790
Otto, A. F.
Chicago, Ill., c. 1856
Oudin, Joseph
Philadelphia, Pa., c. 1810
Oves, George
Lebanon, Pa., c. 1800
Owen, E.
n.p.; n.d. May have been dial maker.
Owen, George
Winsted, Conn., c. 1870
Owen, George B.
New York, N.Y., c. 1850
Owen, Griffith
Philadelphia, Pa., c. 1790. Maker of excellent tall clocks.
Owen, John
Philadelphia, Pa., c. 1815
Owen, M. T.
Abbeville, S.C., c. 1845

Owen, Charles F. & Co.
New York, N.Y., c. 1850
Owen & Clark
New York, N.Y., c. 1850
Owen, G.B. & Co.
New York, N.Y., c. 1850
Owen & Read
Cincinnati, Ohio, c. 1830
Owen & Sile
Chester, Pa., c. 1810
Owens, Williams
Utica, N.Y., c. 1840
Oyster, Daniel
Reading, Pa., c. 1799
Oyster, John
Herndon, Va., n.d.

Pace, C.
San Francisco, Calif., c. 1850
Packard, Isaac
Brockton, Mass., c. 1820. Worked with Rodney Brace.
Packard, Jonathan
Albany, N.Y., c. 1810. With Packard and Brown. Moved to Rochester, N.Y., c. 1815.
Packard and Brown
Albany, N.Y., c. 1810
Packard and Schofield
Rochester, N.Y., c. 1818
Paillot, Leon
Baltimore, Md., c. 1840
Paine & Heroy
Albany, N.Y., c. 1813
Palmer, John
Philadelphia, Pa., c. 1795
Palmer, John C.
Oxford, Haywood, Salisbury, and Raleigh, N.C., c. 1830
Palmer, Samuel
Dedham, Mass., n.d.
Palmer, Samuel A.
Monticello and Tallahassee, Fla., c. 1855
Palmer, William
New York, N.Y., c. 1800. Probably casemaker only.
Palmer and Clapp
New York, N.Y., c. 1830
Palmer and Company
Boston, Mass., c. 1825
Palmer and Hanks
Cincinnati, Ohio, n.d.
Palmer and Owen
Cincinnati, Ohio, n.d.
Palmer and Ramsey
Raleigh, N.C., c. 1845
Palmer, W. and Company
Boston, Mass., c. 1857
Panet, Philip H.
Cincinnati, Ohio, c. 1830
Pardee, Enoch
Poughkeepsie, N.Y., c. 1840
Pardee, William
Albany, N.Y., c. 1830
Park & Ells
Troy, N.Y., c. 1850
Parke, Augustus
Philadelphia, Pa., c. 1815
Parke, Charles B.
Philadelphia, Pa., c. 1800
Parke, Seth
Parktown, Pa., c. 1790

Parke, Solomon
Newtown, Pa., c. 1780; to Philadelphia c. 1790
Parke, Solomon & Company
Philadelphia, Pa., c. 1795
Parke, Solomon and Son
Philadelphia, Pa., c. 1805
Parke and Son
Philadelphia, Pa., c. 1805
Parker, Daniel
Boston, Mass., c. 1760. Also goldsmith and silversmith.
Parker, Gardiner
Westborough, Mass., c. 1790
Parker, George
Ithaca, N.Y., c. 1830; moved to Utica, N.Y.
Parker, Isaac
Deerfield, Mass., c. 1780
Parker, Isaac
Philadelphia, Pa., c. 1815
Parker, Joseph
Princeton, N.J., c. 1785
Parker, Noah
Portsmouth, N.H., c. 1765. Dealer in parts.
Parker, Samuel
Philadelphia, Pa., c. 1795. Dealer in parts.
Parker, T. H.
Philadelphia, Pa., c. 1830
Parker, Thomas
Philadelphia, Pa., c. 1790. Apprenticed to Rittenhouse.
Parker, Thomas, Jr.
Philadelphia, Pa., c. 1815
Parker, William
Portsmouth, N.H., c. 1783
Parker, William
Philadelphia, Pa., c. 1820
Parker, William, Jr.
Philadelphia, Pa., c. 1835
Parker Clock Co.
Meriden, Conn., c. 1890
Parker and Pierce
Boston, Mass., c. 1805
Parker & Co., Thomas
Philadelphia, Pa., c. 1819
Parker and Whipple Co.
Meriden, Conn., c. 1865. Later became Parker Clock Co.
Parkins, Joseph
Philadelphia, Pa., c. 1835
Parks, Augustus W.
Philadelphia, Pa., c. 1820
Parks, G. D.
Cincinnati, Ohio, c. 1850
Parks, Hugh
New York, N.Y., c. 1840
Parks, Jonas
Bennington, Vt., c. 1775
Parlin, A. S.
Norwich, Conn., c. 1860
Parmalee, Abel
Branford, Conn., c. 1765. Apprenticed to his uncle, Ebenezer.
Parmalee, Ebenezer
Guilford, Conn., c. 1725. Also cabinetmaker. Made first tower clock in Connecticut, on exhibition at Henry Whitfield House in Guilford.
Parmier, John Peter
Philadelphia, Pa., c. 1790

Parrot, Frederick
Philadelphia, Pa., c. 1845
Parry, John
Trenton, N.J., c. 1790
Parry, John F.
Philadelphia, Pa., c. 1820
Parry, John J.
Philadelphia, Pa., c. 1795
Parsons, Henry R.
Philadelphia, Pa., c. 1840
Parsons, John H.
Windsor, Conn., n.d. Casemaker.
Parsons, Silas
Swanzey, N.H., c. 1810
Partridge, Horace
Bristol, Conn., c. 1860
Pass and Stow
Philadelphia, Pa., c. 1760. Bell casters. Made bells and parts for clocks. Recast the Liberty Bell.
Patchin, T. A.
Syracuse, N.Y., c. 1840
Patten, Richard
New York, N.Y., c. 1820
Patten, Zebulon
Bangor, Me., 1830s–1870
Patten and Ferris
New York, N.Y., c. 1820
Patterson, John
Alexandria, Va., n.d.
Patton, Abraham
Philadelphia, Pa., c. 1800
Patton, David
Philadelphia, Pa., c. 1800
Patton & Jones
Baltimore, Md., and Philadelphia, Pa., c. 1800
Pavey, John
Philadelphia, Pa., c. 1800
Paxton, John
Danville, Va., c. 1820
Payne, Lawrence
New York, N.Y., c. 1735
Peabody, Asa
Wilmington, N.C., c. 1820
Peabody, John
Woodstock, Vt., c. 1810
Peabody, John
Fayetteville, N.C., c. 1820
Peabody, Moody
Amherst, N.H., c. 1810
Peale, Charles W.
Annapolis, Md., c. 1760. Noted as a portrait painter. Started career as clockmaker.
Peale, James
Philadelphia, Pa., c. 1810
Pearce, William
Charleston, S.C., c. 1785
Pearman, William
Richmond, Va., c. 1830
Pearsall, Joseph
New York, N.Y., c. 1770
Pearsall, Thomas
New York, N.Y., c. 1770
Pearsall & Embree
New York, N.Y., c. 1785
Pearsall, Joseph & Thomas
New York, N.Y., c. 1765
Pearse, Isaac T.
Enfield, Conn., c. 1830
Pearson, Charles
Concord, N.H., n.d.

Pearson, Isaac
Burlington, N.J., c. 1740
Pearson, William
New York, N.Y., c. 1765
Pearson & Grey
Georgetown, S.C., c. 1765
Pearson & Hollinshead
Burlington, N.J., c. 1750
Pease, Isaac and Comp.
Enfield, Conn., c. 1835(?)
Peaseley, Robert
Boston, Mass., c. 1732
Peck, Edson C.
Derby, Conn., c. 1825
Peck, Elijah
Boston, Mass., c. 1785
Peck, Epaphroditus
Bristol, Conn.(?), c. 1840. Sold clocks for other companies.
Peck, Timothy
Middletown and Litchfield, Conn., c. 1795
Peck, Julius & Co.
Litchfield, Conn., c. 1820
Peck, Hayden & Co.
Saint Louis, Mo., c. 1838
Peck & Holcomb
Sanbornton, N.H., c. 1810
Peck, S. & Co.
New Haven, Conn., c. 1860
Peckham & Knower
Albany, N.Y., c. 1815. Clock dealers.
Peele, J. B.
Salem, Mass., c. 1815
Pelham & Comp.
Cold Spring, N.Y., c. 1865. Probably dealer.
Penfield, Josiah
Savannah, Ga., c. 1820
Penfield, Sylvester
New York, N.Y., c. 1840
Penhallow, E. and B.
Portsmouth, N.H., c. 1795. Dealers in parts.
Penniman, John R.
Boston, Mass., c. 1805. Dial painter. Did work for Simon Willard.
Pennwood Co., The
Pittsburgh, Pa., c. 1940
Pennypacker, William
Frederick, Pa., c. 1860
Pepper, H. J.
Philadelphia, Pa., c. 1850
Pepper, H. S.
Philadelphia, Pa., c. 1835
Pepper, Henry J. & Son
Philadelphia, Pa., c. 1845
Perkins, John
Fitzwilliam, N.H., c. 1820
Perkins, Robinson
Jaffrey, N.H., c. 1820
Perkins, Thomas
Philadelphia, Pa., c. 1785; to Pittsburgh, c. 1815
Perkins & Co., Thomas
Pittsburgh, Pa., c. 1836
Perpigan, Peter
Philadelphia, Pa., c. 1805
Perret, Philip H.
Cincinnati, Ohio, c. 1820
Perrigo, James
Wrentham and Dedham, Mass., c. 1760

Perrigo, James, Jr.
Wrentham, Mass., c. 1800
Perrine, W. D.
Lyons, N.Y., c. 1850
Perry, Albert
Salem, Mass., c. 1850
Perry, Elias
Philadelphia, Pa., c. 1800
Perry, Marvin
New York, N.Y., c. 1765
Perry, Thomas
New York, N.Y., c. 1749
Peters, A. R.
Marietta, Lancaster Co., Pa., c. 1850
Peters, Edward
New York, N.Y., c. 1840
Peters, James
Philadelphia, Pa., c. 1830
Peterson, Henry, Jr.
Alexandria, Va., c. 1785
Pettee, Simon
Wrentham, Mass., n.d.
Pettibone, Lyndes
Brooklyn, N.Y., c. 1830
Pettibone and Peters
New York, N.Y., c. 1845
Petty, Henry
Philadelphia, Pa., c. 1825
Petz, John
Nicholasburg, Pa., n.d.
Pfaff, August
Philadelphia, Pa., c. 1830
Pfaff, Henry
Philadelphia, Pa., c. 1830
Pfalt, John W.
Baltimore, Md., c. 1800; Alexandria, Va., c. 1805
Pfaltz, J. William
Baltimore, Md., c. 1805
Pflueffer, Hermann
Philadelphia, Pa., c. 1845
Pharr, Benjamin Y.
Atlanta, Ga., c. 1825
Phelps, Silas
Lebanon, Conn., c. 1740
Phelps & Bartholomew
Ansonia, Conn., c. 1880
Phelps and White
Northampton, Mass., c. 1828
Philip, John
New York, N.Y., c. 1717. Brass founder; made parts for clocks.
Phillipe & Le Gras
Baltimore, Md., c. 1790
Phillips, James
Charleston, S.C., c. 1780
Phillips, Joseph
New York, N.Y., c. 1710
Phinney and Meade
East Randolph, Vt., n. d.
Phinney, Walker and Co.
New York, N.Y., c. 1900
Phoenix Manufactory
New York, N.Y., c. 1840. Probably dealers.
Phyfe, Duncan
New York, N.Y., c. 1770. Cabinetmaker.
Piaget, L.A. and Co.
Paterson, N.J., n.d.
Picard, J. C.
Cincinnati, Ohio, c. 1830
Pickering, George
Cincinnati, Ohio, c. 1850

Pickering, John
Cincinnati, Ohio, c. 1830

Pickering, Joseph
Philadelphia, Pa., c. 1820

Pickett, Richard, Jr.
Newburyport, Mass., c. 1835

Pickrell, J. L.
Greenville, S.C., c. 1850

Pierce, Preserved
Swanzey, Mass., c. 1770

Pierce, William S.
Philadelphia, Pa., c. 1840

Pierpont & Co.
Unionville, Conn., c. 1840

Pierret, Henry S.
Portland, Me., c. 1830

Pierson, Henry S.
Portland, Me., c. 1834

Piggot, Samuel
New York, N.Y., c. 1830. Also silversmith.

Pike, William
Pennsylvania, c. 1790

Pine, David
Strasburg, Lancaster Co., Pa., c. 1770

Pink, Osborne & Conrad
Philadelphia, Pa., c. 1840

Pinkard, Jonathan
Philadelphia, Pa., c. 1770

Pinkham and Bradford
Auburn, Me., c. 1835. Casemakers.

Piper, James
Chestertown, Md., c. 1770

Pitel, K. C.
n.p.; c. 1860

Pitkin, Levi
Montpelier, Vt., n.d.

Pitman, John
Philadelphia, Pa., c. 1820

Pitman, Saunders
Providence, R.I., c. 1780

Pitman, William R.
New Bedford, Mass., c. 1830. Also silversmith.

Pitman & Dorrance
Providence, R.I., c. 1800

Pitt, W.
New York, N.Y., c. 1850

Pittman, John
Alexandria, Falmouth, and Fredericksburg, Va., c. 1790. Dates in each town uncertain.

Place, W. S.
Charlestown, Md., c. 1850

Platt, Alanson S.
Bristol, Conn., c. 1845

Platt, Augustus
Columbus, Ohio, c. 1840

Platt, Benjamin
Danbury, Conn., to 1776, Lanesboro, Mass., to 1779; New Fairfield, Conn., 1779–1817; Columbus, Ohio, after 1817

Platt, Calvin
Columbus, Ohio, c. 1840

Platt, Ebenezer
New York, N.Y., c. 1775

Platt, John
Philadelphia, Pa., c. 1840

Platt, Samuel
Boston, Mass., c. 1825

Platt, William A., Jr.
Columbus, Ohio, c. 1840

Platt, William Augustus, Sr.
Columbus, Ohio, c. 1840

Platt & Blood
Bristol, Conn., c. 1845

Platt, G.W. & N.C.
New York, N.Y., c. 1832

Plelpa, Carl
New York, N.Y., c. 1900

Plumb, James M.
Berlin, Conn., n.d.

Plummer, Elijah T.
Atlanta, Ga., c. 1870

Plunkett, R.
Boston, Mass., c. 1850

Poindexter, William
Lexington, Ky., c. 1820

Polack, Francis C.
York, Pa., c. 1850

Pollhans, Adam
Saint Louis, Mo., c. 1879

Pollhans, Henry
Saint Louis, Mo., c. 1860

Polsey, J.
Boston, Mass., c. 1840

Pomeroy, Chauncey
Bristol, Conn., c. 1835

Pomeroy, Eltwood
Clockmaker and gunsmith of Massachusetts Bay Colony, 1640s.

Pomeroy, Hunt
Elmira, N.Y., c. 1830

Pomeroy, Noah
Bristol, Conn., c. 1860. In various clock companies in Bristol.

Pomeroy and Hill
Bristol, Conn. (?), c. 1850

Pomeroy, John & Co.
Bristol, Conn., c. 1840

Pomeroy, Noah & Co.
Bristol, Conn., c. 1849

Pomeroy & Parker
Bristol, Conn., c. 1855

Pomeroy & Robbins
Bristol, Conn., c. 1847

Pond, John
Portsmouth, N.H., c. 1809. Probably dealer.

Pond, L. A.
Boston and Chelsea, Mass., c. 1840

Pond, Philip
Bristol, Conn., c. 1840

Pond, William
Boston, Mass., c. 1840

Pond and Barnes
Boston, Mass., c. 1845

Pond, C. H.
New Haven, Conn., c. 1885. Made master clocks.

Ponson, Peter
Philadelphia, Pa., c. 1795

Pool, David L.
Salisbury, N.C., c. 1830

Pool, James
Washington, N.C., c. 1845

Pool, Thomas
Cincinnati, Ohio, c. 1830

Poole Clock Co.
Westport, Conn., c. 1900

Pope, Joseph
Boston, Mass., c. 1790

Pope, Robert
Boston, Mass., c. 1785

Porter, Daniel
Williamstown, Mass., c. 1790

Porter, Edward, Rev.
Waterbury, Conn., c. 1805. With Eli Terry, made 4,000 clocks.

Porter, George
Boston, Mass., c. 1830

Porter, George
Utica, N.Y., c. 1830

Porter, Rufus
Billerica, Mass., c. 1830

Porter, William
Waterbury, Conn., c. 1815

Porter, Abel and Co.
Waterbury, Conn., c. 1805

Porter and Atkins
Bristol, Conn., n.d.

Porter, Carter and Co.
Otis, Mass., c. 1825. Probably dealer.

Porter, Horace and Co.
Boston, Mass., c. 1830

Posey, F. J.
Hagerstown, Md., c. 1830

Post, Samuel
New London, Conn., c. 1780; later, to Philadelphia, Pa.

Potter, Eli
Williamstown, Mass., n.d.

Potter, Ephraim
Concord, N.H., c. 1775

Potter, H. J.
Bristol, Conn., c. 1845

Potter, John
Farmington, Conn., c. 1770

Potter, John
Brookfield, Mass., c. 1775

Potter Brothers
Chicago, Ill., c. 1870

Potter, J.O. & J.R.
Providence, R.I., c. 1848

Potts, Thomas
Norristown, Pa., c. 1760

Poultney, John
Philadelphia, Pa., c. 1780

Pound, Isaac
Charleston, S.C., c. 1745

Pound, John
South Carolina, c. 1745

Powell, John
Baltimore, Md., c. 1745

Powell, John
Annapolis, Md., c. 1750

Powers, Hiram
Cincinnati, Ohio, c. 1822. Apprenticed to Luman Watson.

Praefelt, John
Philadelphia, Pa., c. 1895

Pratt, Azariah
Marietta, Ohio, c. 1790

Pratt, Daniel, Jr.
Reading, Mass., c. 1830. Associated in various companies.

Pratt, Joseph
Boston, Mass., n.d.

Pratt, N., Jr.
East Haddam, Conn., n.d.

Pratt, Phineas
Saybrook, Conn., c. 1760

Pratt, William
Boston, Mass., c. 1840

Pratt, William T.
Washington, N.C., c. 1830

Pratt, Betts & Co.
Alliance, Ohio, c. 1860

Pratt, Daniel & Sons
Reading, Mass., c. 1860

Pratt and Frost
Reading, Mass., c. 1832
Pratt and Walker
Boston, Mass., n.d.
Pratt, William, & Brother
Boston, Mass., c. 1847
Prenot, Henry
New York, N.Y., c. 1800
Prentiss, C. M.
n.p.; c. 1870
Prentiss, John H.
Utica, N.Y., c. 1830
Prentiss Calendar and Time Co.
New York, N.Y., c. 1880
Prentiss Clock Co.
New York, N.Y., c. 1870. Name
changed to Prentiss Calendar and
Time Co.
Prescott, Jonathan
Kensington, N.H., c. 1760
Preston, J. W.
Castleton, Vt., c. 1830
Preston, Paul
Buckingham, Bucks Co., Pa., c. 1750
Preston, Stephen
New York, N.Y., n.d.
Prevear & Harrington
Amherst, Mass., c. 1840
Prey, H. W.
Newport, R.I., c. 1830
Preyle, J.
Charleston, S.C., c. 1780
Price, Benjamin
Philadelphia, Pa., c. 1825
Price, E. D.
Kingston, N.Y., c. 1850
Price, Isaac
Philadelphia, Pa., c. 1790
Price, Joseph
Baltimore, Md., c. 1790
Price, Philip
Philadelphia, Pa., c. 1810; Cincinnati,
Ohio, c. 1820; Lebanon, Ohio, c. 1823
Price, Philip, Jr.
Philadelphia, Pa., c. 1815
Price, Robert
New York, N.Y., c. 1820
Price, William H.
West Chester, Pa., c. 1820
Priest, Joseph
Port of Bristol, Md., c. 1775
Prim, William W.
West Chester, Pa., c. 1820
Prince, George W.
Dover, N.H., c. 1825
Prince, Isaac
Philadelphia, Pa., c. 1790
Pringle, John
New York, N.Y., c. 1830
Priollaud, E.
New Orleans, La., c. 1850
Prior, Daniel
New Haven, Conn., c. 1840
Pritchard, Buel
Dayton, Ohio, c. 1820
Pritchard & Holden
Dayton, Ohio, c. 1838
Pritchard & Munson
Bristol, Conn., c. 1844
Pritchard & Spining
Dayton, Ohio, c. 1830. Probably deal-
ers.
Probasco, Jacob
Philadelphia, Pa., c. 1820

Probosco, John
Trenton, N.J., c. 1800; to Lebanon,
Ohio, 1823
Proctor, Cardan
New York, N.Y., c. 1745
Proctor, G. K.
Beverly, Mass., c. 1850
Proctor, William
New York, N.Y., c. 1740
Proctor, G.F. and Co.
Beverly, Mass., c. 1860. Burglar and
protective alarm clocks.
Progressive Manufacturing Co.
Pana, Ill., c. 1880
Prontaut, Anthony
New York, N.Y., c. 1840
Proud, John
Newport, R.I., c. 1720
Proud, Robert
Newport, R.I., c. 1770
Proud, William
Newport, R.I., c. 1750
Pudney, G.
New York, N.Y., c. 1820
Pulsifer, F.
Boston, Mass., c. 1850
Purcell, Charles
Richmond, Va., c. 1820
Purington, Elisha
Kensington, N.H., c. 1740
Purington, Elisha, Jr.
Kensington, N.H., c. 1750
Purington, James
Kensington, N.H., c. 1690
Purington, James
Kensington, N.H., c. 1790; later to
Marietta, Ohio
Purington, Jonathan
Kensington, N.H., c. 1750
Purse, John
Philadelphia, Pa., c. 1800
Purse, Thomas
Baltimore, Md., c. 1790
Purse, W.
Charleston, S.C., c. 1790
Putnam, Jonathan
New York, N.Y., c. 1840
Pyle, Benjamin
Washington, N.C., c. 1790
Pyle, Benjamin, Jr.
Fayetteville, N.C., c. 1835

Quandale, Lewis
Philadelphia, Pa., c. 1810
Quest, Henry
Marietta, Pa., c. 1810
Quest, Samuel
Maytown, Pa., c. 1813
Quimby, Henry
Portland, Me., c. 1830
Quimby, Phineas
Belfast, Me., c. 1830
Quimby, William
Belfast, Me., c. 1821
Quincy, Henry
Portland, Me., c. 1834
Quinn, Thomas
New York, N.Y., c. 1775; to Philadel-
phia, Pa., c. 1780

R. & J. Clock Co.
Pittsfield, Mass., c. 1840 (?)
Racine, Daniel
Baltimore, Md., c. 1790

Radcliff, J. N.
Birchrunville, Pa., c. 1875
Rahmer, G.
New York, N.Y., c. 1840
Raine, Nathaniel
Philadelphia, Pa., c. 1775. Apprenticed
to Jacob Godshalk.
Rait, Robert and Co.
New York, N.Y., n.d.
Ralph, S. W.
Mecca, Ohio, c. 1885
Ramaal, G.W. and Co.
Chicago, Ill., c. 1900
Ramsay, Walter
Raleigh, N.C., c. 1830. With several
companies.
Ramsdell & Whitcomb
n.p.; c. 1865
Ramsden, Wright
Brooklyn, N.Y., c. 1830
Rand, Daniel
Boston, Mass., c. 1825
Randall, I. and Company
St. Albans, Vt., c. 1829
Rankin, Alexander
Philadelphia, Pa., c. 1830
Rankin, John A.
Delaware and Elkton, Md., c. 1870
Ranlet, Charles, Jr.
Gilmanton, N.H., c. 1800
Ranlet, Noah
Gilmanton, N.H., c. 1790
Ranlet, Samuel
Monmouth District, Me., c. 1800
Ransinger, M.
Elizabethtown, Pa., c. 1850
Rapp, William
Philadelphia, Pa., c. 1830
Rathburn, Valentine W.
Stonington, Conn., n.d.
Rauch, James K.
Bethlehem, Pa., c. 1860
Raus, Emanuel
Philadelphia, Pa., n.d.
Rawson, Jason R.
Holden, Mass., and Saxton, Vt., c. 1830
Rawson, S. E. F.
Saratoga Springs, N.Y., c. 1867
Ray, Daniel
Sudbury, Mass. (?), c. 1790
Ray and Ingraham
Bristol, Conn., c. 1840
Raymond, Freeman C.
Belfast, Me., and Boston, Mass.,
c. 1820
Raynes, Joseph
Lowell, Mass., c. 1835
Rea, Archelaus
Salem, Mass., c. 1789. Also a black-
smith.
Rea, George
Flemington, N.J., c. 1795
Read, Daniel I.
Philadelphia, Pa., c. 1795
Read, Isaac
Philadelphia, Pa., c. 1820
Read, Silas
New Brunswick, N.J., c. 1810
Read, Thomas
New York, N.Y., c. 1840
Read, Wm. H. J.
Philadelphia, Pa., c. 1830
Read, Watson & Chamberlain
Cincinnati, Ohio, c. 1810

Reasnors, John
Rochester, N.Y., c. 1840
Reed, Daniel
Philadelphia, Pa., c. 1795
Reed, Ezekiel
North Bridgewater, Mass., c. 1780
Reed, Frederick
Philadelphia, Pa., c. 1820
Reed, Isaac
Stamford, Conn., c. 1760
Reed, John W.
Philadelphia, Pa., c. 1845
Reed, Osmon
Philadelphia, Pa., c. 1830
Reed, Simeon
Cummington, Mass., c. 1770
Reed, Stephen
New York, N.Y., c. 1810
Reed, Zelotus
Goshen, Mass., c. 1795
Reed, Isaac & Son
Philadelphia, Pa., c. 1835
Reed, James R. & Co.
Pittsburgh, Pa., c. 1840. Probably dealer only.
Reet, George P.
Melrose, Mass., c. 1805
Reeve, Benjamin
Philadelphia, Pa., c. 1750; later at Greenwich, N.J.
Reeve, George
Philadelphia, Pa., c. 1800
Reeve, George
Zanesville, Ohio, c. 1805
Reeve, Joseph
Brooklyn, N.Y., c. 1840
Reeve, Richard
Philadelphia, Pa., c. 1800
Reeve, Richard
Zanesville, Ohio, c. 1815
Reeve, Thomas
New York, N.Y., c. 1840
Reeve, Y.
Philadelphia, Pa., c. 1805
Reeve & Co.
New York, N.Y., c. 1850
Reeves, David
Philadelphia, Pa., c. 1830
Reeves, Elijah
Bellefonte, Pa., c. 1810
Reeves, Stephen
Bridgeton, N.J., c. 1735
Regally, M.
Boston, Mass., c. 1840
Regensburg, Moses A.
West Chester, Pa., c. 1835
Reibley, Joseph
Philadelphia, Pa., c. 1840
Reichwine, Isaac
Paradise, Pa., c. 1850
Reiley, John
Philadelphia, Pa., c. 1785
Reiley, William
Newtown, Pa., c. 1745
Reilly & Co., J.C.
Louisville, Ky., c. 1810
Reineman, Conrad
Chambersburg, Franklin Co., Pa., c. 1835
Reiser, Augustin
Philadelphia, Pa., c. 1770
Remington, O. H.
Akron, Ohio, c. 1860

Rentzheimer, Henry
Sansbury Twp., Pa., c. 1785
Revere Clock Co., The
Cincinnati, Ohio, c. 1930. Electric shelf clocks.
Reymond, M.
Charleston, S.C., c. 1785
Reynolds, Henry
Rochester, N.Y., c. 1845
Reynolds, John
Hagerstown, Md., c. 1790
Reynolds, Thomas
New York, N.Y., c. 1890
Reynolds & Benton
Rochester, N.Y., c. 1850
Rice, Charles
Lewiston, Minn., last half 19th century
Rice, Gideon
New York, N.Y., c. 1840
Rice, H. P.
Saratoga Springs, N.Y., c. 1825
Rice, Joseph
Baltimore, Md., c. 1795
Rice, Joseph T.
Albany, N.Y., c. 1815
Rice, Luther
Lowell, Mass., c. 1835
Rice, Phineas
Charlestown, Mass., c. 1830
Rice, William
Philadelphia, Pa., c. 1835
Rice & Barry
Baltimore, Md., c. 1780
Rice and Johnson
New York, N.Y., c. 1840
Rich, Alexander
Charleston, S.C., c. 1790
Rich, Gideon
New York, N.Y., c. 1840
Rich, John
Bristol, Conn., c. 1820
Rich and Williard (B.F.)
Boston, Mass., c. 1840
Richard, C. A.
Columbus, Ohio, c. 1835
Richards, Alanson
Bristol, Conn., c. 1825
Richards, Bryan
Bristol, Conn., c. 1823
Richards, Frank
Boston, Mass., n.d.
Richards, S. R.
Philadelphia, Pa., c. 1800
Richards, Samuel
Paris, Me., c. 1850
Richards, Seth
Bristol, Conn., c. 1815
Richards, Thomas
New York, N.Y., c. 1800
Richards, William, Jr.
Philadelphia, Pa., c. 1815
Richards, William R.
Bristol, Conn., c. 1830
Richards, B. & A.
Bristol, Conn., c. 1820
Richards & Co.
Chester, Conn., c. 1830
Richards & Morrell
New York, N.Y., c. 1832
Richards, Seth & Son
Bristol, Conn., c. 1815
Richards, W. & S.R.
Philadelphia, Pa., c. 1820

Richardson, Francis
Philadelphia, Pa., c. 1715. Also silversmith and engraved dials.
Richardson, George
Nashua, N.H., c. 1865
Richardson, John
Boston, Mass., c. 1800
Richardson, Joseph
Philadelphia, Pa., c. 1730. Engraved dials. Associated with his father, Francis.
Richardson, Joseph, Jr.
Philadelphia, Pa., c. 1775
Richardson, Martin
Little Falls, N.Y., c. 1835
Richardson, William
Norfolk, Va., c. 1795
Richardson, J. & H.
Boston, Mass., c. 1800
Richman, Isaac
Philadelphia, Pa., c. 1845
Richmond, A.
Providence, R.I., c. 1810
Richmond, Franklin
Providence, R.I., c. 1825
Richmond, G.
Providence, R.I., c. 1810
Richter, Joseph
Baltimore, Md., c. 1817
Ricksecker, Israel
Dover, Ohio, c. 1830
Riddell, Crawford
Philadelphia, Pa., c. 1840
Riddle, James
Fermanagh Twp., Pa., c. 1780
Rider, Arthur
Baltimore, Md., c. 1822
Ridgway, C. T.
Nashua, N.H., c. 1840
Ridgway, John and Son
Boston, Mass., c. 1840
Riel, George
Philadelphia, Pa., c. 1805
Riesle, Egidius
New York, N.Y., c. 1840
Riggs, William H. C.
Philadelphia, Pa., 1820-1860. Made regulator clocks for railroads, etc.
Riggs & Brother (Daniel & Robert Riggs)
Philadelphia, Pa., c. 1865
Riggs Brothers
Philadelphia, Pa., c. 1860
Riggs, Daniel & Co.
Philadelphia, Pa., c. 1860
Riggs and Son
Philadelphia, Pa., c. 1860
Rihl, Albert
Philadelphia, Pa., c. 1850
Riley, John
Philadelphia, Pa., c. 1780
Riley, Riley
New York, N.Y., c. 1805
Riley, Robert
Philadelphia, Pa., c. 1805
Riou, E.
New York, N.Y., c. 1840
Riou & Boell
New York, N.Y., c. 1830. Probably importers.
Ritchie, Benjamin
Maryland, c. 1770
Ritchie, F. J.
n.p.; c. 1870

Ritchie, George
  Philadelphia, Pa., c. 1785
Rittenhouse, Benjamin
  Philadelphia, Pa., c. 1770. Brother of
  David. Instrument maker. Worked in
  gun factory.
Rittenhouse, David
  Philadelphia and Norristown, Pa.,
  c. 1750. Astronomer and surveyor.
  Maker of instruments. His masterpiece
  is in the Drexel Institute.
Ritterband, Henry
  New York, N.Y., c. 1830
Roath, R. W.
  Norwich, Conn., c. 1832. Casemaker.
Robbins, George
  Philadelphia, Pa., c. 1830
Robbins, W. H.
  Vandalia, Ill., c. 1830
Roberts, Candace
  Bristol, Conn., c. 1810. Daughter of
  Gideon. Worked for clockmakers as
  dial and tablet painter.
Roberts, Elias
  Bristol, Conn., c. 1740. Father of Elias
  and Gideon.
Roberts, Enoch
  Philadelphia, Pa., c. 1815
Roberts, F.
  Philadelphia, Pa., c. 1820
Roberts, G. E.
  New Milford, Conn., n.d.
Roberts, Gideon
  Bristol, Conn., c. 1780. Established
  first Bristol Clock Factory.
Roberts, Jacob
  Easton, Pa., c. 1810
Roberts, John
  Philadelphia, Pa., c. 1795
Roberts, Joseph
  Newburyport, Mass., c. 1849
Roberts, Oliver
  Lancaster, Pa., c. 1790; moved to
  Eaton, Ohio
Roberts, Silas
  Trenton, N.J., c. 1790
Roberts, Thomas
  Easton, Pa., c. 1812
Roberts, Titus M.
  Bristol, Conn., c. 1835
Roberts, William
  Annapolis, Md., c. 1750
Roberts, William
  Philadelphia, Pa., c. 1810
Roberts, William
  Philadelphia, Pa., c. 1820
Roberts, Wyllys
  Bristol, Conn., c. 1795. Son of Gideon.
Roberts & Co., E.
  Bristol, Conn., c. 1815
Roberts and Lee
  Boston, Mass., c. 1770
Robertson Clock & Instrument Co.
  Detroit, Mich., c. 1929
Robeson, Isaac
  Philadelphia, Pa., c. 1840
Robie, J. C.
  Binghamton, N.Y., c. 1835
Robie, John
  Plattsburgh, N.Y., c. 1815
Robinson, Anthony
  Trenton, N.J., c. 1785

Robinson, Isaac
  Philadelphia, Pa., c. 1825
Robinson, Jacob F.
  Wilmington, Del., c. 1840
Robinson, Jeremiah A.
  Lowell, Mass., c. 1835
Robinson, John
  Haverhill, Mass., c. 1640
Robinson, Obed
  Attleboro, Mass., c. 1790
Robinson, Samuel
  Pittsburgh, Pa., c. 1830
Robinson, William
  Chillicothe, Ohio, c. 1805
Robinson, William F.
  Philadelphia, Pa., c. 1830
Robinson, William K.
  Brownville, N.Y., c. 1825
Robinson and Collins
  New York, N.Y., c. 1840
Robjohn, Thomas
  New York, N.Y., c. 1840
Rockwell, Henry
  New York, N.Y., c. 1840
Rockwell, Samuel
  Providence, R.I., 1745–1760; Middle-
  town, Conn., c. 1760
Rode, William
  Philadelphia, Pa., c. 1780
Rodgers, William
  Philadelphia, Pa., c. 1820
Rodman, Isaac Pearson
  Burlington, N.J., n.d.
Rodman, John
  Burlington, N.J., c. 1760
Rodman, Thomas
  Burlington, N.J., n.d.
Rogers, Abner
  Berwick, Me., c. 1820
Rogers, Caleb
  Newton, Mass., 1785–1790
Rogers, Ebenezer
  Norwich, Conn., c. 1800
Rogers, George W.
  Concord, N.H., c. 1810. Casemaker.
Rogers, Isaac
  Marshfield, Mass., c. 1805
Rogers, James
  New York, N.Y., c. 1820
Rogers, James M.
  Troy, N.Y., c. 1830
Rogers, John
  Billerica, Mass., c. 1765; to Newton,
  Mass., c. 1770. Also worked in Boston.
Rogers, Nathaniel
  Windham, Me., c. 1792
Rogers, Paul
  Berwick, Me., c. 1795
Rogers, Peter
  New York, N.Y., c. 1820
Rogers, Samuel
  Plymouth, Mass., c. 1790
Rogers, Thomas
  New York, N.Y., c. 1820
Rogers, William
  Hartford, Conn., c. 1835. Probably
  dealer only.
Rogers, William
  Boston, Mass., c. 1860
Rogers, William H.
  Brooklyn, N.Y., c. 1850
Rohr, John
  Philadelphia, Pa., c. 1806

Roi, Henry
  Hamburg, Pa., c. 1820
Roland, Henry
  Albany, N.Y., c. 1832
Ronson, Peter
  Philadelphia, Pa., c. 1795
Roome, James H.
  New York, N.Y., c. 1850
Roorback, M.
  New York, N.Y., c. 1760
Root, E. G.
  Forestville, Conn., c. 1865
Root, Joel
  Bristol, Conn., c. 1850
Root, Lafayette
  New Haven, Conn., c. 1850
Root, Samuel E.
  Bristol, Conn., c. 1840. Nephew of
  C. Ives.
Root, Sylvester S.
  Bristol, Conn., c. 1840
Rose, Daniel
  Reading, Pa., c. 1780
Rose, Daniel, Jr.
  Reading, Pa., c. 1820
Ross, Alexander C.
  Zanesville, Ohio, c. 1830
Ross, Robert
  New York, N.Y., c. 1850
Rosselot, P. A.
  New York, N.Y., c. 1840. Dealt in
  clock parts.
Rosset and Mulford
  Elizabethtown, Pa., c. 1860. Cabinet-
  makers.
Roth, Harry
  New York, N.Y., c. 1850
Roth, N.
  Utica, N.Y., c. 1840
Rothrock, Joseph
  York, Pa., c. 1780
Roulstone, John
  Boston, Mass., c. 1770
Rouse, Emanuel
  Philadelphia, Pa., c. 1750
Rouse, William M.
  Charleston, S.C., c. 1830
Rowlands, Henry
  Albany, N.Y., c. 1832
Royce, Charles
  Jersey City, N.J., n.d.
Royce, Harvey
  Morrisville, N.Y., c. 1830
Roydor, Francis
  Boston, Mass., c. 1830
Rudisill, George
  Manheim, Lancaster Co., Pa., c. 1810
Rudolph, Samuel
  Philadelphia, Pa., c. 1800
Rudolph, William
  Delaware, n.d.
Rue, Henry
  Philadelphia, Pa., c. 1830
Rugheimer, Moses
  New York, N.Y., c. 1850
Russel, Jonathan
  Geneva, N.Y., c. 1800
Russel, Samuel
  Middleton, Mass., c. 1840
Russel and Clark
  Woodstock, Vt., c. 1830
Russell, A. L.
  Lynn, Mass., n.d.

Russell, Charles
  Lynn, Mass., c. 1850
Russell, George
  Philadelphia, Pa., c. 1830
Russell, John
  Deerfield, Mass., c. 1760
Russell, Thomas
  Charleston, S.C., c. 1850
Russell, William
  Augusta, Ga., c. 1820
Russell and Jones Clock Co.
  Pittsfield, Mass., c. 1884. Successors to Terry Clock Co.
Ruth, Jacob
  Mount Joy (Elizabethtown), Pa., c. 1825
Rutter, Moses
  Baltimore, Md., c. 1800
Ryerson, Lucas
  Manchester, N.J., c. 1805

Saber, George
  Reading, Pa., c. 1800
Sadd, Harvey
  New Hartford, Conn., 1798–1829; Austinburg, Ohio, 1829–1840. Active in the foundry business.
Sadtler, Philip B.
  Baltimore, Md., c. 1804
Safford & Kail
  Kingston, N.Y., c. 1850. Probably dealers only.
Sage, A. and Co.
  Savannah, Ga., n.d.
Sagey (or Sayey), John
  Germantown, Pa., n.d.
Sagsmuller, George
  Rochester, N.Y., c. 1875. Also instrument maker
Sailor, Washington
  Philadelphia, Pa., c. 1820
Salmon, Alfred
  Cincinnati, Ohio, c. 1820
Salmon, William H.
  Morrisville, N.Y., c. 1820; to Cazenovia, N.Y., c. 1830
Salybacker, I.
  Columbia, S.C., c. 1850
Sample, William
  Boston, Mass., c. 1850
Sampson, Alexander
  Hagerstown, Md., c. 1799
Sampson, William
  Philadelphia, Pa., c. 1800
Samuel, Hyman
  Charleston, S.C., c. 1805
Samuels and Dunn
  New York, N.Y., c. 1840. Dealers. Sold clocks with fake labels.
Sandell, Edward
  Baltimore, Md., c. 1815
Sandoz, Charles
  Philadelphia, Pa., c. 1800
Sandoz, Frederick
  Charleston, S.C., c. 1790
Sandoz, Louis
  Philadelphia, Pa., c. 1840
Sands, Stephen
  New York, N.Y., c. 1770
Sanford, Abel
  Hamilton, N.Y., c. 1830
Sanford, Eaton
  Plymouth, Conn., c. 1800

Sanford, Judson
  Hamilton, N.Y., c. 1840
Sanford, Ransom
  Plymouth, Conn., c. 1840. Made clock parts for other makers.
Sanford, Samuel
  Plymouth, Conn., c. 1840
Sanfords, T. and E.
  Goshen, Conn., c. 1820
Sangamo Electric Co.
  Springfield, Ill., c. 1926. Electric clocks.
Sanson, John
  New York, N.Y., c. 1840. Casemaker.
Sargeant, Jacob
  Mansfield, Conn., c. 1784; Springfield, Mass., c. 1787; Hartford, Conn., c. 1795. Also dealer.
Sargeant, Joseph
  Hartford, Conn., c. 1800
Sargeant, Thomas
  Springfield, Mass., n.d.
Sargent, Ebenezer
  Newbury (now Newburyport), Mass., c. 1750
Sartwell & Chappell
  Chautauqua Co., N.Y., and Busti, N.Y., n.d.
Sauer, Christopher (name spelled various ways)
  Germantown, Pa., c. 1725. Printed first Bible in Colonies. Also M.D. and oculist.
Sauer, Frederick
  West Chester, Pa., c. 1850
Sausse, Richard
  Philadelphia, Pa., c. 1770; later to New York
Sauter, Richard
  Hanover, Pa., c. 1770
Savage, John
  Raleigh, N.C., c. 1865. Also silversmith.
Savage, W. M.
  Columbus, Ohio, c. 1835
Savage, William
  Glasgow, Ky., c. 1810
Savoy, N.
  Boston, Mass., c. 1830
Saw, William
  New Haven, Conn., c. 1840
Sawin, John
  Boston, Mass., c. 1822. With Dyer in Sawin and Dyer. Made clocks for Aaron Willard, Jr.
Sawin, Silas
  New York, N.Y., c. 1820
Saxton, Joseph
  Philadelphia, Pa., c. 1820. Later associated with I. Lukens. Made balances for U.S. Mint.
Saxton & Lukens
  Philadelphia, Pa., c. 1820
Sayre, Charles
  Easton, Pa., n.d.
Sayre, Elias
  Elizabethtown, N.J., n.d.
Sayre, John
  New York, N.Y., c. 1800
Sayre & Richards
  New York, N.Y., c. 1805
Schaffer, T. C.
  Portsmouth, N.H., c. 1840
Schaffenberger, J.
  Philadelphia, Pa., c. 1805

Scharf, J.
  Selinsgrove, Snyder Co., Pa., c. 1810
Scheid, Daniel (name spelled various ways)
  Sumneytown, Pa., c. 1850
Schell, Samuel F.
  Philadelphia, Pa., c. 1825
Schem, J. F.
  Charleston, S.C., c. 1785
Schem & Falconnet
  Charleston, S.C., c. 1790
Scherr, Lewis
  Philadelphia, Pa., c. 1840
Schey, F.
  Lewes, Delaware, c. 1850
Schinkle, John
  Philadelphia, Pa., c. 1810
Schmalze, F.
  Freytown, York Co., Pa., c. 1858
Schmid, John G.
  Philadelphia, Pa., c. 1845
Schmidt, John
  Lakecourt, Calif., n.d.
Schmidt and Taylor
  New York, N.Y., n.d.
Schmoltz, William
  San Francisco, Calif., c. 1850
Schneider, Jacob
  Reading, Pa., c. 1785
Schneider, Peter
  Pennsylvania, c. 1840
Schoemaker, Peter
  New York, N.Y., c. 1810
Schollaberger, John
  Pennsylvania, c. 1800
Schollet, John B.
  Boston, Mass., c. 1795
Schomo, Thomas (name spelled various ways)
  Philadelphia, Pa., c. 1820
Schreiner, Charles W.
  Philadelphia, Pa., c. 1810
Schreiner, Henry M.
  Lancaster, Pa., c. 1850
Schreiner, Martin, Sr.
  Lancaster, Pa., c. 1795. Clocks were numbered. Later made fire engines, with his sons. Father of Martin, Jr., and Philip.
Schreiner, Martin, Jr.
  Lancaster, Pa., c. 1850. Worked with his father and brother.
Schreiner, Philip
  Lancaster, Pa., c. 1830. Worked with his father and brother.
Schreiner, Thomas
  Philadelphia, Pa., n.d.
Schreiner, Martin and Philip
  Lancaster, Pa., c. 1830
Schreiner, P. and Son
  Columbia, Pa., c. 1850
Schroeter, Charles
  Baltimore, Md., c. 1815
Schuller, J.
  Philadelphia, Pa., c. 1840
Schultz, Gottlieb
  Philadelphia, Pa., c. 1820
Schultz, Jacob
  Lancaster, Pa., c. 1850
Schuyler, P. C.
  New York, N.Y., c. 1800
Schwalbach, M.
  n.p.; c. 1880

Schwartz, George
  York, Pa., c. 1775
Schwartz, Peter
  York, Pa., c. 1760. Brother of George.
Schwetzer, George
  Fredericktown, Md., c. 1690
Schwing, John G.
  Louisville, Ky., c. 1800
Scott, Alexander
  Chambersburg, Franklin Co., Pa.,
  c. 1800. Also silversmith.
Scott, Anne
  Harrisburg, Pa., c. 1850
Scott, David
  Greensboro, N.C., c. 1825
Scott, John
  Chambersburg, Pa., c. 1790
Scott, John
  Charleston, S.C., c. 1800
Scott, Robert
  Richmond, Va., c. 1780
Scott, Samuel
  Concord, N.C., c. 1825
Scott, Thomas
  Downingtown, Pa., c. 1834
Scott, William D.
  Louisville, Ky., c. 1840
Scott and Anderson
  Greensboro, N.C., c. 1825
Scott, W.D. and Co.
  Louisville, Ky., c. 1840
Scovil, David
  Oswego, N.Y., c. 1845
Scoville Manufacturing Co.
  New York, N.Y., c. 1870
Scrafton, Wilson
  Wilmington, Del., c. 1850
Scribner, Levi
  New York, N.Y., n.d.
Scudder, John
  Westfield, N.J., c. 1760. Casemaker
  who put his name on clocks. Made
  cases for Brokaw and others.
Seaman, Thomas
  Edenton, N.C., c. 1790
Seaman, Thomas
  New York, N.Y., c. 1840
Sears, John
  Chillicothe, Ohio, c. 1810
Searsall, Thomas
  New York, N.Y., c. 1780
Searson, John
  New York, N.Y., c. 1750
Seddinger, Margaret
  Philadelphia, Pa., c. 1845
Sedgwick & Bishop
  Waterbury, Conn., c. 1820
Sedgwick and Botsford
  Watertown, Conn., c. 1820
Seely and Freeman
  Ogdensburg, N.Y., c. 1830
Segar, Dornick
  Cleveland, Ohio, c. 1830
Seger, James
  New York, N.Y. (?), c. 1830
Seip, David
  Northampton (now Allentown), Pa.,
  n.d.
Self Winding Clock Co.
  Bristol, Conn., n.d.
Selkirk, Samuel
  Kalamazoo, Mich., c. 1850
Sells & Schofield
  Augusta, Ky., c. 1860

Sema, J. K.
  Canton, Pa., c. 1865
Seng & Hess
  New York, N.Y., c. 1850
Sennert, F. L.
  Lititz, Pa., c. 1850
Servoss, Benjamin
  Philadelphia, Pa., c. 1830
Servoss, Charles
  Philadelphia, Pa., c. 1840
Servoss, Joseph
  Philadelphia, Pa., c. 1850
Sessions, Calvin
  Burlington, Conn., c. 1840
Sessions, William E.
  Bristol, Conn., c. 1860
Sessions Clock Company
  Bristol, Conn., c. 1903
Seward, Joshua
  Boston, Mass., c. 1830
Sexton, Noah
  Paterson, N.J., c. 1820
Seymour, Henry A.
  Bristol, Conn., c. 1845
Seymour, Ball and Co.
  Unionville, Conn., c. 1830
Seymour & Churchill
  Bristol, Conn., c. 1846
Seymour, Williams & Porter
  Unionville, Conn., c. 1835. Probably
  worked in Farmington, Conn., also.
Seymoure, Robert
  Waterbury, Conn., c. 1815
Seymoure, Sylvester
  Pittsburgh, Pa., c. 1840
Shade, Daniel
  Sumneytown, Montgomery Co., Pa.,
  n.d.
Shade, John
  Philadelphia, Pa., c. 1840
Shadforth, Whitacker
  Richmond, Va., c. 1795
Shaeffer, Benjamin
  Elizabethtown, Lancaster Co., Pa.,
  c. 1850
Shaffer, Philip
  Lancaster, Pa., c. 1788
Shallenberger, Jonathan
  n.p.; c. 1830
Sharf, John
  Mifflinburg, Pa., c. 1820
Shaver, Michael
  Abington, Va., c. 1800
Shaw, B. E.
  Newport, Vt., c. 1850
Shaw, Caleb
  Kingston, N.H., c. 1740
Shaw, David
  Plainfield, Mass., c. 1825
Shaw, George
  New York, N.Y., c. 1840
Shaw, John
  Philadelphia, Pa., c. 1815
Shaw, Joseph Kernberg
  Philadelphia, Pa., c. 1760
Shaw, P.
  Olney, Ill., c. 1860. Probably dealer
  only.
Shaw, Seth
  Providence, R.I., c. 1850
Shaw, G. and A.
  Providence, R.I., c. 1810
Shay, Michael
  Lancaster, Pa., c. 1850

Sheam, Francis
  New York, N.Y., c. 1810
Shearer, Marvin
  Akron, Ohio, 1930. Made novelty elec-
  tric clock for 1933 Century of Progress
  in Chicago.
Shearman, M.
  Andover, Mass., c. 1840
Shearman, Martin
  Hingham, Mass., c. 1820
Shearman, Robert
  Wilmington, Del., c. 1770. Also worked
  in Philadelphia.
Sheidt, Daniel
  Sumneytown, Pa., c. 1790
Shenk, Henry
  Lancaster, Pa., c. 1850
Shepard, Noah
  Waterbury, Conn., c. 1810
Shepard, Timothy
  Utica, N.Y., c. 1830
Shepard and Porter
  Waterbury, Conn., c. 1800
Shepherd, Matthew
  New York, N.Y., c. 1760; Charleston,
  S.C., c. 1770
Shepherd, Nathaniel
  New Bedford, Mass., c. 1810
Shepherd & Boyd
  Albany, N.Y., c. 1810
Sherbourne, James
  Paterson, N.J., c. 1830
Sherman, Joseph
  Lancaster, Pa., c. 1825
Sherman, Robert
  Philadelphia, Pa., c. 1795
Sherman, William
  Philadelphia, Pa., c. 1810
Sherman, C.R. and Co.
  New Bedford, Mass., c. 1860
Shermer, John
  Philadelphia, Pa., c. 1810
Sherry & Byram
  Sag Harbor, L.I., N.Y., c. 1840. Made
  clocks for churches, public buildings,
  etc.
Sherwin, William
  Buckland, Mass., c. 1820
Sherwood, R.
  San Francisco, Calif., c. 1850
Shethar, Samuel
  Litchfield, Conn., c. 1790
Shide, Charles
  Sumneytown, Pa., c. 1800. Could be
  another spelling for Scheid.
Shidet, V.
  Shreveport, La., c. 1850
Shields, Thomas
  Philadelphia, Pa., c. 1765
Shimer, John
  Philadelphia, Pa., c. 1810
Shinkle, John P.
  Philadelphia, Pa., c. 1820
Shipherd, Arthur
  New York, N.Y., c. 1760
Shipman, Nathaniel
  Norwich, Conn., c. 1785. Apprenticed
  to Thomas Harland.
Shipman, Thomas
  Norwich, Conn., c. 1810. Son of Na-
  thaniel.
Shipman & Son, N.
  Norwich, Conn., n.d.

Shipp, S. A.
Cincinnati, Ohio, c. 1820
Shipp & Collins
Cincinnati, Ohio, c. 1820
Shippen, William A.
Philadelphia, Pa., c. 1815
Shoemaker, Abraham
Philadelphia, Pa., c. 1800
Shoemaker, Benjamin
Philadelphia, Pa., c. 1800
Shoemaker, David
Newtown, Bucks Co., Pa., c. 1815
Shorey, Edwin
Bluehill, Me., c. 1840
Short, John
Halifax, N.J., c. 1790; later to Alexandria and Norfolk, Va.
Shourds, Samuel
Bordentown, N.J., c. 1740
Shreiner: See Schreiner
Shreve, G.C. & Co.
San Francisco, Calif., c. 1860
Shrewsbury Clock & Instrument Co.
New York, N.Y., c. 1935
Shrocter, Charles
Baltimore, Md., c. 1807
Shuler, David
Trappe, Pa., c. 1865
Shuler, John
Philadelphia, Pa., c. 1850
Shuman, John
Easton, Pa., c. 1790
Shurley, John
Albany, N.Y., 1835
Shutz, Gustave
Philadelphia, Pa., c. 1820
Shutz, Peter
York, Pa., c. 1758
Sibley, Asa
Woodstock, Conn., c. 1784; Rochester, N.Y., c. 1815
Sibley, Clark
New Haven, Conn., c. 1810
Sibley, Gibbs
Canandaigua, N.Y., c. 1785
Sibley, James
Rochester, N.Y., c. 1845
Sibley, Richard S.
Boston, Mass., c. 1840
Sibley, Stephen
Great Barrington, Mass., c. 1790
Sibley, Timothy
Sutton, Mass., n.d.
Sibley & Marble
New Haven, Conn., c. 1800. Also made swords, surgical instruments, etc.
Sidle & Barlberger
Pittsburgh, Pa., c. 1840
Sidle, Matthias & Nicholas
Pittsburgh, Pa., c. 1850. Also worked individually.
Sidney Advertising Clock Company
Sidney, N.Y., c. 1885
Sigourney, Charles, Jr.
Hartford, Conn., c. 1800. Importer of parts.
Sill, M. & F.
New York, N.Y., c. 1840
Sillcocks and Cooley
New York, N.Y., c. 1885
Silver, M. A.
New York, N.Y., c. 1840
Silver & Way
Bristol, Conn., c. 1860

Silverthaw and Son
New Haven, Conn., c. 1845
Simmons, Abel
Buffalo, N.Y., c. 1835
Simnet, John
Providence, R.I., c. 1765; to New York, N.Y., c. 1770
Simnet, John
Albany, N.Y., c. 1780
Simons, Elijah
Massachusetts, c. 1800
Simons Brothers
Philadelphia, Pa., n.d.
Simonton, Gilbert
New York, N.Y., c. 1820
Simplex Company
Gardner, Mass., c. 1880. Made time recorders.
Simpson, Alexander
Hagerstown, Md., c. 1795; later to Cincinnati, Ohio
Simpson, Jonathan
Kentucky, c. 1820
Simpson, William
Philadelphia, Pa., c. 1800
Simpson & Johnston
Hagerstown, Md., c. 1800
Sinclair, William
Philadelphia, Pa., c. 1835
Sindler, Andrew
New Church, Va., n.d.
Sines, Hiram L.
Philadelphia, Pa., c. 1850
Singer, George
Baltimore, Md., c. 1840
Singleton, Robert
Greensboro, N.C., c. 1835
Sinnett, John: See Simnet
Sinnott, Patrick
Philadelphia, Pa., c. 1755; then Baltimore, Md., c. 1760
Sinwell, Richard
Pittsburgh, Pa., c. 1835
Skellhorn, Richard
New York, N.Y., c. 1775
Skidmore, Thomas
Lancaster, Pa., c. 1765
Skinner, Alvah
Boston, Mass., c. 1830
Skinner, G. M.
Montpelier, Vt., n.d.
Skinner and Sawyer
Boston, Mass., n.d.
Slagele, George W.
New York, N.Y., c. 1880
Slicer, William
Annapolis, Md., c. 1760. Casemaker.
Sligh, Samuel
West Cahn, Chester Co., Pa., c. 1790
Slover & Kortwright
New York, N.Y., c. 1800
Smallwood, W. R.
Towanda, N.Y., c. 1890. Made clock for World's Columbian Exposition in 1893.
Smart, George
Lexington, Ky., c. 1790
Smart, John
Philadelphia, Pa., c. 1835
Smart, Thomas
New York, N.Y., c. 1770
Smith
Sudbury, Mass., c. 1640

Smith, A.
Boston, Mass., c. 1850
Smith, A. B.
New York, N.Y., c. 1835
Smith, A. D.
Cincinnati, Ohio, c. 1860
Smith, Aaron
Ipswich, Mass., c. 1800
Smith, B.
New York, N.Y., c. 1820
Smith, B.
Philadelphia, Pa., c. 1835
Smith, C. C.
Fayetteville, N.C., c. 1840
Smith, Charles
Reading, Pa., c. 1810
Smith, Charles A.
Brattleboro, Vt., c. 1900
Smith, Charles N.
Philadelphia, Pa., c. 1830
Smith, Daniel
Lancaster Boro, Pa., c. 1820
Smith, Daniel T.
Salem, Mass., c. 1845
Smith, E.
New Haven, Conn., c. 1820. Casemaker.
Smith, Ebenezer
Brookfield, Conn., c. 1790
Smith, Edmund
New Haven, Conn., c. 1835
Smith, Edward A.
Salem, Mass., c. 1850
Smith, Elias
Philadelphia, Pa., c. 1840
Smith, Elisha
Sanbornton, N.H., c. 1800
Smith, Ernest
Philadelphia, Pa., c. 1830
Smith, F. C.
Philadelphia, Pa., c. 1840
Smith, George
Carlisle, Pa., c. 1780
Smith, H. C.
New York, N.Y., c. 1840
Smith, Henry A.
Rochester, N.Y., c. 1830
Smith, Henry C.
Waterbury, Conn., c. 1810; Plymouth Hollow, Conn., c. 1840
Smith, Hezekiah
Philadelphia, Pa., c. 1840
Smith, I.
Skippackville, Pa., n.d.
Smith, Isaac
Philadelphia, Pa., c. 1840
Smith, J.
Concord, Mass., c. 1790
Smith, James
Philadelphia, Pa., c. 1840
Smith, James C.
Bristol, Conn., n.d.
Smith, Jesse
Concord, Mass., c. 1800. Apprenticed to Levi Hutchins.
Smith, Jesse, Jr.
Salem, Mass., c. 1830. In partnership with Benjamin Balch.
Smith, John
Lancaster, Boro, Pa., c. 1817
Smith, John
New York, N.Y., c. 1840

Smith, John
Charleston, S.C., c. 1850
Smith, John Creagh
Philadelphia, Pa., c. 1830
Smith, John W.
Stowe, Vt., c. 1870
Smith, Joseph
Chester, Pa., c. 1750
Smith, Joseph
Earl, Pa., c. 1820
Smith, Joseph
Brooklyn, N.Y., c. 1830
Smith, Josiah
Reading, Pa., c. 1800
Smith, L.
New York, N.Y., c. 1839
Smith, Levi
Bristol, Conn., c. 1842
Smith, Luther
Keene, N.H., c. 1790
Smith, Lyman
Stratford, Conn., c. 1800
Smith, Nathaniel
Columbus, Ohio, c. 1810
Smith, Philip
Marcellus, N.Y., c. 1825. Probably cased movements.
Smith, R.
Hartford, Conn., c. 1830
Smith, Ransom
New York, N.Y., c. 1840
Smith, Robert
Philadelphia, Pa., c. 1820
Smith, S.
Lyons, N.Y., c. 1830
Smith, Sam
Brooklyn, N.Y., n.d.
Smith, Samuel
New York, N.Y., c. 1795
Smith, Samuel
Philadelphia, Pa., c. 1850
Smith, Samuel G.
Coatesville, Pa., c. 1865
Smith, Simon
Suffield, Conn., c. 1775
Smith, William
New York, N.Y., c. 1810; later to Philadelphia, Pa.
Smith, William
New York, N.Y., c. 1810. Cabinet-maker.
Smith, Zebulon
Bangor, Me., c. 1830
Smith, Blakesley and Co.
Bristol, Conn., c. 1840 and New York, N.Y.
Smith & Brother
Philadelphia, Pa., c. 1840
Smith and Brothers
New York, N.Y., c. 1840
Smith Brothers Clock Establishment
New York, N.Y., n.d.
Smith, Clark & Co.
New York, N.Y., c. 1840
Smith and Company
Canton, Ohio, c. 1830
Smith Company
Philadelphia, Pa., c. 1840
Smith, E.A. and D.T.
Salem, Mass., c. 1850
Smith and Fenn
Baltimore, Md., c. 1840
Smith & Goodrich
Forestville, Bristol, Conn., c. 1847

Smith & Goodrich
Philadelphia, Pa., c. 1850
Smith and Holman
Hartford, Conn., n.d.
Smith, R. & Co.
Waterbury, Conn., c. 1830
Smith and Root
New York, N.Y., n.d.
Smith, S.B. & Co.
New York, N.Y., c. 1850. Probably tablet painters.
Smith & Sears
Rochester, N.Y., c. 1830
Smith & Sill
Waterbury, Conn., c. 1830
Smith & Taylor
New York, N.Y., c. 1840
Smith, Tuttle and Blakeslee
Oswego, N.Y., c. 1850
Smith's Clock Establishment
New York, N.Y., c. 1830
Smitten, R. T.
Philadelphia, Pa., c. 1840
Snatt, John
Ashford, Mass., c. 1700
Snow, Benjamin
Augusta, Me., c. 1780
Snow, Jeremiah
Springfield, Mass., n.d.
Snow, William
Kalamazoo, Mich., c. 1850
Snow, R.R. & Son
Ripon, Wis., n.d.
Snyder, George
Philadelphia, Pa., c. 1800
Snyder, John B.
Pottstown, Pa., c. 1860
Snyder, Peter, Jr.
Exeter Twp., Berks Co., Pa., c. 1780
Solliday, Benjamin (name spelled various ways)
Rock Hill, Pa., c. 1790. Brother of Jacob.
Solliday, Calvin
Lambertville, N.J., c. 1900
Solliday, Charles
Doylestown, Pa., c. 1830
Solliday, Christopher
Lambertville, N.J., c. 1910. Son of Calvin.
Solliday, Daniel H.
Sumneytown, Montgomery Co., Pa., c. 1820
Solliday, Eli
New Hope, Pa., c. 1830
Solliday, Frederick
Bedminster, Bucks Co., Pa., c. 1740
Solliday, George
Montgomeryville, Montgomery Co., Pa., n.d. Son of Benjamin.
Solliday, George, Jr.
Precise information not available.
Solliday, Henry
Towamencin, Pa., n.d.
Solliday, Jacob
Bedminster, Pa., c. 1783; also at Northampton (now Allentown), Pa.
Solliday, John
Richland Twp., Pa., c. 1780
Solliday, John
Reading, Pa., c. 1800; later to Bucks Co.

Solliday, John
Bucks and Northampton Cos., Pa., c. 1830
Solliday, Peter
Bedminster, Pa., c. 1790. Son of Jacob.
Solliday, Samuel
Doylestown, Bucks Co., Pa., c. 1828. Son of Benjamin.
Solliday, William
Pennsylvania, n.d.
Solliday and Son
Dublin, Pa., c. 1830
Soloman, Henry
Boston, Mass., c. 1820
Solomon, Parke & Co.
Philadelphia, Pa., c. 1796
Somers, Albert
Woodbury, N.J., c. 1820
Somers & Crowley
Philadelphia, Pa., c. 1825
South, James
Charlestown, Mass., c. 1810
Southern Calendar Clock Company
Saint Louis, Mo., c. 1880. Calendar clocks. Used Seth Thomas movements.
Southwich, A. W.
Boston, Mass., c. 1865
Southworth, Elijah
New York, N.Y., c. 1790
Souza, Samuel
Philadelphia, Pa., c. 1820
Spackman, George
Philadelphia, Pa., c. 1820
Spangler, Jacob
York, Pa., c. 1788. Son of Rudi Spangler.
Spangler, Rudi
York, Pa., c. 1760
Spangler, Rudolph: 1738–1811
York, Pa., c. 1760. Rudolph Spengler (also spelled Spangler) was a clock-maker and silversmith. His clocks are inscribed "Rudy Spengler, York Town." In the Revolution he was a captain of Sixth Company, York County Militia, which marched to easterrn New Jersey in 1776 to form the Flying Camp
Sparck, Peter
Philadelphia, Pa., c. 1795
Spaulding, Abraham
Brooklyn, N.Y., c. 1830
Spaulding, Edward
Providence, R.I., c. 1770
Spaulding, Edward, Jr.
Providence, R.I., c. 1800
Spaulding and Co.
Providence, R.I., c. 1800
Speciale, Michael and Son
New York, N.Y., c. 1905
Spellier, Louis H.
Doylestown, Bucks Co., Pa., c. 1870
Spence, Gavin
New York, N.Y., c. 1810
Spence, James
Flemington, N.J., c. 1800
Spence, John
Boston, Mass., c. 1820
Spencer, Julius
Utica, N.Y., c. 1820
Spencer, Noble
Wallingford, Conn., c. 1796; Stratford, Conn., c. 1797

Spencer, Hotchkiss & Co.
Salem Bridge, Conn., c. 1830

Spencer, Hotchkiss and Wooster
Naugatuck, Conn., c. 1840

Spencer, Wooster and Co.
Salem Bridge, Conn., c. 1828

Sperry, Anson
Waterbury, Conn., c. 1820

Sperry, C. S.
New York, N.Y., c. 1840

Sperry, Elijah M.
New York, N.Y.., c. 1840

Sperry, F. S.
New York, N.Y., c. 1850

Sperry, Henry
New York, N.Y., c. 1850

Sperry, J. T.
New York, N.Y., c. 1810

Sperry, Silas
New Haven, Conn., c. 1840

Sperry, Timothy S.
New York, N.Y., c. 1848

Sperry, W. S.
New York, N.Y., c. 1840. Probably casemaker.

Sperry, William
Baltimore, Md., c. 1840

Sperry, William
Philadelphia, Pa., c. 1840

Sperry & Bryant
Long Island, N.Y., c. 1850

Sperry and Bunker
New York, N.Y., c. 1845

Sperry & Gaylord
New York, N.Y., 1850

Sperry, Henry & Co.
New York, N.Y., c. 1840

Sperry & Shaw
New York, N.Y., c. 1840. May have been dealers.

Spice, William
Hanover, Pa., c. 1820

Spiller, John
New York, N.Y., c. 1820

Spratt, I. M.
Epping, N.H., n.d.

Spratt, Samuel L.
Elkton, Md., c. 1825

Spring, Solomon C.
Bristol, Conn., c. 1835. In several companies. Worked with E. Welch.

Spring, Solomon C. & Co.
Bristol, Conn., c. 1864. Formed Welch, Spring and Company with E. Welch.

Sprogell, John
Philadelphia, Pa., c. 1700

Sprunk, Peter
Philadelphia, Pa., c. 1790

Spurch, Peter
Philadelphia, Pa., c. 1795

Spycher, Peter, Jr.
Tulpehocken, Pa., c. 1785

Spyers, Moses
Philadelphia, Pa., c. 1825

Squire & Bros.
New York, N.Y., c. 1845

Squire, Horatio N. and Son
New York, N.Y., c. 1838

Squire and Lane
New York, N.Y., c. 1850

Stadlinger, Jno. R.
Buffalo, N.Y., c. 1891

Stadt, J.
New York, N.Y., c. 1810

Stadter, P. B., & Co.
Baltimore, Md., c. 1870

Standard Electric Time Co.
New Haven, Conn., c. 1888; also Springfield, Mass. Manufactured electrically wound clocks.

Stanley, J.
Chillicothe and Zanesville, Ohio, c. 1800

Stanley, Phineas
Lowell, Mass., c. 1835

Stanley, Salmon
Cazenovia, N.Y., c. 1830

Stanton, George S.
Providence, R.I., c. 1820

Stanton, Job
New York, N.Y., c. 1810

Stanton, W.
Providence, R.I., c. 1810

Stanton and Brother
Rochester, N.Y., c. 1845

Stanton, W.P. & H.
Rochester, N.Y., c. 1825

Stanwood, Henry B., & Co.
Boston, Mass., c. 1850

Staples, John I., Jr.
New York, N.Y., c. 1790

Staples and Dobbs
New York, N.Y., c. 1780

Stark, W. T.
Xenia, Ohio, c. 1830

Starr, Frederick
Rochester, N.Y., c. 1830

Starr, Theodore
New York, N.Y., n.d.

Starrett, James
East Nantmeal Twp., Chester Co., Pa., c. 1800

Statzell, P. M.
Philadelphia, Pa., c. 1840

Stauffer, Samuel C.
Manheim, Lancaster Co., Pa., c. 1810. Worked with C. Eby.

Stauffer & Eby
Manheim, Pa., c. 1800

Stebbins, Lewis
Waterbury, Conn., c. 1810

Stebbins and Co.
New York, N.Y., c. 1830

Stebbins and Howe
New York, N.Y., c. 1830

Steckell, Valentine
Frederick, Md., c. 1793

Steckman, H.
Middletown, Pa., c. 1850

Stedman, D. B.
Boston, Mass., c. 1860

Stedman, John C.
Raleigh, N.C., c. 1819

Steel, Joseph
Carlisle, Pa., n.d.

Steel, R. F.
Adams, N.Y., c. 1850

Steel, Samuel
New Haven, Conn., c. 1840

Steel, William
Albion, Mich., c. 1860

Steele, Thomas
Hartford, Conn., n.d.

Steele and Crocker
Hartford, Conn., n.d.

Steickleader, John
Hagerstown, Md., c. 1791

Stein, Abraham
Philadelphia, Pa., c. 1795

Stein, Albert
Norristown, Pa., c. 1835

Stein, Daniel
Norristown, Pa., c. 1830

Stein, George
Allentown, Lehigh Co., Pa., c. 1820. Son of Jacob.

Stein, Jacob
Allentown, Pa., c. 1815

Stein, Jacob and Son
Allentown, Pa., c. 1820

Steinman, George
Lancaster, Pa., n.d. Casemaker.

Steinseiffer, John
Hagerstown and Williamsport, Md., c. 1770

Stekman (Steckman), H.
Middletown, Pa., c. 1858

Stellwagen, Charles K.
Philadelphia, Pa., c. 1840

Steman, Henry
Lancaster Boro, Pa., c. 1829

Stephens, William
Albany, N.Y., c. 1840

Stephens, T.C. and D.
Utica, N.Y., c. 1840

Stephenson, Howard and Davis
Boston, Mass., c. 1849. Makers of tower and other clocks.

Sterling, Richard
South Woodstock, Vt., c. 1811

Stern, William
Philadelphia, Pa., c. 1820

Stertz, Martin
Rapho (Manheim), Pa., c. 1842

Stevens, Aaron
Pomfret, Conn., c. 1790

Stevens, B. F.
Peabody, Mass., n.d.

Stevens, Charles G.
New York, N.Y., c. 1840

Stevens, E.
West Springfield, Mass., c. 1790

Stevens, George M.
Boston, Mass., c. 1880

Stevens, J. P.
Utica, N.Y., c. 1835

Stevens, John
Bangor, Me., c. 1830

Stevens, John
Salem, Mass., c. 1830

Stevens, John
New Haven, Conn., c. 1840

Stevens, M.
Chillicothe, Ohio, c. 1810

Stevens, S.
Lowell, Mass., c. 1853

Stevens, Thomas
Amherst, N.H., c. 1795

Stevens and Heath
Chillicothe, Ohio, c. 1815

Stevens, Hodges and Co.
New York, N.Y., c. 1870

Stevens and Lakeman
Salem, Mass., c. 1819

Stevenson, George
  Albany, N.Y., c. 1850
Stever, Jeremiah
  Bristol, Conn., c. 1851
Stever and Bryant
  Burlington, Conn., c. 1845
Stevers and Hill
  Bristol, Conn., c. 1850
Stevers and Prindle
  Burlington, Conn., c. 1850
Stevers and Way
  Bristol, Conn., c. 1860
Steward, Aaron
  Philadelphia, Pa., c. 1840
Steward, D. M.
  Shelbyville, Ind., c. 1860
Stewart, Arthur
  New York, N.Y., c. 1820
Stewart, James
  Baltimore, Md., c. 1790
Stewart, William P.
  Funkstown, Md., c. 1820
Stewart and Co.
  Philadelphia, Pa., c. 1820
Stichler, John
  Marietta, Lancaster Co., Pa., c. 1850
Stickney, Moses P.
  Boston, Mass., c. 1823
Stiles, Samuel
  Windsor, Conn., c. 1795
Stiles and Baldwin
  Northampton, Mass., c. 1791
Stillas, John
  Philadelphia, Pa., c. 1785; later to
  Baltimore, Md.
Stillman, Barton
  Westerly, R.I., c. 1810
Stillman, Ira
  Newport, R.I., c. 1840
Stillman, Paul
  Westerly, R.I., c. 1803
Stillman, William
  Burlington, Conn., c. 1780
Stillson, David
  Rochester, N.Y., c. 1830
Stockell, I.
  New York, N.Y., c. 1870
Stocking, Abner
  Amber, N.Y., n.d.
Stockton, Samuel
  Philadelphia, Pa., c. 1820
Stoddard
  Litchfield, Conn., c. 1820
Stoddard & Kennedy
  New York, N.Y., c. 1790
Stokeberry, George
  Philadelphia, Pa., c. 1835
Stokel, John
  New York, N.Y., c. 1820
Stoll, George
  Lebanon, Pa., c. 1850
Stoll & Funk
  Lebanon, Pa., c. 1850
Stollenwerck, P. M.
  Philadelphia, Pa., c. 1813; New York,
  N.Y., 1820
Stollenwerck & Bros.
  New York, N.Y., c. 1820
Stone, Ezra
  Boston, Mass., c. 1810
Stone, J. W.
  East Randolph, Vt., n.d.

Stone, Jasper
  Charlestown, Mass., c. 1853
Stone, William G.
  Somers, N.Y., c. 1805
Stone and Marshall
  Cazenovia, N.Y., c. 1850
Stoner, Rudi
  Lancaster, Pa., c. 1750
Storrs, C. D.
  Portland, Me., n.d.
Storrs, N.
  Utica, N.Y., c. 1800
Storrs, Nathan
  Northampton, Mass., c. 1790
Storrs, Samuel
  Utica, N.Y., c. 1805
Storrs, Thomas
  Boston, Mass., c. 1800
Storrs and Cook
  Northampton, Mass., c. 1827
Story, Gustavus
  Lebanon, Pa., n.d.
Stout, Samuel
  Princeton, N.J., 1779–1795
Stow, D. F.
  New York, N.Y., c. 1830. Probably
  dealer only.
Stow, P. M.
  Philadelphia, Pa., c. 1810
Stow, Solomon
  Southington, Conn., 1832. Cabinet-
  maker.
Stowe, L. G.
  South Gardner, Mass., n.d.
Stowee, Frederick
  Philadelphia, Pa., c. 1800
Stowell, A.
  Worcester, Mass., c. 1790; Boston,
  Mass., c. 1800
Stowell, Abel
  Worcester and Boston, Mass., c. 1820
Stowell, Abel, Jr.
  Boston, Mass., c. 1830
Stowell, John
  Boston and Medford, Mass., c. 1815
Stowell, John
  Charlestown, Mass., c. 1825
Stowell, John J.
  Boston and Charlestown, Mass., c. 1830
Stowell, A. & Son
  Charlestown, Mass., c. 1845
Stoy, Gustavus
  Lancaster, Pa., c. 1790; Lebanon, Pa.,
  c. 1810; Schnitz Creek, Pa., c. 1820
Straede, Charles
  Lititz, Pa., c. 1850
Stratton, Charles
  Worcester, Mass., c. 1820
Streeter, George L.
  New Haven, Conn., c. 1865
Stretch, Isaac
  Philadelphia, Pa., c. 1752
Stretch, Peter
  Philadelphia, Pa., 1690–1740. Appren-
  ticed to his uncle, Samuel. Excellent
  clocks.
Stretch, Samuel
  Philadelphia, Pa., c. 1711. Uncle of
  Peter Stretch.
Stretch, Thomas
  Philadelphia, Pa., 1720–1760. Son of
  Peter. One of the founders of the Penn-
  sylvania Hospital.

Stretch, William
  Philadelphia, Pa., c. 1720. Son of Peter
  Stretch.
Strieb, C. H.
  Wooster, Ohio, c. 1822–1847
Strieby, George
  Pennsylvania, n.d.
Strieby, Michael
  Greensburg, Pa., c. 1790
Strong, Peter
  Fayetteville, N.C., c. 1788
Stuart, James
  Philadelphia, Pa., c. 1830
Stuart, Thomas
  Philadelphia, Pa., c. 1835
Studley, David
  Hanover, Mass., c. 1810. Brother of
  Luther. Apprenticed to John Bailey.
Studley, Luther
  Brockton, Mass., c. 1840
Stump, Joseph
  Reading, Pa., c. 1820
Stuntz, C.W., & Keath, T.C.
  Pittsylvania, Va., n.d.
Sturgeon, Samuel
  Shippensburg, Pa., c. 1810
Sturgis, Joseph
  Philadelphia, Pa., c. 1810
Stutson, James
  Rochester, N.Y., c. 1835
Suggs, G.W., & Co.
  Yorkville, S.C., n.d.
Suley, John
  Baltimore, Md., c. 1810
Sullivan, J. T.
  Saint Louis, Mo., c. 1850
Sullivan, C.D., & Co.
  Saint Louis, Mo., c. 1850
Summerhays, John
  New York, N.Y., c. 1810
Sutton, Enoch
  Boston, Mass., c. 1820
Sutton, Robert
  New Haven, Conn., c. 1825
Swaim, James
  Philadelphia, Pa., c. 1830
Swain, Reuben
  Kensington, N.H., c. 1775
Swan, Benjamin
  Haverhill, Mass., c. 1810; Augusta,
  Me., c. 1830
Swan, Justus
  Richmond, Va., c. 1820
Swan, Moses
  Augusta, Me., c. 1850
Swan, Timothy
  Suffield, Conn., c. 1785
Swan, B. and M.M.
  Augusta, Me., n.d.
Swartz, Abraham
  Lower Salford, Pa., n.d.
Swartz, Peter
  York, Pa., c. 1780
Sweeney, J. C.
  Houston, Tex., c. 1890
Sweet, James S.
  Boston, Mass., c. 1810
Sweney, Thomas
  Philadelphia, Pa., c. 1850
Swift, A. L.
  Chicago, Ill., c. 1890
Swift, John D.
  Cazenovia, N.Y., c. 1815

Swing Clock Co.
Chicago, Ill., c. 1960

Syberberg, Christian
New York, N.Y., c. 1756; Charleston, S.C., c. 1760

Syderman, Philip
Philadelphia, Pa., c. 1785

Sykes, William
Beverly, Mass., c. 1805

Symmes, Cleadon
Newton, N.J., c. 1785. Brother of Daniel.

Symmes, Daniel
Newton, N.J., c. 1792. Son of Timothy.

Symmes, Timothy
Newton, N.J., n.d.

Taber, Elnathan
Roxbury, Mass., c. 1800. Simon Willard considered him one of his best apprentices. Purchased Willard's tools when he retired. Also made clocks for Simon Willard and Son.

Taber, H.
Boston, Mass., c. 1850. Son of Elnathan.

Taber, J.
Saco, Me., c. 1810

Taber, Rubine
Hingham, Mass., c. 1800

Taber, Stephen
New Bedford, Mass., and Providence, R.I., c. 1790. Brother of Elnathan.

Taber, Thomas
Boston, Mass., c. 1854. Son of Elnathan.

Taf, John James
Philadelphia, Pa., c. 1790

Talbot, Sylvester
Dedham, Mass., c. 1815

Tallmadge, Elliott
Wolcottville, Conn., n.d.

Tannehill, Z. B.
Pittsburgh, Pa., c. 1825

Tappan, Ebenezer
Manchester, Mass., c. 1780. Cabinet-maker.

Tappan, Israel
Manchester, N.H., c. 1800. Cabinet-maker.

Tappan, J. F.
Manchester, Mass., c. 1815 (?)

Tappan, William B.
Philadelphia, Pa., c. 1818

Tappen, John
Flemington, N.J., c. 1840

Tarbox, H. & D.
New York, N.Y., c. 1832. Probably importer.

Taylor, Andrew
New York, N.Y., c. 1850

Taylor, Charles
Sedalia, Mo., c. 1860

Taylor, Henry
Philadelphia, Pa., c. 1780

Taylor, John
York, Pa., c. 1775

Taylor, Joseph
York, Pa., c. 1780

Taylor, Luther
Philadelphia, Pa., c. 1820

Taylor, Noah
Salisbury, N.C., c. 1840

Taylor, Richard
Boston, Mass., c. 1660. Doubtful whether he actually made clocks.

Taylor, Richard
York, Pa., c. 1785

Taylor, Samuel
Worcester, Mass., c. 1810

Taylor, Samuel E.
Bristol, Conn., c. 1858

Taylor, W. E.
New York, N.Y., n.d.

Taylor, William
Buffalo, N.Y., c. 1835

Taylor and Baldwin
Newark, N.J., c. 1820

Taylor and Company
Providence, R.I., c. 1870

Taylor and Hinsdale
Newark, N.J., c. 1810

Taylor, P.L. & Co.
Brooklyn, N.Y., c. 1820

Tazewell, Samuel O.
Philadelphia, Pa., c. 1810

Tazewell, S. S.
Bridgeton, N.J., c. 1864

Tebbets, George
Newmarket, N.H., c. 1830

Templeton, Robert
Newport, R.I., c. 1770

Tennent, Thomas
San Francisco, Calif., c. 1850

Terhune, H.
New York, N.Y., c. 1850

Terhune and Edwards
New York, N.Y., c. 1860

Ternbach, M.
Saint Louis, Mo., c. 1820

Terry, Eli
Plymouth, Conn., c. 1790. Apprenticed to Daniel Burnap and Thomas Harland. First tall clock made c. 1792. Perfected pillar-and-scroll clock. Taught his sons Eli, Jr., and Henry. Also made tower clocks.

Terry, Eli, Jr.
Plymouth, Conn., c. 1820. Worked with his father and M. Blakeslee.

Terry, Eli III
Bristol, Conn., c. 1840. Grandson of Eli and son of Eli, Jr.

Terry, Henry
Plymouth, Conn., c. 1820. Son of Eli, Sr. Worked with his father. Went into woolen business c. 1836.

Terry, John Burnham
Bristol, Conn., c. 1825. Son of Samuel. Later became doctor.

Terry, Lucien
Albany, N.Y., c. 1830

Terry, Ralph E.
Bristol, Conn., c. 1830. Son of Samuel. In several clock companies.

Terry, Samuel
Plymouth and Bristol, Conn., c. 1810. Brother of Eli, Sr. In several clock companies. Made pillar-and-scroll shelf clocks.

Terry, Samuel S.
Plymouth, Conn., c. 1830. Son of Samuel.

Terry, Silas B.
Plymouth, Conn., c. 1830. Son of Eli.

Terry, Solon M.
Waterbury, Conn., c. 1865. Son of Silas B. Terry.

Terry, Theodore
Ansonia, Conn., c. 1830

Terry, Thomas
Boston, Mass., c. 1825

Terry, William
Washington, N.Y., c. 1790

Terry, William A.
Bristol, Conn., c. 1850. Son of Samuel S.

Terry & Andrews
Bristol, Conn., c. 1840

Terry & Barnum
East Bridgeport, Conn., c. 1855. Doubtful whether any clocks were made.

Terry Clock Co.
Winsted, Conn., c. 1855

Terry Clock Co.
Waterbury, Conn., c. 1868; Pittsfield, Mass., c. 1880

Terry, Downs & Burwell
Bristol, Conn., c. 1851

Terry, Downs and Co.
Bristol, Conn., c. 1853

Terry, E. and Sons
Plymouth, Conn., c. 1825

Terry, Eli, Jr., and Co.
Plymouth, Conn., n.d.

Terry, Eli, Jr., and Henry
Plymouth, Conn., c. 1822

Terry, Eli & Samuel
Plymouth, Conn., c. 1824

Terry, Eli & Sons
Plymouth, Conn., c. 1818

Terry, Fairbanks and Co.
Chesterville, Conn., n.d.

Terry, Ralph & John B.
Bristol, Conn., c. 1835

Terry, S.B. and Co.
Terryville, Conn., c. 1840

Terry, Thomas and Hoadley
Plymouth, Conn., c. 1810

Terryville Clock Co., The
Terryville, Conn., c. 1850

Terryville Manufacturing Co.
Terryville, Conn., c. 1851

Teufel, H.
Chicago, Ill., c. 1856

Tewkesbury, Thomas
Meredith, N.H., c. 1820

Thatcher, George
Lowell, Mass., c. 1850

Thaxter, Samuel
Boston, Mass., c. 1830

Thayer, Eli
Boston, Mass., c. 1810

Thayer, Eliphalet
Williamsburg, Mass., c. 1830

Thayer, H. C.
Kennebunkport, Me., c. 1835

Thayer, E. & Co.
Williamsburg, Mass., c. 1830

Thoma and Cottell
Piqua, Ohio, c. 1930

Thomas, Enos
Willistown, Pa., c. 1800. Son of Isaac.

Thomas, Isaac
Willistown, Pa., c. 1770

Thomas, Isaac, Jr.
Worcester, Mass., c. 1800. Printer of clock labels. Son of Isaac.

Thomas, Isaiah
Philadelphia and Lancaster, Pa., c. 1860

Thomas, Joseph
Whitpain or Norristown Twp., Montgomery Co., Pa., c. 1830

Thomas, Mordecai
Willistown, Chester Co., Pa., c. 1790. Son of Isaac.

Thomas, Seth
Plymouth, Conn., c. 1805. Tall case, pillar-and-scroll, and other shelf clocks. Worked with Terry and Hoadley. Plymouth Hollow renamed Thomaston in 1866. Organized Seth Thomas Clock Co.

Thomas, William
Trenton, N.J., c. 1780

Thomas and Hoadley
Greystone, Conn., c. 1810

Thomas, Seth and Sons
New York, N.Y., and Thomaston, Conn., c. 1865

Thomas, Seth Clock Co.
Plymouth, Conn., c. 1853. Organized by Seth Thomas.

Thompson, Avery J.
Cherry Valley, N.Y., c. 1875

Thompson, Avery J., Jr.
Cherry Valley, N.Y., c. 1900

Thompson, Harry
Bristol, Conn., c. 1840

Thompson, Henry
Philadelphia, Pa., c. 1845

Thompson, Hiram
Bristol, Conn., c. 1860

Thompson, Isaac
Litchfield, Conn., c. 1795

Thompson, James
Baltimore, Md., c. 1790; Pittsburgh, Pa., c. 1810

Thompson, John
New York, N.Y., c. 1780

Thompson, John
Philadelphia, Pa., c. 1820

Thompson, Lyman W.
Cherry Valley, N.Y., c. 1850

Thompson, S. N.
Roxbury, Mass., c. 1850

Thompson, Silas G.
New Haven, Conn., c. 1840

Thompson, William
New York, N.Y., c. 1775. Also made instruments.

Thompson, William
Baltimore, Md., c. 1765

Thompson, William
Carlisle, Pa., c. 1790

Thompson, William
Paterson, N.J., c. 1830

Thompson & Ranger
Brattleboro, Vt., c. 1850

Thomson, James
Pittsburgh, Pa., c. 1815

Thomson, Simon
Philadelphia, Pa., n.d.

Thomson, William
Wilmington, N.C., c. 1830

Thorne, Robert
Albany, N.Y., c. 1850

Thornton, Andrew
Philadelphia, Pa., c. 1810

Thornton, Joseph
Philadelphia, Pa., c. 1820

Thorp, H. W.
Beaver Dam, Wis., c. 1870

Thorpe, E., & Co.
Upper Alton, Ill., c. 1860

Thownsend, Charles
Philadelphia, Pa., c. 1819

Thownsend, Charles, Jr.
Philadelphia, Pa., c. 1829

Thownsend, John, Jr.
Philadelphia, Pa., c. 1820

Thrasher, Samuel
New Haven, Conn., c. 1890

Thrasher Clock Company
Manchester, Conn., c. 1910

Thrasher Time System, Inc.
New Haven, Conn., c. 1900

Threadcraft, B.
Charleston, S.C., c. 1790

Thum, Charles
Philadelphia, Pa., c. 1800

Tice & Roberts
Brooklyn, N.Y., c. 1840

Tichenor, David
Newark, N.J., c. 1820

Tiebout, Alexander
New York, N.Y., c. 1790

Tierney, John
Philadelphia, Pa., c. 1820

Tiffany, Charles
New York, N.Y., c. 1850. Founded Tiffany & Co., jewelers and silversmiths.

Tiffany, D. B.
Xenia, Ohio, c. 1885

Tiffany, George S.
New York, N.Y., c. 1900

Tiffany & Co.
New York, N.Y., c. 1880

Tiffany Electric Manufacturing Company
Buffalo, N.Y., c. 1900. Makers of battery clocks.

Tiffany Never Wind Clock Corp.
Buffalo, N.Y., c. 1900. Battery clocks.

Tifft, Horace
North Attleboro, Mass., c. 1800

Tilden, Thurber
Providence, R.I., c. 1855

Timby, Theodore R.
Baldwinsville, N.Y., c. 1850. Inventor of the Timby solar clock. Also made revolving gun turrets, etc.

Timby Globe Timepiece
Invented and made by T. R. Timby and L. E. Whiting. Were numbered from 1 to about 600. Globes made by Gilman Joslin in Boston.

Timme, M.
Brooklyn, N.Y., c. 1840

Timson, William W.
Newburyport, Mass., c. 1855

Tinges, Charles
Baltimore, Md., c. 1780

Tisdale, Benjamin H.
Newport, R.I., c. 1820

Tisdale, Ebenezer Dawes
Taunton, Mass., c. 1870

Tisdale, Nathan, Col.
New Bern, N.C., c. 1795

Tisdale, William, Jr.
Washington, N.C., c. 1816; New Bern, N.C., c. 1821

Tisdale, William II
Washington and New Bern, N.C., c. 1820

Tissot, Alexander
New York, N.Y., c. 1805

Titcomb, Albert
Bangor, Me., c. 1850

Titcomb, Enoch J.
Boston, Mass., c. 1830

Titus, James
Philadelphia, Pa., c. 1830

Tobias, M.I. and Co.
New York, N.Y., c. 1825

Todd, M. L.
Beaver, Pa., c. 1830

Todd, Richard
Strasburg, Pa., c. 1770

Todd, Richard
New York, N.Y., c. 1830

Todd, Tracy
Lexington, Ky., c. 1840

Tolford, Joshua
Kennebunk and Portland, Me., c. 1815

Tolles, Nathan
Plymouth, Conn., c. 1830

Tolman, Jeremiah
Boston, Mass., c. 1805

Tompkins, George S.
Providence, R.I., c. 1820

Tonchure, Francis
Baltimore, Md., c. 1810

Tork Clock Co., Inc.
Mount Vernon, N.Y., c. 1920

Torrey, Benjamin B.
Hanover, Mass., c. 1810

Tower, Reuben
Plymouth, Hingham, Hanover, and Kingston, Mass., 1810–1830. Noted maker of dwarf tall case clocks.

Tower and Frisbie
New Hartford, Conn., c. 1840

Town, Ira S.
Montpelier, Vt., c. 1860

Townsend, Charles
Philadelphia, Pa., c. 1800

Townsend, Charles, Jr.
Philadelphia, Pa., c. 1830

Townsend, Christopher
Newport, R.I., c. 1770

Townsend, David
Philadelphia, Pa., c. 1785

Townsend, Elisha
Philadelphia, Pa., c. 1825

Townsend, H.
Conway, Mass., c. 1850

Townsend, Isaac
Boston, Mass., c. 1790

Townsend, John
Philadelphia, Pa., c. 1810

Townsend, John, Jr.
Philadelphia, Pa., c. 1815

Townsend, Joseph
Baltimore, Md., c. 1790

Tracy, Erastus
New London and Norwich, Conn., c. 1790

Tracy, Gurdon
New London, Conn., c. 1790. Brother of Erastus. Apprenticed to Thomas Harland.

Tracy, William
Philadelphia, Pa., c. 1840

Trahn, Peter C.
Philadelphia, Pa., c. 1845

Trahn, Co., Peter
Philadelphia, Pa., c. 1840

Trampleasure, J.
Jersey City, N.J., c. 1850

Travis, John
New York, N.Y., c. 1859

Treadwell, Oren
Philadelphia, Pa., c. 1840

Treat, George
Newark, N.J., c. 1850

Treat, Orrin
New Haven, Conn., c. 1840

Treat, Sherman
Bristol, Conn., c. 1825

Treat and Bishop
Bristol, Conn., c. 1830. Probably made movements for other makers.

Trenchard, Richard
Salem, Mass., n.d.

Tribe, Gilbert
Newark, N.J., c. 1850

Trone, Peter
Philadelphia, Pa., c. 1840

Troth, James
Pittsburgh, Pa., c. 1810

Troth, Thomas
Pittsburgh, Pa., c. 1815

Trott, Andrew C.
Boston, Mass., c. 1799

Trott, John Proctor
New London, Conn., c. 1790

Trott, Jonathan
New London, Conn., c. 1791

Trott, Peter
Boston, Mass., c. 1800

Trott, A.C. & Co.
Boston, Mass., c. 1805

Trott & Cleveland
New London, Conn., c. 1792

Trotter, Jeremiah
New York, N.Y., c. 1820; Cincinnati, Ohio, c. 1830

Trow, Ephraim
Haverhill, Mass., c. 1830

Truax, DeWitt
Utica, N.Y., c. 1840

Truman, Jeffery
Waynesville, Ohio, c. 1820

Trumball & Haskell
Lowell, Mass., c. 1860

Tucker, J. W.
San Francisco, Calif., c. 1850

Tuerlings, James
New York, N.Y., c. 1850

Tuller, William
New York, N.Y., c. 1830

Turell, Andrew C.
Boston, Mass., c. 1790

Turell, Samuel
Boston, Mass., c. 1780

Turnbull, John
Baltimore, Md., c. 1780

Turner, Allison
Ashtabula, Ohio, c. 1830

Turner, Franklin
Cheraw, S.C., c. 1814

Turner, J. S.
New Haven, Conn., c. 1860

Turner, John
New York, N.Y., c. 1845

Turrett & Marine Clock Co.
Boston, Mass., c. 1860. Partnership of C. Stevens and M. Crane.

Tusten, Hiram S.
Abbeville, S.C., c. 1840

Tustin, Septimus
Baltimore, Md., c. 1815

Tuthill, Daniel M.
Saxtons River, Vt., c. 1840

Tuttle, Elidia
Owego, N.Y., c. 1820. Probably dealer only.

Twin Face Clock Co.
New York, N.Y., c. 1920

Twiss, Hiram
Meriden, Conn., c. 1830

Twiss, B. and H.
Meriden, Conn., c. 1828

Twitchell, Marcus
Utica, N.Y., c. 1825

Twombly & Cleaves
Biddeford, Me., c. 1870

Tyler, David
Sandusky, Ohio, c. 1833 and Clarksburg, Ohio

Tyler, E. A.
New Orleans, La., c. 1840

Tyson, Leech
Philadelphia, Pa., c. 1820

Ulrich, Jacob
East Donegal, Pa., c. 1842

Ulrich, Valentine
Reading, Pa., c. 1760

Umbrect, John B.
Chicago, Ill., c. 1878. Casemaker.

Underhill, Daniel
New York, N.Y., c. 1810

Underhill, George H.
Young America, Ill., c. 1860

Underhill, W. J.
New York, N.Y., n.d.

Union Clock Co.
Bristol, Conn., c. 1840

Union Clock Co.
Chicago, Ill., c. 1940. Electric clocks.

Union Clock Manufacturing Co.
Bristol, Conn., c. 1845

Union Manufacturing Co.
Bristol, Conn., c. 1843

United Clock Co.
Brooklyn, N.Y., 1905–

United States Clock Co.
New York, N.Y., c. 1870

United States Clock and Brass Co.
Chicago, Ill., c. 1860

United States Clock Case Co.
Cincinnati, Ohio, c. 1870

United States Clock Manufacturing Co.
New Haven, Conn.; later to Austin, Ill., c. 1866

United States Time Corp.
New York, N.Y., c. 1940

Upjohn, James
Augusta, Me. (?), c. 1802

Upson, Lucas
New York, N.Y., c. 1840

Upson Brothers
Bristol, Conn., c. 1830 (?)

Upson, Merrimans & Co.
Bristol, Conn., c. 1830

Urletig, Valentine
Reading, Pa., c. 1755. Arrived Pennsylvania 1754; died 1783.

Vail, Elijah M.
Albany, N.Y., c. 1835

Valentine, William
Boston, Mass., c. 1820

Van Aken, William
Philadelphia, Pa., c. 1840

Van Buren, William
Newark, N.J., c. 1790; New York, N.Y., c. 1795

Van Camp, J. G.
New York, N.Y., c. 1885

Van Cott, A. B.
Racine, Wis., c. 1850

Vanderslice, John
Womelsdorf, Pa., c. 1810

Van Der Veer, Jos.
Somerville, N.J., c. 1820

Van Eps, George K.
New York, N.Y., c. 1840. Importer.

Vanlone, James
Philadelphia, Pa., c. 1770

Van Steenbergh, P.
Kingston, N.Y., c. 1780

Vantine, John L.
Philadelphia, Pa., c. 1825

Van Valkenburgh, Charles
New York, N.Y., c. 1850

Van Vleit, B. C.
Poughkeepsie, N.Y., c. 1830. Also silversmith.

Van Voorhis, Daniel
Philadelphia, Pa., c. 1780; also worked in New York, N.Y., and Princeton, N.J.

Van Wagener, John
Oxford, N.Y., c. 1840

Van Winkle, John
New York, N.Y., n.d.

Van Wyck, Stephen
New York, N.Y., c. 1800

Vaughan, David
Philadelphia, Pa., c. 1695

Veal & Glaze
Columbia, S.C., c. 1835

Veazie, Joseph
Providence, R.I., c. 1805

Verdin, Jacob
Cincinnati, Ohio, c. 1850

Verdin, Michael
Cincinnati, Ohio, c. 1850

Vermont Clock Co.
Fairhaven, Vt., c. 1890. Organized as Fairhaven Clock Company, name changed to Vermont Clock Co. c. 1910.

Vibber, Russell
Westtown, Pa., c. 1810

Vickery, Thomas
New Lisbon, Ind., c. 1860

Vining, L. S.
Cincinnati, Ohio, c. 1830

Vinton, David
Providence, R.I., c. 1790

Vogel, Frederick
Middleburg and Schoharie, N.Y., c. 1820

Voght, Henry
Reading, Pa., c. 1790

Vogt, Ignatius
New York, N.Y., c. 1765

Voight, Henry
Philadelphia, Pa., c. 1785. Also Chief Coiner for U. S. Mint.

Voight, Sebastian
Philadelphia, Pa., c. 1795

Voight, Thomas H.
Reading, Pa., c. 1810. Son of Henry.

Vorhees & Van Wickle
New Brunswick, N.J., c. 1840

Votti, G.
Philadelphia, Pa., c. 1880

Voute, Lewis C.
Bridgeton, N.J., c. 1820; later to Philadelphia, Pa.

Vuille, Alexander
Baltimore, Md., c. 1760

Waage & Norton
Philadelphia, Pa., c. 1790

Wade, Charles
Boston, Mass., c. 1830

Wade, Nathaniel
Stratford, Conn., c. 1790

Wadhams, George D.
Wolcottville, Conn., c. 1825

Wadsworth, Jeremiah
Georgetown, S.C., c. 1820

Wadsworth, Samuel
Keene, N.H., c. 1870. Battery clocks.

Wadsworth, J.C. and A.
Litchfield, Conn., c. 1830

Wadsworth, Lounsbury & Turner
Litchfield, Conn., c. 1830

Wadsworth and Turner
Litchfield, Conn., c. 1820

Wady, James
Newport, R.I., c. 1740

Wahlberg, Victor
Brooklyn, N.Y., c. 1850

Wait, L. D.
Skaneateles, N.Y., c. 1835

Wait, Dewey and Co.
Ravenna, Ohio, c. 1855

Waitley
Worthington, Ohio, c. 1893. Made the Columbus Clock for sale at the Chicago World's Columbian Exposition, 1893–1894.

Wales, Samuel H.
Providence, R.I., c. 1850

Walhaupter, John
New York, N.Y., c. 1800

Walker, A.
Brockport, N.Y., c. 1830

Walker, Isaac
Long Plain, Mass., c. 1800

Walker, J. E.
Zanesville, Ohio, c. 1822

Walker, James
Fredericksburg, Va., c. 1790

Walker, Julius
Buffalo, N.Y., c. 1840

Walker, Thomas
Fredericksburg, Va., c. 1760

Walker and Bailey
Pennsylvania, n.d.

Walker and Carpenter
Boston, Mass., c. 1805

Wall, William A.
Hanover and New Bedford, Mass., c. 1805

Wall and Almy
New Bedford, Mass., c. 1820

Wallace, John
Pittsburgh, Pa., c. 1830

Wallace, Robert
Philadelphia, Pa., c. 1860

Walley, John
Boston, Mass., n.d.

Wallig, Frederick
Warwick, Pa., c. 1805

Wallin, Robert
Philadelphia, Pa., c. 1845

Walls, A.
Bristol, Conn., c. 1840

Walsh
Forestville, Conn., c. 1825

Walter, Jacob
Baltimore, Md., c. 1810

Walter, M. F.
Hartford, Conn., c. 1850

Walters, Charles D.
Harrisburg, Pa., c. 1850

Walters, Henry
Charleston, S.C., c. 1757

Waltham Clock Co.
Waltham, Mass., c. 1915

Walton, Hiram
Cincinnati, Ohio, c. 1820

Walton, S. B.
Livermore Falls, Me., c. 1850

Waples, Nathaniel
Philadelphia, Pa., c. 1820

Ward, Anthony
Philadelphia, Pa., c. 1710; New York, N.Y., c. 1720

Ward, Edward H.
Philadelphia, Pa., c. 1835

Ward, Isaac
Philadelphia, Pa., c. 1813

Ward, James
Hartford, Conn., c. 1790. Probably dealer only.

Ward, Jehu
Philadelphia, Pa., c. 1808. Also silversmith.

Ward, John
Philadelphia, Pa., c. 1800

Ward, Joseph
New York, N.Y., c. 1735

Ward, Joseph
Henniker, N.H., n.d.

Ward, Lauren
Salem Bridge, Conn., c. 1832

Ward, Lewis
Salem Bridge, Conn., c. 1829

Ward, Macock
Wallingford, Conn., c. 1725

Ward, Nathan
Fryeburg, Me., c. 1800

Ward, Richard
Salem Bridge, Conn., c. 1830

Ward, Thomas
Baltimore, Md., c. 1775

Ward, W. D.
Springfield, Ill., c. 1850

Ward, W. W.
Winnsboro, S.C., c. 1840

Ward, William
Salem Bridge, Conn., c. 1830

Ward, William L.
Philadelphia, Pa., c. 1830

Ward & Cox
Philadelphia, Pa., c. 1810

Ward & Govett
Philadelphia, Pa., c. 1815

Ward, J. and Co.
Philadelphia, Pa., c. 1840

Ward, John & William L.
Philadelphia, Pa., c. 1830. Probably dealers.

Ware, Beacon
Salem and Greenwich, N.J., c. 1789

Ware, George
Camden, N.J., c. 1820

Warfe, Joseph
Frederick, Md., c. 1815

Warfield, J. H.
Baltimore, Md., c. 1827

Waring, George
New York, N.Y., c. 1845

Wark, William
Philadelphia, Pa., c. 1845

Warner, Albert
Bristol, Conn., c. 1857

Warner, Aseph
Solesbury, Pa., c. 1780

Warner, Cuthbert
Baltimore, Md., c. 1790

Warner, Elijah
Lexington, Ky., c. 1810

Warner, George
New York, N.Y., c. 1790

Warner, John
New York, N.Y., c. 1790

Warner, Thomas
Cincinnati, Ohio, c. 1820

Warner, Warren
Cincinnati, Ohio, c. 1830

Warner, A. & H.A.
Boston, Mass., c. 1865

Warner & Reed
New York, N.Y., c. 1802

Warner & Schuyler
New York, N.Y., c. 1795

Warner and Winthrop & Co.
Bristol, Conn., c. 1850

Warren Clock Co.
Ashland, Mass., c. 1910. Organized by Henry Warren. Experimented with electrically driven clocks.

Warriner, Chauncey
Washington, D.C., n.d.

Warrington, John
Philadelphia, Pa., c. 1811

Warrington, Samuel R.
Philadelphia, Pa., c. 1829

Warrington, John & Co.
Philadelphia, Pa., c. 1825

Warrington, John & S. R.
Philadelphia, Pa., c. 1822

Warrington, S. R. & Co.
Philadelphia, Pa., c. 1830

Wasbrough & Son
Bristol, Conn., c. 1760

Waterbury, M.
Amber, N.Y., c. 1830

Waterbury Clock Co.
Waterbury, Conn., c. 1857. In 1892 began to manufacture watches for Robert Ingersoll. Purchased the business in 1922. Later U.S. Time Corporation.

Waterbury Clock Co.
New York, N.Y. Sales agent for Waterbury Clock Co.

Waterbury Clock Co.
Winsted, Conn., c. 1850. Stock company.

Waterbury Clock Company
Waterbury, N.Y., c. 1880

Waterman, Henry
Millbury, Mass., c. 1810

Waters, George
Exeter, N.H., n.d.

Waters, Thomas
  Frederick, Md., c. 1785
Watson, G.
  Cincinnati, Ohio., c. 1820. Dealer only.
Watson, J.
  Chelsea, Mass., c. 1845
Watson, James
  New London, Conn., c. 1796; Philadelphia, Pa., c. 1800
Watson, James
  Philadelphia, Pa., c. 1820
Watson, John
  Boston, Mass., c. 1842
Watson, Luman
  Cincinnati, Ohio, c. 1820. Prolific maker of wood-movement clocks.
Watson, Thomas
  Cincinnati, Ohio, c. 1809. Father of Luman.
Watson, William
  Philadelphia, Pa., c. 1860
Watson, Luman and Son
  Cincinnati, Ohio, c. 1835
Watson and Reed
  Albans, Ohio, c. 1828
Watt, John Irvine
  Pennsylvania, n.d.
Wattles, W. W.
  Pittsburgh, Pa., c. 1850
Wattles, W. W. and Son
  Pittsburgh, Pa., c. 1850
Watts, Charles
  Rochester, N.Y., c. 1844
Watts, Stuart
  Boston, Mass., c. 1740
Waugh, John
  Schenectady, N.Y., c. 1800
Way, John
  Waggontown, Chester Co., Pa., c. 1796
Weatherly, David
  Philadelphia, Pa., c. 1800
Weaver, Christian
  New Castle, Del., c. 1790
Weaver, Holmes
  Newport, R.I., c. 1775
Weaver, Nicholas
  Rochester, N.Y., c. 1825
Weaver, William
  Wilmington, Del., c. 1800
Webb, Isaac
  Boston, Mass., c. 1690
Webber, William
  Norwalk, Ohio, c. 1830
Webster, H.
  Bristol, Burlington, and Farmington, Conn., n.d.
Weeks, Jason
  Bangor, Me., c. 1840
Wehrle, Joseph
  Belleville, Ill., c. 1850. Probably dealer only.
Weida, Solomon
  Rochester, N.Y., c. 1847
Weidemeyer, John M.
  Fredericksburg, Va., c. 1790
Weigel, Henry
  York, Pa., c. 1827
Weiss, Jedediah
  Bethlehem, Pa., c. 1815. Continued business of Samuel Krause when he died.
Weiss, John G.
  Bethlehem, Pa., c. 1795. Father of Jedediah. Also gun- and locksmith.

Weiss, Joseph
  Allentown, Pa., c. 1840
Weiss, Joshua
  Allentown, Pa., n.d.
Weisser, Martin
  Allentown, Pa., c. 1830
Welby Clock Company
  Elgin, Ill., c. 1905
Welch, Elisha N.
  Bristol, Conn., c. 1840. One of the largest manufacturers of Connecticut shelf clocks. Also a partner in various companies.
Welch, George
  York, Pa., c. 1825
Welch, George W.
  New York, N.Y., c. 1850
Welch, John
  Fincastle, Va., c. 1820
Welch, Vine
  Norwich, Conn., c. 1750
Welch, William
  New York, N.Y., c. 1810
Welch, E.N. Manufacturing Co.
  Bristol, Conn., c. 1864. Later, The Sessions Clock Company.
Welch and Gray
  Bristol, Conn., c. 1830. Probably assemblers only.
Welch, H.M. and Company
  Plainville, Conn., c. 1840. Brother of Elisha.
Welch, Spring and Company
  Forestville, Conn., c. 1868. Manufacturers of regulator and calendar clocks. E. N. Welch in partnership with Solomon Spring.
Weldon, Oliver
  Bristol, Conn., c. 1841
Weller, Carter A.
  Stockbridge, N.Y., n.d.
Weller, Francis
  Philadelphia, Pa., c. 1775
Welles, Gelston & Co.
  Boston, Mass., c. 1825. Probably importer and dealer.
Wells, A.
  Bristol, Conn., c. 1825
Wells, Alfred
  Boston, Mass., c. 1800
Wells, C. H.
  Colebrook, Conn., c. 1840
Wells, Calvin
  Watervliet, N.Y., c. 1810. Made Shaker-style clocks.
Wells, D.
  Ogdensburg, N.Y., c. 1810
Wells, Joseph A.
  Bristol, Conn., c. 1830. Partner in Boardman and Wells, and Wells, Hendrick & Co.
Wells & Foster
  Cincinnati, Ohio, c. 1830
Wells, Hendrick & Co.
  Bristol, Conn., c. 1832
Welsh, Alex
  Baltimore, Md., c. 1800
Welsh, Bela
  Northampton, Mass., c. 1810
Welsh, David
  Lincolnton, N.C., c. 1849
Welsh, George
  New York, N.Y., c. 1850

Welton, Herman
  New York, N.Y., c. 1840
Welton, Merit
  New York, N.Y., c. 1845
Welton, H. & Co.
  Terryville, Conn., n.d. Also known as H. and H. Welton & Co., and Hiram and Herman Welton.
Wendell
  Albany, N.Y., c. 1840
Wentwell, H.
  Charleston, S.C., c. 1800
Wentworth, Joshua L.
  Lowell, Mass., c. 1830
Wentworth, R.
  n.p.; n.d.
Wentz, Hilary
  Philadelphia, Pa., c. 1820
Wenzel, Herman
  San Francisco, Calif., c. 1850. Made pneumatic impulse clocks and clock systems.
Wenzel Company
  Washington, D.C., c. 1880. Promoted pneumatic clocks.
West, Benjamin
  Southbridge, Mass., c. 1820
West, Edward
  Virginia, c. 1780; to Lexington, Ky., c. 1788. Also made gunsmith tools.
West, H.
  Southbridge, Mass., c. 1830
West, James L.
  Philadelphia, Pa., c. 1830
West, John
  Bloomingdale, Ill., n.d.
West, Josiah
  Philadelphia, Pa., c. 1780
West, Josiah
  Philadelphia, Pa., c. 1798
West, Josiah
  Philadelphia, Pa., c. 1830
West, Robert
  Potsdam, N.Y., c. 1860
West, S. B.
  Odessa, Del., c. 1850
West, Thomas
  Philadelphia, Pa., c. 1820
Westclox
  LaSalle, Ill., c. 1895. Manufacturers of alarm clocks.
Westcott, J.
  Brooklyn, N.Y., c. 1849
Western Clock Co.
  LaSalle, Ill., 1895–1930
Western Clock Mfg. Co.
  Peru and La Salle, Ill., c. 1888. Name changed to Western Clock Co., 1895.
Westgate, Baldwin & Co.
  Fall River, Mass., c. 1870
Weston, James
  Boston, Mass., c. 1850
Weston Brothers
  Boston, Mass., from 1860s
Weston, James and Son
  Boston, Mass., c. 1849
Westphall, Ferdinand
  Philadelphia, Pa., c. 1815
Wetherell, Nathan
  Philadelphia, Pa., c. 1830
Wetherell & Mead
  Montpelier, Vt., c. 1840
Wharfe, Joseph
  Fredericktown, Md., c. 1820

Wheaton, Caleb
Providence, R.I., c. 1785. An outstanding maker of clocks.
Wheaton, Calvin
Providence, R.I., c. 1790
Wheaton, Godfrey
Providence, R.I., c. 1790
Wheaton, Caleb & Son
Providence, R.I., c. 1800
Wheaton, Godfrey and Son
Providence, R.I., c. 1810
Wheeler, Charles
New Brunswick, N.J., n.d.
Wheeler, D. C.
New London, Conn., c. 1860
Wheeler, Henry
Boston, Mass., c. 1820
Wheeler, Samuel, Jr.
Rochester, N.Y., c. 1840
Wheeler, Brooks & Co.
Livonia, N.Y., c. 1835
Wheeler & Son
Salem, N.J., n.d.
Wheelock, George
Wilmington, Del., c. 1790. Probably cabinetmaker only.
Wherritt, Samuel A.
Richmond, Ky., c. 1820
Whetcroft, William
Annapolis, Md., c. 1773; Baltimore, Md., 1778. Probably importer of parts, etc.
Whinston, George
Winchester, Conn., c. 1835. Cabinetmaker. Apprenticed to Henry B. Horton.
Whipple, Arnold
Providence, R.I., c. 1810
Whitaker, George
Providence, R.I., c. 1800
Whitaker, Josiah, Gen.
Providence, R.I., c. 1800
Whitaker, Thomas
Providence, R.I., c. 1800. Purchased assets of N. Dodge.
Whitcomb, A.
Stow, Mass., n.d.
White, Charles
New York, N.Y., c. 1870
White, D. C.
Newark, N.J., c. 1830
White, F.
Brooklyn, N.Y., c. 1810
White, Francis
Philadelphia, Pa., c. 1850
White, J.
Brooklyn, N.Y., c. 1830
White, John
Boston, Mass., c. 1780
White, John
New York, N.Y., c. 1810
White, Joseph
Philadelphia, Pa., c. 1800
White, L. W.
North Adams, Mass., c. 1850
White, Matlock
New York, N.Y., c. 1770
White, N. H.
Newark, N.J., c. 1870
White, Peregrine
Woodstock, Conn., c. 1770
White, Sebastian
Philadelphia, Pa., c. 1790

White, Thomas
Philadelphia, Pa., c. 1810
Whitear, Benjamin
Fairfield, Conn., c. 1770
Whitear, John
Fairfield, Conn., c. 1730. Maker of wheel blanks.
Whitear, John, Jr.
Fairfield, Conn., c. 1762. Bell founder.
Whitehead, John
Norristown, Montgomery Co., Pa., c. 1830
Whitehead, John
Philadelphia, Pa., c. 1848
Whitehead, William W.
Philadelphia, Pa., c. 1850
Whiting, Adna
Bristol and Farmington, Conn., c. 1845
Whiting, K.
Winchester, Conn., c. 1800
Whiting, Lewis E.
Saratoga Springs, N.Y., c. 1865. Maker of the Timby clock.
Whiting, Riley
Winchester and Winsted, Conn., c. 1810. In partnership with Hoadley. Made wood-movement clocks, both shelf and tall case.
Whiting, Samuel
Concord, Mass., c. 1808. In partnership with Nathaniel Munroe.
Whiting and Marquand
Fairfield, Conn., c. 1790
Whiting & Munroe
Concord, Mass., c. 1800
Whiting, William and Co.
Buffalo, N.Y., c. 1850
Whitman, Benjamin
Reading, Pa., c. 1770
Whitman, Ezra
Bridgewater, Mass., c. 1800
Whitney, Asa
New York, N.Y., c. 1798
Whitney, Eben
Norwalk, Conn., c. 1845
Whitney, Ebenezer
New York, N.Y., c. 1810
Whitney, George
Boston, Mass., c. 1800
Whitney, M. F.
Schenectady, N.Y., c. 1820
Whitney, Moses
Boston, Mass., c. 1820
Whitney, William
Rochester, N.Y., c. 1845
Whittacker & Co.
Providence, R.I., c. 1824
Whittaker, William
New York, N.Y., c. 1730
Whittaker and Dana
Providence, R.I., c. 1800
Whittemore, J.
Boston, Mass., c. 1850
Whittemore, Thomas
Pembroke, N.H., c. 1800. Probably casemaker only.
Whittle, John
Hopkinton, N.H., c. 1845
Whitton, E. J.
Boston, Mass., n.d.
Whyler, John
Norwalk, Milan, and Fitchville, Ohio, n.d.

Wickens, Obed
New York, N.Y., c. 1840
Widdifield, William
Philadelphia, Pa., c. 1815
Widdifield, William, Jr.
Philadelphia, Pa., c. 1820
Widdifield and Gaw
Philadelphia, Pa., c. 1820
Wiedemeyer, J. M.
Baltimore, Md., c. 1800
Wieland, Frederick
Philadelphia, Pa., c. 1845
Wieland, Johann G.
Salem, Mass., c. 1780
Wiggins, Henry
Newfields, N.Y., c. 1810. Casemaker.
Wiggins and Company
Philadelphia, Pa., c. 1830
Wiggins, T. and Co.
Philadelphia, Pa., c. 1830
Wightman, Allen J.
New York, N.Y., c. 1840
Wightman and Sperry
New York, N.Y., c. 1840
Wiland, John G.
Salem, Mass., c. 1780
Wilbur, Charles
New York, N.Y., c. 1825. Probably dealer.
Wilbur, Job B.
Newport, R.I., c. 1815
Wilcox, A.
New Haven, Conn., c. 1820. Also worked in Fayetteville, N.C.
Wilcox, Cyprian
New Haven, Conn., c. 1825
Wildbahn, Thomas
Reading, Pa., c. 1785
Wilder, Charles
New York, N.Y., c. 1840
Wilder, E. E.
Rochester, N.Y., c. 1860
Wilder, Ezra
Hingham, Mass., c. 1825. Son of Joshua Wilder. Married a daughter of Reuben Tower, also a clockmaker.
Wilder, Joshua
Hingham, Mass., c. 1815. Prolific maker of dwarf tall case clocks.
Wilder, T.
Hingham, Mass., c. 1780(?)
Wilder, Joshua and Ezra
Hingham, Mass., c. 1840
Wilkins, Asa
Wiscasset, R.I., c. 1800
Wilkinson, Charles
Canton, N.Y., c. 1815
Wilkinson, W.S. & J.B.
Chicago, Ill., c. 1880

The **Willards**, a family of famous clockmakers, were descendants of Major Simon Willard, the founder of Concord, Mass. They were the children of Benjamin and Sarah Willard and were all born in Graftton, Mass.

Benjamin, the third child, was born March 19, 1743, and died in Baltimore, Md., September 28, 1803. His one son, Benjamin, died at the age of 13.

Simon, the eighth child, was born April 3, 1753, and died in Boston, Mass.,

August 30, 1848. Of the 11 children by his second wife, 3 became associated with the clock business.

Ephraim, the ninth child, was born March 18, 1755. The location and date of his death are unknown.

Aaron, the tenth child, was born October 13, 1757, and died in Boston, Mass., May 20, 1844. Of the 2 children born to his first wife, Aaron, Jr., became a clockmaker. Of the 7 children born to his second wife, Henry was prominent in the allied trade of cabinetmaker. In this he was outstanding, making clock cases for his father, brother, cousin, and other outstanding clockmakers.

For a more complete story of the Willards, the book *Simon Willard and His Clocks* (1968), by John Ware Willard, is recommended reading.

Willard, Aaron
Grafton, Mass., c. 1770; Roxbury, Mass., c. 1780; Boston, Mass., c. 1798. Apprenticed to his brothers, Benjamin and Simon. The Massachusetts shelf clock is credited to him. Father of Aaron, Jr., and Henry, a cabinetmaker. Aaron retired in 1823; his business was taken over by Aaron, Jr.

Willard, Aaron, Jr.
Boston, Mass., c. 1810. Son of Aaron, who taught him clockmaking. Took over his father's business in 1823. Development of lyre wall clock is credited to him. Aaron, Jr., retired in 1850.

Willard, Alexander T.
Ashburnham, Mass., c. 1796; Ashby, Mass., c. 1800. Made both wood and brass movements. Descendant of Col. Simon Willard.

Willard, B.
New York, N.Y., c. 1820

Willard, Benjamin
Grafton, Lexington, and Roxbury, Mass., c. 1765. Possibly apprenticed to the Cheneys of East Hartford, Conn. Older brother of Simon, Aaron, and Ephraim and, undoubtedly, was their teacher. Several musical clocks made by Benjamin are known.

Willard, Benjamin F.
Boston, Mass., c. 1825. Son of and apprenticed to Simon Willard.

Willard, Ephraim
Grafton, Medford, Roxbury, and Boston, Mass., c. 1775. Brother of Benjamin, Simon, and Aaron. Probably taught clockmaking by Benjamin. Not many clocks by him are currently known.

Willard, Henry
Boston, Mass., c. 1825. Cabinetmaker. Made cases for his father, Aaron, brother, Aaron, Jr., and Simon Willard and Son in addition to W. Cummens and E. Tabor.

Willard, John M.
Boston, Mass., c. 1825. Tablet painter. Son of Simon.

Willard, Philander J.
Ashburnham and Ashby, Mass., c. 1775. Brother of Alexander.

Willard, Simon
Grafton and Roxbury, Mass., c. 1765. Made his first clock at age 17. Probably taught by his brother, Benjamin, and a Mr. Morris. Had many apprentices, the most famous being Levi and Abel Hutchins, Elnathan Taber, and Daniel Munroe, Jr. Patented "Improved Patent Timepiece" in 1802. Also made clock jacks, powered by a clock movement, for roasting meats. Made tall clocks, Massachusetts shelf clocks, the improved patent timepiece, gallery clocks, lighthouse clocks, and tower clocks. When he retired in 1839, he sold his tools to Elnathan Taber. Taber was also allowed to use Simon's name on his clocks. Of all the clocks made by the Willards, those of Simon and Aaron are the most sought after.

Willard, Simon, Jr.
Roxbury, Mass., c. 1817; New York, N.Y., c. 1826; Boston, Mass., c. 1828. Son of Simon, to whom he was apprenticed. Was in charge of the tower clocks in Boston and clocks at Harvard University. Learned chronometer making in New York City.

Willard, Sylvester
Bristol, Conn., c. 1830

Willard, Zabadiel
Boston Mass., c. 1845. Son of Simon, Jr., from whom he learned clockmaking. Last of the Willard clockmakers.

Willard and Nolen
Boston, Mass., c. 1806. Dial painters. Members of this firm were Aaron Willard, Jr., and his brother-in-law, Spencer Nolen.

Willard and Son
Boston, Mass., c. 1824. Members of this firm were, undoubtedly, Simon and Simon Willard, Jr. Banjo or improved patent timepieces are known.

Willbank, John
Philadelphia, Pa., c. 1840. Bell caster.

Willcox, Alvin
Norwich, Conn., c. 1805; Fayetteville, N.C., c. 1819; New Haven, Conn., c. 1825

Willey, Stephen
Dover, N.H., c. 1830

Williams, Andrew L.
Newark, N.J., c. 1850

Williams, Benjamin
Elizabeth Town, N.J., c. 1780. In partnership with William J. Leslie.

Williams, David
East Cahn, Chester Co., Pa., c. 1790

Williams, David
Newport and Providence, R.I., c. 1825

Williams, George R.
Charleston, S.C., c. 1780

Williams, Hinds
Boston, Mass., c. 1855

Williams, Ichabod
Elizabeth, N.J., c. 1830

Williams, J.
Alexandria, Va., c. 1795

Williams, Jehu
Lynchburg, Va., c. 1815. Worked with John Victor.

Williams, John
Philadelphia, Pa., c. 1820

Williams, N.
Portsmouth, N.H., n.d.

Williams, Nathaniel
Taunton and Dighton, Mass., c. 1770

Williams, Nicholas
Liberty Town, Frederick Co., Md., c. 1790

Williams, Stephen
Providence, R.I., c. 1799. Partner of N. Dodge.

Williams, Thomas
Flemington, N.J., c. 1792. Joachim Hills was an apprentice.

Williams, William
Alexandria, Va., c. 1810

Williams & Hatch
North Attleboro, Mass., c. 1840

Williams and Leslie
New Brunswick, N.J., c. 1780; to Trenton, N.J., c. 1791

Williams, Orton and Preston & Co.
Farmington, Conn., c. 1820. Made wood-movement clocks.

Williams & Victor
Lynchburg, Va., c. 1800

Williamson, Henry
Baltimore, Md., c. 1805

Willis, John
Burlington, N.J., c. 1745

Willmott, Benjamin
Easton, Md., c. 1795

Willock, John
Pittsburgh, Pa., c. 1830. Possibly dealer only.

Wills, Joseph
Philadelphia, Pa., c. 1725

Wilmer, Andrew
Philadelphia, Pa., c. 1818

Wilmer, George
Philadelphia, Pa., c. 1820

Wilmirt, John
New York, N.Y., c. 1795

Wilmot, Samuel
New Haven, Conn., c. 1815; also Georgetown and Charleston, S.C.

Wilmot and Richardson
Savannah, Ga., c. 1850

Wilmott, Benjamin
Easton, Md., c. 1790

Wilmurt, Stephen M.
New York, N.Y., c. 1800

Wilson, Andrew
Providence, R.I., c. 1890

Wilson, Hosea
Baltimore, Md., c. 1817

Wilson, James
Trenton, N.J., c. 1770

Wilson, Robert
Philadelphia, Pa., c. 1830

Wilson, William B.
Newtown, Bucks Co., Pa., c. 1825

Wilson & Dunn
New York, N.Y., c. 1840

Wilson T. and J.
Philadelphia, Pa., c. 1795

Wiltberger, Charles H.
Washington, D.C., c. 1825

Wing, Moses
  Windsor, Conn., c. 1790
Wingate, Frederick B.
  Augusta, Me., c. 1800
Wingate, George
  Baltimore, Md., c. 1815
Wingate, Paine
  Boston, Mass., c. 1790. Moved to Augusta, Me., c. 1810. Brother of Frederick.
Winkley, John
  Canterbury, N.H., c. 1790
Winship, David
  Litchfield, Conn., c. 1830. Casemaker and dealer in clocks.
Winslow, Ezra
  Westborough, Mass., c. 1860
Winslow, Jonathan
  New Salem, Worcester, and Springfield, Mass., c. 1810
Winstanley, Henry
  Brooklyn, N.Y., c. 1840
Winston, Alanson
  Bristol, Conn., n.d.
Winston, A.L. & W.
  Bristol, Conn., c. 1840
Winterbottom, Thomas
  Philadelphia, Pa., c. 1750
Winterhalder, Charles
  Santa Cruz, Calif., c. 1860
Wintermute, O.
  Newton, N.J., c. 1870. Probably dealer only.
Winterrode, Jacob
  Dauphin County, Pa., n.d.
Winters, Christian
  Easton, Pa., c. 1800
Wise, William
  Brooklyn, N.Y., c. 1834. Later William Wise and Sons, active to c. 1930.
Wismer, Henry
  Plumstead, Bucks Co., Pa., c. 1800
Wister, Charles J.
  Germantown, Pa., c. 1820
Witherill & Co.
  South Bend, Ind., c. 1850
Withington, Peter
  Mifflinburg, Pa., c. 1820
Witman, Benjamin
  Reading, Pa., c. 1800
Witmer, Abel
  Ephrata, Lancaster Co., Pa., c. 1785. Mostly 30-hour clocks.
Witt, Christopher
  Germantown, Pa., c. 1720. Also doctor and scientist. Probably painted first portrait done in oils in this country, 1706.
Wittenmyer, Michael
  Doylestown, Pa., c. 1810
Witwer, Isaac
  New Holland, Pa., c. 1850
Wohlschlangler, B.
  Carondelet, Mo., c. 1860
Wolf, Henry
  Marietta, Lancaster Co., Pa., c. 1850
Wolf, Jacob
  Waynesburg, Pa., n.d.
Wolf, Theodore
  Lancaster, Pa., c. 1850
Wolf, Thomas D.
  Westtown, Chester Co., Pa., c. 1810

Woltz, George Elie
  Hagerstown, Md., c. 1820. Son of George Woltz.
Woltz, John
  Shepherdstown, W.Va., c. 1800. Son of George Woltz.
Woltz, John G.
  Hagerstown, Md., c. 1770
Woltz, Samuel
  Hagerstown, Md., c. 1800
Woltz, William
  Oakland, Md., c. 1825. Son of George Woltz.
Wood, B. B.
  Boston, Mass., c. 1840
Wood, B. F.
  Winchester, N.H., n.d.
Wood, David
  Newburyport, Mass., c. 1790. Maker of beautiful shelf clocks, also made banjo and tall case clocks.
Wood, James
  New York, N.Y., c. 1875
Wood, John
  Philadelphia, Pa., c. 1770
Wood, John
  New York, N.Y., c. 1775 (?)
Wood, John
  Mount Holly, N.J., c. 1800
Wood, John, Jr.
  Philadelphia, Pa., c. 1780
Wood, Josiah
  New Bedford, Mass., c. 1800
Wood, M.
  Rockport, Ind., c. 1840
Wood, N. G.
  Boston, Mass., c. 1850
Wood and Foley
  Albany, N.Y., c. 1850
Wood & Hudson
  Mount Holly, N.J., c. 1790
Wood, John and Son
  Philadelphia, Pa., c. 1755
Woodcock, William
  Baltimore, Md., c. 1820
Woodcock and Company
  New Haven, Conn., c. 1870
Woodford, Isaac
  New Haven, Conn., c. 1840
Woodin, Riley L.
  Decatur, N.Y., c. 1830
Wooding, E.
  Torrington, Conn., c. 1820
Woodruff, Enos
  Cincinnati, Ohio, c. 1820
Woodruff, Isaac B.
  Winsted, Conn., c. 1880
Woodruff, Jesse
  n.p.; c. 1765
Woodruff, John II
  New Haven, Conn., c. 1840
Woodruff and White
  Cincinnati, Ohio, c. 1840
Woodward, Antipas
  Bristol and Middletown, Conn., c. 1790
Woodward, Isaac
  Amherst, N.H., n.d.
Woodward, James
  Philadelphia, Pa., c. 1795. Cabinetmaker.
Woolf, B.
  Charleston, S.C., c. 1800

Woolson, Thomas, Jr.
  Amherst, N.H., c. 1805
Woolston, R.
  Glastonbury, Montgomery Co., Pa., n.d.
Woolworth, Chester
  New Haven, Conn., c. 1840
Woolworth, R. C.
  Philadelphia, Pa., c. 1815
Worden, C. M.
  Bridgeport, Conn., c. 1850
Worton, Robert
  Philadelphia, Pa., c. 1840
Wriggins, Thos., & Co.
  Philadelphia, Pa., c. 1830
Wright, Charles C.
  New York, N.Y., c. 1800; Utica, N.Y., c. 1812
Wright, Filbert
  Bristol, Conn., c. 1850. Son of Harvey Wright.
Wright, Harvey
  Bristol, Conn., c. 1831. Made wood movements.
Wright, John
  New York, N.Y., c. 1715
Wright, Julius
  Bristol, Conn., c. 1850. Son of Harvey Wright.
Wright, Samuel
  Lancaster, N.H., c. 1810
Wright, T. H.
  Lancaster, N.H., c. 1800
Wright, William
  Baltimore, Md., c. 1805
Wruck, F. A.
  Salem, Mass., c. 1860
Wvuille, Theophile
  Philadelphia, Pa., n.d.
Wyand, John
  Philadelphia, Pa., c. 1845
Wyleys
  Charleston, S.C., c. 1785
Wyman, Benjamin
  Boston, Mass., n.d.
Wyman, Charles
  Saint Albans, Vt., n.d.
Wyman, Isaac
  Boston, Mass., c. 1835
Wyman, Rogers and Cox
  Nashua, N.H., c. 1830
Wynn, Christopher
  Baltimore, Md., c. 1840
Wynne, Robert
  Salisbury, N.C., c. 1825

Yale, Charles M.
  New Haven, Conn., c. 1865
Yale Clock Co.
  New Haven, Conn., c. 1881
Yarnall, Allen
  Sugartown and West Chester, Pa., c. 1825
Yates, Edward J.
  Freehold, N.J., c. 1805
Yates, Erastus
  Butternuts, N.Y., c. 1825
Yates, John B.,
  New York, N.Y., c. 1890
Yates, Joseph
  Trenton, N.J., c. 1780; Freehold, N.J., after 1805

Yates and Kent
Trenton, N.J., c. 1796

Yeadon, Richard
Charleston, S.C., c. 1770

Yeager, William
Philadelphia, Pa., c. 1835

Yeakel, Abraham
Perkasie, Bucks Co., Pa., c. 1865

Yeakel, Solomon
Northampton (now Allentown), Pa. c. 1815

Yeakle, Abraham
Doylestown, Pa., c. 1870

Year Clock Co.
New York, N.Y., c. 1840. Made Crane's torsion pendulum clock.

Yeiser, Frederick
Lexington, Ky., c. 1850

Yeomans, Elijah
Hadley, Mass., c. 1760; Middletown, Conn., c. 1780

Yeomans, James
New York, N.Y., c. 1771

Yeomans and Collins
New York, N.Y., c. 1767

Yerkes, William
Pennsylvania, c. 1770 (?)

Yodder
Philadelphia and Bethlehem, Pa., n.d

Yerkee, Jacob
Manheim, Pa., c. 1790

Yost, Samuel M.
Mount Joy, Donegal, Pa., c. 1834

You, Thomas
Charleston, S.C., c. 1750

Young, Charles
Chambersburg, Pa., c. 1750

Young, David
Hopkinton, N.H., c. 1800. Cabinet-maker.

Young, Francis
Philadelphia, Pa., c. 1775

Young, Francis
New York, N.Y., c. 1785

Young, Jacob
Elizabethtown, N.J., c. 1750

Young, Jacob
Hagerstown, Md., c. 1775

Young, Jacob
Northern Liberties, Philadelphia, Pa., c. 1760

Young, John
Norwalk, Ohio, n.d.

Young, Joseph
Newburgh, N.Y., n.d.

Young, S. E.
Laconia, N.H., c. 1850

Young, Samuel
Charlestown, W.Va., c. 1790

Young, Stephen
New York, N.Y., c. 1810

Youngs, Benjamin
Windsor, Conn., c. 1757; Schenectady, N.Y., c. 1767; Watervliet, N.Y., c. 1780. Joined the Shakers, making plain clocks.

Youngs, Benjamin
New York, N.Y., c. 1800

Youngs, Ebenezer
Hebron, Conn., c. 1775

Youngs, Isaac
New Lebanon, N.Y., c. 1800. Son of Benjamin.

Youngs, Joseph
Windsor, Conn., n.d.

Youngs, Seth
Windsor, Conn., c. 1730; later at Torrington, Conn.

Youngs, Seth, Jr.
Windsor, Conn., c. 1800

Zahm, G. W.
Lancaster, Pa., c. 1850. Retail jeweler, silversmith, and clockmaker.

Zahm & Co.
Lancaster, Pa., c. 1850

Zahm, H. L. and E.J.
Lancaster, Pa., c. 1850

Zahm and Jackson
Lancaster, Pa., c. 1850

Zeissler, G. A.
Philadelphia, Pa., c. 1848

Zilliken, William
Pittsburgh, Pa., c. 1850

Zimmerman, Anthony
Reading, Pa., c. 1765

Zimmerman, C. H.
New Orleans, La., c. 1850

Zuber, John J.
Upper Hanover, Pa., n.d.

GLOSSARY

Alarm: An attachment to a clock whereby, at a predetermined time, a bell is sounded.

Anchor escapement: Resembles a ship's anchor in appearance. Invented about 1671, and enabled the clockmaker to use a long pendulum.

Arbor: The axle on which the gears or wheels are mounted.

Backplate: The plate that is farthest from the dial.

Balloon clock: A clock case somewhat resembling the shape of a hot-air balloon.

Banjo clock: Common name for Simon Willard of Boston's "Patent Improved Timepiece" patented in 1802.

Barrel: The drum containing the springs of a clock or watch.

Basket top: The top of a bracket clock, which resembles an inverted basket.

Beat: The rhythmic sound of the pallets on the escape wheel.

Beetle hand: The hour hand, shaped like a stag beetle, frequently found on early Massachusetts shelf clocks and other early clocks. Generally used with a poker or straight minute hand.

Bell top: The top of a bracket clock, resembling a bell.

Bezel: The metal or wood ring that holds the glass over the dial.

Bob: The weighted end of a pendulum. Usually held on the threaded rod by a nut, thus enabling it to be raised or lowered for time adjustment.

Boss: The round disk applied to the arch of a dial on which is usually recorded the maker's name. Usually used on early brass dials.

Bracket clock: A form of clock that sits on a table or bracket.

Bushing: That part of a clock plate, usually reinforced with metal, in which the arbors are inserted.

Calendar: An attachment on clocks that indicates the date, etc. Calendar clocks with separate calendar dials were made in profusion after about 1860.

Center-seconds hand: Sometimes called sweep-seconds hand. Mounted on the center post of clocks and watches.

Chapter ring: That part of a dial on which are marked the hours and minutes. In early clocks it was a separate piece attached to the dial.

Clepsydra: A form of clock using water, instead of sand, that falls from one container to another at a given rate.

Click: A pawl, held by spring tension to the ratchet, enabling the clock to be wound.

Clock: A timepiece to which a strike train has been added.

Collet: A brass ring or washer used in front of the pin for fastening the minute hand and/or gears.

Count wheel: A locking wheel that controls the striking mechanism of a clock. Has twelve slots, each of which becomes progressively wider, into which a claw drops.

Crown-wheel escapement: So called because of its resemblance to a crown. Another name for verge escapement.

Crutch: The arm at the end of a pallet arbor through which the pendulum passes.

Date dial: An accessory dial marked with the dates of the month. Usually moved twice every 24 hours.

Deadbeat escapement: Invented by George Graham of London, an escapement in which there is no recoil. Used on expensive movements.

Drum: The cylinder on which the cord of a weight-driven clock is wound.

Escapement: A means by which the pendulum allows the going train to operate at a regular interval, thus controlling the passage of time.

Fly: A fan or type of air brake used to regulate or slow the speed of the strike train.

Foliot: An early type of pendulum used in verge escapements; later used on the Columbus clock. It has two arms with adjustable weights on the ends and swings in a horizontal plane.

Front plate: The plate next to the dial in which the arbors are held.

Fusee: A cone-shaped device made to equalize the spring tension on spring-driven clocks and watches. By this means a constant force is exerted on the train, enabling it to run at a constant speed.

Gathering pallet: A part of the rack-and-snail strike train. A small metal bar that rotates once for each strike and gathers one tooth of the rack until the striking is completed.

Gimbal: A device, similar to a universal joint, that keeps a clock level. Usually used in ships' chronometers.

Girandole clock: A variant of the banjo clock. Invented by Lemuel Curtis and, as far as can be determined, made only by him in Concord, Massachusetts.

Grande sonnerie: A type of striking in which the last hour struck is repeated at each quarter.

Grandfather clock: Popular name for the tall case clock.

Grandmother clock: Popular name for the dwarf or miniature tall case clock.

Gravity escapement: A type of escapement used on tower clocks. The impulse is given to the pendulum directly by a small falling weight that is raised by the going train after each beat of the pendulum.

Great wheel: The first wheel in the going train.

Gridiron pendulum: A series of steel and brass rods in the pendulum to counteract the heat and cold to which it is subjected. By this means the pendulum length is kept constant. Invented by John Harrison of London.

Hollow-column clock: A type of shelf clock in which the weights fall through a hollow column situated on either side of the case.

Hourglass: An early form of timekeeper in which sand falls at a given rate from one container to another through a slender glass neck.

Kidney dial: So called because of its shape. Usually used on the Massachusetts shelf clock.

Kitchen clock: A particular style of case popular from about 1865 or 1870 to about 1910.

Lantern clock: So called because of its resemblance to a lantern. The early ones had only one hand. First appeared in England around 1630. Although probably made in this country at one time, no known examples have survived.

Lantern pinion: Instead of teeth or leaves as in a common pinion, the lantern pinion had a series of metal pins held in place with two end plates.

Leaf pinion: The teeth are leaves as opposed to pins.

Lighthouse clock: A style of case devised by Simon Willard of Boston in 1822. It follows the general lines of the Eddystone Lighthouse at Plymouth, England. As it was not popular, very few were made.

Locking plate: Common name for the count wheel, in the strike train.

Lunette: The half circle above the dial. Usually contains a phase of the moon or ornamentation.

Lyre clock: A variation of the banjo, usually attributed to Aaron Willard, Jr., of Boston.

Mainspring: Source of power for spring-driven clocks.

Maintaining power: A device in a clock that provides sufficient power to keep it going while being wound.

Massachusetts shelf clock. A particular style of clock thought to have been developed by the Willards of Boston. Often called box-on-box or half clock.

Mean time: Days and hours of equal length as opposed to solar time where the days are not of equal length.

Movement: The assembly of gears between two plates in such a fashion as to provide the transmitting of power from either the weights or the springs. Sometimes called "works."

New Hampshire mirror clock: A type of clock thought to have originated in New Hampshire and attributed to Benjamin Morrill of Boscawen.

Ogee: A series of convex and concave moldings in the form of an S. There is also a reverse ogee molding.

Oil sink: An indentation at the pivot hole of a clock used for the retention of oil.

Orrery: A device that shows the positions of the planets in relationship to each other.

Pallets: That part of the escapement that either locks or receives impulse from the escape wheel.

Pendulum: A rod, either of metal or wood, with a spring at one end connected to the escapement and a movable bob at the other end, which controls the rate of the clock.

Pillar-and-scroll clock: A type of case design that has been attributed to Eli Terry of Plymouth, Connecticut. Usually had a thirty-hour wood movement. Made by many makers with variations.

Pinion: The smaller of two wheels, made up of leaves or small pieces of wire, mounted on a single arbor.

Plates: Flat plates between which are held the gears of a clock.

Pull repeater: A device whereby the striking mechanism of a clock is set in motion between the hours.

Quarter strike: A clock that strikes the quarter hours, usually on two bells.

Rack and snail: A device that controls the striking mechanism of a clock as opposed to a count wheel. Allows for repeat striking. The rack is a piece of metal with teeth on one edge that is moved by the gathering pallet; the snail is roughly in the shape of a snail and mounted on the center post. It selects the number of times a clock will strike.

Rattrap striking: A strike train with only one wheel in the train. Used by Benjamin Morrill of Boscawen on New Hampshire mirror clocks.

Regulator: A weight-driven clock of great accuracy. Usually without a striking attachment and always with a deadbeat escapement, and a compensating pendulum.

Reverse fusee: A type of fusee where the chain or gut is crossed, allowing the springs to unwind in opposite directions.

Ripple front: The wavy part of the clock case, usually applied. Commonly used on the beehive and steeple cases.

Roman strike: A rare form of striking usually found on English clocks by Joseph Knibb. The striking takes place on two bells of different tones. All Is are represented by a stroke on the small bell. All Vs are represented by a stroke on the larger bell and X is represented by two strikes on the large bell. IIII is represented as IV. This method was devised to conserve power in the strike train.

Sheep's-head clock: A lantern clock in which the chapter ring is wider than the rest of the clock.

Shelf clock: A type of case designed to sit on a shelf as opposite to a tall clock.

Solar time: A solar day is the period that elapses between two successive returns of the sun to the meridian.

Spandrel: The four corners of a square clock dial in which designs are painted or fancy metalwork is applied.

Splat: The decorator piece at the top of a clock case.

Spring barrel: The metal container for springs in a spring-driven clock.

Strike train: The added gears used to operate the striking mechanism of a clock.

Suspension spring: The piece of metal or spring on which the pendulum rod is mounted.

Sweep-seconds hand: A seconds hand mounted in the center of the dial.

T-bridge: The double bridge from which the pendulum rod is suspended.

Tick-tack escapement: A type of escapement found on late-seventeenth-century bracket clocks. Rarely used, it is similar to the anchor escapement but covers only one and one-half teeth in the escape wheel.

Timepiece: A device for recording time.

Tower clock: A public clock. Usually on church steeples, public buildings, etc.

Train: The gears that make up the going and strike mechanism of a clock.

Verge escapement: See crown-wheel escapement.

Wagon spring: A series of flat springs used to supply power to a movement as opposed to a coil spring. Attributed to Joseph Ives of Bristol, Connecticut.

Wall clock: A clock that was designed to be hung on the wall, such as the banjo, schoolhouse clock, etc.

Warning: In striking clocks, the strike train is set in motion to strike a few minutes before the hour but is stopped short until released by the minute hand.

Weights: A source of power for the movement in clocks, as opposed to springs.

SELECTED BIBLIOGRAPHY

Bailey, Chris H. *Two Hundred Years of American Clocks and Watches.* Englewood Cliffs, N.J.: Prentice-Hall, 1975.

Baillie, G. H. *Watchmakers and Clockmakers of the World.* London: Methuen and Co., Ltd., 1929.

Battison, Edwin A., and Kane, Patricia F. *The American Clock, 1725–1865.* Greenwich, Conn.: New York Graphic Society, 1973.

Britten, F. J. *Old Clocks and Watches and Their Makers.* 8th ed. New York: E. P. Dutton & Co., Inc., 1973.

Bruton, Eric. *The Longcase Clock.* New York: Frederick A. Praeger, 1968.

Carlisle, Lilian B. *Vermont Clocks and Watchmakers, Silversmiths and Jewelers.* Lunenburge, Vt.: Stonehour Press, 1970.

Cescinsky, H. *Old English Master Clockmakers.* London, 1938.

————, and Webster, M. *English Domestic Clocks.* London, 1913.

Chandlee, E. E. *Six Quaker Clockmakers.* Philadelphia: Historical Society of Pennsylvania, 1943.

Chappius, Alfred, and Droz, Edmund. *Automata. A Historical and Technological Study.* London: B. T. Batsford, 1958.

Dreppard, Carl W. *American Clocks and Clockmakers.* Boston: C. T. Branford Company, 1958.

Drost, William E. *Clocks and Watches of New Jersey.* Elizabeth, N.J.: Engineering Publishers, 1966.

Dworetsky, Lester, and Dickstein, Robert. *Horology Americana.* Roslyn Heights, N.Y.: Horology Americana, 1972.

Eckhardt, George M. *Pennsylvania Clocks and Clockmakers.* New York: Devin-Adair Company, 1955.

Edwards, Ernest L. *The Grandfather Clock.* Altrincham, England, 1952.

Gordon, G. F. C. *Clockmaking, Past and Present.* London, 1949.

Hering, Daniel W. *The Lure of the Clock.* New York: New York University Press, 1932.

Hoopes, Penrose R. *Connecticut Clockmakers.* New York: Dodd, Mead and Company, 1930.

————. *Shop Records of Daniel Burnap, Clockmaker.* Hartford, Conn.: Connecticut Historical Society, 1958.

Hummel, Charles F. *With Hammer in Hand. The Dominy Craftsmen of East Hampton, L.I.* Charlottesville, Va.: The University of Virginia Press, 1968.

James, Arthur E. *Chester County Clocks and Their Makers.* West Chester, Pa.: Chester County Historical Society, 1947.

Jerome, Chauncey. *History of the American Clock Business for the Past Sixty Years and Life of Chauncey Jerome.* New Haven, Conn.: F. C. Dayton, Jr., 1860.

Joy, Edward T. *The Country Life Book of Clocks.* Feltham, Middlesex, England: Country Life Books, 1967.

Lloyd, H. Alan. *Chats on Old Clocks.* Philadelphia: Historical Society of Pennsylvania, 1951.

————. *The Collectors Dictionary of Clocks.* New York: A. S. Barnes and Company, 1964.

Maust, Don. *Early American Clocks.* Uniontown, Pa.: E. G. Warman Publishing Company, 1971.

Milham, Willis. *Time and Timekeeping.* New York: The Macmillan Company, 1923.

Miller, Andrew H., and Miller, Dalia M. *Survey of American Clocks, Calendar Clocks.* Elgin, Ill., 1972.

Moore, N. Hudson. *The Old Clock Book.* New York: Frederick A. Stokes, 1911.

Nutting, Wallace. *The Clock Book.* Framingham, Mass.: Old America Company, 1924.

————. *Furniture Treasury.* 3 vols. Framingham, Mass.: Old America Company, 1933.

Palmer, Brooks. *The Book of American Clocks.* New York: The Macmillan Company, 1959.

————. *A Treasury of American Clocks.* New York: The Macmillan Company, 1967.

Roberts, Kenneth D. *The Contributions of Joseph Ives to Connecticut Clock Technology, 1810–1862.* Bristol, Conn., 1970.

————. *Eli Terry and the Connecticut Shelf Clock.* Bristol, Conn., 1973.

Schwartz, Marvin D. *Collectors' Guide to Antique American Clocks.* Garden City, N.Y.: Doubleday and Company, Inc., 1975.

Terry, Henry. *American Clock Making.* Waterbury, Conn., 1870.

Ullyett, Kenneth. *In Quest of Clocks.* London, 1951.

Wenham, Edward. *Old Clocks for Modern Use.* London, 1951.

Willard, John W. *A History of Simon Willard, Inventor and Clockmaker.* New York: Dover Publications, 1968.

INDEX

Note: The illustration number for each clock is designated by the figures in boldface type; the page on which the illustration appears is shown by the figures in parentheses.